*Richard M. Gula, S.S.*

# REASON INFORMED
# BY FAITH
Foundations
of
Catholic
Morality

New York          PAULIST PRESS          Mahwah

## ACKNOWLEDGMENTS

Excerpts from Bernard Häring, *Free and Faithful in Christ*, Vol. 1: *General Moral Theology* (New York: Crossroad Publishing Co., 1978), used by permission of Crossroad Publishing Co. Excerpts from Robert Bolt, *The Man for All Seasons* (New York: Random House, 1962), used by permission of Random House, Inc. The diagram of the structure of moral theology has been adapted from the doctoral dissertation of Charles M. Swezey which examined the correlations more extensively, *What Is Theological Ethics? A Study of the Thought of James M. Gustafson* (Ann Arbor: University Microfilm International, 1978), used by permission of Charles M. Swezey.

*Book design: Ellen Whitney*

Library of Congress Cataloging-in-Publication Data

Gula, Richard M.
    Reason informed by faith : foundations of Catholic morality / by
Richard M. Gula.
      p.   cm.
    Includes bibliographies and index.
    ISBN 0-8091-3066-1
    1. Christian ethics—Catholic authors.   2. Catholic Church—
Doctrines.   I. Title.
BJ1249.G82 1989
241'.042—dc19                                        89-30053
                                                           CIP

Published by Paulist Press
997 Macarthur Boulevard
Mahwah, NJ 07430

Printed and bound in the
United States of America

*Marge*
*Panwar 1407—*

# CONTENTS

Introduction . . . . . . . . . . . . . . . . . . . . . . . . . . . . . . . . . . . 1

1. THE NATURE OF MORAL THEOLOGY . . . . . . . . . . . . . . 6
2. THE TASK OF THE MORALIST . . . . . . . . . . . . . . . . . . . 13
3. THE CONTEXT OF CONTEMPORARY MORAL
   THEOLOGY . . . . . . . . . . . . . . . . . . . . . . . . . . . . . . . . . 25

PART ONE: THE NATURE OF THE GOOD

4. FAITH AND MORALITY . . . . . . . . . . . . . . . . . . . . . . . . 43

PART TWO: THE NATURE OF THE HUMAN
          PERSON

5. THE HUMAN PERSON . . . . . . . . . . . . . . . . . . . . . . . . . 63
6. FREEDOM AND KNOWLEDGE . . . . . . . . . . . . . . . . . . . 75
7. A SENSE OF SIN . . . . . . . . . . . . . . . . . . . . . . . . . . . . . 89
8. KINDS OF SIN . . . . . . . . . . . . . . . . . . . . . . . . . . . . . . 106
9. CONSCIENCE . . . . . . . . . . . . . . . . . . . . . . . . . . . . . . . 123
10. THE FORMATION OF CONSCIENCE . . . . . . . . . . . . . . 136
11. CONSCIENCE AND CHURCH AUTHORITY . . . . . . . . . 152

PART THREE: CRITERIA OF JUDGMENT

12. SCRIPTURE IN MORAL THEOLOGY . . . . . . . . . . . . . . 165
13. JESUS AND DISCIPLESHIP . . . . . . . . . . . . . . . . . . . . . 185
14. THE CHURCH AND THE MORAL LIFE . . . . . . . . . . . . . 199
15. THE NATURAL LAW IN TRADITION . . . . . . . . . . . . . . 220
16. NATURAL LAW TODAY . . . . . . . . . . . . . . . . . . . . . . . 231
17. LAW AND OBEDIENCE . . . . . . . . . . . . . . . . . . . . . . . 250
18. THE MORALITY OF HUMAN ACTION . . . . . . . . . . . . . 265

19.  MORAL NORMS  ..................................... 283
20.  MORAL DECISION MAKING AND PASTORAL MORAL
     GUIDANCE  ........................................ 300
21.  DISCERNMENT OF SPIRITS  ......................... 314

Index  .................................................. 330

# Introduction

Since the Second Vatican Council (1962–1965) a ferment of thinking and research has been enriching Catholic moral theology. Before the council, the moral theology of the manuals tended to separate reflection on the moral life from its roots in our Christian convictions and commitment. The mandate of the council, however, called for a radical revision of the moral manuals—the "classical moral theology" of the Roman Catholic tradition.

The first phase of renewal began in the 1940s and 1950s and continued through the years immediately following the Council. It set out to "Christianize" morality by rooting it more deeply in scripture and the mysteries of faith. However, the direction of the early attempts at renewal shifted in the late 1960s and early 1970s to a more philosophical orientation. The second phase ushered in the movement of "autonomous ethics," so called because the emphasis was not so much on the God who reveals morality, but on the human person who discovers it. Since the demands of morality are equally accessible to all through reason, autonomous ethics claimed that the special character of Christian morality lies in something other than its content, especially if the content is limited to norms, values, or cases.

Vincent McNamara attributes the shift to a philosophical orientation—not only to the undercurrents of secularizing tendencies in theology generally, but even more to some enthusiastic but uncritical analyses and expressions produced by the first phase of renewal. It seems that efforts at renewing moral theology were creating a form of sectarianism which would be counterproductive to the Catholic desire to be in critical dialogue with all people of good will and to be in solidarity with the genuinely human concerns facing the world.[1]

Autonomous ethics was in turn challenged by the movement called "faith ethics" which claimed that revelation has a specific contribution to make in knowing what morality requires. Faith ethics wanted to restore the direction and spirit of the early efforts at renewing Catholic moral theology by integrating scripture and the mysteries of faith into moral reflection.[2] Today Roman Catholic moral theology is marked by the creative tension of trying to include the orientation of faith ethics, while preserving at the same time reason's critical reflection on human experience which characterizes autonomous ethics. In other words, today we want to avoid separating morality into either a natural "rational morality" or a revealed "faith morality." The former yields a pure humanism, the latter a sectarianism. When taken alone, neither is faithful to the deepest desire of the Catholic moral tradition to

1

address genuine human concerns as a believing community in a language accessible to nonbelievers as well.

Moreover, the most distinctive characteristic of the Catholic theological tradition is its insistence on "both/and" thinking and the incarnational or sacramental principle of mediation, which means that God comes to us through us. The Catholic tradition insists on the "and" which yokes together two seeming opposites such as scripture and tradition, faith and reason, nature and grace, church and world, faith and works. In the Catholic tradition, the "and" ought never become an "or." Also, traditional Catholic moral theology insists as well on the principle of mediation by claiming that we come to know moral truth not only by appealing to revelation but also by reflecting on human nature.

The insistence on mediation continues to characterize Catholic moral theology today. We continue to insist on the significance of the human but try to do so in a way which is integral with a total faith perspective. Both faith and human resources are constitutive dimensions of discovering the moral demands of being human. That is why we speak of "reason informed by faith" as the characteristic approach of Roman Catholic moral theology. This approach is identified in some recent official statements: *Humanae Vitae* (1968) is "founded on the natural law as illuminated and enriched by divine revelation"; the Declaration on Procured Abortion (1974) "teaches moral principles in the light of faith" and cites scripture frequently; the "Letter to Bishops on the Pastoral Care of Homosexual Persons" (1986) is written from the moral viewpoint "founded on human reason illumined by faith" and it appeals to "the solid foundation of a constant biblical testimony" to establish the basis of its moral position; the instruction on bioethics, "Respect for Human Life in Its Origin and on the Dignity of Procreation" (1987), asserts that "the magisterium of the Church offers to human reason in this field too the light of revelation."

How does faith inform Catholic morality? What relation do religious convictions have to Catholic moral thinking which prides itself on being "rational" and based on "nature"? How are the sources of faith, such as scripture, Christ, the church, and the magisterium, integrated into moral thinking and the moral life? How do we integrate into a perspective informed by faith the aspects of a "rational" morality, such as natural law, positive law, moral action, moral norms, and methods of making a decision? These are the kinds of questions which direct this study of the foundations of Catholic morality.

These probing questions bring us to the center of investigation in Roman Catholic moral theology today. Only if we can answer them can we qualify our ethics as "Christian" or "theological." Showing the relation of faith to judgments of value is the unfinished task in the renewal of Roman Catholic moral theology. Exploring this issue promises to make even more profound the ecumenical breakthroughs which have already happened and which continue in moral theology. This is as it should be, since an adequate Catholic morality ought to draw on the full breadth of Christian experience and tradition. Catholic moral theology today is a markedly ecumenical endeavor. We are experiencing a convergence of Protestant and Catholic thinking in more and more areas, especially in one of the major areas of concern in this book—the integration of the rational aspects of morality with a perspective of faith. Therefore, while the primary emphasis here is on the foundations of Roman Catholic morality, many Protestant voices will be heard throughout.

Most of the public attention in matters of morality focuses on controversies surrounding specific issues. Any reader of *USA Today*, the *New York Times*, or *Time* magazine is already familiar with some of the controversies on specific issues—sexual matters, respect for human life, nuclear war, economic justice, and the like. The difficulty in agreeing on specific moral issues reflects a much deeper dispute about the nature and method of moral theology itself. How we think and argue is as crucial as the conclusions we draw. This book does not hope to resolve disputes about specific issues. It hopes to lay out in a somewhat coherent way the foundations of Catholic morality as they are being explored by a great majority of moral theologians. Laying out the foundations will provide the context for the controversies on specific issues, and it will help to make following the debates on specific issues a little easier.

Clearly, this book cannot offer an exhaustive study of moral theology. Bernard Häring has already tried something like that with his recent three volume work, *Free and Faithful in Christ*.[3] Germain Grisez promises such a study and has already completed the first volume of that enormous task.[4] On a lesser scale, this book will organize developments in fundamental moral theology into an overview of the present state of the discipline.

After introducing the nature of moral theology, the task of the moralist, and the context in which moral theology is being done today, I have organized this book into three major parts, corresponding to the three formal elements of the discipline of ethics.

*Part One: The Nature of the Good* treats God as the center of value. This part establishes God as the central point of reference for objective morality. It then gives particular attention to the relation of faith and morality in order to understand the distinctiveness of Christian morality.

*Part Two: The Nature of the Human Person* treats the human person from the theological perspective of the image of God. It explores the aspects of the human person "adequately considered" as the foundations for a personalistic morality. It gives substantial attention to the aspects of freedom and knowledge in the moral life, and to the notions of sin and conscience which follow from this foundation.

*Part Three: Criteria of Judgment* explores the major points of reference in the moral life and the process of making a moral decision. It begins with the specifically theological sources of faith—scripture, Jesus, and the church—to show their relation to the moral life. Then, in the perspective of faith, it takes up aspects of rational morality—natural law, positive law and obedience, the morality of human action, moral norms, and moral decision making. The final chapter repositions the entire discussion of the book within the perspective of faith by treating the theological notion of the discernment of spirits.

I have written this book to make accessible the ideas of those who have significantly influenced the direction and shape of Roman Catholic moral theology since the council. It is written for those who are seriously interested in Catholic morality but who do not have the time to make their way through all the scholarly work which has gone on in Catholic moral theology. Given all the significant changes which have occurred since the council, many who were trained in the pre-conciliar era may be wondering where we are now and what we have done to get here. Those who have come on the scene more recently are curious about the "why" behind the "what" of the controversies which are receiving so much public attention. Professional ministers who are trying to update themselves on the developments in moral theology, as well as those preparing to be professional ministers, have often approached me asking for a book which makes the specialized knowledge and discussions of moral theologians accessible to people like themselves. Other lay and professional persons who are struggling with contemporary ethical issues have also sought the same kind of help. I hope this book will be the one they can use. It is written with them in mind.

This book is the result of the help of many people with different gifts and perspectives. Most of their names appear in the notes at the end of each chapter. In a more personal way I am deeply grateful to some others. Fr. Philip Keane, S.S. and Fr. Richard Sparks, C.S.P. graciously read the entire manuscript and offered many valuable suggestions. Also, Fr. Peter Chirico, S.S. spent many hours in conversation with me helping to clarify my understanding of some difficult issues and then read sections of the manuscript to offer further helpful suggestions. Sr. Joan Marie O'Donnell, S.M. read the chapters as they were being written and constantly challenged me not to forget to write for the "people in the pews" who would also be interested in this book. Fr. Steve Rowan patiently read the entire manuscript and offered many helpful suggestions to make the book clearer. To all these people and more who took an interest in this project and encouraged me along the way, "Thanks."

## Notes

1. Vincent MacNamara, *Faith and Ethics* (Washington: Georgetown University Press, 1985), pp. 38–39. Part One is an excellent overview of the renewal movement and the reactions it provoked.

2. The debates between autonomous ethics and faith ethics focused on the distinctiveness of Christian ethics. For some of the significant essays which contributed to this debate, see Charles E. Curran and Richard A. McCormick, eds., *Readings in Moral Theology No. 2: The Distinctiveness of Christian Ethics* (Ramsey: Paulist Press, 1980).

3. Häring, *Free and Faithful in Christ* (New York: Seabury Press, 1978, 1979, 1981).

4. Grisez, *The Way of the Lord Jesus*, Vol. 1: *Christian Moral Principles* (Chicago: Franciscan Herald Press, 1983).

# 1   $T$he Nature of Moral Theology

*T*his kind of book—an exercise in fundamental moral theology—is often mistaken for a work in moral philosophy, or ethics. Since moral theology is a species of ethics, it will necessarily share an affinity with the formal structure and the formal interests of that discipline. However, moral theology is sufficiently different from philosophical ethics to warrant its being treated separately. The purpose of this first chapter, then, is simply to provide a brief description of what we mean by moral theology, its relationship both to moral philosophy and to theology, its nature, range of interest, divisions, and structure. Perhaps such a description will also help focus the larger project of this work as well.

## The Range of Interest in Moral Theology

Christian theology itself is a discipline in which the commitment of faith seeks to understand God's revelation of divine love in Christ Jesus and through the Spirit. Systematic theology is the overarching discipline of theology which tries to work out a coherent view of the world by integrating the truths of faith with all other truths we can know. Moral theology (sometimes called Christian or theological ethics) is a particular expression of systematic theology which focuses on the implications of faith for the way we live. As a formal theological discipline, it is concerned with God's revelation of divine love in Jesus and through the Spirit as an invitation calling for our response. It regards the response to the initiative of God's offer of love as the very soul of the moral life.

Moral philosophy, or philosophical ethics, can reflect quite well on the nature of the moral life and what constitutes right and wrong behavior without any reference whatsoever to God's revelation and to Christian beliefs. Moral theology, however, as a "theological" discipline cannot. In short, Christian moral theology wants to know what difference being a Christian believer makes for the way we live our lives. Therefore, it is interested in the implications of Christian faith for the sorts of persons we ought to be (this is often called "the ethics of being" or "character ethics") and the sorts of actions we ought to perform (this may also be called "the ethics of doing"). Both being and doing, or character and action, constitute interdependent concerns and must be taken together in any complete project of moral theology. The sort of person one is depends to a great extent upon the sorts of decisions and actions one has taken, and conversely, the sorts of decisions and actions which one has taken depend in part upon the sort of person one is.[1]

## Ethics of Being

Morality is often associated exclusively with behavior guided by rules. But to focus on behavior and rules is not sufficient for understanding the scope of moral reflection. If we talk too exclusively of actions, we are in danger of regarding them as something outside ourselves and as having a reality of their own. But actions are always expressions of a person. Moral goodness is a quality of the person, constituted not by rule-keeping behavior alone, but by cultivating certain virtues, attitudes, and outlooks. Moreover, if we focus too much on rules, we lose sight of the Christian moral life as pertaining to a way of life guided by the paradigmatic story of Jesus Christ. While we are certainly called to do what is right as Christians, we are first of all called to be loving persons in the imitation of Christ.

Morality, then, has a great interest in the interiority of the person, or the person's character. In other words, who we are matters morally. For this reason, moral theology must also pay attention to "character ethics" or the ethics of being which focuses on what is happening to the person performing actions rather than on the actions the person performs. It focuses on patterns of actions, or the habits we acquire, the vision we have of life, the values and convictions or beliefs we live by, the intentions we have, the dispositions which ready us to act as well as the affections which move us to do what we believe to be right. Here is where we locate the classical idea of the virtues— those personal qualities disposing us to act in certain ways.[2] The "ethics of being" in a Christian context asks "What sort of person should I become because I believe in Christ?"

Perhaps one of the reasons we have not paid enough attention to character in morality is that we have relegated the interiority of the person to considerations of spirituality. When the manuals of moral theology were introduced after the Council of Trent, spirituality and moral theology went separate ways. Bringing them together again would be the natural result of retrieving the tradition of virtue and addressing questions about who we are supposed to become. The unity of the moral and spiritual life is emerging again through attention on the virtues and is in need of further development in the Roman Catholic tradition.

## Ethics of Doing

Yet, interiority, such as good intentions and sensitive dispositions, does not cover the whole territory. Interiority gets expressed in behavior. The biblical metaphor that the good tree bears good fruit and the bad tree bears bad fruit teaches that right actions come from good persons. An "ethics of being" focuses on the good person; an "ethics of doing" focuses on right actions. In a Christian context, it asks, "What sort of action should I perform because I believe in Christ?"[3]

The interest of the ethics of doing is with making a decision to resolve conflicts of moral values so that we might do the right action. From this perspective, moral theological reflection attends not only to the duties and obligations of the person acting but also to the circumstances which make up the moral situation. These are considered in light of the moral norms or principles which guide us through the resolution of conflicting values. In some respects, the interest of the ethics of doing has affinity with the interests of canon law and jurisprudence in general, and, in fact, moral theology was governed for a long time by a juridical perspective.

In sum, moral theology as a whole seeks to relate Christian faith to the complex realities of living in the world. It asks, "What sorts of persons ought we to be, and what sorts of actions ought we to perform by virtue of being believers in Christ?" As a discipline of theology, it presupposes a commitment of faith by which we accept the mystery of Christ as the full revelation of God and accept the sources of faith as valid sources of coming to the truth about God, being human, and living in the world. Moreover, since the incarnational principle, or the principle of mediation, tells us that only through the human, always and everywhere already graced by God, do we come to know God and respond to what God is enabling and requiring us to be and to do, moral theology also takes seriously critical reflection on human experience as a valid source for coming to know what is morally required.

## Divisions of Moral Theology

From the time it became a separate theological discipline after the Council of Trent (1545–1563), moral theology has included concerns of a general or fundamental nature as well as those of a particular or special nature. These two types of concerns have given rise to the twofold division of the discipline of moral theology into *fundamental moral theology* and *special moral theology*.

While these two need to be carefully related, they can be treated separately. This book is an example of fundamental moral theology. As such it will not address the concrete moral issues which arise pertaining to sexuality, medical practice, business relations, or social living, for example. The particular treatment of issues of this sort pertains to works of special moral theology. Since fundamental moral theology is intricately related to special moral theology, this book will, from time to time, refer to concrete issues to show the implications of the foundational concerns of moral theology.

One of the objectives of fundamental moral theology is to show the "why" behind the "what" of special issues. Moreover, disagreement at the level of concrete issues often can be traced to different understandings of the foundational concerns of morality, such as those which make up this book. So anyone who wants to participate in or, at least, to follow the debates on special issues will need to keep pace with the developments occurring at the foundational level of moral theology.

## Structure of Moral Theology

The outline of this book reflects the formal structure of the discipline of ethics according to one of America's leading Protestant ethicians, James M. Gustafson.[4] Since moral theology is a species of ethics, it shares the same formal structure. According to Gustafson this entails a dialectical relationship of theory and practice, or more specifically, of *ethics* and *morals*.[5] However, not everyone adheres to Gustafson's distinctions, and so we frequently find these terms used interchangeably.

*Ethics*, according to Gustafson, explores the theoretical foundations of moral theology. It involves a level of thinking prior to making a decision and taking action. It develops the standards or provides the framework, or presuppositions, for answering the practical question of morals, "What should I do?" According to Gustafson, *ethics* is made up of three formal elements: (1) an understanding of the good as the goal of the moral life and the basic reason for being moral; (2) an understanding of the human person as a moral agent; (3) and the points of reference which serve as the criteria for a moral judgment.[6]

*Morals*, in Gustafson's definition, is the practical level of moral theology. *Morals* is concerned with giving direction to human behavior in light of what one believes to be right or good. The fundamental concern of *morals* is to answer the practical question, "What should I do?" To answer this question adequately, one must consider the relevant aspects of at least the following four points: (1) fundamental convictions or religious beliefs—these influence the interpretation the agent makes of the moral situation and the direction the agent takes in life; (2) the character of the moral agent who must decide and act—this involves a consideration of the agent's uniqueness as manifest in capacities, dispositions, intentions, affections, and the like; (3) the situation in which the conflict of values arises—this involves a careful gathering of data in order to get the lay of the moral land; (4) appropriate norms—this enlightens and guides the agent by drawing on the accumulated wisdom of the moral community in order to ensure that significant values are properly respected.[7]

Moral theology, then, is a twofold enterprise of ethics and morals. It is concerned with clarifying the foundations of the moral life on the basis of Christian religious convictions (*ethics*) and with interpreting how to judge and act in light of these convictions (*morals*). Perhaps an example can show their interrelationship. At the level of practice (*morals*), we appeal to the norm "life is sacred and ought to be respected" to give a reason for not taking innocent life. At the level of theory (*ethics*), we try to show the accuracy of this position by giving some account of the good (life is a gift of God), of the nature of the human person (an especially sacred being made in the image of God), and of criteria of judgment (in the situation of an unjust attack on innocent life, the norm of protecting life applies).

Moral theology, or Christian ethics, is not unique by virtue of having convictions about the good, the human person, or criteria of judgment. Moral theology is distinguished as Christian, and even more specifically as Catholic or Protestant, on the basis of the sources of ethical wisdom to which one appeals to give content to the formal elements of *ethics* and *morals*. Insofar as these formal elements are informed, in part at least, by Christian experience and beliefs, we have Christian ethics or morals. If they are informed, in part at least, by a particular Catholic experience or source of wisdom, such as the magisterium, we have Catholic ethics or morals.

Characteristically, Catholic moral theology relies on "mediation" for coming to know God and what faith requires. This means that it takes seriously not only revelation and the tradition of the Church, but also critical reflection on ongoing human experience as well. Both faith and reason, then, are the fundamental sources to which we appeal in giving content to *ethics* and *morals* within Catholic moral theology.

Because *ethics* and *morals* consider the same subject matter differently, each perspective must be used and allowed to inform the other. This makes the inquiry that constitutes the field of moral theology a dialectic of theory and practice. This inquiry can be diagrammed as indicated in Figure 1.[8]

The lines show the relationships of theory and practice. Solid lines indicate direct relationships; dotted lines indicate other possibilities. Since all the elements interrelate, we can begin our inquiry at any one of the elements and from either perspective. Only when we have interrelated the elements of both perspectives, however, do we have a fully critical moral analysis. Although this book cannot draw out all the possible correlations, I hope to give some understanding of the content of these elements along with some correlations. For example, Part One of the book shows some of the relationships between

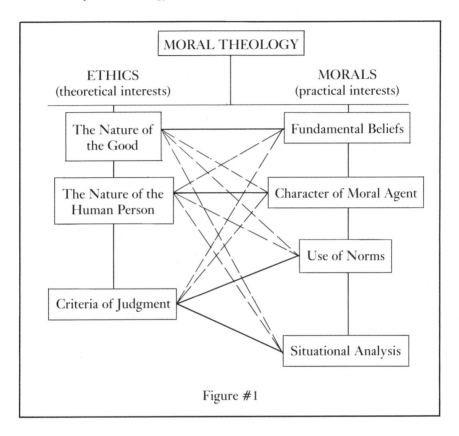

Figure #1

the nature of the good and religious beliefs in God; Part Two, between the nature of the human person and being a moral agent; Part Three, between criteria of judgment and the sources of moral guidance in scripture, Jesus, church, natural law, positive law, moral norms, and the discernment of spirits.

In addition to a general description of the nature of moral theology, an introduction to this discipline also needs to consider the tasks of one who engages in moral theological reflection as well as the significant features of the context in which moral theological reflection is being done today. These will be the focus of the next two chapters.

## Notes

1. For a further discussion of this distinction, see Bruce C. Birch and Larry L. Rasmussen, *Bible and Ethics in the Christian Life* (Minneapolis: Augsburg, 1976), pp. 79–123.

2. On virtue in St. Thomas, see *ST*, I–II, qq. 55–67. For a review of current literature reflecting the discussion on the nature of virtue and character, see John W. Crossan, *What Are They Saying About Virtue?* (Ramsey: Paulist Press, 1985).

3. The distinction between the ethics of being and the ethics of doing also helps us understand the distinction between a "right" action (or judgment of moral rightness) and a "good" action (or judgment of moral goodness). The term "right" answers "What should I do?" by pointing to actions. The term "good" answers the same question by pointing to what falls under the notion of virtue—such as motives, dispositions, and intention. Morality in the strict sense pertains to the person, to character. Actions are moral only in a derived or secondary sense because the person expresses himself or herself in actions. Strictly speaking, "good" and "bad" properly refer to the person; "right" and "wrong" refer to the action. For a detailed discussion of the moral goodness/moral rightness distinction, see Bernard Hoose, *Proportionalism* (Washington: Georgetown University Press, 1987), pp. 41–67; for a briefer treatment of the same theme, see Josef Fuchs, "Morality: Person and Acts" in *Christian Morality: The Word Became Flesh*, translated by Brian McNeil (Washington: Georgetown University Press, 1987), pp. 105–117.

4. Gustafson's two most significant books which illustrate the structure and interrelationship of parts in the field of moral theology are *Christ and the Moral Life* (New York: Harper and Row, 1968; reprint edition Chicago: University of Chicago Press, Midway Reprint, 1976), and *Can Ethics Be Christian?* (Chicago: University of Chicago Press, 1975). For a succinct article on this distinction, see "Theology and Ethics" in *Christian Ethics and the Community* (Philadelphia: United Church Press, 1971), pp. 83–100.

5. "Theology and Ethics," in *Christian Ethics and the Community*, p. 85.

6. See especially *Christ and the Moral Life*, pp. 1–4.

7. Three articles by Gustafson in which these four base points appear, although in slightly different form, are "Moral Discernment in the Christian Life" in *Theology and Christian Ethics* (Philadelphia: United Church Press, 1974), pp. 99–119; "Context Versus Principles: A Misplaced Debate in Christian Ethics" in *Christian Ethics and the Community*, pp. 101–126; and "The Relationship of Empirical Science to Moral Thought" in *Theology and Christian Ethics*, pp. 215–228.

8. This diagram is adapted from the doctoral dissertation of Charles M. Swezey which examines the correlations more extensively. See *What Is Theological Ethics? A Study of the Thought of James M. Gustafson* (Ann Arbor: University of Microfilm International, 1978), pp. 26–33; see especially p. 30. Used by permission.

# 2 The Task of the Moralist

Given the previous description of moral theology, what can we expect from one who engages in moral theological reflection? Do we expect the moralist to know better than anyone else who we ought to be and what we ought to do? Do we expect the moralist to be a moral virtuoso or to be the most competent judge of the rightness or wrongness of every human action? While these may be noble goals for anyone to achieve, and some will achieve them in modest proportions, a more realistic task of the moralist is to be one who can be a resource for moral living by bringing *sensitivity*, *reflection*, and *method* to discerning the sorts of persons we ought to be and the sorts of actions we ought to perform when we face conflicting moral values.[1] Anyone who is willing and able to engage the requirements of these tasks can do moral analysis. Moral disagreement occurs primarily because of some flaw in doing any one of these tasks or because of disagreement over what belongs to the content of them. Because sensitivity, reflection, and method are important for understanding the nature of morality and moral reflection, we need to take a closer look at each.

## Sensitivity

Sensitivity is fundamental. It implies that moral living begins in the heart and not with an abstract principle about the nature of being human from which we draw crisp conclusions. Morality pertains to value, particularly the value, sacredness, or worth of persons and what befits their well-being. The foundational experience that awakens our moral consciousness and gives a basis in reality to our moral judgments is the experience of the sacredness of human life, or the value of persons as persons.[2] All morality is organically linked to this foundational experience. The value of persons as persons can only be appreciated. It is not something we reason to or can

13

prove with the satisfaction of a logical syllogism. That is why the foundational moral experience is a matter of the heart. It is affective, intuitive, imaginative, somatic. To bring sensitivity to moral analysis, then, is to engage artistic or mystical insight in the service of the moral life and moral reflection.

Not until we have imagined with sensitivity the value of persons and what befits their well-being will we have reached the sort of experience that makes authentic moral living and moral reflection possible. All the intricacies of moral reflection have developed in response to the need to bring the meaning of this foundational experience to specific cases. Whether the issue is abortion or euthanasia, nuclear war or the economy, moral discussion tries to express what the foundational experience of human value demands of us. The whole purpose of moral dialogue is to discover what best befits persons in all their sacredness. By exploring this foundational experience we discover not only what morality is but also what love is, since to be moral and to be loving imply one another.

The capacity for love, that is, the ability to appreciate and respond to love in all its forms, is the beginning of moral consciousness. Carol Gilligan's studies of moral development have shown that authentic moral living is not possible until a person is capable of empathy.[3] When empathy is born, care is born, and with it, morality. Morality explores the implications of the discovery and appreciation that someone other than one's self is real and valuable.

Our grasp of the moral quality of a person and our convictions about what befits a person's well-being do not come merely by way of thinking through some rational argument, nor do they end there. Rather, our moral knowledge and moral convictions come by way of affective experiences. That is to say, we are "awestruck" by the value of a person or the quality of an action and commit ourselves to them. Our affective commitment to and care for the value of persons and what befits their well-being are "reasons of the heart" which ultimately cannot be proven, yet which will always remain the final court of appeal for our moral judgments. We appeal to "reasons of the head," or our rational arguments, to confirm and demonstrate in a way that can be convincing to another what we already know by heart. In the moral life, head and heart work together.

The final appeal to reasons of the heart is aptly demonstrated in an exchange between Thomas More and his beloved daughter, Margaret, in a scene from Robert Bolt's play, *A Man for All Seasons*. The scene takes place in a jail cell when Margaret comes to persuade her father to sign an Act of State which goes contrary to More's most deeply held beliefs.

> MARGARET: In any State that was half good, you would be
> raised up high, not here, for what you've done already. It's not

your fault the State's three-quarters bad. Then if you elect to suffer for it, you elect yourself a hero.

MORE: That's very neat. But look now . . . If we lived in a State where virtue was profitable, common sense would make us good, and greed would make us saintly. And we'd live like animals or angels in the happy land that needs no heroes. But since in fact we see that avarice, anger, envy, pride, sloth, lust and stupidity commonly profit far beyond humility, chastity, fortitude, justice and thought, and have to choose, to be human at all . . . why then perhaps we must stand fast a little—even at the risk of being heroes.

MARGARET: (*Emotionally*) But in reason! Haven't you done as much as God can reasonably *want?*

MORE: Well . . . finally . . . it isn't a matter of reason; finally it's a matter of love.[4]

This exchange helps explain, in part at least, the futility of trying to argue with someone who does not have an affective appreciation of the basic values at stake in a moral conflict. We live and reflect morally in the first place not because we have reason but because we have an affective commitment to what we care about. We are enough alike in what we care about to make ethical agreement possible. However, we experience disagreement, in part at least, because of the different degrees to which we care about the same things.

In the abortion debate, for example, we find many people caring about human life and even agreeing on the basic scientific facts pertaining to the development of human life; however, people share different affective commitments to these things and so come to different moral conclusions as to whether abortion befits human well-being in any way whatsoever. Not until heart speaks to heart will we be able to come to the sort of moral conversion which changes where we stand in a moral debate or even allows us to make any progress in it.

The sensitivity required for the moralist to engage in moral "theological" reflection is a sensitivity of the heart attuned to the presence of God. Such sensitivity requires prayer. A heart sensitive to God is born in prayer and is nurtured by prayerful attention to the presence of God in the diverse experiences of living. A heart so sensitive is alert to the diverse ways of God and can read the signs of God's presence and action in the world. Without this prayerful attentiveness to God, moral reflection stops short of attending to the fullness of the relationships which make up the moral life.

The task of a moralist, then, involves learning to live in a way attuned to one's heart. Heartfelt experiences of values evoke a sense of awe in the presence of what is fitting. This is the mystical and artistic side of moral reflection. Moral judgments and moral convictions spring from a pre-reflective grasp of value and are nurtured both by an affective commitment to what we care about and by critical reflection which enables us to understand, assess, and communicate what we know in a pre-reflective way. The place of sensitivity in moral reflection helps us to appreciate moral judgments as more like the artist's aesthetic judgment of beauty than they are the referee's judgment of playing by the rules. Without sensitivity to moral values we risk becoming hardened to the subtleties of the moral dimension in experience. For example, in health care we see medical management problems, but not moral ones; in the arms race, we see the political issues, but not the moral ones; in trying to feed the hungry, we see the economic issues, but not the moral ones. However well informed we may be about the medical, political and economic issues, and even about the moral rules, our moral awareness and judgment depend on our moral instinct, or fine feeling for moral truth which is born in the heart.

## Reflection

Along with sensitivity comes reflection which explores and extends into all areas of life the primary affective experiences which have generated an awareness of basic values and a commitment to them. We turn to the language of the mind when we want to support, analyze, and communicate what we grasp by heart. The work of reflecting morally on affective experiences of value involves reflecting as well on questions of moral knowledge, objectivity, and truth.

Within the Catholic moral tradition, the fundamental axiom that "morality is based on reality"[5] makes assumptions which take us to the core of the task of reflection. Implied in this axiom are basic questions pertaining to knowledge: How do we know reality? What can we know? How reliable is our knowledge? Our goal is to know reality as completely as possible before making a moral judgment. Often the differences in moral positions today, even among those who share profound affective experiences of the value of persons, can be traced to differences in the work of "reflection" seeking a judgment about what does or does not befit human well-being.

Various philosophies seek to explain our moral knowledge. One of these is the relativistic school of thought. *Social relativists* look to what society approves in order to know what is morally right or wrong. For them, the moral and the customary are synonymous so that sociological studies are enough to confirm whether moral claims are true and reliable or not. *Personal relativists* use the criterion of self-satisfaction to confirm what is right or wrong. "Do your own thing" is their familiar slogan. For them, the tools of psychology would be sufficient to determine whether a person is really satisfied or not. Not far behind these approaches is the *emotivist* school which claims "The good is what I feel comfortable with." This school regards all moral evaluations as simply expressions of emotions, but not as statements which could be true or false.

Ethical relativisms such as these will always be a seductive force in a confusing world. If any of these were to reign as the way to moral knowledge, however, we would have no grounds for claiming that any actions "ought" to be (the purpose of normative ethics). In that case, we would have no grounds to carry on any public discussion about different moral judgments, since all of our moral claims would be subject to custom, to personal satisfaction, or to subjective emotion. This would leave us no basis either for moral creativity or criticism.

In contrast to these approaches are those which claim some form of objective grounding to morality. If our moral evaluations rest on some common, objective human reality, then, in principle at least, we ought to be able to reach universal agreement about the truth or falsity of our moral claims. What allows for universal agreement is the single source to which we are appealing for determining what is morally right. For some this is the universal human capacity to accept intuitively that a rational order of the world is objectively there. For others, it is God's will commanding what is right and understood only by those who have an authentic experience of God. Neither of these positions is being adopted by Roman Catholic moral theologians today. These, along with the relativistic approaches, are inadequate shortcuts in our effort to know moral reality in a critical fashion.

Another form of an objective approach which does have great appeal to Roman Catholic moral theology is *critical realism*. In a more satisfying way than the extremes of subjectivism and objectivism, critical realism seeks to grasp the whole of moral reality and to probe the natures of moral knowledge, objectivity, and truth. This approach to moral evaluation follows the invariant structure of human knowing and implies a rather complex cognitional theory well developed by Bernard Lonergan.[6] For our purposes only a brief sketch of this theory will have to suffice in order to show that how we know reality is the root issue in fulfilling this task of reflection.

According to critical realism, *experience* is the beginning of knowledge. Experience seems to tell us that the knowledge we have is based on something that is really out there. The senses are stimulated and we are registering the sensations. But looking at what is out there and seeing it are only the first operations in the act of knowing. They only "input" the data; that is all, nothing more.

Beyond gathering data and registering it, we want to "understand" the data, to "see into" it. *Understanding* is called forth by the question, "What is it?" Understanding puts the separate parts of the data into some kind of order so that we can grasp the whole of what is given. To understand, to answer the question "What is it?" we begin to sift through the data, to walk around it and look at it from all different sides and at all its relationships. In going through this process we come to what Lonergan calls "insight": a new way of seeing what we first experienced just by looking. Now, we understand.

Understanding raises another question: "Is it so?" This is the question of adequacy, of truth. We want to have some assurance that what we have "looked at" and "understood" is so. Does our understanding reflect reasonably the reality of what we have experienced? To answer this question is to make a *judgment*. In making an accurate judgment we try to ask as many questions as we can about our understanding.[7] Only when we reach such a critical judgment do we attain knowledge of reality in the proper sense. From this knowledge we move on to deciding and acting.

Through experience we gather data, and through our understanding and judgment we try to account for as much data as possible. But the accounts of our experience, understanding, and judgment do not catch the whole of reality at once. Grasping the whole is something like fishing. We have to throw the line in many times before we have a catch. This means that we have many experiences, create many accounts, or formulate many hypotheses. Each of these needs to be tested. We are constantly refining our hypotheses or formulations in order to give a better account of the data. To make progress toward truth, we must be free of preconceived notions that would control from within our understanding of the data. One such bias is reflected in those famous seven last words, "We've never done it that way before." Such an attitude can block us from ever seeing a new set of relationships or being open to a new kind of experience.

When we have an accurate grasp of reality and assent to its truth by an accurate judgment, we want to rest in it. But the rest stop, this partial yet reliable grasp of truth, is less like a comfort station and more like a launching pad. We have not yet arrived at the whole of reality or truth; we have reached instead a new point of departure. Lonergan's cognitional theory as well as the sociology of knowledge clearly shows us that the whole is bigger than any partial grasp of it or of our effort to give an account of it.[8] The search for the whole goes on. New experiences bring new data which require revision of any previous grasp of reality.

A new experience, or a new look at an old experience, may force us to review the process by which we came to our former conclusions, as well as the conclusions themselves. In this review, we may discover that we missed some clues, or that we have found new ones. We may also recognize that we allowed irrelevant ideas to contaminate our analysis, or we may see that we were not all that free from blinding prejudices. Also, thoughtful but dissenting voices may cause us to reconsider our account and give attention to the truth grasped by another's contribution. In these ways we are led to revise our former ideas, formulations, or conclusions and to realize that we do not grasp the whole of reality through any one experience or express it in any one formulation. After these experiences, we should not be surprised that much of what we know remains open to revision because the process of knowing is ongoing.

This theory of how we know and what we know has important implications for moral theology, especially for the interpretation of "objectivity" in morality. In raising questions about our experience, understanding, and judgment, we are all wrapped up with the object we are trying to know. This means that we have no true grasp of reality apart from being involved in it. We have no way of separating the "knowing subject" from the "object known." The very process by which we have come to knowledge and truth has so involved us in a relationship with the object that we can no longer be separated from it. For this reason we cannot really distinguish "objectivity" from its relationship to "subjectivity."[9] We either get to "know" reality, and so get caught up in a relationship with what we are trying to know, or we do not know at all. We just take a look and move on.

According to Lonergan's theory, "objectivity" is not to be equated with what is out there to be seen.[10] For example, in morality we have often located "objectivity" merely in the physical structure of an act, such as an act of reproduction by means of artificial insemination. We then proceeded to prescribe or proscribe "objective" morality with norms derived from these physical actions alone: for example, "Do not use artificial means of reproduction." However, neither the physical act alone nor the behavioral norm derived from it expresses the complete objective moral reality. If we think they do, then we have stopped too soon and have committed the common fallacy in moral thinking of substituting a part for the whole.

Lonergan's cognitional theory holds a significant place for the subject (the person) in the process of grasping the meaning of reality. Moral theology today is overcoming the dualism of the subject-object split by giving significant attention to the role of the person in moral action (notice the emphasis being placed on intention, dispositions, capacities) and to the experience of moral persons in the formulation of its moral positions (notice the method of consultation used by the American bishops to write their pastorals on nuclear war, the economy, and women's concerns).

Furthermore, contemporary moral theology tries to be more modest in its claim to grasp the whole truth about moral reality. At any one time our knowledge of the values important to the full development of human life is by no means exhaustive. We continue to seek their meaning. While the knowledge we do have at any one time may be accurate and reliable, it is also partial. Our moral beliefs are approximations to the truth and therefore need to be revised in light of better evidence and improved reflection. While we have genuine insight into moral values, our formulations of them never succeed in capturing all the intricacies and complexities of what these values demand. These limitations to our knowledge and to our ability to express what we know call for some humility in our theological discussions, an openness to revising our formulations, and a necessary tentativeness in our moral judgments.

Moreover, contemporary theology recognizes that everyone is involved in the effort of coming to truth. Everyone contributes according to his or her own proper competence, while respecting differences in authority and responsibility.[11] Mutual sharing of experience, insight, and judgment is how we come toward a more complete grasp of truth. For this we need the collaboration of various perspectives, different experiences, years of testing, the raising of new questions, coming to a rest stop, and launching on ahead. Our greatest danger is to stop too soon and to claim too much on the basis of too little.

Reflection which respects the very structure of how we know and come to truth promises to yield moral judgments which are reliable and which, in principle at least, can be endorsed universally. Reflection leads to method.

## Method

Thus far we have seen that the moralist's task begins with sensitivity, since morality is born in the heart, and moves on to a process of reflection in order to confirm and demonstrate as well as we can what we know in an affective way. Now that we have judged a certain value to be true and worthy of our attention (for example, the value of persons and what befits their well-being), we need to do something about it. For this we need a method—a strategy which helps us to love well in the midst of conflicting values. If we must do the truth in love, then how do we justify our actions? This question asks for a method. Just as insensitivity or inadequate reflection can block effective moral discernment and cause moral disagreement, so too can an inadequate method for loving. In fact, one outcome of the "new morality" debates has been more awareness of how much the method used is the central reason for moral disagreement.

Three principal methods have emerged to help us organize the data of moral experience for the purpose of making a moral decision. These methods received their classical formulation in H. Richard Niebuhr's *The Responsible Self.*[12] They are the teleological, deontological, and responsibility styles of moral decision making. Only a brief description of each is necessary here since we will meet these again in Chapter 20 when we take up the issue of making a moral decision.

The *teleological* position finds its analogy for moral decision making in the act of building. As a style, it fits what Niebuhr called "man-the-builder," the person who constructs things with an end in view.[13] (The word "teleology" comes from the Greek word, *telos*, for goal.) The teleological method is primarily concerned with determining which action would bring about the goal being sought, and so approaches the question "What ought I to do?" by raising and answering the question "What is my goal?"

The *deontological* method finds its closest analogy in the working of the law. According to Niebuhr, this style fits best what he called "man-the-citizen," the one who comes to self-awareness in the midst of commandments and rules.[14] (The word "deontology" comes from the Greek word, *deon*, for duty or obligation.) Deontology seeks to establish the law, duty, right, or obligation in question on the basis of the intrinsic aspects of an act rather than on its consequences. Therefore, a deontologist approaches the question "What ought I to do?" by first asking and answering the question "What is the law?" or "What is my duty?" Traditionally, Roman Catholic moral theology, while fundamentally teleological in its basic orientation, has been commonly identified with this method for making a moral decision.

The third method of decision making is the *responsibility* model. Its closest analogy is to an aesthetic experience, and as a style it appeals to what Niebuhr called "man-the-answerer," the person who acts in a way that fits what is going on.[15] The question "What ought I to do?" is preceded by the question "What is happening?" Moral persons are seen as ones who are acted upon and then must respond in accordance with their interpretation of what is happening to them. In this model, the right thing to do is properly harmonious with the full relational context. The responsibility model does not look at competing rights, rules, obligations, or consequences only. The consequences and duty continue to have an important place in the moral life, but neither can be taken apart from the person's relatedness to others, to the world, and to God.

Since aspects of all three strategies are integral to moral experience, we would expect to find elements of each always taken into consideration. Yet we sometimes find moralists guided by a preference for one method over another. In Chapter 20 we will take a look at each strategy again and give preference to the responsibility model for making a moral decision and draw out its implications for giving pastoral moral guidance.

The purpose of this chapter has been to spell out in some detail the three primary tasks of anyone who wishes to engage in moral reflection. Engaging these tasks today occurs in a new context which has wide-ranging implications for the meaning and significance of the way we think about moral matters and of the positions we hold. To complete this introduction to moral theology, then, we need to consider some of the major aspects of the contemporary context in which moral theology is done.

## Notes

1. This threefold task of ethics is an expansion of Daniel C. Maguire's proposal that the task of ethics is to bring "sensitivity and method to the discernment of moral values." *The Moral Choice* (Garden City: Doubleday and Company, Inc., 1978), p. 110. By adding "reflection" to the task of the moralist, I am incorporating aspects of the "science" component of Maguire's notion of ethics as an "art-science" and I am expanding on his requirements of method.

2. According to Maguire, "The foundation of morality is the experience of the value of persons and their environment." *Ibid.*, p. 72. Another way of expressing this experience is in the symbol, "sanctity of life." See *ibid.*, p. 83.

3. Gilligan, *In a Different Voice* (Cambridge: Harvard University Press, 1982).

4. Robert Bolt, *A Man for All Seasons* (New York: Random House, Inc., Vintage Books, 1962), p. 81.

5. Maguire has explored the implication of this axiom to great benefit for understanding how to do ethics. See *The Moral Choice*, especially Chapter Five, pp. 128–188, though the whole book is rooted in this axiom.

6. Lonergan's most extensive treatment of his cognitional theory is in *Insight* (New York: Philosophical Library Inc., 1957); a more succinct treatment is in his essay "Cognitional Structure," *Collection*, edited by F.E. Crowe (New York: Herder and Herder, 1967) pp. 221–239. James J. Walter and Stephen Happel have drawn upon this theory to show the foundations it provides for moral theology and Christian doctrine. See their *Conversion and Discipleship: A Christian Foundation for Ethics and Doctrine* (Philadelphia: Fortress Press, 1986).

7. This is the sense of Lonergan's notion of coming to a "virtually unconditioned judgment" which is a key notion in his epistemology. See the short section, "The General Form of Reflective Insight" in *Insight*, pp. 280–281.

8. *Ibid.* The sociology of knowledge has helped us realize that our knowledge is limited by where we stand (intellectually, socially, geographically, or otherwise). Our knowledge changes as we move from one place to

another. But since we cannot see reality from all points of view at once, we must remain open to a revision and expansion of our knowledge.

9. This position is evident in Lonergan's epistemology. See, for example, the reflective study of John P. Boyle, "Lonergan's Method in Theology and Objectivity in Moral Theology," *Thought* 37 (July 1973): 599–601. This understanding of the relationship of "objectivity" to "subjectivity" is also confirmed by the sociology of knowledge. See, for example, Werner Stark, *The Sociology of Knowledge* (London: Routledge and Kegan Paul, 1967); also, see Peter Berger and Thomas Luckmann, *The Social Construction of Reality* (Garden City: Doubleday, 1967).

10. Bernard Lonergan distinguishes two disparate meanings of the term "object," and two different criteria of "objectivity." "Object" can refer to the world of immediacy or to the world mediated by meaning. In the world of immediacy, the criterion of objectivity is the proper functioning of our senses. In the world mediated by meaning, the criteria of objectivity are the data of sense and of consciousness, the operations of intelligence and reasonableness, and the result of combining these two. Lonergan concludes: "For it is now apparent that in the world mediated by meaning and motivated by value, objectivity is simply the consequence of authentic subjectivity, of genuine attention, genuine intelligence, genuine reasonableness, genuine responsibility. Mathematics, science, philosophy, ethics, theology differ in many manners; but they have the common feature that their objectivity is the fruit of attentiveness, intelligence, reasonableness, and responsibility": *Method in Theology* (New York: Herder and Herder, 1972), pp. 262–265, quotation at p. 265. An attempt to rethink the meaning of moral objectivity by giving significant place to the subject has been evident in the work of Stanley Hauerwas. See his *Character and the Christian Life* (San Antonio: Trinity University Press, 1975), *Vision and Virtue* (Notre Dame: Fides Publishers, Inc., 1975), *Truthfulness and Tragedy*, co-authored with Richard Bondi and David B. Burrell (Notre Dame: University of Notre Dame Press, 1977), and *A Community of Character* (Notre Dame: University of Notre Dame Press, 1981).

11. In recent years, theologians have frequently spoken of the inseparability of the teaching-learning function in the church. For a few examples, see Richard A. McCormick, "The Magisterium and Theologians," *CTSA Proceedings* 24 (1969): 239–254; also his "Moral Notes," *Theological Studies* 29 (December 1968): 714–718; and 30 (December 1969): 644–648; also, his "The Contemporary Moral Magisterium," *Lectureship* (St. Benedict, Oregon: Mount Angel Abbey Press, 1978) pp. 48–60.

Some documents of Vatican II have also witnessed to the importance of drawing upon different competencies in coming to truth. See especially *Gaudium et Spes*, n. 62, which advocates not only freedom of inquiry but also the need for all who search for truth to share resources and points of view proper to different areas of competence. *Lumen Gentium*, n. 37, encourages ongoing dialogue between the laity and clergy for the sake of promoting the mission of the church and sharing in the apostolate of the hierarchy.

12. Niebuhr, *The Responsible Self* (New York: Harper and Row, 1963).

13. *Ibid.*, pp. 49–50.

14. *Ibid.*, pp. 51–52.

15. *Ibid.*, p. 56.

# 3    The Context of Contemporary Moral Theology

*N*ow that we have a general overview of the nature of moral theology and of the tasks of one who engages in it, we may be able to understand more clearly what is happening in contemporary moral theology if we examine some of the main lines of its development. This chapter, then, will look first at the shape moral theology took between the Council of Trent and Vatican II. Then it will sketch some of the main features which characterize the renewal of moral theology since Vatican II and which make up the general context in which moral theology is being developed today.

## Historical Background

### From Trent to Vatican II

The moral theology which shaped the Catholic world prior to the renewal of the Second Vatican Council (1962–1965) came rather late in our tradition. Moral theology emerged as a discipline distinct from other theological disciplines after the Counter-Reformation Council of Trent (1545–1563). Prior to that time, reflections on the practical concerns of Christian living were, by and large, normally integrated into the one larger theological reflection on the mysteries of faith. Such integration is especially evident in the patristic literature and in the great summas such as the *Summa Theologica* of Thomas Aquinas. However, the Penitential Books of the early Middle Ages (sixth to ninth centuries) represent a deviation from this norm. These books, though not theological works strictly speaking, did have an influence on the future development of moral theology. They were primarily lists of typical sins with a corresponding penance. These Penitentials were designed as handbooks for confessors during the emergence of private, frequent, individual confession of sins. As such they had an influence on shaping a moral perspective which focused on individual acts, on regarding the moral life as a matter of avoiding sin, and on turning moral reflection into an analysis of sin in its many forms.[1]

At the time of the Council of Trent, the Church took up a defensive posture to protect itself from the Reformation. The Council of Trent sought to provide clear lines which would distinguish Protestant protest from Catholic doctrine. To assure the continuation of teaching clear and consistent doctrine, the Council established the seminary system for the training of priests. As a result, the world of Catholic theology shifted from the university to the seminary and became highly influenced by the pastoral agenda of training priests. In the seminary, the teaching of morality became closely allied with canon law and liturgical rubrics. These disciplines shared the common concerns of determining clear and concise guides for the kinds of behavior which were allowed and forbidden in different states of life and for determining the appropriate penalties for breaking the law. To have the same person teach morality, canon law, and liturgical rubrics would not be unusual in seminaries marked by the Tridentine spirit.

The origins of Roman Catholic moral theology as a distinct discipline go hand in hand with the Council of Trent's decrees regarding the sacrament of penance. Trent reasserted the norm of the Fourth Lateran Council (1215) requiring the confession to one's pastor of all mortal sins according to number, kind, and circumstances. This required a deeper probing into moral problems with an emphasis on forming a proper conscience, on solving cases of conscience, and on making a precise determination of sins so as to make a proper confession. As a result, the Council of Trent placed the accent in moral theology on the seminary's need to train priests to serve as confessors. The practical problem the confessor had to solve was whether the penitent had sinned or not. As a result, the primary focus of moral theology was to determine the sinfulness of actions and the principles underlying the correct solution of cases.

For these purposes handbooks for confessors, a byproduct of the earlier forms of the Penitential Books, quickly emerged in the form of manuals of moral theology. These manuals were prepared to meet the pastoral need of priests who were supposed to play a significant role in the formation of consciences and who were to judge the degree of sinfulness of specific human acts. As such the manuals were oriented toward the individual and focused on acts in order to determine their degree of sinfulness. As a result, the tone of the manuals was minimalistic and their method was casuistic. That is, they tried to determine within the limits established by laws or principles what was permitted or forbidden. The challenge to the moral life put forth by the manuals was the matter of discovering the appropriate law for each situation and assessing its binding force in the circumstances. The primary questions which helped to make such an assessment were "What am I doing? Is it allowed? How far can I go?" Such casuistry gave the impression that living within the limits of the law is really what the Christian moral life is all about.

The result was the gradual development of an independent and self-sufficient moral theology. This separation was strengthened by the division of theology into different disciplines. Moral theology became isolated from the influence of scripture, the great mysteries of faith, and spirituality. Moreover, the source of moral knowledge was reduced to knowledge of the law—divine, natural, ecclesial, and civil. Even scripture was taken as a collection of laws which could be used to enforce natural law principles. Natural law itself was understood as a codified system of laws known by reason, and the declarations of the magisterium were interpreted also in the perspective of abiding laws. In short, classical Roman Catholic moral theology became separated from other branches of theology and rooted in an unchanging vision of an objective natural order which could be known largely by reason. The structures of the natural order were understood to support laws which demanded conformity, even at the level of very specific judgments.

The legalistic tendency of moral theology had a seriously confining effect on moral perspectives and moral thinking. For example, reason, nature, and law held a place of primacy while other vital concerns in moral theology, such as the development of moral character and the life of virtue, were treated lightly, if at all (even though St. Thomas himself had a substantial treatment of the virtues in his *Summa*). Moreover, the legalistic tendencies showed an excessive concern with absolute moral certainty. This led to a carefully constructed system of abstract principles which would yield clear conclusions to take the place of the judgment of conscience.

Because of this history, Roman Catholic moral theology on the eve of the Second Vatican Council reflected a moral perspective that was individualistic, act-centered, law-oriented, and sin-conscious. For example, nearly 80% of Nolden-Schmitt, a standard manual used in seminaries at the time of the council, is devoted to acts, law, and sin. The other 20% deals with aspects of the moral person and virtue.[2] Even as recently as 1958, the moral compendium of the influential John C. Ford and Gerald Kelly reiterate the principal goal of moral theology to be the forming of confessors to determine the limits of sin and to educate consciences in the sacrament of penance.[3] The method and tone of the manuals not only have influenced the moral perspective and thinking of generations of priests, but also, through being enshrined in popular catechisms, have shaped the minds and hearts of generations of lay Catholics as well.

The manuals, with their focus, worldview, and method, form the immediate background to the renewal of moral theology called for by the Second Vatican Council. By the time of the Council there was widespread dissatisfaction with what passed for Christian morality in the Catholic Church, and the conviction was growing that Christian morality had much more to offer than what was contained in the manuals. A change was long overdue.

## The Renewal of Moral Theology

To say that great changes have occurred in Catholic moral theology since Vatican II is a commonplace. As a result of the council, the manuals were abandoned as standard texts for teaching moral theology and with that at least three major changes occurred: (1) a shift in focus, (2) a shift in worldview, and (3) a shift in method. The remainder of this chapter will summarize some of the outstanding features of these shifts in order to establish the context of contemporary moral theology and its ongoing renewal.

### A Shift in Focus

One of the criticisms directed against the manuals is that they represent an understanding of moral theology that is too narrow in scope and in purpose. Moral theology needed to be transformed from a discipline for confessors to one of a critical understanding of faith for Christian living. For this to happen, moral theology would have to be integrated with the great mysteries of faith. Another criticism of the manuals is that their so-called "moral theology" was not "theology" at all. It could more accurately be described as moral philosophy pursued by believers. The content of the manuals was too separated from the great mysteries of faith to be theological, and scripture appeared in the form of random quotations to support positions arrived at on the basis of philosophy. The moral reflection in the manuals was primarily rational reflection on human nature. Faith did not seem to make a difference.

The renewal of moral theology has radically changed the manualist focus of an isolated, individualistic, act-centered, and sin-oriented approach to morality and the moral life. The primary tenet of the renewal of moral theology has been that morality worthy of the modifier "Christian" ought to be integrated with revelation and the great mysteries of faith. The efforts at renewing moral theology try to take seriously the claim of *Gaudium et Spes* that "Faith throws a new light on everything, manifests God's design for man's total vocation, and thus directs the mind to solutions that are fully human" (n. 11).

The possibility of integrating moral theology with scripture and the great mysteries of faith was prepared for by a renewed interest in biblical studies. Remote inspiration came from Leo XIII with his encyclical *Providentissimus Deus* (1893) which declared scripture the "soul of theology." In 1943 Pius XII issued *Divino Afflante Spiritu* to open the way for Catholic scholars to take critical approaches to the biblical text. This gave a powerful boost to all of theology, not just to the study of the Bible. It opened the way for the council's decree on revelation, *Dei Verbum*, to declare that "Sacred theology rests on the written word of God, together with sacred tradition as its primary and perpetual foundation. . . . The study of the sacred page is, as it were, the soul of sacred theology" (n. 24). With regards to moral theology in particular, the only explicit statement of the council comes from *Optatum Totius*, the Decree on Priestly Formation:

> Special attention needs to be given to the development of moral theology. Its scientific exposition should be more thoroughly nourished by scriptural teaching. It should show the nobility of the Christian vocation of the faithful, and their obligation to bring forth fruit in charity for the life of the world (n. 16).

The challenge issued by this statement to enrich moral theology with teaching drawn from scripture had already begun prior to the council. One thinks particularly of the work of Emile Mersch who influenced the idea of a morality based on the notion of the mystical body (1937),[4] and Gerard Gilleman who put love at the center of the moral life in his major book of moral reform, *The Primacy of Charity in Moral Theology* (1952),[5] or Fritz Tillman's stress on morality as the imitation of Christ in *The Master Calls* (1960).[6] However, the most significant work for the renewal movement was Bernard Häring's *The Law of Christ*, which first appeared in German in 1954. Few works were as popular as that one, and no one contributed more to the general spirit of renewal in moral theology than did Bernard Häring. This "charter document" of renewal in moral theology retained an interest in the concerns of the manuals but approached these interests with a new spirit. Häring's work shows, if even at times in an uncritical fashion, what a moral theology might look like which returns to its sources, notably the Bible, and which is integrated with the great mysteries of faith.

Since Häring's groundbreaking work in the mid-1950s, many other attempts have been made to integrate moral thinking with scripture and the great mysteries of faith. *Covenant, vocation, responsibility, conversion, discipleship,* and *the imitation of Christ* are only some of the themes contemporary moral theology is developing in the effort to root morality in scripture and to integrate it with the great mysteries of faith. Developing these themes leads not only to a closer dependence of moral theology on scripture but also to a close relationship with systematic theology, which elaborates dogmatic understandings with fidelity to scripture.

In short then, the renewed moral theology, rooted in the Bible and integrated with the great mysteries of faith, focuses on the total human vocation of living in response to God's self-communication to us in creation, in history, and most fully in Jesus. As such, moral theology deals with what God's offer of divine love enables us to be and to do. In this renewed morality, values are primary; laws are secondary. The fundamental value is the sacred value of persons as the image of God. By promoting and protecting whatever befits the well-being of persons we are responding to the presence of God in our midst. In this way, the moral life becomes largely the matter of promoting positive human relationships which allow the full potential of one's own and another's gifts to flourish. With its attention to relationships and responsibility, our renewed moral theology is much more socially conscious than the individualistic morality of the manuals. (manuals of moral Theology)

In the renewed moral theology, the act-centered question of the ethics of doing, "What am I doing?" is no longer enough to cover the scope of morality. We must also ask from the ethics of being, "What is my doing doing to me? What sort of person am I becoming?" These call for much greater attention to character and virtue than the manuals gave. The renewed view of moral theology sees the moral life reflected more in the quality of our character and our relationships than in isolated actions we may do. Living morally is a matter of appropriating the values which promote positive moral character and life-giving human relationships. As such the moral life is a matter of an ongoing process of conversion so that who we are and what we do becomes more and more a response to divine love.

## A Shift in Worldview

Perhaps the most important shift in theology which affects the entire enterprise of contemporary moral theology is the shift in ways of looking at the world. Since the roots of moral misunderstanding and disagreement often lie in a conflict of worldviews, we need to give a little more attention to what is entailed in this shift than we are giving to the other two.

When I try to explain "worldview" and a shift in worldviews, a clip from *Peanuts* comes to mind. Linus is struggling with his introduction to new math. In his frustration he exclaims, "How can I do 'new math' problems with an 'old math' mind!" Linus has it exactly right. The issue is his "worldview" (also called "point of view" or "consciousness"). Something like the old math/new math shift has occurred in theology.

Bernard Lonergan characterizes this shift from the old theology to the new as a move away from a "classicist" worldview to one marked by "historical consciousness."[7] The Age of Enlightenment marks the beginning of this shift; the development of empirical science and philosophy's "turn to the subject" were major influences. These movements called into question the great conceptual systems of well-defined essences expressed in abstract, universal concepts. The impact of these movements and the shift in worldviews have been strongly reflected in the theology of Vatican II and in subsequent theological reflection.

Stated briefly, the classicist worldview assumes that the world is a finished product. In principle, everything that can be done has been done; "there is nothing new under the sun." Moreover, the classicist worldview mistakes knowing for looking. One only needs to look upon the world to discover its order because a good look grasps the unchanging principles of the moral order. Since the natural, unchanging principles remain valid forever, they yield a high degree of certitude in the conclusions which are deduced from them. According to this worldview, moral living requires that we reproduce the order given in the world and learn to live by it. The Greek Parthenon and the Roman Forum are symbols of the classicist worldview. Each represents a world standing in well-balanced proportions. Stability is the principal virtue; change is a threatening vice. "Abstract," "universal," "eternal," "necessary," "essential," and "fixed" are adjectives which characterize the classicist worldview. It is most reluctant to admit that moral theology itself could change or that the specific conclusions drawn in one historical period may not be valid in another era. From this point of view, moral theology only needs to make different applications of its eternal principles to the new problems and questions which may emerge.

The modern, historically conscious worldview, on the other hand, sees each thing as part of a whole which has yet to be discovered. Since life is an ongoing process of knowing more and more, thinking in developmental terms is quite natural. The historically conscious view conceives the person as growing closer to the truth but not being so bold as to know the whole of it anywhere along the way. This point of view recognizes that all knowledge is conditioned by time and place, limited self-awareness, and limited grasps of reality. "Specific," "individual," and "changing" are adjectives which characterize this point of view. Change, development, and revision are not signs of imperfection but ways of coming to the truth. This point of view believes that, although we come to possess truth slowly, we are not wandering aimlessly with nothing to give us direction. The truth can be grasped in some reliable way, allowing us to obtain a foothold in our journey before moving on to new discoveries.

Historical consciousness recognizes that humanity is both a product and a maker of history. For this reason, historical consciousness requires that all statements of moral teaching be interpreted from within their context and for a new audience. Since it does not absolutize any one particular culture or one particular moment in history as having grasped the whole of truth, the modern worldview is not satisfied with the mere repetition of the formulations of another age for a new era with new people and new experiences. Historical consciousness employs an inductive method which takes seriously the diversity of human experience based on historical and cultural differences. Since moral theology is reflecting on the lived experience of the Christian community, it will inevitably be influenced by the very context in which it finds itself. As a result, its practical conclusions will also be colored by the limitations of historically and culturally conditioned experiences and expressions of value within that community. For this reason, it has greater difficulty than does the moral theology of the classicist worldview in reaching an absolute certitude which excludes the possibility of error even in specific complex instances.

The accompanying chart sketches some prominent features of both worldviews. Laying out so cleanly the differences in the two worldviews can

| FEATURES | CLASSICIST WORLDVIEW | MODERN WORLDVIEW |
|---|---|---|
| A. *CHARACTERISTICS* | Views the word as complete and fixed for all eternity | Views the world as dynamic and evolving through historical development |
| | The world is marked by harmony of an objective order | The world is marked by progressive growth and change |
| | Speaks of the world in terms of well-defined essences using abstract, universal concepts | Speaks of the world in terms of individual traits using concrete, historical concepts |
| B. *METHOD* | Begins with the abstract and derives principles from universal essences | Begins with experience and derives principles from accumulated experience |
| | Primarily deductive | Primarily inductive |
| | Conclusions will remain the same | Some conclusions will change as empirical evidence changes |
| | Conclusions are always secure as long as deductive logic is correct | Leaves room for incompleteness, possible error, open to revision; conclusions are as accurate as evidence will allow, but these are accurate enough |

| FEATURES | CLASSICIST WORLDVIEW | MODERN WORLDVIEW |
|---|---|---|
| C. *MORAL THEOLOGY AND THE MORAL LIFE* | Abstracts from the concrete to deal with issues in the abstract and universal realm | Deals with issues in the concrete particularity of historical moment |
| | Deals with universals of humanhood by deriving principles from the physical nature of being human | Deals with the historical person in historically particular circumstances |
| | Conforms to authority and to pre-established norms | Formulations of norms are historically conditioned |
| | Emphasis on duty and obligation to reproduce established order | Emphasis on responsibility and actions fitting to changing times |
| | Lacks integration with the great mysteries of faith and a critical biblical orientation | More soundly integrated with the mysteries of faith and critical use of the Bible |
| D. *ADVANTAGES* | Clear, simple, and sure in its view of reality and in its conclusions about what to do | Respects the uniqueness of the person and the peculiarities of historical circumstances |
| | | Emphasis on the moral life as incomplete and in need of conversion |
| E. *DISADVANTAGES* | Tends to be authoritarian in the sense of claiming to have answers suitable for all time | Tends to be relative in the sense that everything is conditioned |
| | Tends to be dogmatic in the sense of having the last word | Tends to be antinomian in the sense that all laws are relative |

be deceiving since it might suggest that either of these appear in persons and documents in their pure form. The more likely situation is to find these worldviews adopted in different degrees and in various ways.

The shift of worldviews has been reflected in the theology of the documents of Vatican II and in subsequent theological reflection. *Gaudium et Spes*, the Pastoral Constitution on the Church in the Modern World, is an excellent example. It makes its call to "read the signs of the times" with some credibility because the document itself recognizes that "the human race has passed from a rather static concept of reality to a more dynamic, evolutionary one" (n. 5). Other signs of an historical consciousness at work in the conciliar documents are the fundamental acceptance of a readiness for change, the call for the church to undergo continuous reform, the use of a dynamic image for the church such as a "pilgrim people of God," the call for ongoing dialogue as a method of teaching and learning, the centrality of conversion in the moral life, and an openness to reformulating long-standing principles.

The church has officially recognized that historical consciousness can and must be taken into account in formulating and interpreting official teachings. The official documents which endorsed and encouraged the biblical renewal in the Roman Catholic Church, for example, hold this regarding teachings pertaining to the Bible. *Divino Afflante Spiritu* (1943) was the charter document in this matter. Likewise, the Instruction of the Pontifical Biblical Commission, "The Historical Truth of the Gospels" (1964), and Vatican II's *Dei Verbum*, the Constitution on Divine Revelation (1965), recognized that the books of the Bible contain the word of God in the limited words of men and women of various ages. To discover God's revelation we must take into account the historical situation, the philosophical worldview, and the theological limitations of those who wrote these books. The same limiting conditions which affect the Bible, its composition and its interpretation also affect the dogmatic and moral teaching of the church.

Some evidence of historical consciousness at work in the moral teaching of the magisterium can be found in the following examples. In social ethics we have, in addition to *Gaudium et Spes* of Vatican II, the encyclical of Paul VI in 1971, *Octogesima Adveniens* (popularly known as "A Call to Action"), which said: "In the face of such widely varying situations it is difficult for us to utter a unified message and to put forward a solution which has universal validity. Such is not our ambition, nor is it our mission" (n. 4). The American bishops have worked out of the framework of historical consciousness in developing their three pastoral letters of the 1980s on nuclear war, the economy, and women's concerns. The process by which these letters were written demonstrated a commitment to the inductive method of historical consciousness by consulting broadly and openly with experts as well as with the wider community of faith.

In medical ethics, too, historical consciousness is at work. The Vatican *Declaration on Euthanasia* (1980), for example, shows a commitment to this point of view in the way it faces the question of life-support technology. It wants to uphold the substance of the teaching enshrined in the principle of the distinction between ordinary and extraordinary means of treatment but recognizes the ambiguity and inadequacy of expressing it in this language. The document suggests a new formulation of the substance of that teaching in the language of "proportionate" and "disproportionate" means.

Interestingly, official Catholic teachings in the area of sexual morality show less of a commitment to historical consciousness. By and large, they reflect a mix of worldviews with a bias toward classicism. For example, the "Declaration on Sexual Ethics," *Persona Humana* (1975), reflects a classicist worldview with its emphasis on the eternal and the immutable:

> Of course, in the history of civilization many of the concrete conditions and needs of human life have changed and will continue to change. But all evolution of morals and every type of life must be kept within the limits imposed by the immutable principles based upon every human person's constitutive elements and essential relations—elements and relations which transcend historical contingencies (n. 3).

The "Letter to the Bishops of the Catholic Church on the Pastoral Care of Homosexual Persons" in 1986 admits to some degree of historical consciousness when it points out that challenges to its teaching on homosexuality come from recognizing earlier condemnations to be historically bound by culture. It acknowledges that the biblical condemnations upon which it relies must be understood as products of different historical periods reflecting great cultural and historical diversity and differing in many ways from the world today (n. 5). However, the document does not follow through with its recognition of historical consciousness when it applies the biblical material: "What should be noticed is that, in the presence of such remarkable diversity, there is nevertheless a clear consistency within the scriptures themselves on the moral issue of homosexual behavior" (n. 5).

In a similar fashion, the Congregation for the Faith's instruction on bioethics, "Instruction on Respect for Human Life in Its Origin and on the Dignity of Procreation" (1987), is not consistently committed to historical consciousness. Its introductory section reflects historical consciousness at work by recognizing that progress has been made in the biomedical sciences and that new data, experience and research must be taken into account in any moral position (Introduction, n. 1). However, the subsequent sections on specific technologies reflect a shift to the classicist method of deduction and to the moral viewpoint of a fixed, non-relational moral order. For example, its position on specific technologies is deduced from "laws inscribed in the very being of man and of woman" (II-B, n.4; cf. II-B, n.7). The document basically applies principles formulated by the magisterium prior to the new evidence which the document's Introduction acknowledges must be taken into account. The classicist moral viewpoint of a fixed, non-relational moral order is also evident in its judgment of homologous "in vitro" fertilization:

> The process of IVF [in vitro fertilization] and ET [embryo transfer] must be judged in itself and cannot borrow its definitive moral quality from the totality of conjugal life of which it becomes part nor from the conjugal acts which may precede or follow it (II-B, n. 5).

The ongoing revision of Catholic moral theology today is an effort to incorporate in a coherent way the insights and advantages of the historically conscious worldview while not ignoring the perduring values of the classicist worldview. Contemporary moral theology wants to preserve the clarity, consistency, and precision of the classicist worldview while at the same time respecting human freedom, the uniqueness of the historical moral situation, and the unfinished character of the moral life so valued by the historically conscious worldview. Contemporary moral theology is not concerned with ignoring either classicism or historical consciousness. As Richard P. McBrien points out, the relationship of classicism to historical consciousness in contemporary theology is one of dialectical tension.[8] That is to say, values are present in both approaches which should not be ignored.

However, McBrien also points out that there is perhaps one irreconcilable difference between the two worldviews: "The classicist assumes that one can know and express absolute truth in ways that are essentially unaffected by the normal limitations of our human condition."[9] Because the classicist rejects in principle the assertion that the perception and expression of truth is historically conditioned, moral theology cannot follow classicism alone in formulating its moral positions. Classicism would be generally indifferent to the sociology of knowledge and to the findings of the empirical sciences as well as to the impact of ongoing experience on the meaning and limits of already formulated moral teaching. And yet, moral theology today cannot follow historical consciousness alone, for that would underestimate the ability of well-established moral norms to provide continuity and stability for the moral life and to counter tendencies toward subjectivism and relativism in moral matters. Catholic moral theology today respects the continuity of tradition and the discontinuities of human experience.

## The Shift in Method

The third shift behind the changes in moral theology is that of method. This has already been suggested by the shift in worldviews and logically follows from it. Contemporary theology's method is reflected in *Gaudium et Spes*. Before taking its reading of the signs of the times in Part II, the document states its method in an introductory paragraph saying that it is going to consider the urgent needs of the present age "in the light of the gospel and of human experience" (n. 46). This statement tips the document's hand showing its favor for a more historically conscious, inductive method in theology.

What is this method like? Perhaps a study in contrasts will show its points of emphasis. The moral manuals reflect the classicist worldview. Their method is deductive. The classicist worldview presumes that we can have a clear grasp of the essence of reality, human nature, and the human good in a clear and distinct way. By starting with an abstract principle, such as give to each his or her due, or artificial means of reproduction are prohibited, deduction yields practical conclusions which claim always to be valid. Abstract principles of human nature and moral action form the basis of universal and unexceptional moral teaching. This leaves little room for taking seriously historical development, uncertainty, the complexities of human existence, or being tentative about the application of moral norms to different and complex moral situations.

The historically conscious worldview of contemporary moral theology supports a method that is empirical and inductive. This is not to say that deductive reasoning has no place in modern moral theology. It still does. But moral theology today is more likely to begin with historical particulars, the concrete, and the changing.[10] It is reluctant to draw conclusions independently of a consideration of the human person and the complexities of human existence. This requires a greater concern for the developmental, personalistic, and social structural dimensions of lived experiences. In order to gain access to this experience, the social sciences must form an integral part of the reflection on complex moral issues.

The inductive method in moral theology has a significant implication for understanding and using moral norms—those standards of judgment of who we ought to be and what we ought to do. Since the inductive method gives such significant attention to the concrete and the historical, we can no longer expect our behavioral norms to spell out everything in advance. To think that they did or could do so would be to take our hospital code of ethics as the sure answer to all the doctor's dilemmas, or it would make our norms of social justice determine specific social policy. The inductive method helps us to avoid claiming absolute certainty where we cannot get it. Also, it does not bring us to moral conclusions with the unambiguous, comfortable clarity we may wish to have. It forces us to be more modest in our moral claims, to be tentative in our moral conclusions, and to be open to revising our positions if the evidence warrants it.

Another implication of the inductive method is that it requires moral theology to pay attention, in a critical way, to contributions from the empirical sciences and from the testimony of people of good will. We cannot adequately arrive at a moral position apart from considering empirical data, the data of human experience. The very structure of the knowing process demands it. In moral matters, experience is a valid source of moral knowledge about the human good and a valid source for confirming moral judgments.[11] This means that we ought to pay closer attention to the experience of the moral community and the consequences of what helps and what hinders the full development of human life in the process of formulating and interpreting our moral teaching. This is precisely what the American bishops have tried to do in the way they went about producing their pastoral letters of the 1980s. The high acclaim given to these documents is due largely to the method used to arrive at their teaching more than to the actual positions taken themselves.[12]

Greater appeal to the empirical sciences and to the experience and testimony of people of good will affects the way we formulate new teachings and assess past ones. For example, some matters about which we have made unambiguous moral judgments in the past (such as masturbation, contraception, sterilization, religious liberty, and usury) are now seen to be much more complex realities than previous formulations admitted. The appeal to empirical data and the testimony of people of good will softens the severity of some of our formulations and weakens their claims for certain, universal application. The inductive method is, in many ways, forcing us to bring the ancient and honorable prudential process to center stage.

Furthermore, an inductive method encourages the learning-teaching process of coming to truth. The conclusions of an inductive method do not claim to be absolutely certain and free from error. An inductive method accepts limitations of conclusions based on the possibility of limited evidence and insight. Mistakes are the way to fuller understanding. A dissenting opinion which comes at the end of careful deliberation and honest effort to appropriate the official position as valid becomes itself a new datum to be interpreted, evaluated, and appropriated for its kernel of truth. The inductive method assumes that its conclusions are, at best, tentative summaries of the present state of the question. An inductive method does not claim to solve a problem completely or to close a discussion. It always remains open to new experience and insight because it proposes its conclusions as identifying the way things appear to be at the present time.[13]

At this point the three principal shifts in moral reflection should be clear at least in outline. The further significance of these shifts will be sketched out through the remainder of this book.

## Notes

1. For more detailed overviews of the development of moral theology, see Bernard Häring, *The Law of Christ*, Vol. 1: *General Moral Theology* (Westminster: Newman Press, 1963), pp. 3–33; Häring, *Free and Faithful in Christ*, Vol. 1: *General Moral Theology* (New York: The Seabury Press, 1978), pp. 28–58. For an excellent treatment of the development of moral theology from a thematic point of view, see John Mahoney, *The Making of Moral Theology: A Study of the Roman Catholic Tradition* (Oxford: Clarendon Press, 1987).

2. H. Nolden, *Summa Theologiae Moralis*, 3 vols., 28th edition revised by A. Schmitt (Barcelona: Herder, 1951), Vol. 1.

3. John C. Ford and Gerald Kelly, *Contemporary Moral Theology*, Vol. 1: *Questions in Fundamental Moral Theology* (Westminster: Newman Press, 1958), pp. 97–98.

4. Mersch, *Morale et Corps Mystique* (Paris: Desclée de Brouwer, 1937). *Morality and the Mystical Body*, translated by Daniel F. Ryan (New York: P. J. Kenedy & Sons, 1939).

5. Gilleman, *The Primacy of Charity in Moral Theology*. French edition (Paris: Desclée de Brouwer et Cie, 1952). Translated from second French edition by William F. Ryan and Andre Vachon (Westminster: Newman Press, 1959).

6. Tillman, *The Master Calls*. Translated by Gregory J. Roettger (Baltimore: Helicon Press, 1960).

7. See Bernard Lonergan, "Theology in Its New Context," *Theology of Renewal*, Vol. 1: *Renewal of Religious Thought*, edited by L.K. Shook (New York: Herder and Herder, 1968), pp. 34–46; also his "The Transition from a Classicist World-View to Historical Mindedness," in *Law for Liberty*, edited by James E. Biechler (Baltimore: Helicon Press, 1967) pp. 126–133; also, his "Dimensions of Meaning," in *Collection*, edited by F. E. Crowe (New York: Herder and Herder, 1967), pp. 252–267.

8. McBrien, *Catholicism*, Vol. 2 (Oak Grove: Winston Press, 1980), p. 942.

9. *Ibid.*, p. 943.

10. For a more thorough analysis of these contrasts, see Charles E. Curran, "Absolute Norms in Moral Theology," *Norm and Context in Christian Ethics*, edited by Gene Outka and Paul Ramsy (New York: Charles Scribner's Sons, 1968), pp. 139–173, especially pp. 166–173. More recently see his

*Classicist world view —*
*Modern world view —*
*Inductive method of Theology*

"Natural Law," in *Directions in Fundamental Moral Theology* (Notre Dame: University of Notre Dame Press, 1985), pp. 119–172; see especially pp. 137–157.

11. John G. Milhaven has consistently urged that more attention be given to experience and empirical evidence in moral matters. See his "Toward an Epistemology of Ethics," *Theological Studies* 27 (June 1966): 228–241. This was reprinted as "Criticism of Traditional Morality" in his book, *Toward a New Catholic Morality* (Garden City: Doubleday, 1970), pp. 127–139. He has continued to show the significance of experience and empirical evidence in his "Objective Moral Evaluation of Consequences," *Theological Studies* 32 (September 1971): 407–430; also, "The Voice of Lay Experience in Christian Ethics," *CTSA Proceedings* 33 (1978): 35–53. Also, Daniel C. Maguire has shown the significance of individual and group experience as a valid source of knowledge for making a moral choice. See his *The Moral Choice* (Garden City: Doubleday and Co., 1978), especially Chapter Ten, pp. 309–342.

12. Edward V. Vacek, "Authority and the Peace Pastoral," *America* 149 (October 22, 1983) pp. 225–228.

13. The use of the inductive method to promote the teaching-learning process of coming to moral truth has been a consistent theme of Richard A. McCormick. See, for example, "The Magisterium and Theologians," *CTSA Proceedings* 24 (1969): 239–254; also, his "Moral Notes," *Theological Studies* 29 (December 1968): 714–718; and 30 (December 1969): 644–648; also, his "The Contemporary Moral Magisterium," *Lectureship* (St. Benedict, Oregon: Mount Angel Abbey Press, 1978) pp. 48–60.

# PART ONE: THE NATURE OF THE GOOD

| The Nature of the Good | Fundamental Beliefs |
|---|---|

# 4   Faith and Morality

*T*he good is the foundation and the goal of all moral striving. Ethics, then, whether philosophical or theological, must in some way be specific about what the good is and where it can be found. The basic conviction of Christian faith is that God is good. God is the only center of value, the fixed point of reference for Christian morality. As a result, our convictions about God, which are formed and mediated by the experience of the Israelite community, Jesus, the apostolic community, and the subsequent tradition of the church ought to make a difference in the moral life.

To say that our convictions about the good are based on our beliefs about God puts us at the heart of relating faith and morality. After establishing the basic Christian conviction that God is the center of value, this chapter draws out the implications for relating faith and morality. In light of many arguments over how one can claim some distinctiveness for Christian morality, this chapter presents one way of relating faith and morality so that religious beliefs might play an integral role in moral reflection.

## God—The Center of Value

The convictions of philosophers about the good have long influenced moral dispositions and actions. For Aristotle, the good is happiness; for hedonists it is pleasure; for utilitarians it is in what is most useful. The scholastic philosophy of the Roman Catholic tradition sets up an identity between "good" and a "being's own perfection" (ST. I, q.5). That is, the nature of the good is the full actualization of any being's potential, or to achieve perfection. The innate tendency within the human person to seek perfection is the ontological basis for the fundamental moral obligation—to realize one's potential, or to be all that one can be. Actions are moral which flow out of this innate tendency and contribute to the full actualization of human potential (*agere sequitur esse*). With faith informing reason on the nature

43

of the good, the believer sees God as the fullness of being and sees God's actions as good because they flow from the divine nature—which is love.

Christians, or theologians, then, are not distinguished by the fact of having convictions about the good. Rather, they are distinguished by the kinds of convictions they have. The Christian conviction about the good is governed by the religious beliefs expressed in the stories of the Bible, especially in Jesus, and further expounded in the theological tradition of the church. The basic Christian conviction about what is good and where it can be found is that God is good. Anything else is good only in relation to God as a reflection or mediation of God. The monotheistic faith of Christianity tolerates only one center of value.[1] All other forms of goodness are always a derived goodness dependent upon the prior goodness of God. So, to establish anything other than the God of Abraham, Isaac, Jacob, and Jesus as the center of value is idolatrous.

The goodness of God is disclosed in scripture, pre-eminently in Jesus the Christ. Our knowledge of God's goodness is given, then, in our knowledge of Jesus in scripture, and in the interpretation of human experience in light of Jesus and the scripture. The convictions we have about God form the presuppositions of the moral life. The basic conviction that God is good, the only center of value and the fixed point of reference for morality, makes Christian morality an objective morality. It also makes responding to God an unconditional moral obligation.

Moreover, the belief in God as the center of value gives the Christian a reason for being moral. As James Gustafson suggests, the Christian answers the question, "Why be moral?" in terms of his or her experience and belief in the goodness of God. The Christian is moral because God is good, and because the goodness of God, always and everywhere present to us, enables and requires us to be responsible for the goodness of the world.[2] This conviction about the goodness and presence of God yields a normative statement about the moral life informed by faith: Human moral striving ought to be responsive to God and to be governed by what we can know of the goodness of God and of God's own good activity. The basic question this perspective raises for morality is "What is God enabling and requiring me to be and to do?" To answer this question, ongoing discernment must be a necessary feature of the moral life in order to discover the ways which would be most responsive to God.

From a theological perspective, what God "enables and requires"[3] of us becomes the norm of the moral life. Whether one experiences God, how one experiences God, and what beliefs one holds about God will have a pervasive, though not exclusive, effect on the sort of person one is and what one does. The extent to which we lack a vivid sense of God's loving presence (or grace), to that extent the tone and quality of our moral lives wither. Morality itself (from "mores" or "customs") means to make "customary," or we might say "to ritualize," in the actions of our lives the experiences which we have of knowing and being loved by God. In this sense, the moral life is like worship. It is a response to an experience of God. The moral life has a different quality when an awareness of God is lost: sin becomes the infraction of a rule rather than the turning away from God; moral actions become so many "works" of moral rightness rather than grateful responses to the goodness of God; moral deliberation becomes a computer-like problem-solving rather than a prayerful discernment of what God enables and requires.

For the Christian believer, then, morality cannot but be closely related to experiences of God and beliefs about God. The Christian cannot do justice to his or her moral experience and moral worldview without seeing all things as being dependent on God and without referring to God in some way as the source and goal of it all. God is the horizon within which the believer sees and values all things. As a result, the morality of those whose imagination is influenced by the religious beliefs of the Judaeo-Christian tradition has a distinctively theological element to it.

Morality for the religious believer is not authorized merely by social conventions, or merely by the desire for self-fulfillment, or merely by the requirements of general rules of conduct which reason demands. Though all of these are legitimate ways to authorize morality, they are not sufficient from a theological point of view. From a theological point of view, God authorizes and requires morality. As a result, moral responsibilities are not merely to oneself or other persons, nor are they only to the demands for rationality. They are, rather, responsibilities to God. Moral actions are judged wrong not because of harms they cause to self or others, or because they violate rational rules of conduct. Actions are wrong because they are not properly responsive to what God enables and requires. This theological dimension distinguishes the morality of persons who live by religious beliefs from those who do not. Also, the theological point of view most distinguishes a moral theologian from a moral philosopher.

To say that morality is closely related to experiences of God and beliefs about God is not to say that faith is the sole source of moral knowledge or the only justification of moral activity. To say that religious beliefs have an essential role to play in morality is not to say that they have the only role. To make morality solely dependent on faith would require that one be religious in order to be capable of arriving at moral wisdom and of living in a moral way. The Catholic tradition has not maintained such a complete dependence of morality on faith. It holds to a relative autonomy for faith and morality. Faith informs reason, but it does not replace it. Faith *and* reason are the two sources of moral knowledge to which the Catholic tradition appeals.

In the renewal of moral theology, the moral manuals were criticized for concentrating too much on reason, or natural law, as the way to know the purposes of God and to live in communion with God. The manuals' adherence to natural law resulted in giving too little attention to ways of conceiving morality and of doing moral reflection informed by faith, such as including the full range of one's religious beliefs for shaping one's moral perspective, or the significance of one's religious imagination in the process of making a moral judgment, and the dynamic of moral discernment for knowing what God requires. Reason informed by faith in the renewal of moral theology is trying to bring such considerations to the forefront. The challenge to moral theology today lies in maintaining the proper relationship of faith and reason for determining what constitutes morally good character and right moral action. This brings us to the issue of relating faith and morality.

## Faith and Morality

Most people who hold to Christian religious beliefs have a sense that their beliefs ought to make a difference in the way they understand themselves and conduct their lives. The conviction that our religious commitment sanctions certain kinds of moral behavior shows itself in a number of ways. For example, in Dostoevsky's classic, *The Brothers Karamazov*, Ivan expresses the attitude that if God does not exist, then everything is permissible. This can be taken to mean that we have no morality unless we believe that some forms of behavior are sanctioned by God.

Ordinary experience also evidences some sort of relationship between faith and morality. How often we hear remarks such as, "A Christian would never think that way," or, "That was certainly a Christian thing to do." Such remarks suggest that the speaker assumes Christianity at least entails and sanctions moral behavior, and, perhaps, that something distinctive about Christian morality can be identified either at the level of one's point of view, in one's reasons for acting, or in one's actions themselves.

Another sign of the conviction that a certain morality is entailed in religious beliefs is the disappointment one feels with religious people who are not commendably moral. Such a reaction assumes that practice is the authentic test of the sincerity and depth of a person's faith.

Religious schools are another sign that morality is in some way related to religion. Some parents want a religious education for their children because they hope that learning about God and the Bible will make their children better in a moral sense.

On the other hand, it is also true that one does not need to be religious to be moral. As surprised as some seem to be by the fact, a moral person does not need to have any religious affiliation. In fact, society expects those who have no allegiance to any religion to be as responsible for their conduct as are those who do. This would be a preposterous expectation unless it were possible to understand right and wrong, good and bad, apart from a religious commitment.

So, if one does not have to be religious to be moral, what difference can and ought one's religious beliefs make for the sort of person one is and the kinds of actions one does? This question forces us to look at the kind of dependence morality has on faith. The relation of faith and morality is not as simple and as direct as ordinary discourse sometimes makes it seem.

## The Debate on the Distinctiveness of Christian Morality

In recent years a number of Christian theologians have shown an interest in the relationship of faith and morality by contributing to the debate on the distinctiveness of Christian morality. The early years of the renewal of moral theology pursued a common insight: faith ought to affect morality. The early attempts at renewal held for a morality which would be different from a natural law, or secular morality because its primary source would be the Bible and its most important feature would be the guidance of faith. However, a reaction to this first phase of renewal almost reversed the direction of the renewal efforts.

Seeking to preserve the tradition that grounded morality in "natural" considerations, some theologians of the late 1960s and early 1970s ushered in the movement of "autonomous ethics." In Europe this movement is identified largely with Alfons Auer, Josef Fuchs, and Bruno Schuller. In the United States, Charles E. Curran and Richard A. McCormick are its prominent defenders.[4] While each of these theologians contributes his own nuances to the way of approaching the issue of distinctiveness, each shares with the others the main features of this movement.

Autonomous ethics emphasizes the human person as the discoverer of morality over God as the revealer of it and the common morality of all people over the specific morality of Christians. Its concern is that Christians be able to dialogue with all people of good will and to agree on common matters of public policy. So the movement stressed that every demand of Christian morality must be accessible to everyone through reason. Its claim is that the content of Christian and non-Christian morality at the level of concrete norms and values is substantively the same. Stated boldly, this means that the fact of being a Christian offers no specific content to the moral solutions of human problems which are not also available to the non-Christian. What Christian faith does do is to provide a distinctive context in which one lives the moral life, a religious motivation for living morally, a self-understanding informed by faith, and a specific religious intentionality, namely union with

God. In short, faith left the specific content of morality untouched. Distinguishing the specific content of morality from its context reflects a very loose relationship between faith and morality. As a result, Christian morality could easily be detached from Christian faith and presented to the world as entirely reasonable and accessible for anyone to use in addressing the problems of the world.

A stiff opposition to autonomous ethics appeared in the movement of "faith-ethics," an extension of the early phase of renewal which had begun in the 1940s and 1950s. Joseph Ratzinger and Philip Delhaye are two of its leading representatives.[5] The faith-ethics movement stresses that Christian morality cannot be completely discovered by reason but relies on faith as well. Its main thesis is that faith has such a bearing on moral discernment that some moral solutions can only be understood within the framework of faith. It claims that the content of Christian morality cannot be converted entirely into philosophical ethics. In short, the distinctiveness of Christian ethics cannot be limited to context, motivation, moral self-understanding, or intentionality. If the source of Christian morality and the norms for moral living come from the midst of faith, then Christian morality can and ought to have a distinctive content.

The specific details of this debate need not detain us here.[6] For our purposes, we need only to attend to a related issue stimulated by this debate—an understanding of how faith qualifies morality. In other words, I am asking, "What real difference can and ought the qualifier 'Christian' make when we put it before 'ethics' or 'morality'?"

All the participants in the debate acknowledge that morality is in some way dependent on some aspect of Christian faith. Given the complexity of both faith and morality, we can readily expect the dependence to operate in a wide variety of ways. James J. Walter has sorted out seven ways that Christian morality depends upon faith: (1) empirical, (2) linguistic, (3) logical, (4) ontological, (5) epistemological, (6) psychological, and (7) normative.[7] In the debate on the distinctiveness of Christian ethics, the most problematic issues pertain to logical dependence (how to account for the "therefore" which links morality to faith) and to epistemological dependence (how to know what counts for content in morality). These two cannot be easily separated.

## Linking Morality to Faith

Philosophers of language tell us that belief statements, such as "God is Creator" or "Jesus is Lord," are not like scientific statements, which are flat, testable assertions that something is true. Rather, statements of religious belief involve the believer in commitments of certain kinds.[8] Thus, the "therefore" which links morality to religious beliefs is not by way of a strict inference of syllogistic logic. The inference is made by way of what Donald D. Evans calls "the logic of self-involvement."[9] Whereas syllogistic logic is concerned with the relation between propositions, the logic of self-involvement is concerned with the ways in which language may involve something more than merely making an assertion about the way things are. The self-involving statement commits the speaker to a certain manner of living and to having certain attitudes and feelings.[10] To say, for example, "God is Creator," involves the believer in certain kinds of activity (obedience), certain attitudes (reverence), and certain feelings (awe). Therefore, to commit oneself to certain religious beliefs is to do more than to assert that such-and-such is the case. Part of the meaning of a religious belief is to commit the believer to certain intentions, attitudes, and future actions which are consistent with what the belief asserts.[11]

In addition to implying a particular style or spirit, the attitudes expressed in a religious belief are linked with a worldview which, in turn, influences the way the believer perceives the situation in which a moral decision has to be made. The religious statement or belief is a perspective on the situation, or, as Donald Evans calls it, an "onlook," expressed by the linguistic form "I look on *x* as *y*."[12] As Evans explains, when we look on *x* as *y* ". . . we assume that there is an appropriate way of thinking and behaving in relation to *y*, so that we are committing ourselves to a similar way of behaving and thinking in relation to *x*."[13] For example, the good Samaritan looked on the victim in the ditch as himself and so took care of him in the way he would take care of himself. For this reason, Jesus holds him up as a model of what it means to love God and neighbor as you love yourself. Therefore, "onlooks" provide not only a way of knowing the situation at hand but also an implicit commitment to behave in a certain way. In short, through onlooks, ". . . deciding-that and deciding-to, 'is' and 'ought,' come together."[14]

Scripture and theological tradition provide an abundance of religious onlooks through parables, symbols, and creeds. When religious beliefs form a great part of the framework within which the moral agent looks on experience, they become a powerful influence on moral character and action. By governing the moral imagination, they connect the many dimensions of experience with certain values and intentions entailed in the beliefs to shape the way one interprets the experience and responds to it. Since onlooks nuance one's conception and evaluation of circumstances in favor of certain judgments, the use of religious symbols in the moral life eliminates the possibility of ever judging and acting on the basis of a neutral description of a situation. By means of the imaginative process, the moral agent combines the most relevant aspects of the situation with the attitudes and actions which are entailed in the religious symbol. Using a Christian symbol of some sort to look on a situation, then, will determine to some extent what one sees and what one does.

The insights of the sociology of religion make a similar claim for the function of religious symbols. From the point of view of sociology, religious beliefs give a particular view of what it means to be human; they influence the attitudes one ought to have toward the world; they help us interpret the morally relevant factors of a situation; they can provide reasons for acting in a certain way; and, they are co-determiners of the response one makes to the world.[15] So the person who holds Christian religious symbols in his or her imagination will look on the world differently than someone whose imagination is not influenced by Christian beliefs. Consequently, he or she may respond differently.

One comes to know the self-involving meaning of the religious symbol by participating in the life of the community which is formed by those beliefs. This points to the important role of the Church in the moral life which we will consider in Chapter 14. Also, one comes to know the self-involving meaning of a religious belief by means of developing a personal openness and affinity with God. In turn, the importance for developing a rapport with God points to the importance of prayer, private and liturgical, and other spiritual disciplines as an integral part of the moral life. We will meet this again in the treatment of the use of scripture in the moral life and in the treatment of the discernment of spirits at the end of the book.

Practicing one's faith, i.e., participating in the life of the church and exercising a regular discipline of prayer, expands one's capacity to perceive the meaning of religious beliefs by directing one's sensibilities and imagination to the religious symbol or "onlook." What happens in relationship to God is analogous to what happens when we develop a deep personal relationship with others. For example, a mother and father's love for their children qualifies their understanding of the children and what their well-being requires. The parents' love affects both what they see in their children and how they relate to them. James Gustafson claims that practicing our faith in like manner qualifies our perceptions and sensibilities of what believing in God enables and requires.[16]

However, while we may claim that religious beliefs entail certain intentions, attitudes, and actions as part of their meaning, the logic of self-involvement does not guarantee that the believer will become existentially involved in his or her professed beliefs. How one lives morally is not necessarily predictable from the religious beliefs one holds. More than logic is involved in living morally. In other words, existential self-involvement does not necessarily accompany linguistic self-involvement. More than the rational ability to draw moral inferences from religious beliefs is necessary to become a morally sensitive and morally committed person.

The degree of a person's existential involvement depends on many factors. The biological, psychological, and social-cultural conditioning on an individual have a great deal to do with the extent to which one is able to appropriate and live by the value component of religious beliefs. For example, some people are too psychologically crippled, or too turned in on themselves, to be morally sensitive people.[17] The decisiveness of religious beliefs on one's moral life also depends a great deal on the depth or sincerity of one's commitment to faith. As James Gustafson puts it, "Proper doctrine without a passionate relationship to the God whom the doctrine seeks to delineate hardly leads to Christian moral intentions and actions."[18]

At this point, a few examples will help to illustrate how morality is linked, at least intellectually, to religious beliefs about God's nature, will, and activity. Without pretending to be exhaustive, James Gustafson in his book *Can Ethics Be Christian?*[19] draws out some of the moral implications of certain beliefs about God. Three of his examples will suffice here.

## God as Creator

The person nurtured by the Judaeo-Christian tradition perceives that nothing which exists has chosen to be, but that all is radically dependent on the source of being, God the creator. The belief that God is creator engenders a sense of dependence upon one another, and ultimately upon God. It entails the self-awareness of human persons as stewards of creation who seek to preserve the good which God has created. It also provides a reason for being moral, namely, to express one's allegiance to the one who provides all things. Dependence also engenders an attitude of living with the limitations of created reality, of being critical about ourselves and what we produce, and of fostering interdependence with one another and with all creation. Our ecological concerns teach us what is at stake when we lose a sense of interdependence and fall to the temptation of radical self-sufficiency. Self-criticism cautions against any insensitivity to the tendency to dominate others or any segment of creation. Self-criticism also checks any tendencies we might have to absolutize any human creation as eternally valid. The sense of dependence also engenders the disposition to trust in God. This virtue releases the freedom to risk something new and to act under conditions of less than complete certainty with the confidence that God continues to provide new possibilities for sustaining the well-being of creation.

## God as Beneficent

The belief that God is beneficent is the belief that God gives freely and in love. No one has to earn God's love. We only have to appropriate and participate in what God gives freely. The belief that God wills the well-being of all calls forth the pivotal virtue of the moral life—gratitude. In thankfulness to God for gifts freely bestowed, we ought to use our gifts for the well-being of all. What we have received freely, we ought to give freely. The experience of God giving graciously implies that we ought to care for what has been given to us, and we ought to share it freely, justly, and lovingly. This is especially true when we remember that God is the ultimate good, the center of value, and that to be like God is to live within the good we most desire. What has been given to us is not for serving our own interests at the expense of others. We are to be concerned for the well-being of others the way God has been concerned for ours.

## God as End of All Creation

The belief that God is the end of both human persons as well as the rest of creation engenders a sense of direction in the moral life. This belief about God is familiar to Roman Catholics reared on the moral manuals. Human persons are to act in accord with their final end—communion with God. To have one's fundamental intention in the moral life oriented toward God gives a sense of integrity and coherence to the moral life. The moral life which has God as its end is guided by those principles which are in accord with God's purposes. Also, it seeks to realize those moral values which are in accord with what God values. More specifically, to be oriented toward God who is loving, who is just, and who wills the well-being of creation is to be oriented in one's moral life toward what benefits the well-being of the human community and the interdependence of all creation.

These are but three examples of moral implications from beliefs about God. Others could be given. In the next chapter I will pick up on the master image of "God is love" as it has been formulated in the trinitarian doctrine and show its implications for understanding the human person as a moral agent.

## Christian Faith and the
## Content of Morality

On the basis of linguistic and sociological analysis, then, we have an insight into how religious beliefs can qualify the content of morality. I have already introduced what pertains to the content of morality in the first chapter under the heading "The Range of Interest of Moral Theology." There I showed that the content of morality includes all that pertains to the morality of being (which deals with character), and to the morality of doing (which deals with action and decision-making). Christian faith informs both aspects.

## Faith and Character

What one perceives in a situation, and the responsibilities one believes he or she has, depend on one's character. Character in turn shapes one's decisions and actions. As soon as we include character and vision as important aspects of morality and not just norms and values guiding decisions leading to actions, we must pay attention to all that shapes the moral character from which decisions and actions derive. The Christian mysteries, symbols, or stories which one appropriates through living in the Christian community influence one's moral imagination. They form, in part at least, the perspective from which decisions and actions are made. According to Charles E. Curran, the fivefold Christian mysteries of creation, sin, incarnation, redemption and resurrection destiny are the constitutive elements of a Christian perspective, horizon, or "stance" as he prefers to call it.[20]

Since all evaluations are made in the light of some criteria, Christian religious beliefs, such as those used by Charles Curran, can serve as providing some of the "light" in which interpretations are made. Because of one's religious stance, a Christian may make a different choice than a non-believer, or he or she may make the same choice but for different reasons. For example, the way a Christian approaches the medical options and the suffering which accompany the condition of terminal cancer may be influenced by the paschal mystery of Jesus and the symbols of the cross and resurrection. The dying Christian need not try to stave off death at all costs because Christian beliefs insist that death is not as final as it may seem. Through symbols of faith, the Christian may face death with hope because of his or her belief that death does not have the last word. Part of what it means to have a Christian character is to be able to live with the disposition of hope without crippling anxiety. So when one's religious beliefs inform one's basic stance toward the world, his or her moral reasoning, judgment, and behavior will inevitably be qualified by religious faith. As long as one's religious stance is part of the overall vision linked to one's justification of a moral position, we can rightly include it as part of the content of morality.

## Faith and Actions

Making a moral decision is also qualified by faith, but not in the sense that faith gives the Christian an additional capacity for discernment. James Gustafson insists that the Christian must rely on the same processes of discernment as anyone else.[21] However, Christian faith aids in discernment by helping the believer to order a plurality of values, to remain focused on basic human values, and to rank moral options. In these ways and others, Christian beliefs help one to make a decision. Of course, the same practical conclusion may be achieved apart from Christian faith, but this does not deny that Christian beliefs can also assist in determining a moral judgment for the Christian.

Christian beliefs also directly influence decision making and action at the level of specific obligations which arise because one is Christian. This would include acts directed to God, such as prayer and worship, as well as acts which are proper to belonging to a certain Christian community, such as providing a religious education. Also included under obligations which arise only within a Christian consciousness would be those which come out of the teachings of Jesus, such as the call to renounce power, to do penance, to seek the good of others and not one's own good, and to love your enemies. Therefore, certain limited moral obligations are specifically dependant on being Christian and would not always also be justified on the basis of rational self-interest.

In conclusion, then, Christian beliefs are not accidental or incidental to the morality of the Christian. James Gustafson's analysis of the distinctiveness of Christian ethics provides a succinct picture of what is at stake. For him, Christian beliefs can and do make a difference at the level of the three substantive concerns of ethics.[22] First, at the level of the good, Christian beliefs offer distinctive reasons for being moral based on one's experience of the reality of God in Jesus and through the Spirit as the ultimate good. Second, at the level of the person, moral character can be distinguished by the perspectives, dispositions, affections, and intentions which Christian beliefs engender. Third, at the level of criteria of judgment, Christian beliefs offer a distinctive point of reference used to give guidance or to provide criteria for moral actions. In some instances, these points of reference indicate courses of action which may not satisfy the desire for rationality or universal applicability, but they do have a binding force on those committed to Christian beliefs which have shaped a Christian imagination. In short, Christian morality cannot be converted completely into a rational ethics. If it could, then the experience of God in Christ, and the mediation of that experience through scripture, the church, and human experience, would have no particular ethical significance for the Christian community. To be a Christian believer carries a particular commitment to becoming a certain sort of person living a way of life which entails certain reasons for being moral and certain practices which follow from Christian beliefs.

## Faith and Morality:
## Critical-Dialogical Relationship

So far, we have seen how faith qualifies morality. But the relationship between faith and morality is not all one way. One's religious commitment not only informs experience and leads to action, but new experiences may also lead to a weakened or to a more profound religious commitment. The religious person's understanding of God arises out of the symbols we use to express the human experiences which open us to the reality of God—such as loving, creating, judging, and doing good. For example, the belief that God is beneficent is evoked and enabled by analogy to human experiences of goodness through one's family and friends. Occasions for thankfulness in human experience are (at their depths) occasions of thankfulness to God present and working in and through those human experiences. However, the graves of Auschwitz, the bombing of Hiroshima, the arms race between the superpowers, the starving children in Ethiopia, and apartheid in South Africa, for example, are incidents of malice which detract from any easy claims about God's beneficence. They force one to raise questions about the validity and worth of the belief "God is beneficent." All of a sudden, in the face of such horrendous expressions of evil, believing in God as beneficent becomes a problem.

How does one face such a challenge to one's belief about God and the adequacy of one's religious symbols? One extreme is to let go of one's beliefs as untrue. This is to lose one's faith. The other extreme is to deny the validity of one's experience of the world and to hold on to one's faith as the only source of truth. In between these extremes is a way of understanding the relation of faith and morality which lets one's beliefs become a challenge to see new dimensions of the world at the same time that one's experiences of the world open up new dimensions of religious belief itself.[23]

James Walter speaks of such a relationship as a "critical-dialogical" one.[24] This means that faith and morality remain relatively autonomous but continuously interact to shape and reshape the understanding of one another. While religious symbols give form and content to moral experience, moral experience moves toward faith in order to give new insight into the content of the religious symbols and to correct any misperceptions which might be contained in them. But the religious symbols people ultimately use to express their experiences of God and to interpret their moral experiences are the ones which make sense or "ring true" to their human experience.[25] If the symbols used to express the nature and actions of God do not find confirmation in and through one's own experiences, then we should not be surprised to find that the reasons for being moral, the principles and values inferred from these symbols, and the actions required by them will have no persuasive power over one's life. But if the symbols do ring true in the moral agent's life, then we can expect that his or her moral life will be truly qualified by religious beliefs and will receive content from them.

The movement back and forth between religious symbols and experience is at the heart of the life of the church and is the basic dynamic of any ministry of the word. Chapter 12 takes up the role of the church in the moral life. At this point we only need to indicate that the church is necessary for the moral life to be informed effectively by religious beliefs. The church is both a community of belief and a community of action. As a community of belief it supports the religious self-understanding of its members and a religious understanding of human experience. As a community of action, it witnesses to the moral meaning of religious beliefs and, in so doing, it provides human support to sustain beliefs and to enrich their meaning even in the face of conflict.[26] If we are to live as moral persons informed by our faith, we will only be able to do so as active members of a believing community.

## Conclusion

This chapter has shown that when the nature and locus of the good is God, then one's moral life will inevitably be qualified by the experiences one has of God and the beliefs one holds about God. While the Christian tradition does not make morality entirely dependent on religion, it challenges any attempt to separate too cleanly "religious acts" (such as believing in God) and "moral acts" (such as seeking the well-being of creation). If one is religious in the Judaeo-Christian way, then the sort of person one ought to be and the kinds of actions one ought to do can and ought to be qualified by one's religious beliefs. Experiences of God and beliefs about God are integral to the tone and quality of the moral life. The moral challenge to Christians is to open their moral imaginations to the symbols of Christian faith and to allow their moral vision and its demands to be influenced by them.

But to say that faith informs morality does not mean that all who share the same religious beliefs will draw out the same moral implications. A certain plurality of moral responses is possible within the Christian community. Christians can and do differ on the moral meaning of their faith. The one faith supports a stress on different elements of the moral life. One of the great challenges to Roman Catholic moral theology is to show the ways that the central symbols of faith should be interpreted so as to bring the moral meaning of faith into clearer focus.

Since faith and morality intersect in the moral agent, we need to turn next to an understanding of the human person and those aspects of moral character which are subject to the influence of the religious beliefs by which one lives.

## Notes

1. The expression is from H. Richard Niebuhr. See especially his "The Center of Value," *Radical Monotheism and Western Culture* (New York: Harper & Row, 1970), pp. 100–113.

2. I am following the sense of the religious reason for being moral as developed by James M. Gustafson, "Theology and Ethics," *Christian Ethics and the Community* (Philadelphia: United Church Press, 1971), p. 88.

3. I am following this expression of Gustafson's to express the normative requirement of an ethics centered on God. He favors it over Karl Barth's "what God commands" or Paul Lehmann's "what God is doing" because it better respects the transcendence of God and the freedom of the moral agent to determine one's own actions. Furthermore, since the presence of God is always filtered through human mediations, we do not have the absolute certainty that we know what God "commands" or is "doing." To discern what God "enables" requires other resources of moral knowledge, not just the resources of revelation. For Gustafson's use of this expression and his criticism of the others, see *Can Ethics Be Christian?* (Chicago: University of Chicago Press, 1975), pp. 156–157.

4. The debate on the distinctiveness of Christian ethics was opened by Alfons Auer in Germany with *Autonome Moral und Christlicher Glaube* (Dusseldorf: Patmos-Verlag, 1971). For some of the major articles which express the movement developing autonomous morality as well as the counter-movement of faith-ethics, see the collection edited by Charles E. Curran and Richard A. McCormick, *Readings in Moral Theology No. 2: The Distinctiveness of Christian Ethics* (Ramsey: Paulist Press, 1980).

5. See, for example, their representative articles in *ibid.*

6. The debate on the distinctiveness of Christian ethics is well summarized and assessed by Vincent MacNamara, *Faith and Ethics* (Washington: Georgetown University Press, 1985). Also, see Lucien Richard, *Is There a Christian Ethics?* (Mahwah: Paulist Press, 1988).

7. James J. Walter, "The Dependance of Christian Morality on Faith: A Critical Assessment," *Eglise et Théologie* 12 (1981): 237–277.

8. See, for example, Dallas High, *Language, Persons, and Belief* (New York: Oxford University Press, 1967), Chapter 5, "Belief Utterances," pp. 133–163, and Chapter 6, "I Believe in . . .': Creedal and Doctrinal Understanding," pp. 164–184. Also, J. L. Austin, *How to do Things with Words*, ed. J. O. Urmson (Oxford: The Clarendon Press, 1962).

9. Evans developed this kind of logic most thoroughly in his book by the same title, *The Logic of Self-Involvement* (London: SCM Press, Ltd., 1963).

10. Donald D. Evans, "Philosophical Analysis and Religious Faith: Some Retrospective Reflections," *Faith and the Contemporary Epistemologies*, eds. Jean-Louis Allard, François Duschesneau, and Jean Theau (Ottawa: University of Ottawa Press, 1977), p. 12. Also, his "Differences Between Scientific and Religious Assertions," *Science and Religion*, ed. Ian G. Barbour (New York: Harper & Row, 1968), pp. 101–133.

11. Evans, *The Logic of Self-Involvement*, pp. 27–46; and, "Differences

Between Scientific and Religious Assertions," in *Science and Religion*, ed. Barbour, p. 112.

12. Evans, *The Logic of Self-Involvement*, p. 131.

13. *Ibid.*

14. Evans, "Does Religious Faith Conflict with Moral Freedom?" in Gene Outka and John P. Reeder, Jr., eds. *Religion and Morality* (Garden City: Doubleday & Co., Inc., 1973), p. 378; cf. Evans, "Philosophical Analysis and Religious Faith: Some Retrospective Reflections," in *Faith and the Contemporary Epistemologies*, p. 12.

15. For a succinct account of the role of religious symbols from a sociological point of view, see Gregory Baum, "Foreword," in Andrew Greeley, *The New Agenda* (Garden City: Doubleday & Co., Inc., 1973), pp. 24–34. James P. Hanigan has made an effective use of the meaning and function of religious symbols from a sociological point of view in the second chapter of his *As I Have Loved You* (Mahwah: Paulist Press, 1986); see pp. 25–38.

16. Gustafson uses the family relationship analogy for this purpose in "Two Approaches to Theological Ethics," *Christian Ethics and the Community*, pp. 135–136; and "Moral Discernment in the Christian Life," *Theology and Christian Ethics* (Philadelphia: United Church Press, 1974), p. 114.

17. Donald Evans has explored at great length the psychological conditions of human fulfillment which are the conditions for understanding the moral meaning of religious beliefs in his *Struggle and Fulfillment: The Inner Dynamics of Religion and Morality* (Philadelphia: Fortress Press, 1979).

18. James M. Gustafson, "Christian Conviction and Christian Action," *The Church as Moral Decision-Maker* (Philadelphia: United Church Press, 1970), p. 98.

19. Gustafson, *Can Ethics Be Christian?* pp. 87–114.

20. Charles E. Curran, "The Stance of Moral Theology," *Directions in Fundamental Moral Theology* (Notre Dame: University of Notre Dame Press, 1985) pp. 29–62.

21. Gustafson, "Moral Discernment in the Christian Life," *Theology and Christian Ethics* (Philadelphia: United Church Press, 1974), p. 109.

22. Gustafson develops his position most thoroughly in *Can Ethics Be Christian?* See especially his summary statement, pp. 169–179.

23. James P. Hanigan identifies four ways of responding to a challenge to one's religious symbols in much the same way as I indicate here. However, he regards the relationship between beliefs and experience as a dialectical one. However, "dialectic" does not adequately express the correcting function which moral experience has on faith claims, and vice versa. See *As I Have Loved You*, pp. 34–38.

24. James J. Walter, "The Relation Between Faith and Morality: Sources for Christian Ethics," *Horizons* 9 (Fall 1982), pp. 263–270.

25. On the necessity of subjective validation of a religious symbol, see Gustafson, *Can Ethics Be Christian?* pp. 86–87, 91, 122–123, 161.

26. On the church as a community of belief and action, see James M. Gustafson, *Treasure in Earthern Vessels* (Chicago: University of Chicago Press, "Midway Reprint," 1976), pp. 86–97.

# PART TWO: THE NATURE OF THE HUMAN PERSON

| The Nature of the Human Person | Character of the Moral Agent |
|---|---|

# 5 The Human Person

Since Vatican II, a significantly broad consensus in moral theological literature suggests that the human person is the most appropriate point of departure for elaborating on the meaning of morality in general and for providing the fundamental criteria which are necessary for dealing with specific moral questions. Of course, the human has always been taken seriously in Roman Catholic moral theology because, for Catholics, to take the human seriously is to take seriously the creator God who became incarnate in the humanity of Jesus. However, the most striking feature about the renewal in moral theology since the council is the noticeable shift from using the language of "human nature" to that of the "human person."

This shift affected profoundly the way the human person serves as the criterion for determining proper moral behavior. For example, from its perspective on human nature which emphasized the natural tendencies of common bodily structures and functions, Catholic moral thinking derived absolute, universal norms. Morally right actions were those which were done in accord with the natural end of each faculty. The moral absolutes in Catholic sexual ethics, for example, are determined on this basis.

The shift to the human person, however, has allowed a movement away from basing moral conclusions on the finality of bodily structures and functions taken independently of the totality of the person. A personalistic foundation for morality was laid by the Second Vatican Council in *Gaudium et Spes*, especially in Part I. The personalistic criterion was employed in Part II of that document when dealing with issues pertaining to marriage and the family:

> Therefore when there is a question of harmonizing conjugal love with the responsible transmission of life, the moral aspect of any procedure . . . must be determined by objective standards. These, based on the nature of the human person and his acts . . . (n. 51).

Louis Janssens, who has studied the official commentary of *Gaudium et Spes*, finds that this expression applies to the entire domain of human activity, and not just to sexual activity. Also, this principle is affirmed by the expression that "human activity must be judged insofar as it refers to the human person integrally and adequately considered."[1] In other words, in personalistic morality the human person adequately considered is the criterion for discovering whether an act is morally right.

This chapter considers the anthropological basis of personalistic morality. It begins with the theological foundations by presenting an understanding of the human person as the image of God. Its second section briefly describes the fundamental dimensions of "the human person adequately considered": a relational being, an embodied subject, an historical being, and a being fundamentally equal to others but uniquely original. Finally, it will briefly state the personalistic criterion which is to be applied in making a moral judgment about human acts.

## Image of God

To say that the person adequately considered is the norm of morality does not dethrone God and raise the human person to the level of supreme value. God remains supreme, the ultimate center of value. In fact, the biblical witness to the mystery of creation provides the theological foundation for understanding the ultimate place of God and human life as a reflection of God. The story of creation tells us that at the summit of creation stands woman and man, made in God's image (Gn 1:26–27). Through the motif of the image of God (cf. Ps 8:5; Wis 2:23; 1 Cor 11:7; Jas 3:9), the Bible vigorously affirms the sacredness or dignity of every person prior to any human achievement. The Catholic tradition, as reflected for example in the Vatican *Declaration on Abortion* (n. 5) and in the pastoral letter *Economic Justice for All* (n. 32, 79), has based its claims for fundamental human dignity and human rights on this theological foundation.

To say that the human person is the "image of God" is first a theological statement before it is an anthropological one. This means that it says something about the relation between God and us which has implications for what it means to be human. For example, one thing it says is that God has so established a relationship with us that the human person cannot be properly understood apart from God. God sustains this relationship by divine faithfulness and love. As long as God offers divine love (i.e., grace), humans will ever remain God's image and enjoy a sacred dignity whether in sin or not, whether acting humanly or not. The biblical truth about the human person is that being the image of God is irreversible.

As an anthropological statement, "image of God" says that we all share in a common human condition which has a common end, namely God. It also says that human dignity does not depend ultimately on human achievements, but on divine love. We have witnessed the moral implications of this in arguments against abortion, in defense of care for handicapped newborns, and in reflection on issues of economic and social justice for all regardless of race or human attributes.

Further implications of the image of God motif for a personalistic morality can be drawn out of elaborations of the central symbols for God in the Christian faith. For example, the root symbol of God is "God is love" (1 Jn 4:8 and 16), i.e., God is the one who is perfectly self-giving. This claim leads to the Trinity which is the theological code word for the freedom and totality of God's self-giving. It means that God is eternally the giver or lover (Father), the receiver or beloved (Son), and the gift or love which binds them together (Spirit). When God expresses divine love outside the Trinity, nature comes into being, with the human person being the point at which nature reaches self-consciousness.

As Michael and Kenneth Himes have shown, our understanding of the triune nature of God (both the immanent and the economic Trinity) can shed light on the true meaning of being human. For example, by putting this great symbol of the Christian tradition into dialogue with the economic and ethical themes of the pastoral letter, *Economic Justice for All*, they point out that

> if God is triune, if God is the perfect relationship of the love and the beloved and the love which unites them, then to maintain that the human being is created in the image of God is to proclaim the human being capable of self-gift. The human person is the point at which creation is able to acknowledge gratefully the divine self-gift and to respond by giving oneself in return.[2]

Likewise, the trinitarian doctrine implies a communitarian understanding of being human. The trinitarian vision sees that no one exists by oneself, but only in relationship to others. To be is to be in relationship. The individual and the community co-exist. Humanity and relatedness are proportional so that the deeper one's participation in relationships is, the more human one becomes. Since community is necessary to grow in God's image, the fundamental responsibility of being the image of God and for living in community is to give oneself away as completely as possible in imitation of God's self-giving. The freedom which humans need for living morally is the freedom to give themselves more completely. A deeper participation in the human community enhances the humanity of each person while the failure to establish community diminishes the humanity of all.[3]

From this trinitarian vision of the human person as the image of God we can see that the fundamental dynamic of a personalistic morality is the dynamic of receiving and giving love. The Johannine version of the great commandment captures it exactly: "As I have loved you, so you must love one another" (Jn 13:34). We first receive love and then are to love in imitation of the love we have been given. It is like the basic rhythm of life—breathing in and breathing out. When either part of this dynamic movement ceases, life ends. The trinitarian vision of the person tells us that to be the image of God is not only a gift but also a responsibility. The moral life lived out of the image of God not only rejoices in what one has received as gift, but also promises to use these gifts well in communion with others.

This theological vision of the person helps us to see that our fundamental relationship to God gets expressed in and through the ways we use our gifts and enhance the giftedness of others. To be the image of God is an imperative calling us to live out of the fullness of the gifts we have received by moving out of ourselves and into the world of our relationships. To withdraw into ourselves, to hoard our gifts, and to cut off the dynamic of receiving and giving love by refusing to gift another is to abort our gifts and to mock God. It is sin, simply put. It denies the sort of self-giving which being the image of God demands, and it blocks the movement toward living fully in communion with God and others. The judgment parable which Jesus told of the talents given to the three servants in Matthew 25:14–30 is a powerful indictment of this kind of life.

A personalistic morality with theological foundations in the image of God asks: Have we accepted our gifts, and how well do we use them to contribute to positive, life-giving relationships and to the development of the human environment? In other words, the moral implications of the trinitarian vision of the human person as the image of God have to do with the quality of our relationships and with how our actions build up or destroy the network of relationships which make up human life.

## The Person Adequately Considered

The human person "adequately considered" is the person as understood by reason informed by faith. The biblical truth about humanity being the image of God is the conviction of faith which informs reason's grasp of the human person. If we are irreversibly the image of God, then we are so in the totality of our personalities and not just in certain aspects, such as intellect and will. So all the fundamental dimensions which constitute the person "integrally and adequately considered" participate in the human person's imaging God.

In this section, I am deeply indebted to the work which Louis Janssens has done to elaborate the concept of the person adequately considered. He based his analysis on the teaching of Vatican II, especially *Gaudium et Spes*.[4] He says, in brief, that the human person is adequately considered when taken as an historical subject in corporeality who stands in relation to the world, to other persons, to social structures, and to God, and who is a unique originality within the context of being fundamentally equal with all other persons. To say that these dimensions constitute an "integral and adequate" consideration of the person means that the human person is always, and at the same time, every one of these dimensions interacting to form a synthesis which is the integral human person. My separating them here is purely for purposes of discussion. Since Janssens does not claim a hierarchy for these dimensions, I will present them in a manner slightly different from his own by organizing them under four major groups: a relational being, an embodied subject, an historical being, and a being fundamentally equal to others but uniquely original.

## A Relational Being

The trinitarian vision of God in its implications for humanity underscores very clearly the relational dimension of being human. Human existence does not precede relationship, but is born of relationship and nurtured by it. To be a human person is to be essentially *directed toward others*. We are communal at our core. The image of being human in the creation story is a communal one: "And now we will make human beings; they will be like us and resemble us. . . . Male and female, God created them" (Gn 1:26–27). Personal existence, then, can never be seen as an "I" in isolation, but always as "I" and "you" in relationship.

The significance of being directed toward others has wide-ranging moral implications. In medical moral matters, for instance, it has implications for both judging the appropriateness of using life-sustaining treatments and for determining death. If someone's capacity for relationships, i.e., one's capacity to receive love and to give love, never develops (as in the case of the anencephalic fetus) or is irreversibly lost (as in the case of those in a chronic vegetative state) can we say that he or she enjoys human life in such a personal way that it ought to be sustained at all costs? An awareness of justice also shows us that personal existence is a shared existence. Through interdependence we discover that we bear mutual responsibilities. Our pursuit of individual ends can be justified only to the extent that we respect the patterns of inter-dependence which make up our relational selves. From the point of view of justice, then, we need to ask whether our moral choices and actions detract from the value of true community or promote the kind of self-giving which sustains the well-being of life together.

As relational, social beings, human persons need *to live in social groups with appropriate structures* which sustain human dignity and the common good. The moral significance of this aspect of being human is that we must respect the laws and institutions of society which promote communal living and uphold the common good. But we must be careful not to absolutize any one cultural form. The need for social structures demands that structures be renewed, and at times revised, according to changing circumstances and the growing demands of human dignity. For example, slavery was once an accepted social institution in biblical times as well as in the formative years of this country; however, it is no longer accepted because the sense of what human dignity demands could not support it. Likewise, many today find the laws favoring capital punishment to be suspect in light of new structures of law enforcement as well as a heightened sense of the respect due the dignity of human life. The moral significance of living with appropriate structures in social groups is that in making moral choices, we need to ask whether our actions will preserve or undermine the basic structures (such as marriage and the family) which we need in order to safeguard and promote human well-being.

The relational dimension of being human reaches its high point in our *relationship to God* in faith, hope, and love. Each person has eternal significance and worth. The moral import of this aspect of the person is that all relationships must find their source and fulfillment in God. After all, the fundamental conviction of our faith is that human life is fulfilled in knowing, loving, and serving God in communion with others.

## An Embodied Subject

To speak of the human person as a *subject* is to say that the person is in charge of his or her own life. That is, the person is a moral agent with a certain degree of autonomy and self-determination empowered to act according to his or her conscience, in freedom, and with knowledge. The Catholic tradition has been clear that we cannot speak of morality in any true sense apart from human persons who are able to act knowingly and willingly (cf. *ST.* I–II, prologue).

The great moral implication of the person as subject is that no one may ever use a human person as an object or as a means to an end the way we do other things of the world. Every right entails a duty, and the rights that belong to the person as subject entail the duty of demanding respect for them. And so we must respect the other as an autonomous agent capable of acting with the freedom of an informed conscience. Exploitation of human persons for one's own advantage is never allowed. We show respect for the human person as a subject by guaranteeing that he or she can act on the basis of a duly informed and free conscience. Since the importance which the Catholic tradition has given to the person as moral subject requires more attention, the subsequent chapters on freedom and knowledge, sin, and conscience will explore this aspect at greater length.

To speak of the human person as an *embodied* subject is to use a more unitive expression than the familiar one of "body and soul," the Greek version of this aspect of being human. "Embodied subject" implies that our bodies are not accessories. They are not merely something we have to house our subjectivity, but are essential to our being integrated persons. We express ourselves as the image of God through our bodies. What concerns the body inevitably concerns the whole person, for our bodies are essential to being human and to relating in human ways. The fact that we have bodies affects every expression of ourselves in relationship. The affection of love, for example, needs to be expressed in bodily ways, such as through a gift, or a kiss, or an embrace, or sexual intercourse. God so loved us as to come to us in bodily form so that we could know divine love in the only way humans can know it—in an embodied form.

The fact that we have bodies and cannot enter into relationships apart from them entails a number of moral demands. Since our bodies are symbols of interiority, bodily expressions of love in a relationship ought to be proportionate to the nature of the commitment between persons. Also, bodily existence means that we must take seriously the limits and potential of the biological order. Since the body is subject to the laws of the material world, we must take these laws into account in the way we treat our bodies. We are not free to intervene in the body in any way we want. For example, to flood the blood system with toxic drugs means to so damage the body as to kill ourselves. To relate well to others we must take care of our bodily health and respect bodily integrity. Bodily existence also means that we must accept our genetic endowment which sets the baseline for certain possibilities and limitations to our physical, intellectual, and psychological capacities. We have the moral responsibility to live well within these limits and not to push ourselves to become or to do what our genotypes, taken together with our environment, would not support.

As body persons we are a *part of the material world.* To be a part of the material world holds both great potential and serious limitation. The potential is that, created in God's image with the mandate to bring the earth under human control, we can act as co-agents with God to make the world a continuously more livable place. The developments of science and technology are certainly helping us to do that. But human creations are ambiguous. Herein lies the serious limitation. The very products which help us to improve communication, production, and prosperity can be detrimental to our corporeality and communality by entailing negative effects such as traffic congestion, air, water, and noise pollution, land erosion, and the accumulation of toxic waste. Likewise, the very techniques which are being developed in the life sciences to benefit the human community, such as developments in reproductive technology and genetic engineering, can easily be extended to produce disturbing results for the wholeness of society and the common good. Being part of the material world requires moral agents to consider the negative effects necessarily entailed in the positive discoveries of technology and to weigh their moral importance.

## An Historical Subject

An embodied spirit is necessarily an *historical* subject. While the spirit enables us to become more than ourselves, our bodies anchor us in the here and now. To be an historical subject, then, means to be relentlessly temporal, seizing each opportunity of the present moment as part of a progressive movement toward our full human development. Much of spiritual theology today has capitalized on this characteristic of the person by using the metaphors of life as a journey and of each person as a pilgrim made to rest only in God. Narrative theology, too, reflects on the temporality of human existence when it talks about the "narrative quality of experience,"[5] i.e., every moment of life is in tension with the past and the future. When we integrate our past into the person we are becoming we move into the future not only with a sense of integrity but also with a coherent sense of direction.

The moral imperative of being an historical subject is to integrate the past into the person we are becoming so as to shape a future rather than to settle into a static condition. The moral significance of the personal historical process is that one's moral responsibility is proportionate to his or her capacities at each stage of development. We must be careful to regard moral culpability for behavior relative to each stage of development. Also, the actions of historical subjects have their full moral meaning only when considered in relationship to the total context which includes the future consequences.

Just as persons develop and change, so do cultures. Progress or regress is always possible and the elaboration of new values is never ending. As new possibilities open up to us through science and technology (such as artificial means of reproduction) and as new values emerge (such as a new appreciation for the relational meaning of sexuality), we must constantly discern and order laws and values which will enrich human dignity. As historical subjects, our moral reflection must be as dynamic as the human life which it intends to guide. As we acquire new potential and elaborate new values, we need to discover appropriate ways to integrate them into our uniquely individual but commonly shared lives.

## Fundamentally Equal but
## Uniquely Original

The dimensions of being human considered thus far affirm a *fundamental equality* among human persons. Equality allows us to take an interest in everything that is human and to understand the moral obligations which inform our common humanity. However, human persons are sufficiently diverse so that we must also taken into account the *originality and uniqueness* of each person. This means that while everyone shares certain common features of humanity, each one does so differently and to different degrees.

James M. Gustafson has analyzed a person's unique moral character according to the uncontrollable and the somewhat controllable features.[6] The features of ourselves over which we have no control in establishing our uniqueness are our genetic endowment, our unconscious motives, and the social-cultural conditioning to which we have been subjected in the process of growing up.

Beyond these uncontrollable features are those over which we do have some control. One of these features is our beliefs, or stable convictions, which give direction and meaning to our lives. The extent to which our beliefs influence the originality of our lives depends not only on what beliefs we hold but also on how intensely we hold them. The perspective, or point of view, from which we look on the world also accounts for originality. What we think is important and how we respond to it are influenced by the way we see it. Also, dispositions, or a readiness to act in a certain way, mark our unique character. Affections, or sensitivities, influence the depth and swiftness of our moral responses. Finally, our intention, or the basic direction of our actions governed by our knowledge and freedom, puts the distinctive mark of personal style on what we do.

In each of us, these features are all interrelated through the imagination. Understood in its deepest sense, the imagination is not merely a capacity for frivolity in an otherwise serious world; rather, the imagination is the capacity to construct a world. By means of the imagination we bring together diverse experiences into a meaningful whole. Influenced by the philosophy of Paul Ricoeur, Philip Keane describes the imagination in his study, *Christian Ethics and the Imagination,*

as the basic process by which we draw together the concrete and the universal elements of our human experience. With imagination we let go of any inadequately pre-conceived notions of how the abstract and the concrete relate to one another. We suspend judgment about how to unite the concrete and the abstract. We let the two sides of our knowing play with one another. By allowing this interplay between the two aspects of our knowing, we get a much deeper chance to look at what we know, to form a vision of it.[7]

When we "get the picture" through the imaginative process we come to an image which puts together diverse beliefs and experiences so that we can understand what is going on and relate to it appropriately. When religious beliefs, for example, are part of the imaginative process, they enter into the content of what we experience and contribute toward connecting the many dimensions of experience with the values entailed in those beliefs. This gives us a distinctively religious "picture" of the world and a way of responding to it such as we explored in the last chapter.

Since we are guided and formed by the images which give us a "picture" of the world, the imagination sets the direction and limits of our moral behavior. The imagination informs what we think, what we see, the way we feel, our readiness to act, and the direction of our actions. It gives a definiteness to our characters in such a way that when our master images change, we are significantly changed. Since this is so, we find a clue to ourselves through the master images of the imagination. They help us to organize our lives and influence our moral arguments, choices, and actions.

A person's unique identity within the fundamental equality of a community of persons has profound moral implications, especially for giving pastoral guidance. Because each person embodies the common features of humanity differently, we cannot expect two people to respond to the same situation in the same way. They are simply not capable of it. One's moral character sets the range of possibilities for action. Each person's capacity is limited both by the uncontrollable givens and by the somewhat controllable givens integrated by one's moral imagination. Even though we may all appeal to the same objective norms in relation to the same issue, each of us will only be able to live up to the norm and respond to the issue according to his or her capacity. A person's subjective responsibility for moral behavior is relative to the development of that person's moral capacity. No one can be held responsible for doing what is beyond his or her power to do.

In a pastoral setting, then, the advice of Bernard Häring reflecting the wisdom of St. Alphonsus Liguori is sound, "One should never try to impose what the other person cannot sincerely internalize, except the case of preventing grave injustice toward a third person."[8] We can only hold a person accountable for what is relative to that person's capacity. A person is only morally culpable for failing to do what he or she is capable of doing. Therefore, since each person's actions remain subject to justification in light of objective moral norms, the demands of the situation, and one's capacity, we can expect to find some differences between what a moral situation demands of one person and what it demands of another.

## The Personalistic Criterion

These then are dimensions of the human person adequately considered. When taken together in an integrated way, they form the foundation of a personalistic morality. Louis Janssens has used these essential dimensions of the human person to form this criterion: an action is morally right if it is beneficial to the person adequately considered in himself or herself (i.e., as an unique, embodied spirit) and in his or her relations (i.e., to others, to social structures, to the material world, and to God).[9] For Janssens this is an objective criterion since it is based on the constant dimensions of being human. But since it is a criterion about the human person as an historical being, it requires a regular review of the possibilities we have available to promote the human person so that we can determine whether they truly do so. Janssens recognizes that the application of this criterion is not easy. To use it in a morally responsible way requires wisdom—the special gift of the morally good person who has an affinity for what is right and whose judgment is inspired by a morally good disposition, an attitude which is ready to place our activity as much as possible at the service of the human person adequately considered.[10]

## Conclusion

As we try to understand the human person adequately, we may better appreciate the great advantage of the language of "human person" over "human nature" to express the anthropological foundations of morality. The advantage to "human nature" is that it underscores what is common to all. Its great disadvantage, however, is that it does not adequately express one's fundamental originality. The language of "human person," by contrast, is more adequate because it captures the uniqueness of the person without abandoning those features of the common human condition and the moral demands founded upon them.

A view of the human person such as the one presented here challenges Roman Catholic theology to integrate empirical evidence into its moral assessments. Moral theology from a personalistic perspective must take into account the experiences of people over time in order to determine what sorts of activities best serve the person adequately considered. As a result, moral theology must include not only deductive but also inductive methods in order to take human experience seriously. An inductive approach will yield reliable though tentative conclusions open to revision. New historical experience and new evidence will emerge to reinforce a position already held or to call it into question and ask that it be reformulated or rescinded if necessary.

Even though each of the features of the human person treated above can be given much greater elaboration in order to develop the anthropological foundations of a personalistic morality of responsibility, I will focus in the next chapter only on those which the Catholic tradition has made the indispensable features of the moral subject: knowledge and freedom. For without these we do not have true morality at all. The subsequent chapters on sin and conscience will then consider the person even more adequately in the light of faith and grace.

## Notes

1. Louis Janssens, "Artificial Insemination: Ethical Considerations," *Louvain Studies* 8 (Spring 1980): 4.

2. Michael J. Himes and Kenneth R. Himes, "Rights, Economics, and the Trinity," *Commonweal* 113 (March 14, 1986): 139.

3. *Ibid.*, pp. 139–140.

4. Louis Janssens explored these dimensions in a preliminary way in his "Personalist Morals," *Louvain Studies* 3 (Spring 1970): 5–16. His most worked out version is in the methodological introduction to his treatment of artificial insemination, "Artificial Insemination: Ethical Considerations," *Louvain Studies* 8 (Spring 1980): 5–13.

5. The expression is from Stephen Crites, "The Narrative Quality of Experience," *Journal of the American Academy of Religion* 39 (1971): 291–311.

6. For this analysis of Gustafson's, see his *Can Ethics Be Christian?* (Chicago: University of Chicago Press, 1975), pp. 32–47.

7. Philip S. Keane, *Christian Ethics and the Imagination* (Ramsey: Paulist Press, 1984), p. 81. Some of the influential material from Paul Ricoeur are "The Metaphorical Process as Cognition, Imagination, and Feeling," *Critical Inquiry* 5 (1978), pp. 143–159; also, *Hermeneutics and the Human Sciences*, ed. and trans. by John B. Thompson (Cambridge: Cambridge University Press, 1981).

8. Bernard Häring, *Free and Faithful in Christ*, Vol. 1: *General Moral Theology* (New York: Seabury Press, 1978), p. 289.

9. Janssens, "Artificial Insemination: Ethical Considerations," *Louvain Studies* 8 (Spring 1980): 13.

10. *Ibid.*, pp. 14–15.

# 6 Freedom and Knowledge

*I*n the last chapter we looked at some of the major conditions for being a human person made in the image of God. In this chapter, we will isolate the two indispensable conditions of being a moral subject, freedom and knowledge, especially the kinds of freedom and knowledge necessary for the moral life.

## Freedom

Freedom is so central to the moral life that without it we cannot properly speak of being moral persons at all. If we are beyond freedom, then we are beyond morality. Morality pertains to those areas of our lives where freedom is possible and enables us to actualize our potential as the image of God. Promoting freedom is at the same time promoting the possibility for a moral life.

 We can speak of freedom in the moral life in two ways: as basic freedom, or the freedom of self-determination, and as freedom of choice. In either sense of the word, freedom is so necessary that we can only be morally good not when we reason well to a moral judgment, but only when we use our freedom well.

### Freedom of Self-Determination

In coming to self-awareness, especially through the use of psychological instruments, we recognize the limiting conditions to who we can become and to what it is possible for us to achieve. We know that we are very much the product of what is not ourselves. Consider, for example, the influence of genetics and the social-cultural conditioning to which we are all subject.[1] Our genetic inheritance is unalterable. No amount of willing can change what is given to us through heredity, although we may alter the manner of developing what is there. Genetic predispositions stress our uniqueness and color our

75

potential. But heredity does not predetermine specifically what we will do or who we will become. Our freedom can be exercised across a broad spectrum of genetic possibilities and is subject to environmental influences. We must find our way within the limits of these potentials and the forces of the social-cultural conditions which shape our worldview and influence not only the way we interpret experience but even the kinds of experiences we have. The frequently given advice "Be yourself" is not simply permission to turn in on oneself; it is, instead, an encouragement to express oneself within one's own limits and according to one's own predispositions. Freedom necessarily acts within the given conditions of heredity and environment.

One of the dangers in facing these limitations is that we can sell out to determinism. Selling out is an attempt to escape from freedom by claiming that we are forced to be who we are and to do what we do by heredity or environment. If we sell out, then we claim that we are not responsible for anything we do. In fact, by refusing to accept the freedom which is ours, we show that we are afraid to accept responsibility. One of the tasks of human life is to achieve freedom in those areas where we are not yet free. Therefore, a primary goal of moral education is to free people from becoming directed by the unalterable givens of heredity or by the changeable limits of some external authority. It is to free them to live well within limits.

Of course, the behavioral sciences have clearly shown that our freedom is limited. Our actions fall somewhere on the continuum between absolute freedom and absolute determinism. If this were not so, I suspect we would not have the experience of feeling unsettled or indecisive about our choices. Moreover, we would not have to deliberate about anything if we were completely free or completely determined.

Assuming, then, some freedom of self-determination in the moral life, we recognize that one purpose of this freedom is to appropriate actively what happens to us into the persons we are and can yet become. We do not look on human existence as though we should all be dealt a winning hand. Rather, we see life as a matter of playing well the hand we have been handed. Freedom enables us to integrate the "slings and arrows of outrageous fortune" into our lives so that we might grow toward wholeness and live with peace. This involves making what happens to us part of who we are. Turning necessity into a virtue is one of the signs of a strong moral character, and it is an expression of our capacity for self-determination.

But what does this kind of freedom look like? Stanley Hauerwas tells a story that shows how much the capacity for this freedom is associated primarily with character and not with choices or actions.

I have a friend who, after failing to get tenure at a university as a philosopher, decided to go to law school. He is now an extraordinarily able lawyer and is quite happy he "decided" to go to law school; but in another sense he hardly decided at all. He was forced to go to law school because his teaching career was blocked. The fact that he is now happy as a lawyer means that he has learned to make a virtue out of necessity.[2]

As the old joke would have it, if someone dumps a load of lemons on your porch, don't complain. Make lemonade!

We cannot be held morally accountable for the determining givens of our lives, but since they constitute something of who we are, they need to be appropriated into ourselves. The more we are able to become aware of ourselves and possess ourselves, including all the determining influences, the more we will experience ourselves as responsible for what we do and who we become.

The freedom to decide about oneself and to make someone of oneself brings us squarely in touch with what theologians call *basic* or *core* freedom. Basic freedom is directed toward a loving relationship with God, the ultimate end of our lives. But since we experience God in mediated ways, we ultimately establish our relationship with God in and through the ways we relate to all things. For this reason, basic freedom of self-determination before God is always incarnated in the particular choices we make through life.

But not every choice we make involves us at the deepest levels of our being. For example, consider these two expressions of freedom of choice. At our seminary we take our meals in a cafeteria which always has at least three options for dessert. To illustrate freedom of choice with my students, I ask them if they can remember which dessert they chose for lunch on a certain day of the previous week. Only those who choose jello every day remember! The rest do not. One of the reasons they do not remember their choice of dessert is that such a choice does not demand a very deep involvement of their persons. Freedom of choice, the smorgasbord freedom of choosing among indifferent goods, is like that. It does not demand very much from us.

On the other hand, basic freedom, the freedom of self-determination, involves more. For example, a friend of mine struggled for several years over whether he ought to remain in the seminary and proceed toward priesthood, or withdraw in order to be free to devote his life to working in a third world country through an agency of the United Nations. He chose the latter. Such a choice is an exercise of basic freedom. It demands more personal involvement than choosing jello over cookies in the cafeteria.

The notion of basic freedom, or the freedom of self-determination, rests on an understanding of the human person as a complex multi-leveled being. To illustrate this I like to diagram the human person as a moving spiral. Others prefer to use the food metaphors of an onion, artichoke, or cinnamon roll. The spiral illustrates better our having a common center for each of the levels of our being. Furthermore, with the spiral we cannot tell clearly where one level ends and the next begins. This is closer to real life, I think. With a spiral, too, we know that each level shares a common center and moves out from there without ever being disjointed from the whole. The spiral is "moving" to capture the temporal dimension of being human and the developmental orientation of the moral life. My diagram looks like this:

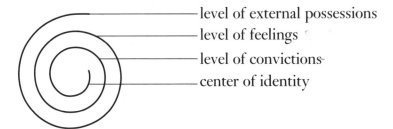

level of external possessions
level of feelings
level of convictions
center of identity

As the diagram shows, our actions can spring from different levels of our being. Not everything we do is a clear and complete embodiment of what springs from the deepest core of our being. Some actions might be rooted there, but most of our actions spring from a more peripheral level. This cautions us to refrain from concluding on the basis of isolated actions alone that anyone has embodied the full meaning and commitment of the self. What seems more likely is that we come to actualize who we are through a whole series of actions which, when taken together, express the basic character or dominant direction of our lives. This basic direction of our lives, which manifests a rather consistent personal indentity, is our *fundamental stance.* Those significant moments of choice in our lives, which establish or affirm more strongly than others the character and direction of our lives, are *fundamental options.*[3]

## The Theory of Fundamental Option

Bernard Häring has gone to great length in the first volume of his *Free and Faithful in Christ* to give a proper understanding of the theory of fundamental option. He shows that contemporary theology finds biblical roots for the theory of fundamental option in the notions of covenant and heart.[4] This theory assumes the basic conviction of the covenantal experience, namely, that we are born graced. That is, God has created us out of love for love. We are the good creation of a gracious God. Without destroying our freedom, God's love for us has so affected us in our innermost being (i.e., our hearts) as to make a claim on us and to give us an orientation toward love and life. Our response is to live out of this orientation in freedom. To agree to live in covenant with God is a basic act of faith—the most self-committing choice we can ever make. This act of faith is "the" fundamental option. Yet we must live out this condition in a broken world—a world where original sin and social sin abound, and a world where many temptations and bad influences arise to contradict the very orientation of our innermost being, or heart.

Though more deeply marked by grace than by sin, we always stand in need of purification and conversion. This gives a dynamic character to a life of constant growth. Traditional moral theology understood this basic condition of being human. The classic moral manuals began with attention on our ultimate end and the necessity to make decisions for that end. From a theological point of view, this end is God calling us into communion with God's self. Our basic decision is whether we will live our lives responding to God in and through all our choices.

## Fundamental Stance

Within the context of the fundamental option theory, "fundamental stance" expresses the sort of person we have chosen to be, the fundamental direction we have chosen for our lives. It brings a stable direction, perduring quality, and personal meaning to our actions. The fundamental stance of the Christian is one which allows the great commandment to function as a critical judge of one's relationships and activities.

Bernard Häring has aligned what is entailed by the fundamental stance with Eric Erikson's notion of identity.[5] By this he means that we cannot lay claims to having achieved a fundamental direction for our lives until we can lay claim to having achieved a stable identity. For neither identity nor stance arises all at once. They come into being through committing oneself to a way of life that is stable enough to sustain a perduring quality of life, and in this way to give personal meaning to actions.

Actions taken by themselves are ambiguous. Situating actions in relation to the fundamental direction of a person's life, however, enables us to discover the personal meaning of actions. Our actions embody, to a greater or lesser degree, the fundamental direction of our lives. They are signs more or less expressive of our interiority. In this sense, our actions are like the tip of an iceberg. They are held above the surface by our attitudes, convictions, and the fundamental direction of our lives which seek external, concrete expression. To get to the true meaning of our actions as expressions of ourselves, we need to look beneath the surface of observable behavior to the attitudes and convictions of the person. These give expression to the fundamental direction of our lives and seek concrete embodiment in particular actions. Only by looking beneath the surface of our actions will we be able to get to the roots of moral conversion, healing, and growth.

When we take such an in-depth look at our actions, we discover that they may be more or less consistent with the fundamental direction of our lives. This is because our actions arise from different levels of our being. Not all our actions spring from the deepest center of ourselves wherein lies the core of our identity. In the biblical sense, this is the "heart"—the deepest source from which we commit ourselves to God and to others and show what we most care about or value. The truest expression of ourselves as moral persons arises from there; it does not lie in our external actions alone. Moral goodness lies in the loving disposition to choose God, while right actions are external expressions of this disposition. The challenge of moral living is to do those actions which are consistent with the love of God. The role of the "heart" in the moral life gives full force to the biblical prayers which beseech God for a "pure heart" and give power to Jesus' sayings, "Where your treasure is, there will be your heart" (Mt 6:21), and "Of what the heart is full, the mouth will speak" (Mt 12:34). The goal of moral growth is to live singleheartedly committed to God so that our actions are consistent with whom we have chosen to be through that commitment.

## Fundamental Option

A choice which arises from such a personal depth that it can significantly reverse or reinforce the fundamental direction of our lives is a fundamental option. To qualify as a fundamental option, a choice must be rooted in a deep knowledge of self and a freedom to commit oneself. Through a fundamental option we express our basic freedom of self-determination to commit ourselves profoundly toward a certain way of being in the world.

Bernard Häring speaks of the "great decisions" as special moments in life which express the fundamental option. These are decisions appropriate to those who have reached the necessary stage of identity and who are able to commit themselves in knowledge and with freedom to a community or to a person. Without any claim to completeness, Häring suggests the following examples:

> I want to point to such fundamental decisions as personal choice of faith in Jesus Christ and in the role and mission of the Church, made by an adult or an adolescent who has already reached the necessary stage of identity. I would list among such choices: adult baptism as sign of personal commitment to Christ and covenant with the Church—and since adult baptism is the exception in the West, I would note confirmation as a mature ratification of what God offers us in baptism; marriage vows; the vows of celibacy for the kingdom of God; a decision that is the test of deep and true

friendship or of self-giving love; the deliberate choice of a profession such as that of a physician or of a politician with a firm commitment to the positive ethos.[6]

Pope John Paul II has used the notion of fundamental option in a similar sense in his document on catechetics, *Catechesi Tradendae*, in 1979. When speaking about the youth, he writes:

> With youth comes the moment of the first great decisions. Although the young may enjoy the support of the members of their family and their friends, they have to rely on themselves and their own conscience and must ever more frequently and decisively assume responsibility for their destiny. Good and evil, grace and sin, life and death will more and more confront one another within them, not just as moral categories but chiefly as fundamental options which they must accept or reject lucidly, conscious of their own responsibility (Par. 39).[7]

These statements of theologian Bernard Häring and of Pope John Paul II suggest that those fundamental decisions which affect the basic direction of our lives are not made quickly, or easily. We must be truly ready for them on all levels of our personality. These statements also show that fundamental choices are deeply rooted in the relational character of our lives. Our basic decisions have to do with our commitment to our own integrity and identity, our commitment to others, and our sense of responsibility to the world around us. If these basic decisions are made soundly and not precipitously, they can well establish the direction of our lives so as to resist those strong determining forces which are constantly warring against us fighting to make us someone else.

## Freedom of Choice

The other kind of freedom at stake in the moral life has to do with realizing our capacity to be ourselves through the particular choices we make. This is what most people call moral freedom, though moralists call it more properly freedom of choice.

Freedom of choice—a smorgasbord kind of freedom—chooses one option from a number of others. This kind of freedom is also subject not only to the hereditary determinants of our basic inclinations, but also to limiting factors such as unconscious motives, peer pressure, drugs, ignorance, passions, fears, blind habits, and the hidden persuaders of the mass media. Yet the more aware we become of these determinants and their influence on us, the more we will be able either to overcome those we can or to live more freely within the limits of those which we cannot overcome.

A powerful scene from *One Flew Over the Cuckoo's Nest* brings home this freedom of choice graphically, and shows what we should all be about in our moral striving as responsible adults. In this novel, McMurphy fakes insanity to escape a penal farm for the softer life of a mental institution. However, he comes to a head-on collision with Big Nurse, the tyrant of the ward who has psychologically emasculated her patients so that they can no longer have freedom to choose. McMurphy begins a one-man campaign against tyranny and for freedom. In one scene he stages a showdown with Big Nurse by calling for a vote which would allow the patients to watch the World Series on TV. He is one vote short of a majority. It is up to Chief, the big Indian who, to escape the pains of tyranny, has retired into a fog where he cannot hear and cannot speak. McMurphy pleads with him to raise his hand. Chief finds his hand going up, and he says to himself:

> It's too late to stop it now. McMurphy did something to it that first day, put some kind of hex on it. . . . McMurphy's got hidden wires hooked to it, lifting it slow just to get me out of the fog and into the open where I'm fair game. He's doing it, wires. . . . No, that's not the truth. I lifted it myself.[8]

This is the goal of moral striving. We need to cut short our attempted escapes from freedom so that we can responsibly claim, "I did it myself!" Freedom and responsibility go hand in hand. Responsible freedom says, "I choose to do this because, as a responsible person, I *want* to do it." This is quite different from the familiar, "I really should . . ." or "I had better . . ." or "I must. . . ." These all indicate motivation from without. Whenever we find ourselves saying "Actually I should . . ." chances are that we really *do not* want to, we feel some external pressure to, there are possible rewards if we do, or punishments if we do not. A cuckoo's nest may be an extreme image for the world in which we live, yet the neurotic is a clear image of the determined conditions which we all share. The neurotic suggests that the tyranny of determining influences over which we seem to have no control has made powerlessness our chief neurosis. We all have a Big Nurse in our lives. That is inevitable. With Chief we often retreat into the fog and attempt to escape from freedom.

However, our freedom to choose this or that—even within limits—is fundamentally a freedom to choose an identity, to become a certain sort of person. We cannot do everything. Determining factors prevent that. But we can pour ourselves into what we do, make it truly our own, choose it as a genuine expression of ourselves which asserts our integrity. The freedom of our moral striving does not mean doing just anything we want to do. Rather, the freedom of our moral striving is wanting to do what we can do. Moral freedom is an act of self-determination, an act which, through all the pathways of particular choices, chooses who we want to be, persons either open or closed to the mystery of our lives and of all life.

# Knowledge

If the actual stuff of moral freedom is not a choice between individual objects, but rather the self-realization of the person choosing, then this element of being a moral person must also be present in moral knowledge. This means that the object of moral knowledge is primarily not something outside the person, but it is the free moral person in all his or her concreteness and possibilities.

The moral life entails two kinds of knowledge: conceptual and evaluative.[9] Conceptual knowledge, the explicitly formulated consciousness of moral reality, is necessary for passing on moral wisdom from generation to generation and for living in a moral community which shares a common discourse about moral experience. But conceptual knowledge is not to be equated with genuine moral knowledge. Evaluative knowledge, on the other hand, counts as genuine moral knowledge for it calls forth decisions and actions expressive of one's moral freedom. Without any degree of evaluative knowledge we could not live as moral persons in the full sense of that term.

## Conceptual Knowledge

Conceptual knowledge in the moral life pertains both to a knowledge of self and to a knowledge of moral values. It is what most people mean when they speak of moral knowledge, though it is not what moralists mean by genuine moral knowledge.

Conceptual knowledge is symbolized by the head.[10] It is the kind of knowledge we have when we have the right information and have mastered the facts. It is the kind of knowledge which is fairly easy to grasp and to verify, for we only need to double check our observations, our facts, our logic. We can easily communicate this kind of knowledge through preaching, teaching, and sharing since we can detach the facts from the knower and the circumstances to make them readily available to anyone who wants them.

Conceptual knowledge of the self comes as a result of being an object of our own scrutiny and being able to express what we discover. Psychological tests, for example, help us to attain this kind of awareness. Through such testing we can know our fundamental limits and basic potentials, our personality preferences, or whether we have any character disorders. Whatever we can do to enhance our critical, conceptual awareness would serve our moral lives well since the basic conditions of our unique identity influence the way we interpret moral reality and the responses we can make.

Conceptual self-awareness has some important implications for the moral life. Right moral living, for instance, involves expressing ourselves according to the capacities we have. While we are morally required to express ourselves according to our capacities, no one is morally obligated to do what he or she is incapable of doing. Sensitive pastoral moral guidance will respect the limited capacity of a person and not impose what a person is incapable of attaining.

Since our predispositions will give us a certain amount of ease or trouble with different virtues, we would do well to know our proclivities so that we will know when we are acting with them or straining against them. We only frustrate ourselves morally by running ahead of our graces, i.e., by trying to live beyond our means. We incur guilt unnecessarily if we compare our own moral efforts with those of someone with a capacity different from our own. We need to learn, then, the limits and potentials which are ours both as humans and as unique individuals. A basic demand of Christian morality is to live according to the graces we have received. The goal of moral striving, then, is to become what God has made us to be by appropriating our capacities and developing our potential within the limits of our natural endowment. In this way we live out of our blessings and give thanks and praise to God by using well what is ours. Living in this way makes the moral life a continuous expression of praise and thanksgiving to God who has endowed us with different gifts or with different degrees of the same gifts.

In matters pertaining to moral values, conceptual knowledge is knowledge about values. It comes with a knowledge of moral rules and the strategies for doing what the rules prescribe. We use conceptual moral knowledge to communicate values and to argue for or against a position.

However, conceptual knowledge is the least convincing kind of knowledge for achieving moral conversion. We do not change what we or another person may value simply on the basis of the right information or rational explanations. We change our values on the basis of experiencing a value as satisfying a basic need. Moreover, we do not make our moral decisions on the basis of bare facts, nor do we exercise our moral freedom in a disinterested way. A mere conceptual grasp that a particular course of action is right or wrong is not enough to ensure that a person will act in a virtuous way. A virtuous response requires that the person has interiorized the values inherent in the action. A personal commitment to value is an essential dimension of moral behavior. So, while conceptual knowledge is important and necessary for the moral life, it alone is not sufficient if we are to act as morally virtuous persons. We also need evaluative knowledge.

## *Evaluative Knowledge*

Moral knowledge, properly so called, is evaluative knowledge.[11] It is the heart's knowledge and so is difficult to express in concepts. We can recognize it in the knowledge lovers have of one another. For example, when we want a friend to know someone we truly love, we excitedly try to give all the descriptions of our love that we can. Try as we might, we cannot close the gap between our personal knowledge of the one we love and our descriptions. Faced with the limitations of conceptual media and the incommunicability of what the heart knows, we finally say in frustration, "You'll just have to meet my love!" That is it exactly. Only through personal encounter will anyone else be able to know what we know by heart. Even then degrees of knowing will differ. That is how evaluative knowledge works.

Evaluative knowledge, symbolized by the heart, is the kind of knowledge we have when we are "caught up" in someone or something through personal involvement or commitment. Evaluative knowledge is more personal, more self-involving than conceptual knowledge of facts or ideas, for it has to do with grasping the quality of a person, object, or event. We do not gain evaluative knowledge by words but by touch, sight, and sound, by experiencing victories and failures, sleeplessness and devotion.

In short, evaluative knowledge is a felt knowledge which we discover through personal involvement and reflection. It is not something which can easily be passed on through statements, formulas, or rules. A *Peanuts* cartoon once captured the sense of evaluative knowledge well in a scene which has Peppermint Patty sitting at her school desk and speaking out to her teacher: "You know what Oscar Wilde said, Ma'am? He said, 'Nothing that is worth knowing can be taught.' Nothing personal, Ma'am . . . Carry on." While we may not want to agree with Oscar Wilde's statement absolutely, it does convey the significance of evaluative knowledge as the kind of knowledge which is not easily taught in a detached way but must be evoked and caught in our experiences. The most we can hope for in trying to communicate evaluative knowledge is to occasion similar experiences of this value for another so as to draw out of another the value experienced.

As it pertains to the self, evaluative knowledge touches the deepest level of ourselves as persons. It is difficult to grasp fully or to express adequately not only for oneself but also for others because it is knowledge of such a deeply personal reality. This implies that we need to refrain from making an absolute and final judgment not only about our own moral status before God but also about someone else's. If we do not have a full or clear grasp of ourselves, how much more difficult it is to have a total, explicit grasp of someone else's true moral self. We have no window into another person's soul which would allow us to see clearly enough where she or he stands before

| FEATURE | CONCEPTUAL KNOWLEDGE | EVALUATIVE KNOWLEDGE |
|---|---|---|
| Symbol | Head | Heart |
| Content | Right information; "master the facts." | Quality or value of someone or something. |
| Verifiable | Easily verified since the facts can be observed and the logic demonstrated. | Difficult to verify since the quality or value escapes easy demonstration and logical exposition. |
| Acquired | Can be easily learned, for right information is ripe for teaching, preaching, and sharing. | Quality and value must be caught through personal interaction and encounter. |
| Communicated | Information or facts are easily detached from the knower and the situation, so they are easy to pass on. | Since quality and value are not easily detached from knower and situation, communication is difficult and must be discovered to be appreciated. |
| Morality | This is the knowledge of rules and the strategies for achieving what the rules prescribe; this is knowledge *about* values. | This knowledge is a personal grasp of value. This is what makes our actions truly our *own*. With this knowledge, we act on the basis of what we truly value. Moral growth and conversion happen through the experience of value and acquiring evaluative knowledge. |

God in order to make a moral judgment of absolute condemnation, even if that person's observable patterns of behavior are destructive of human well-being. The teaching of the Council of Trent on justification claimed as much. It declares that no one but God can know with absolute certitude anyone's condition before God.[12]

As it pertains to value, evaluative knowledge is the self-involving knowledge which makes deciding and acting on behalf of what we value truly our own. Without this knowledge we act merely by hearsay, by what we are told is right, rather than on the basis of what we have discovered to be valuable. This kind of knowledge is not acquired nor altered through rational argument alone, but by personal experience, discovery, and appreciation of moral values.

The accompanying chart summarizes some of the distinguishing characteristics of conceptual and evaluative knowledge. Since these approaches to freedom and knowledge have had a profound effect on the ways we understand and evaluate sin, we turn, next, to the issue of sin.

## Notes

1. On the influence of these "givens," see James M. Gustafson, *Can Ethics Be Christian?* (Chicago: University of Chicago Press, 1975), pp. 32–34; also, Vincent Rush, *The Responsible Christian* (Chicago: Loyola University Press, 1984), pp. 32–48.

2. *The Peaceable Kingdom* (Notre Dame: University of Notre Dame Press, 1983), pp. 37–38.

3. Not all theologians who use the fundamental option theory employ the distinction between fundamental stance and fundamental option as Timothy O'Connell does in his book, *Principles for a Catholic Morality* (New York: The Seabury Press, 1978); see especially pp. 64–66, 70–74. Bernard Häring, for example, gives a lengthy treatment of the fundamental option theory without making this distinction. See his *Free and Faithful in Christ*, Vol. 1: *General Moral Theology* (New York: The Seabury Press, 1978), pp. 164–222. However, I find using the term "option" (which ordinarily connotes a particular moment of choice) to refer to "basic direction" or "orientation" of life to be misleading. O'Connell's distinction seems to capture the heart of the fundamental option theory without building in unnecessary confusion.

4. Häring, *Free and Faithful in Christ*, Vol. 1: *General Moral Theology* (New York: The Seabury Press, 1978), pp. 164–222; for his section on the "heart" as it relates to the theory of fundamental option, see pp. 185–189.

5. *Ibid.*, pp. 168–177, esp. pp. 172–175.

6. *Ibid.*, p. 189.

7. Pope John Paul II, *Catechesi Tradendae*, "Apostolic Exhortation on

Catechetics," issued October 25, 1979 as found in *Official Catholic Teachings, Update 1979* (Wilmington, N.C.: McGrath Publishing Co., 1980), pp. 368–426, quotation at p. 397.

8. Ken Kesey, *One Flew Over the Cuckoo's Nest* (New York: New American Library, 1962), p. 126.

9. The distinction of two different kinds of moral knowledge is based on the distinction of the two different forms of human consciousness developed in the writing of Karl Rahner and subsequent theologians. Rahner used this distinction effectively in his discussion of the knowledge and consciousness of Jesus; see his "Dogmatic Reflections on the Knowledge and Self-Consciousness of Christ," *Theological Investigations*, Vol. V, translated by Karl-H. Kruger (Baltimore: Helicon Press, 1966), pp. 193–215; see esp. pp. 199–201. For a succinct explanation of this distinction and its implications for human existence, see John W. Glaser, "Man's Existence: Supernatural Partnership," *Theological Studies* 30 (September 1969): 473–488. Timothy O'Connell has used this distinction to explore the two kinds of moral knowledge which he calls "speculative" and "evaluative." See O'Connell, *Principles for a Catholic Morality*, pp. 52–55.

10. On this understanding of conceptual knowledge, see Timothy O'Connell, *Principles for a Catholic Morality* (New York: Seabury Press, 1978), p. 52.

11. *Ibid.*, pp. 53–55.

12. The pertinent text reads: "For, just as no pious person should doubt the mercy of God, the merit of Christ, and the virtue and efficacy of the sacraments, so every one, when he considers himself and his own weakness and indisposition, may entertain fear and apprehension as to his own grace [can. 13], since no one can know with the certainty of faith, which cannot be subject to error, that he has obtained the grace of God." *The Sources of Catholic Dogma*, translated by Roy J. Deferrari from the thirtieth edition of Henry Denzinger's *Enchiridion Symbolorum* (St. Louis: B. Herder Book Co., 1957), #802, p. 253.

# 7    A Sense of Sin

$N$o one doubts the presence of evil in the world. We experience it in a variety of ways: national and international conflict; domestic and street violence; political and corporate corruption; and a host of manifestations of sexism, clericalism, racism, ageism, and other violations of justice. All such forms of brutality, disorder, or discrimination, seen from a theological perspective, are rooted in sin. But do we ever recognize the sin and name it as such?[1]

## Retrieving a Sense of Sin

For some reason, sin seems to have lost its hold on us as a way of accounting for and naming so much of the evil we know. Among the many other reasons, the eclipse of a religious worldview through the rise of the secular spirit accounts significantly for the loss of a sense of sin. In fact, in his post-synodal exhortation, *Reconciliatio et Penitentia* (1984), Pope John Paul II credits "secularism" above all with contributing to a loss of a sense of sin.[2] The secular spirit questions the relevance and meaning of all Christian symbols, and even of religion itself. One effect of this secular spirit on the meaning of sin, for example, has been to reduce sin to some form of psychological or social disorder. The therapeutic perspective which pervades the secular spirit looks on behavior as either healthily adaptive problem-solving behavior, or as unhealthy, non-adaptive, and problem-creating behavior.[3] It does not call the latter sin.

Moreover, the secular, therapeutic perspective tends to look on persons more as victims of unconscious or socio-cultural influences than as agents of free action. Psychiatrists Karl Menninger in *Whatever Became of Sin?*[4] and M. Scott Peck in *People of the Lie*[5] want to make full allowance for those conditions which cause people to do evil. Yet both insist on a strip of responsibility which cannot be negotiated away to these determining influences. While the behavioral sciences provide us with helpful explanations of human behavior, they do not give a full account. Sin is real, and we need a fresh way to get at it and call it what it is.

What do we need to grasp in order to retrieve a sense of sin in an adult manner? Contemporary moral theology says a "sense of responsibility." Christian theologians find in "responsibility" the essential theme of Christian faith and the central characteristic of the moral life. A leading American Protestant theologian of this century, H. Richard Niebuhr, has done much to give impetus to the "responsibility" motif in Christian morality.[6] He summarizes the constituents of responsibility by describing an agent's action as a

> response to an action upon him in accordance with his interpretation of the latter action and with his expectation of response to his response; and all of this is in a continuing community of agents.[7]

Since God is present to us in and through all that makes up our lives so that we are never not in the presence of God, our responses to all actions upon us include our response to God. As Niebuhr asserts, "Responsibility affirms: God is acting in all actions upon you. So respond to all actions upon you as to respond to his action."[8] If "being responsible" sums up the quality of character and action marking Christian moral living, sin will mark the failure to be fully responsible.

"Responsibility" as a motif for the moral life has found its way into Catholic moral thinking with the strong support of the biblical renewal in the Catholic Church. Bernard Häring, who has been instrumental in renewing Catholic moral thinking, has used this notion of "responsibility" with great success in restructuring Catholic moral thought. Along with other Catholic theologians, Häring has found in the biblical renewal a fresh theological framework and an orientation for understanding the moral life.[9] We turn, then, to the biblical perspective on sin.

## Sin: The Biblical Perspective

From the Bible we see that Christian morality is primarily a "vocation." This means that our life is a response to the word of God spoken to us pre-eminently in Jesus, but also in and through all the people and events of our lives. From the perspective of vocation, wherein God calls and we respond, responsibility replaces obligation as the primary characteristic of the moral life. Also, the relationship that we establish with God in and through our responses to all things becomes the focal point of the moral life. From this point of view, practicing the presence of God becomes essential for Christian responsibility, Christian moral growth, and our awareness of sin.

A consistent theme of contemporary theology has been that we cannot have a proper understanding of sin unless we have a proper understanding of the nature and implications of the covenant God has established with us. "Covenant" and "heart" are the dominant metaphors of biblical faith for understanding the moral life. They provide the biblical horizon against which to recognize sin.

## Covenant

The two frequently used terms for sin in the Old Testament point to violations of relationships. *Hattah* is the most common term. Its meaning, "to miss the mark" or "to offend," points to a purposeful action oriented toward an existing relationship. The existence of the relationship makes the offense or failure possible. *Pesa*, meaning "rebellion," is a legal term denoting a deliberate action violating a relationship in community. The New Testament term for sin is *hamartia*. It connotes a deliberate action rooted in the heart and missing the intended mark. [10]

These terms acquire theological significance when used in the context of the covenant which expresses the most personal kind of relationship between God and us. The primary claim of the covenant is that God loves us without our having done anything to attract God's attention or to win that love. God's covenant is a bond of completely gratuitous love, pure grace. But God's initiative of love (grace) does not destroy our freedom. Unlike the Godfather, God makes an offer we can refuse. God's offer of love awaits our acceptance. Once we accept the offer of love we commit ourselves to living as the covenant requires.

The covenantal context lifts the notion of sin out of a legalistic framework to set it on a level of a personal relationship with God. In worshiping the golden calf (Ex 32), Israel missed the mark of covenantal love, or sinned, not so much because Israel broke one of the laws of the covenant, but because Israel broke the personal bond of love of which the law was an external expression. The law was not to be the final object of Israel's fidelity. God was. Sin in the Bible is not merely breaking a law. Sin is breaking or weakening the God-given bond of love.

The law was an aid to Israel's fidelity and pointed to the responsibilities of being in relationship to God. But to make the law the end of Israel's loyalty would be to make an idol of the law, or to commit sin. The sense that sin involves a broken relationship with God got lost when the law itself became the absolute object of loyalty. Legalism replaced the religious foundations of sin with juridical ones. Then, when taken to the extreme, sin became a transgression of a legal code rather than a failure to respond to God. To speak of sin in legal terms is to miss the important aspect of sin as a religious, relational reality which expresses our refusal to respond appropriately to God's love and mercy. Sin, simply put, is refusing to live out the gift of divine love.

The response to which the gift of divine love in the covenant calls us may be summarized in a threefold manner: to respect the *worth* of ourselves and others as constituted by God's love; to live in *solidarity* with creation and with one another as covenantal partners; and to develop the virtue of *fidelity* as the proper characteristic of every covenantal relationship.[11] Sin would be to act contrary to these covenantal requirements.

## *Worth*

Our hearts hunger for love. We have a passionate longing to know that we count in the eyes of someone special. We long to know that we are loved, valued, and the source of delight for another. The persistent cry of the heart, "Do you love me?" is asked not just of people significant to us, but ultimately of God.[12] The covenant responds to this cry of the heart longing for worth with a firm "yes." The covenant insists that grace is the first move. We are not so much searchers as the ones searched out. Because God has taken the initiative to enter into covenant with us, we matter to God in a most serious way. This is what it means to have worth. Our worth comes from God's offer of divine love as a free gift and is not conditioned by our own achievement.

Various biblical passages and images help us to understand divine love as our true source of worth and our only security. In Isaiah, for example, we read of God loving the people of the covenant for their own sakes and not for the sake of their being useful or powerful: "I have called you by name—you are mine. . . . I will give up whole nations to save your life, because you are precious to me and because I love you and give you honor" (Is 43:1, 4; cf. Is 41:8–16). Perhaps some of the most powerful texts which communicate that our worth is established by divine love are those which use the image of the child to explain our relationship to God. In Hosea, for example, we read of God's love for a rebellious people being expressed through the tender image of the parent for the child (Hos 11:1–9). In the New Testament, one of the favorite images of Jesus for those whose lives are grounded in God's unconditional love is the child. When Jesus is asked who is the greatest in God's reign, he reaches into the crowd, sets a child beside him and says, "Unless you become like this, you will never understand greatness" (Mt 18:1–5). What makes the child such a powerful image? The child's worth is constituted not by what it achieves, but simply by the generous love of the parents. That is what we are like before God. We are grounded in a love which desires us out of the abundance of love itself, and not because of anything we may have accomplished.

From within this perspective, therefore, we recognize that our worth and security remain grounded in God and not in ourselves. However, the modern heresy of individualism insists that we generate our worth with our own power. The special temptation of this heresy is to believe that our loveableness is really something we make for ourselves. The covenant, however, is set against every notion of independence.[13] The covenant assures us that we are forever established by God: "I will be your God, you will be my people" (Jer 31:33; 32:38; Ez 36:28); "I have called you by name—you are mine" (Is 43:1); "I can never forget you! I have written your name on the palms of my hands" (Is 49:16).

Sin refuses to believe that we are loveable apart from our virtue. Instead of grounding our worth in divine love, sin attempts to establish worth on the basis of surrogate loves which we create for ourselves and by ourselves to give us the security of being loveable and acceptable. But when we rest our worth on something besides divine love, we create an idol. Creating surrogate loves is the sin of idolatry. These loves may be our talent, our goodness, our efficiency, our charm, our wit, our bright ideas, our wealth, our social position and prestige, or whatever else we might create in order to secure our worth and make ourselves somebody.

When we so fill up our lives with these self-created loves, we have no room for divine love. The four blessings and the four woes of Luke (Lk 6:20–26) speak to this condition quite starkly. What is it about being poor, hungry, weeping and rejected that these should be a blessing, whereas those who are rich, filled, happy and praised receive a curse? To be poor, hungry, weeping and rejected are blessings of the reign of God because people in these conditions know they cannot establish themselves on any grounds of their own. Rather, they rely totally on being supported by a love which comes to them out of its own abundance and not out of their own boasting or achievement. On the other hand, the rich, the filled, the happy, and the praised have no room in their lives for such love. They are filled already by their own achievements and, hanging on to these achievements as their sole source of security, are unable to surrender to divine love.

Not until we overcome the temptation to regard ourselves as self-sufficient are we able to let go and surrender to the deepest truths about ourselves as being grounded in divine love. But letting go is hard. We hang on to these surrogate loves out of fear that if we let go we will lose our worth, and no longer be valued or valuable. Yet surrendering is the only way to allow God to secure us in divine love.

Those who establish their worth and security on their own achievements are ultimately not free. They are trapped in the self-absorbing fear which believes that they are not loveable as they are. This fear and its unfreedom drive them to strive for qualities and achievements with which to exalt them-

selves and oppress others. This only results in the self-righteousness which
Jesus singles out as the obstacle to hearing the good news that our worth is
grounded in God's love and not our own. We pronounce a judgment against
ourselves when we refuse to accept this divine love as our only true source of
worth and security. Not until we open ourselves to the source of our worth in
God will we overcome our sin of idolatry and be open to the wider values of
God's creation and God's people.

## Solidarity

The same divine love which calls us into covenant with God and establishes our worth also cultivates the relationship of people with one another
and with all creation. In Jesus Christ we affirm that all creation is under the
covenantal grace of God, and we recognize that our responsibility to care for
all things is related to the sovereignty of God (Col 1:15–20). Because the
covenant is all-inclusive, we have no other way of relating to God except in
and through our relationships with everything else.

God's love in the broadest sense is not limited just to humanity but is
directed also toward all creation. We who consciously accept this covenant
with God accept responsibility for all that is included in God's love. The
lesson this inclusive covenant teaches is the very one we are learning
through our scientific explorations—namely, that every facet of the universe
is bound together by an unbreakable bond of relatedness. A quote from
John Muir inscribed on a metal placard at the beginning of a trail in
Yosemite National Park reminds me of this truth: "When we try to pick out
something by itself, we find it hitched to everything else in the universe."
In short, nothing exists by itself as an independent entity. Everything exists
in dynamic interrelationship.

Obviously, the covenant also includes the human moral community. By
calling us into covenant, God calls us to be social. The moral community
lives by the same covenantal principle which governs the working of the
universe, namely, the principle of cooperative community. Patricia Mische,
in her book *Star Wars and the State of Our Souls*, has summarized this scientific
and covenantal principle and its implications well when she writes,

> Some may call this principle bonding. Some call it electromagnet-
> ism. Some call it attraction. Some communion. Teilhard de Char-
> din looked at this principle and called it love. It may be the most
> fragile of principles governing the universe, but love, cooperation,
> communion, is also what makes the universe work. If the whole
> universe and every cell in our bodies and life itself is possible only

through this principle, we may, like Teilhard, wonder why we ever doubted that we were created in love and for love.[14]

However, to see the universe as a community sounds so antithetical to what we experience. We take independence and separation as the norm, and community as the exception. But according to the covenant and scientific understanding, we have it all backward. The covenantal perspective is that we have no life without community and cooperation. Of course, we have individual differences; diversity and the tension which come with it are part of life. In fact, we can enhance our lives to the extent that we are able to sustain a high degree of diversity within a cooperative community. But our covenantal commitment, like our scientific discoveries, requires that we develop those modes of cooperation which respect the functional integrity of the universe.

The paradigm from human relations which Jesus proposed for covenantal existence is friendship. The amazing grace of the divine choice for us in covenant is God's friendship with us. Jesus summed up the witness his life had given to this divine choice when he said to his disciples, "I no longer call you servants. . . but I have called you friends because everything I have heard from my Father I have shared with you" (Jn 15:15). Jesus' final command to his disciples is to love one another as he has loved them, i.e., with the love of friendship (Jn 15:12). Sandra Schneiders interprets the ecclesial results of this divine choice to be friends as Christian solidarity:

> that mutual interdependence that can put every gift at the service of the community, that can sustain mutual challenge and correction for the good of all, that can enhance the dignity of each without abasing any, that can govern itself without recourse to coercion or violence.[15]

In his social encyclical, *Sollicitudo Rei Socialis* (December 30, 1987), Pope John Paul II spoke of solidarity as a virtue, a moral and social attitude:

> This then is not a feeling of vague compassion or shallow distress at the misfortunes of so many people, both near and far. On the contrary, it is a firm and persevering determination to commit oneself to the common good; that is to say to the good of all and of each individual, because we are all really responsible for all. (n. 38)

The laws of the covenant express what life ought to look like for those who have accepted the offer of divine love and live in solidarity with one another. The covenant is not fully realized until we live out the covenantal commitment to be responsible to and for one another as covenantal partners. The covenantal laws express the responsibility we have to and for one another by virtue of our sharing in the same divine love. This is the core of the inseparability of the great commandment to love God and others as we love ourselves. The great commandment requires that each of us recognize that the other matters for his or her own sake and not just as the means to an end. Pope John Paul II's encyclical on social concerns advocates this same aspect of responsibility in its understanding of solidarity:

> Solidarity helps us to see the "other"—whether a person, people or nation—not just as some kind of instrument, with a work capacity and physical strength to be exploited at low cost and then discarded when no longer useful, but as our "neighbor," a "helper" (cf. Gen 2:18–20), to be made a sharer, on a par with ourselves, in the banquet of life to which all are equally invited by God (n. 39).

Covenantal solidarity means that our lives extend beyond a private relationship with God and our neighbor to embrace the whole social order—social structures, institutional order, economic systems. Our lives are inevitably marked by the structural relationships which can act for or against the fundamental worth and well-being of all. The fruit of covenantal solidarity is shalom—that peace which is not just the absence of violence, but the peace which is the justice of communal wholeness wherein competing claims achieve a proper balance. This is the sense of *opus solidaritatis pax*, peace as the fruit of solidarity, which Pope John Paul II uses in his encyclical on social concerns (n. 39).

Sin, from the perspective of an inclusive covenant and solidarity, affects all the relationships to which we are called. It is rooted in radical independence. Sin fails to respect diversity within a cooperative community by promoting the domination of one form of life. But, as our lessons from ecology teach us, when one form of life dominates in a region, the whole region collapses. Sin adopts simplistically Darwin's perception that only the fittest survive. It overlooks Darwin's other discovery that only those species survive which learn to cooperate.[16] Therefore, from the perspective of covenantal solidarity, sin cannot be limited to breaking the law. Sin is not first and foremost against laws. Sin is against people and, in and through people, against God. Sin is an offense against God, not in the sense of harming God, but in the sense of failing to respect what God loves. Personal sin shows its effects in society and creation as a whole. It shows itself as a violation of the covenant by introducing disorder and strife into the interdependence of covenantal relationships. We have come to recognize the structures which support this disorder as social sin.

Throughout life we have the opportunity to better our world. When we live with indifference, jealousy, envy, contempt, domination, possessiveness, or prejudice and ignore situations of need requiring works of justice, mercy, and love, we are failing to heed the summons of divine-human solidarity. In so doing, we pronounce a judgment against ourselves. One of the meanings of the great judgment scene in Matthew's parable of the sheep and the goats (Mt 25:31–46) is that people did not recognize in the hungry, thirsty, naked, sick and imprisoned the summons of divine-human solidarity. Our obligations inherent in being social are inseparable from the bond that links us to God. Isaiah's image of true fasting, for example, shows that within the covenant, anti-social behavior cannot be distinguished from irreligious behavior. "The kind of fasting I want is this: Remove the chains of oppression and the yoke of injustice, and let the oppressed go free" (Is 58:6). Human solidarity is one piece with our relationship to God. To betray a social commitment demanded by justice is to betray God and to perpetuate social sin.

## Fidelity

The solidarity of covenantal partners who have responsibility to and for one another needs fidelity in order to come to its fullest expression. "What I want is loyalty, not sacrifice" (Hos 6:6). Fidelity, trustworthiness and loyalty are various ways of expressing the central moral virtue of the covenant.[17] From the perspective of virtue, covenantal living asks, "What sort of person should I be?" The answer: be faithful, be trustworthy. Live a life that demonstrates *hesed*, God's faithful love for us. Imitating this faithful love which binds the covenant together is the moral imperative for living in covenant. Fidelity is the very weave of the fabric of the covenant. To rend this fabric through infidelity is to ruin the whole cloth. Therefore, fidelity or trustworthiness binds the covenantal partners together. Dominating control by some and subservient submission by others pulls them apart.

For the covenant to be sustained, each partner must be trustworthy. Where one cannot trust another to be loyal to the covenantal commitment, the relationship of love breaks down. One of the most bitter moments in the lives of those who join in covenant is to find out that the one we believed had been committed to us is not being faithful to that commitment. Such moments arouse our moral indignation at the betrayal of trust. When we experience such betrayal, we sometimes hedge against any future infidelity by making efforts to defend ourselves against the forces of an imbalance of power. This infects all our relationships with the suspicion and the fear that fidelity is not being practiced in our commitments to one another.

We see this virtue of trustworthiness or fidelity played out in the contrast of two garden stories in the Bible, the garden of Eden and the garden of Gethsemane. Both can be seen as stories of what we do with our freedom to live as trustworthy creatures.[18]

We look in on the activity of the garden of Eden on the sixth day, when God entrusted the earth to the care of Adam and Eve and entrusted them to each other. The story implies that everything comes to us as a gift from a free and gracious God. The story of the garden of Eden is pervaded with the sense that humanity is empowered with the capacity to influence creation and one another by being entrusted with gifts, the gifts of creation and the gifts of one another. The serpent enters to sow seeds of distrust. The serpent suggests that God cannot be trusted, and so tempts the creatures with power (the knowledge of good and evil). Adam and Eve choose to believe the snake. In this, they miss the mark of their proper role in the covenantal relationship. The fall is the result of their abuse of power by seeking self-serving ends.

The moment Adam and Eve refuse to believe that God can be trusted and abuse their role in the covenant, they refuse to trust each other also, and so imprison themselves within their own defenses. This is symbolized by Adam's and Eve's hiding in the bushes to protect themselves from God, and by their sewing fig leaves for clothes to hide their nakedness and to protect themselves from one another. To stand naked before another is to leave oneself vulnerable. Adam and Eve could no longer afford to do that. They could no longer allow themselves to be vulnerable by saying to each other, "I trust you." From this point, all of life becomes marked by the suspicion of betrayal and by walls of protection which hedge against infidelity and other abuses of power.

The story of the garden of Gethsemane, on the other hand, is the story of Jesus trusting in God by not abandoning his mission of living to make everyone a friend of God and of one another. Jesus' great act of living by covenantal fidelity was to accept the death on the cross, trusting that his life would not echo into an empty future. Jesus lived his life trusting that he would be sustained by the undefeatable love of God. The resurrection confirms that such trust was not ill-founded.

In the story of the garden of Gethsemane, Judas is an important figure for understanding covenantal fidelity.[19] Judas shows us the real possibility of betrayal. His betrayal provides the contrast to God's faithfulness to Jesus and Jesus' fidelity to God. With Judas in the story, we see more clearly the centrality of fidelity in the lives of those who covenant with Jesus as disciples. To violate fidelity is to violate the call to follow Jesus in the imitation of God's covenantal, steadfast love.

The stories of the garden of Eden and the garden of Gethsemane teach us that we are pursued by the relentless fidelity of God. Sin is the power-play of infidelity. Sin is refusing to believe that God can be trusted and that others are worth trusting. In a covenant, we entrust to one another something of value to ourselves. In God's covenant with humanity, for example, God has entrusted to us divine love, most fully expressed in the person of Jesus. In marriage we covenant with another by entrusting to another our whole selves and our lives. This is symbolized in giving our bodies to each other. In health care, we covenant by entrusting our physical well-being to a health-care professional. In covenants with lawyers, we entrust our legal rights to a legal professional.

In making these acts of trust, we entrust the other with power. We hope that power will not be abused. Sin, however, abuses that power because sin cannot let go of the fear and suspicion which keeps us from coming to know the other as gift. In sin we are unable to live in the freedom of being entrusted by God with personal worth and with the gifts of one another. Sin abuses the power we give to one another when we entrust another with something of value to ourselves: a personal secret, our health, our property, our bodies. Sin abuses this power by not holding in trust that which has been entrusted to us. Rather than living in trust as creatures empowered with gifts to set one another free, we live in suspicion of another's gifts and abuse our power by controlling, dominating or manipulating these gifts to serve our own self-interests. This is sin as infidelity, an arrogant use of power.

## Heart

If covenant is the primary metaphor for the biblical context for sin, then heart is an apt metaphor for the personal relationship to God. The heart is what the divine love of the covenant seeks. Divine love is either embraced or rejected in the heart. According to biblical anthropology, the heart is the seat of vital decisions, for it is the center of feeling and reason, decision and action, intention and consciousness.[20] This makes the heart the ultimate locale of virtue or sin.[21] The American bishops have expressed this biblical insight in their treatment of sin in the pastoral letter on the moral life, *To Live in Christ Jesus*, "We sin first in our hearts, although often our sins are expressed in outward acts and their consequences."[22]

The moral vision of the Bible sees good and evil not just in deeds but in the heart which promotes good and evil actions. The prophets in the Old Testament remind Israel that God complains not so much about perverse actions as about the hardened heart from which such actions arise (Is 29:13). Jesus continues in this tradition with his concern about the filth on the inside of the cup which shows itself on the outside (Mt 23:25–26). This means that from a person's heart come the evil ideas which lead one to do immoral things (Mk 7:21), whereas a good person produces good from the goodness in the heart (Lk 6:45). The Lukan Jesus aptly summarizes the implications of the unity of the person: "Of what the heart is full the mouth will speak" (Lk 6:45).

The hope of the messianic prophecies is for the people to receive a new heart so that their inmost inclinations will be to live out of divine love in loyalty to the covenant (Jer 31:33; Ez 36:26). The Markan summary of Jesus' proclamation of the reign of God is the call for a new heart (Mk 1:15). The very essence of conversion, or *metanoia*, is to live with a new heart in a new spirit, the spirit of Christ living in us (Rom 8:10; Eph 4:17–24). The radical ethical demands of Jesus stress such interior renewal: "If your eye causes you to sin, pluck it out" (Mt 5:29); "If someone slaps you on the right cheek, give your left as well" (Mt 5:39); "Give to everyone who asks" (Mt 5:42); "Do not store up riches on earth" (Mt 6:19). Imperatives like these are not demands to act in these specific ways. Rather, they are paradoxical figures of speech meant to shock the imagination and to reorient the heart.

The biblical vision of the heart focuses on that dimension of us which is most sensitive and open to others. The essential characteristic of the heart is its openness to God—its capacity to receive divine love. Augustine said that our hearts are by nature oriented toward God. Jesus said "Where your heart is, there will be your treasure as well" (Mt 6:21). When our hearts treasure God, all other treasures will be treasured rightly. The heart properly ordered to God as our single center of value will have a certain instinct for what is good relative to God. Such a properly directed heart yields a life of virtue. The misdirected heart produces sin.

## Sin: The Arrogance of Power

Now we are ready to summarize the understanding of sin which emerges from retrieving a sense of responsibility and from situating sin within its biblical context of covenant and heart. Above all, sin is fundamentally a religious reality. This means that sin makes no sense apart from the presence of God in Christ and through the Spirit, and our awareness of being in relationship to God. If an action is not against God, it is not sin. If we use sin in any other way than to refer to this fundamental relationship to God, we are using "sin" only analogously. Three common analogous uses of sin are "original sin" (a theological code word for the human condition of living in a world where we are influenced by more evil than that which we do ourselves), "material sin" (transgressions of a law or acts of wrongdoing such as killing), and "social sin" (the consequences of individual choices which form oppressive social structures such as sexism).

To understand sin primarily as a matter of the quality of our relationships in the covenant suggests both a transcendent and an immanent dimension to sin. The _transcendent_ dimension expresses a break in our relationship to God. This is the "no" we answer to the invitation to live with God in love. But we do not experience or express this relationship to God apart from our relationship with all things, especially other persons. Our sin is our way of rebelling not only against God (which we rarely, if ever, do directly) but also against the living images of God, one another.

This accounts for the _immanent_ dimension of sin. We understand the immanent dimension of sin when we see the importance of the human community as the place in and through which we receive love and give love. Sin in its immanent dimension is the "no" we answer in our relations with our neighbors to be loved and to love. We sin when we choose to turn inward and cut off the dynamics of receiving and giving love. In this sense, sin is always a type of self-absorption. Whenever loving, life-giving relationships are weakened or destroyed, sin is present in some form. Whether that form be lying, gossip, stealing, abusing, ignoring, or whatever is not as important as the result—a life-giving relationship is weakened or broken.

Only when we can understand both the transcendent and immanent dimensions of sin will we be able to grasp the full significance of the American bishops' definition of sin which they stated first in their pastoral letter on the moral life, *To Live in Christ Jesus* (1976), and then repeated in the National Catechetical Directory, *Sharing the Light of Faith* (1979). From their pastoral letter, we read:

> [Personal sin] is different from unavoidable failure or limitation. ... It is a spirit of selfishness rooted in our hearts and wills which wages war against God's plan for our fulfillment. It is rejection, either partial or total, of one's role as a child of God and a member of his people, a rejection of the spirit of sonship, love and life.[23]

We see in this statement that sin is some form of selfishness. Sin as selfishness is first a matter of the heart, before it ever becomes manifest in external actions. We become sinful to the extent that we turn inward, refuse to respond, and so cut off the dynamic of giving and receiving love. This is to "harden one's heart" in the biblical sense. In sin, we cease to pay attention to, or care about, anyone outside ourselves. Selfishness is self-absorption. It is the failure to love and to accept love. All sin springs in some fashion from a love turned in on itself. Several metaphors, drawing upon several types of relationships, have been used to convey this meaning of sin. Principal metaphors used about sin today are rebellion, isolation, alienation, and estrangement. Each expresses a different nuance of love turned in on itself.

I would like to suggest another metaphor which may have rich potential for expressing the reality of sin as selfishness within the context of covenant and heart. That is sin as the "arrogance of power." The covenant says that we are already established as persons of worth by the gratuitous love of God, nothing else. But the heart panics. It does not trust that we are creatures of a gracious God. Life is too ambiguous to assure the heart of being loved without achievement. Since the world we know does not run on unconditional love, the heart finds it hard to accept this gift of love as true. So the heart sets out to secure its loveableness by its own striving. The arrogance of power is the imperial "I" living as though it must make itself great.

Rollo May, in his book, *Power and Innocence*,[24] provides a helpful schema for understanding sin as the arrogance of power. First May establishes the point that all of us have power. But not all of it is demonic. His analysis shatters the commonly held view that the more loving one is the less powerful one is. Love and power, in fact, are not opposites. We need power to be able to love in the first place, since power, as May defines it, is the capacity to influence change in others and situations for good or ill.

Rollo May then distinguishes five kinds of power which can be in all of us at different times.[25] The moral issue is concerned with the proportion of each kind of power within the total spectrum of ways of expressing ourselves in relation to others. *Exploitative* and *manipulative* power are destructive. These are forms of power over another and often can be equated with force or violence. *Competitive* power acts against another. It can act destructively when it puts another down, or it can act constructively to bring out dormant capacities in another and to bring vitality to a relationship. *Nutrient* power acts for the sake of another by giving care. This kind of power is vital in relationships between friends and loved ones. *Integrative* power acts with another to draw out the best in him or her. The arrogance of power in the misdirected heart seeks a greater proportion of exploitative, manipulative and competitive power over nutrient and integrative power.

Sin as the arrogant use of power separates us from life-giving and loving relationships. Our responsibility as covenantal partners is to care for and to serve one another through nurturing and integrative power. Jesus' great commandment of love makes this all clear. Sin arises out of our striving to protect the self we have made in order to guarantee that we are loveable and loved. When we set out to protect the self we have made, we set ourselves against God, against nature, and against one another. Self-serving interests destroy bonds of peace and justice, and spread conditions of fear, hatred, and violence which usher in the disharmony of the world which we know as social sin—the cooperation in the continued maintenance of oppressive structures in society.

We break the dynamic power of sin in our lives when we realize that we are in fact profoundly loved apart from our achievements and our virtue. Only God's love is so permanent and profound as to release us from our sin.

The sacrament of reconciliation becomes the concrete sign that God's love is being offered to us and that it cannot be defeated even by our sin. Through reconciliation, the dynamic of receiving and giving love is renewed and the life-giving relationship we share with God and with others is strengthened.

Divine love is the only love which will satisfy our longing hearts. Divine love opens our hearts to nurture the life-giving potential in ourselves and in others so that we might transform human relationships and institutions. When we accept the gift of divine love, then we are taking Jesus at his word: "No longer do I call you servants; I call you friends" (Jn 15:15). As friends, we become united with the mission of Jesus to use our power so that all may have life in abundance.

Now that we have considered the sense of sin from a biblical perspective, we are ready to take up the various kinds of sin which the moral tradition has distinguished: original sin, actual sin (mortal and venial), and social sin. These kinds of sin will be the focus of the next chapter.

## Notes

1. For a survey of major attempts in the past twenty years to explore the mystery of sin, see James A. O'Donohoe, "Toward a Theology of Sin: A Look at the Last Twenty Years," *Church* 2(Spring 1986): 48–54.

2. The other factors of a non-ecclesial nature which John Paul II lists are errors made in evaluating certain findings of the human sciences, deriving systems of ethics from historical relativism, and identifying sin with neurotic guilt. Within the thought and life of the Church, certain trends have also contributed to the loss of a sense of sin. Among these he lists the movement from seeing sin everywhere to not recognizing it anywhere; from an emphasis on fear of eternal punishment to preaching a love of God that excludes punishment; from correcting erroneous consciences to respecting consciences but excluding the duty to tell the truth. Two other ecclesial factors are the plurality of opinions existing in the church on questions of morality and the deficiencies in the practice of penance. To restore a healthy sense of sin, the pope advocates "a sound catechetics, illuminated by the biblical theology of the covenant, by an attentive listening and trustful openness to the magisterium of the church, which never ceases to enlighten consciences, and by an ever more careful practice of the sacrament of penance." See *Origins* 14 (December 20, 1984): 443–444, quotation at p. 444.

3. The research of the team headed by sociologist Robert Bellah which has produced *Habits of the Heart* (Berkeley: University of California Press, 1985), a study of the American beliefs and practices which give shape to our character and form to our social order, shows that the therapist is the newest

character defining American culture. See Chapter Two "Culture and Character: The Historical Conversation," pp. 27–51, especially pp. 47–48.

4. Menninger, *Whatever Became of Sin?* (New York: Hawthorn Books, Inc., 1973).

5. Peck, *People of the Lie* (New York: Simon and Schuster, 1983).

6. See especially Niebuhr, *The Responsible Self* (New York: Harper & Row, 1963), pp. 61–65.

7. *Ibid.*, p. 65.

8. *Ibid.*, p. 126.

9. Bernard Häring's writings are vast and wide-ranging. His early three-volume work, *The Law of Christ* (Westminster: Newman Press, 1961, 1963, 1966), was one of the first major works by a Catholic moral theologian to rethink morality in light of the biblical renewal. His most recent three-volume work, *Free and Faithful in Christ* (New York: Seabury Press, 1978, 1979, 1981), is an expression of Häring's more mature thought. This work is not a revision of *The Law of Christ*, but a completely new work. Charles E. Curran, a student of Häring, has followed his teacher's lead in making efforts at renewing moral theology in light of the biblical renewal. Some of Curran's pertinent articles are "The Relevancy of the Ethical Teaching of Jesus" and "Conversion: The Central Moral Message of Jesus" in *A New Look at Christian Morality* (Notre Dame: Fides Publishers, Inc., 1968), pp. 1–23 and 25–71.

10. A helpful, succinct interpretation of the terms for sin in the Bible can be found in S. J. DeVries, "Sin, Sinners," *The Interpreter's Dictionary of the Bible*, Vol. 4 (Nashville: Abingdon Press, 1962), pp. 361–376; for the terms, see pp. 361–362, 371.

11. These terms of the covenantal relationship are derived from the analysis of the covenant made by Joseph L. Allen, *Love and Conflict: A Covenantal Model of Christian Ethics* (Nashville: Abingdon Press, 1984). Allen's analysis is based on the six characteristics of God's covenantal love: "God (1) binds us together as members of a covenant community, (2) affirms the worth of each covenant member, (3) extends covenant love inclusively, (4) seeks to meet the needs of each member of the covenant community, (5) is steadfast, and (6) is reconciling." See pp. 61ff. My threefold subdivision captures the scope of these six.

12. Sebastian Moore pursues this theme to great effect in *The Inner Loneliness* (New York: Crossroad Publishing Co., 1982).

13. This is the central thesis of Walter Brueggemann, "Covenanting as Human Vocation: A Discussion of the Relation of Bible and Pastoral Care," *Interpretation* 33 (April 1979): 115–129; his covenantal thesis is stated on p. 116.

14. Mische, *Star Wars and the State of Our Souls* (Minneapolis: Winston Press, 1985), p. 72.

15. Schneiders, "Evangelical Equality," *Spirituality Today* 38 (Winter 1986), p. 301.

16. Mische, *Star Wars*, p. 125.

17. Allen, *Love and Conflict*, p. 72.

18. The interpretation of these garden stories follows that of John Shea, *The Challenge of Jesus* (Garden City: Doubleday & Co., Inc., 1977), pp. 93–113.

19. For this interpretation of the significance of Judas in the story of Gethsemane, see Karen Lebacqz, *Professional Ethics: Power and Paradox* (Nashville: Abingdon Press, 1985), pp. 89–91.

20. Hans Walter Wolff, *Anthropology of the Old Testament* (Philadelphia: Fortress Press, 1974), pp. 40–55.

21. DeVries, "Sin, Sinner," *IDB*, Vol. 4, p. 364.

22. *To Live in Christ Jesus* (Washington: USCC, 1976), p.5.

23. *To Live in Christ Jesus* (Washington: USCC, 1976), p. 5; cf. *Sharing the Light of Faith* (Washington: USCC, 1979), #98.

24. May, *Power and Innocence* (New York: W. W. Norton & Company, Inc., 1972); see especially Chapter Five, "The Meaning of Power," pp. 99–119.

25. *Ibid.*, pp. 105–113.

# 8    K inds of Sin

*I*n moral literature as well as in our conversations about moral living, we find ourselves using "sin" in various ways without taking the time to distinguish clearly what we mean. Perhaps the most familiar use of "sin" is personal sin. This is the classic notion of actual sin (mortal and venial). It refers to personal culpability for choosing, in knowledge and with freedom, to be unloving or selfish. This is the sense of sin we confess. "Sin," however, is also a fact—a force or power in the world which is greater than the sum of individual acts of sin. We recognize this given condition of estrangement or brokenness as "original sin." Theologians speak of this kind of sin generically as "the sin of the world."[1] Today we are hearing more about a third kind of sin which has some features of the sin of the world but which is also related to personal sin in that we share some responsibility for it. This is "social sin." In this chapter we want to explore the meaning of each kind of sin, but to give particular attention to personal sin and social sin, since these are the kinds of sin for which we share some responsibility.

## Original Sin

Insofar as sin has a semi-autonomous existence, we call it "original sin." A great deal of theological debate has gone on trying to discover the best way to interpret the doctrine of original sin.[2] In the midst of it all, we find general agreement that, since original sin exists prior to our personal acts of freedom, it differs in kind from personal sin. Original sin is the theological code word for the human condition of living in a world where we are influenced by more evil than what we do ourselves. Our whole being and environment is infected by this condition of evil and brokenness willy-nilly. We feel the effects of its presence and its poison in our lack of freedom and in our inability to love as we would want. St. Paul knew the force of this evil when he said, "I do not do the good I want to do; instead, I do the evil I do not want to do" (Rom

7:19). As a result of our solidarity in this predicament of brokenness or universal estrangement, we find ourselves somewhat alienated from our deeper selves, from others, and from God. We need redemption, or the healing of divine love.

The full doctrine of original sin tells us that though we may be "broken," we are not disasters. We can still become who we were made to be. The reason for this is that the power of original sin is in tension with the power of God's redeeming love, or grace, which enables us to grow toward wholeness and in communion with ourselves, others, and God. While the energy of original sin pulls us in the direction of radical selfishness and independence, the energy of grace moves us toward inter-dependence and communion. But separation and independence or belonging and inter-dependence do not face us as external objects of choice in the way choosing one make of car over another does. They face us, rather, as a radical dynamism within us with which we can align ourselves to different degrees. Our Christian convictions tell us that these are unequal forces, for God's redeeming love is the more powerful force. This is the sense of St. Paul's conviction that while sin abounds, grace abounds even more (Rom 5:20).

In order to rise above the negative pull of original sin, we need to open ourselves to the presence of redemptive love. This gift of divine love is mediated to us in and through the human community—our families, our neighborhoods, and the wider community which witnesses to justice, truth, peace, and other virtues. In fact, one of the ways of interpreting the effects of baptism is to see it as initiating us into a life-giving, supportive community committed to living according to the gospel. The fact that the power of grace and original sin are part of being human makes responsible moral living a truly demanding task. Because of original sin, struggle and tragedy will always be part of our moral striving. But because of grace, redemption and the resurrection-destiny will always have the last word.

Since original sin makes actual sin and social sin possible and even probable, we need to move on to consider these kinds of sin in greater detail.

## Actual Sin

We have long recognized that sin is a wide-ranging reality with various degrees of gravity. We are familiar with the common distinctions of actual sin as *mortal* and *venial*. Where did we get our distinctions for actual sin, and how might an adult understand mortal and venial sin today?

The Bible shows that the biblical communities were aware of degrees of sin, but not in the sense of the distinctions which I have just mentioned. The Bible does not even support reducing all sins to two categories, and does not offer any quantitative measurement for distinguishing kinds of sin. We have already seen that sin is primarily and always a rupture in our relationship with God. The greatest sin is the direct rejection of God. This is idolatry. The direct rejection of the true God and the setting up of idols are the first offenses mentioned in the ten commandments. One of the great missions of the prophets was to call Israel away from idolatry and back to fidelity to the one true God of the covenant.

In the New Testament, Paul lists those sins which can exclude one from the reign of God (1 Cor 6:9–10; Gal 5:19–21). The synoptics have the saying of Jesus about blasphemy against the Holy Spirit as the sin which will not be forgiven (Mk 3:28–30; Mt 12:31–32; Lk 12:10). This sin will not be forgiven because the person who commits such blasphemy is closed to the power of the Spirit to save. The clearest reference to degrees of sin is found in 1 John 5:16–17. There we find the designation of sins as "deadly" or "unto death" and those which are not "deadly" or "not unto death." But the author gives no examples of either. Theologians today continue to try to bring precision to what this distinction might be.[3]

The terms "mortal" and "venial" came into use as a result of efforts to be precise about the distinction in degrees of sin. Tertullian, a north African apologist of the late second and early third centuries, was the first to refer to some sins as "mortal sins." For him this meant sins for which the church should refuse forgiveness. We must understand that Tertullian and his Montanist party at that time were reacting to the mild manner in which the church was receiving sinners back after serious sin. Tertullian and the Montanists felt that while the church can forgive sins, the church should not forgive some sins lest this be taken as leniency and invite others to sin. The unforgivable sins he called *mortalia* (deadly). On his list of deadly or mortal sins were idolatry, blasphemy, murder, adultery, fornication, false witnessing, fraud, and lying.

During the era of canonical penance from the fourth to sixth centuries, a fundamental principle guiding penitential discipline seemed to be that canonical penance was required for mortal sins, while private mortification was sufficient for venial sins. However, we have no uniform listing of what were regarded as mortal or venial sins since the distinction was not easily made, nor made on the basis of the same criteria.

When the law was established at the Fourth Lateran Council (1215) making annual confession obligatory for those who had committed a mortal sin, the distinction between mortal and venial took on juridical importance. To be able to distinguish between sins now becomes important so that penitents will know which sins must be confessed. The law of obligatory, annual confession of mortal sin requires some way of determining who is subject to the law. Moralists began to turn to quantitative and objective measurements to distinguish mortal and venial sin. As soon as quantitative thinking entered into moral thinking, the minimalist question of legalism, "How far can I go before committing a mortal sin?" was not far behind.

Moralists settled on the three conditions which traditional Catholic moral theology has maintained as necessary for mortal sin: *sufficient reflection, full consent of the will,* and *serious matter.* While prominent moralists of our tradition took all three conditions for mortal sin seriously, the popular mind gradually came to identify serious matter alone as enough for mortal sin. By focusing on matter alone, ready catalogues of sin could easily be devised to aid an examination of conscience. With these examination aides, the personal factors of knowledge and freedom often got lost. By contrast, contemporary moral thinking focuses on personal responsibility and so tries to retrieve the personal factors of knowledge and freedom in order to appreciate the moral significance of an action. In looking further, then, at how contemporary theology speaks about sin, we will focus primarily on what constitutes mortal sin, because personal sin which truly deserves the name "sin" is mortal sin. St. Thomas himself claimed as much (ST I–II, q. 88, a. 1). Venial sin derives its meaning by analogy to mortal sin.

## Mortal Sin

The three conditions which the Catholic tradition has required to be present in order for a sin to be "mortal" are still valuable criteria. However, we need to understand them fully. "Sufficient reflection" and "full consent of the will" have to do with the person. "Serious matter" has to do with the action as an expression of the person. But both the conditions which pertain to the person as well as the condition which pertains to the action must be taken together before we can designate the presence of mortal sin.

Chapter 6 on freedom and knowledge already explored what is entailed in the kinds of freedom and knowledge which pertain to acting in a personally virtuous or sinful way. The condition of "sufficient reflection" is fulfilled when we have reached evaluative knowledge. Only then is mortal sin possible, for only with evaluative knowledge have we reached the kind of knowledge which entails the self-involvement of a personal commitment to a person, event, or action.

The traditional requirement of "full consent of the will" implies personal freedom. The kind of freedom which fulfills the requirement of "full consent of the will" is what theologians call basic or core freedom. This is the freedom of self-determination which gives expression to the basic character or dominant direction of our lives. Basic freedom is at the heart of the fundamental option. It gets expressed in those significant choices which arise from a deep level of self-awareness and self-possession so that they can significantly reinforce or redirect the fundamental direction and commitment of our lives.

Only now are we ready to understand the meaning of "serious matter." The basic question of "serious matter" is not how much of a "big deal" the action is in itself, but how deeply invested we are in the action. The most important feature in the moral life is the sort of person we are becoming by the choices we make and the actions we do. Actions are indeed important for this. But when it comes to determining "serious matter," we need to see our actions in relation to the full development of our knowledge and freedom. Bernard Häring has captured the meaning of "serious matter" well in this statement:

> This approach in no way negates the importance of the object of the act or the gravity of the matter; but gravity or relevance assumes moral meaning only in proportion to the actual development of a person's knowledge and freedom, and to the extent that the deep self-determination that we call fundamental option can be evoked.[4]

On the basis of this way of understanding the traditional criteria for the presence of a mortal sin, we can draw a synthetic view of mortal sin. Some theologians speak of mortal sin in a shorthand way as a negative fundamental option. This means that mortal sin, as an expression of the person from deep levels of knowledge and freedom, is a conscious decision to act in a way which fashions a style of life that turns us away from relating to God, others, and the world in a positive, life-giving way. Through mortal sin we no longer build up and promote wholesome relationships, nor do we contribute to the well-being of the human community and all creation.

The 1975 document on sexual ethics, *Persona Humana*, states its understanding of mortal sin in a way that refers to the theory of fundamental option:

> In reality, it is precisely the fundamental option which in the last resort defines a person's moral disposition. But it can be completely changed by particular acts, especially when, as often happens, these have been prepared for by previous more superficial acts. Whatever the case, it is wrong to say that particular acts are not enough to constitute mortal sin (n. 10).[5]

Clearly, the document accepts at least the essence of the theory of fundamental option. Its treatment reins in and corrects those exaggerated forms of the theory which unreasonably minimize the significance of individual actions in assessing sin. Responsible use of this theory would not accept this minimizing. In fact, the theory of fundamental option, properly understood, can help us to take sin more seriously by showing how sin is truly a corruption of the

person. It can also help restore a balance between the three necessary requirements for mortal sin by showing that actions are indeed important and must
always be considered in the context of the person if we are to determine sin
properly.

The document's use of the fundamental option theory shows us two
extreme ways of committing mortal sin. One way occurs when a person, who
has a sharp awareness that a particular act contradicts the love of God,
decides nevertheless in favor of that act in a way which reaches into the
depths of the heart, and so reshapes his or her whole being. The other way
occurs when mortal sin comes as a result of frequent failures to love and to do
the good within one's reach. This increasing laxity deadens the person's
sensitivity to the good and responsibility to others. A point finally comes
where a particular act embodies more clearly than others the erosion of bonds
of love. This approach to mortal sin does not deny that we may reverse in a
concrete action our fundamental commitment to the good. However, it
shows why we should become concerned with the pattern of our decisions
and actions rather than with individual actions taken in isolation. The theory
of fundamental option admits that individual actions can radically change a
person's fundamental orientation, but these actions are not isolated, self-
contained units of personal meaning. As mortal sins, they are much more the
embodying of accumulated unconcern and seal a process that has already
been going on.

Properly understood, actions cannot be separated from persons and from
a relational context. Single actions are the product of interactions, deliberations, and desires over a period of time. To understand our actions as contex-
tual, we might think of the moral life as a kind of story. Individual actions are
like the incidents which make up the story. No action has its proper moral
significance in isolation from the whole narrative. Since all moral action is
interaction, each individual action finds its proper meaning from within the
total narrative that is the moral life. The plot of our story is the fundamental
orientation which flows from our basic commitment and gives shape to the
stable identity of our moral character. We discover the plot only after we are
well into the story. The plot is unveiled by looking back over what has
happened and how it has happened. By looking back, we are able to draw
from the collection of continuous incidents a plot line on which each incident
is graphically located. The plot, once discovered, yields a sense of integrity to
the narrative and gives each particular incident a significance which reaches
beyond its immediate context. In this way, we see each incident not as an
isolated vignette but as continuous with others as part of the story.

The sinfulness of adultery, for example, does not reside simply in its
being the physical action of intercourse with someone other than one's
spouse. Even this physical act takes its meaning from the larger context of

marital interaction and the experiences of daily neglect, plans to meet someone else, frequent meetings, and other acts of infidelity. In short, spouses do
not break up; they drift apart. The action that we call adultery is the accumulation of a lack of concern and infidelities. We realize the gravity of a single
act only in the context of the general direction of the person's life and within
the larger context of moral growth or decay. Mortal sin, as an individual act,
sums up a deteriorating commitment to life and love so as to identify and seal
the selfishness that has already been developing.

This way of understanding mortal sin should caution us from naming
as "mortal sin" physical actions in themselves apart from the person and the
fuller context of personal interaction. An older Catholic theology appreciated this, too, with its distinction between *formal* and *material* sin. Formal
sin is sin in the true sense. It is precisely the action for which we are
morally culpable because it proceeds from knowledge and freedom and so
carries a significant degree of personal involvement. Material sin, on the
other hand, is "sin" only in an analogous way. A material sin is an act of
objective wrongdoing, an act which may even cause great harm. But the
objective wrongdoing itself does not automatically make one morally culpable or make the actions subjectively sinful. Not until we consider the degree
of self-possession and self-determination that goes into an action are we
truly able to name it sin, or more especially "mortal sin," in its most
complete sense.

Even the gruesome acts we hear reported on the evening news, such as
those of the Trailside Killer, the Manson murders, child molestations, and
rape accompanied by physical mutilations, are all crimes which seem too
much like mental illness or poisoned toxic states to be considered voluntary
acts of final rejection of God. Certainly an individual has a certain degree of
moral culpability for getting into such an out-of-control state by not making
use of necessary help; but once such a person has become drugged or crazed,
then he or she can hardly be free enough to sin voluntarily with full knowledge of what is being done. No doubt these people perpetrate evil and cause
untold harm through this wrongdoing, but can we say they are committing
mortal sin in the fullest sense of that term?

Contemporary theology emphasizes the reality of sin in its proper sense
as expressing the involvement of the person in actions, and argues against
using the term "sin" to describe mere external acts considered apart from the
degree of personal involvement. For this reason, the only possible answer to
the straightforward question, "Is it a sin to do x?" (when "x" is any action
taken in itself, and "sin" is understood to be formal sin) is to say, "It depends." What does it depend on? It depends on the subjective involvement of
the person in doing the action. The most we can say about an action in itself
is that it is objective wrongdoing (material sin) or objective rightdoing. Not

until we consider the degree of involvement of the person can we claim that sin, in its truest sense, is present.

For this reason we should be careful with the way we read and use those actions traditionally listed as "mortal sins" in our catalogues of sins. To say an action is a "mortal sin" presumes that the action is done with evaluative knowledge and basic freedom. Unless this presumption can be verified, we ought to understand these designations of actions by themselves as "mortal sins" in a limited way. That is, they are warnings that these sorts of actions are so potentially disruptive of the development of positive human relationships that we should want to avoid them. Also, if we find ourselves engaging in these sorts of actions, we ought to take a close look at the sorts of persons we are becoming. Bernard Häring, with his characteristic pastoral sensitivity, offers this advice:

> Sensible moralists have always realized that their categories regarding gravity of matter can serve only as a rule of thumb. They could be understood as a form of warning. "Danger." But they become senseless if they are used as criteria by a confessor-judge who wants to control the consciences of the faithful in accordance with these determinations of borderline.[6]

Above all, we need to be careful about ever judging that another person is committing mortal sin. No one holds such a privileged point of view as to be able to judge, as an outside observer, the degree of knowledge and freedom which goes into a particular action. Again, Bernard Häring offers some keen pastoral advice:

> No human being can give an accurate definition of how much freedom and awareness is necessary for a mortal sin that always means a sin proportionate to eternal damnation by an all-holy and all-merciful God. It is my conviction that there can be no mortal sin without a fundamental option or intention that turns one's basic freedom towards evil. And we have at least approximate criteria for determining whether a person lives with a fundamental option against God. That is, to presume that the person has no such option if, soon after the fall, he or she has genuine sorrow for the sin and continues to strive to please God and to do what is right.[7]

In this light, we should be very careful with the way we respond to the straight-on question, "Is this a mortal sin?" In answering, remember what it takes to make a sin mortal. Mortal sin says that this action in itself, or as the summation of a series of actions, is hopelessly destructive. A mortal sin truly belongs to the person as his or her own, and it expresses the sort of person one has become and wants to be. Through mortal sin, the sinner closes the self off from a commitment to life and love. So when we are asked "Is this a mortal sin?" we need to be cautious. We begin to explore questions such as these: "In this action, and as a result of this action, is your relationship with God and neighbor still alive? Are you in fact still trying to love and to serve?" Questions such as these try to reach the true meaning of the action and the person's relationship with God and others. Mortal sin radically disrupts the person's relationship with God and turns the person away from an openness to life and to love. In short, if signs of such a radical closure or destructiveness are not evident, then perhaps we can say that the sinner has not yet destroyed a basic commitment to love God and others. Perhaps we are seriously in the realm of venial sin.

## Venial Sin

Only now that we have taken such an extensive look at mortal sin are we ready to understand venial sin. Venial sin is analogous to mortal sin. We have seen above that mortal sin demands a significant degree of self-awareness, self-possession, and self-determination in order to be an expression of one's whole life in a way that radically reverses one's positive relationship to God. The classic requirements for mortal sin which we explored above tell us that we must enter into mortal sin with a clear head, open eyes, and committed heart.

When we examine ourselves for the hallmarks of mortal sin by asking what have we done that is so monstrously evil, contemplated soberly, and then deliberately committed with the intention of making a personal affront to God, what do we find? Probably not much. Most of our selfish neglect takes less spectacular forms, is less clear-headed and open-eyed. These less spectacular forms put us in the realm of venial sin.

Sin so often enters our lives through some form of avoiding the call of conscience to exercise nutrient power and so to meet the demands of love and justice. We psychologically detach ourselves from these demands and become submerged in our own self-interest. We act against another with destructive forms of competitive power by telling our piece of gossip, delivering a scathing sarcasm, or exercising any other power-play to keep ourselves secure. Our sin only quickly escalates through further defensive efforts to keep guilt away. We persevere in our pride until the fruits of sin come forth—projected blame, self-pity, angry attacks, sarcasm, cruelty, distrust, cynicism about another's goodness, and other forms of arrogant power. While these may not be monstrous evils, they do put us seriously in the realm of venial sin.

Venial sins, however, do not embody the whole of our lives in such a radical way as to turn us away from God. Why does not every act carry such weight as to change radically the direction of our lives? For one reason, many of our choices and actions are not done with the open eyes of clear vision. We often do not see what is before us rightly, and so do not respond to what is really there. Furthermore, many of our daily choices do not appear to our consciousness as so important as to demand the expression of full freedom. Most of our daily choices are not relevant enough to alter in a radical way our whole life plan. Most often these choices and actions spring from a more peripheral level of our being, and are not rooted in our hearts. Another reason that not every choice is an exercise of fundamental option is that we continue to be influenced by impediments to our knowledge and freedom. Impediments prevent our actions from penetrating to the deepest core of our selves.

Simply put, then, venial sin is acting inconsistently with our basic commitment to be for life and love. Venial sin does not spring from the deepest level of our knowledge and freedom so as to change our fundamental commitment to be open to God, others, and the world. For example, while I may be fundamentally a caring person, my occasional acts of aloofness and causing harm do not radically change the sort of person I am, though they may weaken my commitment to love and justice. This gives a serious character to venial sins. Even though they do not carry the weight of radical malice in the way mortal sins do, venial sins cannot be dismissed as being of no account.

If a pattern of actions that we judge to be venially sinful can weaken our commitment to goodness and love, can we objectively determine the borderline between mortal and venial sin? Determining this line is the goal of the minimalistic and legalistic mentality which wants to know "How far can I go?" Theologians today generally agree that we cannot give an exact determination of where venial sin ends and mortal sin begins. The reason seems to lie basically in realizing that sin is not in the action itself, but primarily in the person. As the American bishops put it in their pastoral letter on the moral life, *To Live in Christ Jesus,* "We sin first in our hearts, although often our sins are expressed in outward acts and their consequences."[8] Because of the great diversity of genetic endowment, moral and psychological growth, and environmental influences, we are not able to draw clear objective lines that mark off without ambiguity when we are acting from the depths of our hearts to reverse radically the fundamental orientation of our lives to be for life and love.

These claims, that sin is primarily in the person and that we have no clear objective borderline between mortal and venial sin, in no way suggest that venially sinful actions are of no account. They are. Actions, whether a "big deal" or not, have consequences not only for others but also for ourselves. The daily inch and quarter-inch decisions we make contribute to the sorts of persons we are becoming. We are always actively pursuing a way to be by the individual choices we make. Somewhere in the future lies the realization of being a certain kind of person as a result of the small decisions we have already made. Barnard Häring summarizes well the issues pertaining to having no clear objective borderline between mortal and venial sin and the seriousness with which we ought to take even our venial sins:

> My conviction is that an objective border-line, valid for all, between mortal and venial sin can never be determined. We can, however, say that a relatively small matter normally cannot be the object of a mortal sin. The emphasis is on *relative*, which means in proportion to the moral level, the maturity, the awareness and full use of freedom of the individual person. What one person does not consider as a grave matter can, for a very sensitive person, appear to be absolutely irreconcilable with God's friendship. A relatively small act of goodness will normally not turn a bad fundamental option into a good one, although it can be a first step in that direction. Similarly, each sin, if not soon repented, has the frightening possibility of being a first step or next step towards downfall.[9]

The more clearly we become aware of God's love for us, and the more deeply grateful for that love we become, the more clearly we can recognize our venial sins and the more seriously we will take them. Our venial sins are what weaken the rootedness of our fundamental commitment to God and to being a loving person. The more clearly we become aware of God's love for us and the more seriously we take our venial sins, the more attuned we will become to the call to conversion in our lives. The ongoing need for moral growth, the ongoing conversion which ought to mark our moral lives, is the movement bringing us back in line with our fundamental orientation of being committed to life and love.

## Social Sin

"Social sin" is a relatively new theological concept in Roman Catholic theology, though the reality of which it speaks is as old as human culture itself. The notion of social sin articulates how social structures can shape our existence for the worse. It describes the consequences of individual choices which form structures wherein people suffer various forms of oppression and exploitation. Examples of social sin abound: patterns of racial discrimination, economic systems that exploit migrant farm workers, structures which make it necessary that persons be illegal aliens and that sanctuaries harbor them, and the exclusion of women from certain positions in the church are but a few examples.

## Evolution of the Concept

The newness of this concept for Roman Catholic theology is evident in its noticeable absence as an entry in the *New Catholic Encyclopedia* of 1967. However, the National Catechetical Directory, *Sharing the Light of Faith* (1978), was a breakthrough with four short paragraphs on it (165b). How can we account for the lack of development of this concept in the moral tradition?[10]

One of the leading reasons for its slow development is that, for the most part, our awareness of sin and our ways of talking about sin have been worked out for the purposes of confessional practice. This has supported a rather private, individualistic understanding of sin with emphasis on individual actions (serious matter) and the degree of knowledge (sufficient reflection) and freedom (full consent of the will) supporting these actions. Little attention has been given to their wider, social consequences. As a result, our sense of responsibility has been so limited to private actions that we frequently have little sense of collaborating, even tacitly, in social evils. For example, concern over excessive attachment to material goods may be confessed as a selfish interest, but does such attachment ever open us to the larger issue of the morality of tax reform measures which support the acquisition of material goods as tax shelters? Confessing a private, individual sin does not always open us to an awareness of how we may be collaborating in an inequitable system of distributing goods.

Closely related to the attention we often give to individual actions is the emphasis we place on the conditions limiting guilt for wrongdoing. Our confessional practice taught us to distinguish objective wrongdoing from subjective culpability. We could be excused from doing wrong if we were ignorant of the moral significance of our actions. For example, to draw from the experience of a former era, if, forgetting it was Friday, we had a hot dog at the ball game, we did not have to confess it as a sin on the basis of invincible ignorance, an excusing cause. Since the complexities of social sin are often greater than those of individual actions, we could easily extend invincible ignorance to social issues. As a result, our awareness of contributing to oppressive social structures is much less, and so we have little or no sense of culpability for social sin. If we bought grapes or lettuce, for example, not knowing that they were picked by non-union workers, we would not be aware that we were collaborating with an oppressive structure and contributing to social sin.

These are only two examples of factors present in our moral tradition which have worked against the development of the notion of social sin. While the Catholic community has had some outstanding statements in social ethics, our practical social conscience has not always matched them. However, we are beginning to shift our attention from a disproportionate emphasis on actions to an emphasis on the sort of people we are becoming and the sort of community we are creating through our attitudes and actions. In other words, we are becoming concerned not simply with one-to-one action for the sick, the starving, or the homeless, but also with organizing the corporate power of the community to change the structures which oppress, alienate, and deprive people of their due. In short, we are trying to be much more sensitive to actions on behalf of justice as an integral part of preaching and living according to the gospel. As a result, we are experiencing some changes in our moral consciousness.

The first fruits of the effort of Catholics to reform their moral thinking appeared in the Vatican Council's document *Gaudium et Spes*. There we see early evidence of the awareness of the power of social structures and the relation of personal sin to these structures:

> To be sure the disturbances which so frequently occur in the social order result in part from the natural tensions of economic, political, and social forms. But at a deeper level they flow from man's pride and selfishness, which contaminate even the social sphere. When the structure of affairs is flawed by the consequences of sin, man, already born with a bent toward evil, finds there new inducements to sin, which cannot be overcome without strenuous efforts and the assistance of grace (n. 25).

While this document so linked social structures to sin, we have no further instances of this notion within the council documents themselves.

The notion of social sin developed further thanks to the socially conscious liberation theologies, those reflecting not only the experience and perspective of Latin America but also women's experience and a feminist perspective. Liberation theology in general attempts to understand faith in the midst of the struggle to overcome oppression. It recognizes all forms of institutionalized oppression, injustice, or exploitation as situations of sin. "Liberation" expresses the desire to be free to shape one's own destiny and not to be subject to the controlling forces of outside powers, whether they be the male domination of women or the first world domination of third world economies. Liberation theologies see such self-determination being achieved only through a conversion in our use of power and a change of social structures.[11]

Magisterial documents began to reflect the vision of liberation theology when Pope Paul VI stated at the Medellín conference in Colombia in 1968 that Christians cannot be linked with structures which cover up or favor oppressive inequality among citizens. The awareness of the need to transform social structures became evident in the work of that conference.

The most significant magisterial breakthrough in social consciousness and social sin came with the 1971 synod called by Pope Paul VI to discuss justice in the world. Its document, "Justice in the World," presumes that personal freedom is inescapably social and dependent on social structures. It uses the biblical notion of liberation to speak of the church's mission to free the human race from every oppressive situation. Noteworthy for our purposes is that this document encourages education for justice to be based on recognizing sin in its social manifestations.

Pope John Paul II has also referred to the notion of social sin in his post-synodal exhortation, *Reconciliatio et Penitentia* (1984) and again in his social encyclical, *Solicitudo Rei Socialis* (1988). In both documents, he makes clear the personal moral responsibility for social sin, since social sin is the result of the accumulation of personal sin.[12] His description of social sin is this:

> It is a case of the very personal sins of those who cause or support evil or who exploit it; of those who are in a position to avoid, eliminate or at least limit certain social evils but who fail to do so out of laziness, fear or the conspiracy of silence, through secret complicity or indifference; of those who take refuge in the supposed impossibility of changing the world and also of those who sidestep the effort and sacrifice required, producing specious reasons of a higher order (RP n. 16).

For John Paul II personal sin provides the defining norm for sin so that social sin can be properly understood only in the context of sin as a personal act. In this way, he hopes to avoid making social sin the only kind of sin. If it were, then we could easily lose a sense of individual responsibility for sin by attributing everything to a vague anonymous system. John Paul II rejects the notion of social sin which allows blame to be put on the group or the system rather than on the individual. He favors a sense of distributive moral responsibility. This means that social sin can never be separated from personal moral responsibility.

## *The Notion of Social Sin*

Such is the evolution of the notion of social sin. We can summarize the meaning of this kind of sin by identifying its leading characteristics.[13] Social sin reflects the dialectical nature of human existence: freedom and fate. The social sciences, especially the sociology of knowledge,[14] help us to see that through our freedom we create society by embodying meaning and value in social structures. For example, economic structures (import quotas, income taxes, medicare, and social security benefits), educational structures (compulsory education, busing programs for racial balance), social structures (zoning regulations), and ecclesial structures (an exclusively male clergy) are all embodiments of meaning and value. These structures in turn affect us through the process of socialization to limit our freedom, but not to determine it completely. As a result, what we see, what we think, what we believe, what we value, and what we do depend a great deal on the social context of our lives. By participating in these structures we sustain them and help to produce their effects, whether we want to or not.

Since social structures are the result of acts of personal freedom in the first place, the relationship of personal sin to social sin is inevitable and inseparable. Since we participate in the process of creating society, we share in the responsibility for causing social sin. But being responsible for causing social sin does not automatically mean we are morally culpable for it. Culpability demands knowledge and freedom. So, once we become aware of the social structures which influence our lives for the worse, then we need to be attentive to the further decisions we make and to the actions we take to support such structures which are destructive and oppressive of human well-being. However, as often happens, we get so caught up in the worldview and spirit we have created by these structures that we cannot see clearly the evil we perpetuate. As a result, our moral sensitivity to evil grows dull. Our blindness and ignorance consequently limit our culpability for social sin. But if, after our consciousness has been raised and our imaginations transformed so that we can see clearly the wrongdoing being perpetuated by our social practices, we still do nothing about the oppressive structures, then we are on the verge of culpable personal sin for these social ills. Our liability, or obligation to make reparation for them, becomes proportionate to our degree of culpability.[15]

Since the real responsibility for social sin lies with each individual, sinful structures will not be converted until we who are responsible for them alter the way we use our power to influence change in ourselves, others, and the structures within which we live. The right use of power lies behind the reality of social sin and remains a major moral issue in our world and in the church. If we wish to do anything effective about social sin we certainly need to know something about how societies work. To make business and politics less sinful demands learning lessons of economic and political science. Not all of us will be able to do this with equal competence. What all of us can do, however, is face the challenge to break the cycle of evil by naming the power at work in our personal relationships and in our institutions. Is ours a power that controls, manipulates, dominates, and exploits? Or is ours a power that liberates? As a people who are covenanted together under the power of divine love, we need to take our power seriously, to accept the responsibility we have to use this power to liberate and to give life, and to call others to account for their use of power. When we accept the power that is ours, regardless of the position of authority we may hold in the church or in society, then we are living as a covenanted people who are committed to enhancing human well-being and the quality of relationships in a way which will make a difference for living life in freedom, justice, and peace.

## Notes

1. The notion of "sin of the world" was first popularized by Piet Schoonenberg, *Man and Sin*, translated by Joseph Donceel (Notre Dame: University of Notre Dame Press, 1965), pp. 98–123.

2. For an overview of the theological discussion on original sin, see Brian McDermott, "The Theology of Original Sin: Recent Developments," *Theological Studies* 38 (Spring 1977), pp. 478–512; Battista Mondin, "Original Sin in Contemporary Thought," *Theology Digest* 26 (Summer 1978), pp. 145–149; Christian Duquoc, "New Approaches to Original Sin," *Cross Currents* 28 (Summer 1978), pp. 189–200; more recently, an integrated view of various perspectives can be found in James Gaffney, *Sin Reconsidered* (Ramsey: Paulist Press, 1983), pp. 45–52.

3. After discussing the various theories about this sin, Raymond E. Brown concludes: "The best solution by far is that it is the sin of the secessionists, i.e., refusing to believe that Jesus is the Christ come in the flesh. A refusal to believe kept people away from Jesus during his lifetime and kept people away from Christianity during the early mission; now it has led to a schism within the Johannine Community." *The Anchor Bible*, Vol. 30, *The Epistles of John* (Garden City: Doubleday & Company, Inc., 1982), p. 636. Pheme Perkins is of a like mind: "Originally, the 'sin unto death' was probably the reverse of the belief in Jesus that brings eternal life, that is, denying one's belief in Jesus during persecution." *New Testament Message*, Vol. 21, *The Johannine Epistles* (Wilmington: Michael Glazier, Inc., 1979), p. 65.

4. Häring, *Free and Faithful in Christ*, Vol. 1: *General Moral Theology* (New York: Seabury Press, 1978), p. 403.

5. The document *Lineamenta*, designed by the synod secretariat to promote discussion and input in preparation for the 1983 synod on reconciliation and penance, holds a similar position when it says:

> Certainly the life of a man must be evaluated on the basis of the fundamental option which he makes with regard to God: accepting him as the supreme good or rejecting him. But this fundamental option is not at all reducible to an "intention" empty of any well-defined binding content, to an intention to which an efficacious effort in the various areas of the moral life does not correspond. In reality, the existence of man works itself out within history and

within personal events. For this reason, the fundamental and global orientation of human liberty demands that it be concretized in concrete determinate choices; and also in one of these choices it is possible to effect a revision of the very global orientation, either in the sense of rejecting God or in the sense of returning to him.

In "Reconciliation and Penance in the Mission of the Church," *Origins* 11 (February 18, 1982): 575. Here we find another positive expression of the essence of the fundamental option theory which captures the proper relationship between fundamental option and the person's fundamental orientation, or stance.

However, John Paul II's post-synodal document *Reconciliatio et Penitentia* (1984) has spoken in a negative way about using the theory of fundamental option to explain mortal sin. For a critical assessment of the pope's use of fundamental option, see Norbert Rigali, "Human Solidarity and Sin in the Apostolic Exhortation, 'Reconciliation and Penance'," *The Living Light* 21 (June 1985): 342–343.

6. Häring, *Free and Faithful*, Vol. 1, p. 407.

7. *Ibid.*, p. 215.

8. *To Live in Christ Jesus* (Washington: USCC, 1976), p. 5.

9. Häring, *Free and Faithful*, Vol. 1, pp. 213–214.

10. For an overview of the emergence of the notion of social sin in the Catholic consciousness, see Peter Henriot, "Social Sin: The Recovery of a Christian Tradition," in James W. Whitehead and Evelyn Eaton Whitehead, *Method in Ministry* (New York: Seabury Press, 1980), pp. 127–144.

11. A helpful review of "liberation theology" is in Roger Haight, *An Alternative Vision: An Interpretation of Liberation Theology* (Mahwah: Paulist Press, 1985).

12. For an analysis of the understanding of social sin in *Reconciliatio et Penitentia*, see Norbert Rigali, "Human Solidarity and Sin in the Apostolic Exhortation, 'Reconciliation and Penance'," *The Living Light* 21 (June 1985): 337–344. On the meaning of social sin in *Sollicitudo Rei Socialis*, see n. 36.

13. An excellent analysis of significant aspects of social sin in relation to personal sin can be found in Kenneth R. Himes, "Social Sin and the Role of the Individual," *The Annual: Society of Christian Ethics* (1986): 183–218.

14. See, for example, the still valuable work of Peter Berger and Thomas Luckmann, *The Social Construction of Reality* (New York: Doubleday & Company, Inc., 1967).

15. For a more extensive treatment of personal responsibility, culpability, and liability for social sin, see the excellent analysis of Kenneth Himes, "Social Sin and the Role of the Individual," *The Annual: Society of Christian Ethics* (1986): 183–218.

# 9   Conscience

"Conscience" is another word like "sin"—often used but little understood. Trying to explain conscience is like trying to nail jello to the wall; just when you think you have it pinned down, part of it begins to slip away. This is really no surprise. We all know we have a conscience, yet our experiences of conscience are ambiguous. We struggle with conscience when facing those great decisions of life, such as the choice of a career, or of conscientious objection to war, or whether to pay our taxes which support defense projects. Yet we even feel the pangs of conscience over petty matters, like jaywalking or taking cookies from the cookie jar. We are told that conscience enjoys inviolable freedom, yet we are often given rules so absolute in character that we wonder whether conscience matters at all. What is this thing called conscience? Which is the true conscience?

The first task is to clarify the important distinction between moral conscience and the superego, a psychological notion of conscience. After establishing this distinction, we will be able to appreciate the meaning of personal moral conscience in our theological tradition. Only then will we be ready to consider the critical issue of the formation of conscience. Chapter 10 will be exclusively devoted to that issue. Chapter 11 will consider the relation of personal moral conscience to the moral teaching of the magisterium, the official teaching office of the pope and the bishops.

## Moral Conscience and the Superego

Psychology has helped us greatly in our efforts to be clear about the meaning of conscience. The work of psychologists has helped us to understand the development of a mature conscience which is subject to all the vagaries of the human experience of growth and development. Normally the pattern of growth is from a conscience subject to external control (when the moral backbone is on the outside and we do what we are told to do by someone in authority, or what we see others do) to a more internal, self-directing conscience (when the moral backbone is on the inside and we do what we ourselves perceive to be right and want to do).

In other words, a criterion of a mature moral conscience is the ability to make up one's mind for oneself about what ought to be done. Note: the criterion says *for* oneself, not *by* oneself. The mature conscience is formed and exercised in community in dialogue with other sources of moral wisdom. The criterion also implies that if a person spends his or her whole life doing what he or she is told to do by some authority simply because the authority says so, or because it is expected by the group, then that person never really makes moral decisions which are his or her *own*. For moral maturity one must be one's own person. It is not enough merely to follow what one has been told. The morally mature person must be able to perceive, choose, and identify the self with what one does. On the moral level, we perceive every choice as a choice between being an authentic or an inauthentic person. Or, as some would put it today, we act either in character or out of character. In short, we give our lives meaning by committing our freedom. The morally mature adult is called to commit his or her freedom, not to submit it. As long as we do not direct our own activity, we are not yet free, morally mature persons.

One of the most common errors and sources of confusion in talking about conscience, or in examining conscience, is to mistake what the theologians mean by "moral conscience" with what some psychologists mean about conscience when speaking of the "superego." We can appreciate this goal of committing our freedom, or developing our character, as a morally mature person if we clear up the confusion between moral conscience and superego which contaminates so much of our thinking and conversing about the moral conscience.

The conscience/superego mixup causes confusion about what it is we must form, follow, examine, and whose freedom we must respect as morally responsible adults. So many confessions in the sacrament of reconciliation are more clearly expressions of an overactive superego producing unhealthy guilt than they are the witness of an adult moral conscience renewing itself so that the moral person can serve God more lovingly and faithfully. But the moral conscience is not the superego. What then is the difference between them?

Psychologists of the Freudian school tell us that we have three structures to our personality: the *id*—the unconscious reservoir of instinctual drives largely dominated by the pleasure principle; the *ego*—the conscious structure which operates on the reality principle to mediate the forces of the id, the demands of society, and the reality of the physical world; and the *superego*— the ego of another superimposed on our own to serve as an internal censor to regulate our conduct by using guilt as its powerful weapon. The superego is like an attic in an old house. Instead of furniture, it stores all the "shoulds" and "have-tos" which we absorb in the process of growing up under the influence of authority figures, first our parents but later any other authority figures—teachers, police, boss, sisters, priests, pope, etc. Its powerful weapon of guilt springs forth automatically for simple faults as well as for more serious matter. The superego tells us we are good when we do what we are told to do, and it tells us we are bad and makes us feel guilty when we do not do what the authority over us tells us to do.

To understand the superego we need to begin with childhood. As we develop through childhood, the need to be loved and approved is the basic need and drive. We fear punishment as children not for its physical pain only, but more because it represents a withdrawal of love. So we regulate our behavior so as not to lose love and approval. We absorb the standards and regulations of our parents, or anyone who has authority over us, as a matter of self-protection. The authority figure takes up a place within us to become the source of commands and prohibitions. Gordon Allport tells a delightful tale which illustrates graphically the way an authority figure takes up a place within us so that not only the content of the command but also the voice of the external authority arise from within.

A three-year-old boy awoke at six in the morning and started his noisy play. The father, sleepy-eyed, went to the boy's room and sternly commanded him, "get back into bed and don't you dare get up until seven o'clock." The boy obeyed. For a few minutes all was quiet, but soon there were strange sounds that led the father again to look into the room. The boy was in bed as ordered; but putting an arm over the edge, he jerked it back in, saying, "Get back in there." Next a leg protruded, only to be roughly retracted with the warning, "You heard what I told you." Finally the boy rolled to the very edge of the bed and then roughly rolled back, sternly warning himself, "Not until seven o'clock!" We could not wish for a clearer instance of interiorizing the father's role as a means to self-control and socialized becoming.

At this stage the external voice of authority is in the process of becoming the internal, or appropriate, voice of authority. The parents' task is to enlist the voice in behalf of virtue, as the parents themselves conceive virtue.

To illustrate the prevailing theory at a somewhat later age, let us say the parents take their son into the woods on a family picnic. Under their watchful eyes he picks up the litter after lunch and disposes it. Perhaps a firm warning on a printed sign, or the sight of a passing constable, may also act as a monitor of neatness. Here still the moral backbone is on the outside.[1]

A simplified way of thinking about the difference between superego and moral conscience is to distinguish between the "shoulds" or "have-tos" and the "wants" as the source of commands directing our behavior. "Shoulds" and "have-tos" belong to someone else. "Wants" belong to us. As a friend of mine once reminded me, "Don't 'should' on me. I don't *want* to be the way you think I *should* be." She had it exactly right.

The commands of the superego which tell us what we "should" do come from the process of absorbing the regulations and restrictions of those who are the source of love and approval. We follow the commands of the superego out of the fear of losing love, or out of our need to be accepted and approved. The moral conscience, on the other hand, acts in love responding to the call to commit ourselves to value. The commands of the moral conscience come from the personal perception and appropriation of values which we discover in the stories or examples of persons we want to be like. The moral conscience is the key to responsible freedom of wanting to do what we do because we value what we are seeking. Whereas the "shoulds" and "have-tos" of the superego look to authority, the "wants" of the moral conscience look to personalized and internalized values. The conscience/superego mixup helps us to understand in part what makes a person with an overly developed or overly active superego have a difficult time distinguishing between what God is enabling or calling him or her to do from what someone in authority says he or she "should" do.

John W. Glaser gives a more sophisticated contrast of the differences between superego and moral conscience in his valuable article, "Conscience and Superego: A Key Distinction."[2] In the accompanying chart, I have reconstructed Glaser's nine contrasting characteristics of the superego and moral conscience. This listing is not intended to be exhaustive. I have added emphasis to the points of contrast in Glaser's list, and I have slightly re-worded his characteristics to bring his language into line with what I am using here.

Glaser points out that the failure to distinguish between superego and moral conscience can cause some serious pastoral confusion. For example, the belief that we can make a transition from grace to serious sin and back to grace again easily and frequently leads to the phenomenon of mortal sin on Friday, confession on Saturday, Communion on Sunday, and back to sin again on Monday. However, the approach to serious sin which respects the dynamics of the theory of fundamental option, together with an understanding of the difference between superego guilt and genuine moral guilt, challenges such a belief that one can sin seriously, repent, only to sin seriously

| SUPEREGO | CONSCIENCE |
|---|---|
| 1. *Commands* us to act for the sake of gaining approval, or out of fear of losing love. | 1. *Responds to an invitation* to love; in the very act of responding to others, one becomes a certain sort of person and co-creates self-value. |
| 2. *Turned in toward self* in order to secure one's sense of being of value, of being lovable. | 2. *Fundamental openness* that is oriented toward the other and toward the value which calls for action. |
| 3. Tends to be *static* by merely repeating a prior command. Unable to learn or function creatively in a new situation. | 3. Tends to be *dynamic* by a sensitivity to the demand of values which call for new ways of responding. |
| 4. Oriented primarily *toward authority:* not a matter of responding to value, but of obeying the command of authority "blindly." | 4. Oriented primarily *toward value:* responds to the value that deserves preference regardless of whether authority recognizes it or not. |
| 5. Primary attention is given to *individual acts* as being important in themselves apart from the larger context or pattern of actions. | 5. Primary attention is given to the *larger process* or *pattern.* Individual acts become important within this larger context. |
| 6. Oriented toward the *past:* "The way we were." | 6. Oriented toward the *future:* "The sort of person one ought to become." |
| 7. *Punishment* is the sure guarantee of reconciliation. The more severe the punishment, the more certain one is of being reconciled. | 7. Reparation comes through *structuring the future* orientation toward the value in question. Creating a new future is also the way to make good the past. |
| 8. The transition from *guilt to self-renewal* comes fairly easily and rapidly by means of confessing to the authority. | 8. *Self-renewal* is a gradual process of growth which characterizes all dimensions of personal development. |
| 9. Often finds a *great disproportion* between feelings of guilt experienced and the value at stake, for extent of guilt depends more on the significance of authority figure "disobeyed" than the weight of the value at stake. | 9. Experience of *guilt is proportionate* to the degree of knowledge and freedom as well as the weight of the value at stake, even though the authority may never have addressed the specific value. |

again—and do all this within a matter of days! The nature of genuine moral conscience which we are exploring in this chapter, together with the dimensions of human freedom which we explored in Chapter 7, do not support such an easy and frequent transition.

Another area of pastoral confusion pertains to the appropriate form of moral counseling. An approach which services superego needs would be oriented primarily toward individual actions apart from their total context in one's life. Moral counseling sensitive to moral conscience and moral growth would pay attention to the larger context of the person's life and to the values that deserve preference in this context.

What would this distinction between superego and moral conscience look like when dealing with a pastoral problem? Glaser offers some illuminating pastoral approaches to certain issues of sexuality (an area notoriously susceptible to the tyranny of superego) which respect the difference between superego and moral conscience. For example, an actual case dealing with masturbation was resolved by the counselor's refusing to respect the superego as if it were the conscience. It went like this:

> A counselor told me of a case in which a happily married man with several children had been plagued by masturbation for fifteen years. During these fifteen years he had dutifully gone the route of weekly confession, Communion, etc. The counselor told him to stop thinking of this in terms of serious sin, to go to Communion every Sunday and to confession every six weeks. He tried to help him see his introversion in terms of his own sexual maturity, in terms of his relationship to his wife and children. Within several months this fifteen-year-old "plague" simply vanished from his life. By refusing to follow a pattern of pastoral practice based on the dynamics of superego, this counselor was able to unlock the logjam of fifteen years; by refusing to deal with the superego as if it were conscience, he freed the genuine values at stake; he allowed them to speak and call the person beyond his present lesser stage of sexual integration. We can pay rent to the superego but the house never becomes our own possession.[3]

Although basically a principle of censorship and control, the superego still has a positive and meaningful function in our personalities. In children, the superego is a primitive but necessary stage on the way to genuine conscience. In adults, the superego functions positively when integrated into a mature conscience to relieve us from having to decide freshly in every instance those matters which are already legitimately determined by convention or custom.

The difference between the working of the superego in the child and the adult is one of degree and not of kind. In concrete cases, the superego and moral conscience do not exist as pure alternatives in undiluted form. We experience a mixture of these in our deliberations. Fr. Frank McNulty provides an illuminating example of this mixture in his account of the interior dialogue he experiences in trying to decide whether to attend a wake service or not. The issue emerged when he did not think he would be able to go to the wake because of a meeting he already had to attend. But the meeting broke up early, and thus the need for the decision. Here is the account of his interior dialogue:

"Good. I will have a chance to attend that wake." (Conscience at work, saying, in effect: "Frank, my friend just lost his father. Go to the wake; it will mean something to him.")

"Wait a minute. I can't go to that wake. I'm not wearing clerical clothes. Priests don't go to wakes dressed like this." (Superego warning about making a "bad" appearance, facing disapproval.)

"Why not? The important thing is consoling the bereaved. It's an act of charity. Look at Jesus and his example in Scripture, at how good he was to Mary and Martha when Lazarus died. Did he worry about what he was wearing?" (Conscience back again.)

"What will people think? Remember I was taught that a priest should even carry a hat to a wake. I don't have to do that, but at least I have to wear my clericals." (Superego)

"But I gotta go. I have the time. The family would like to see me there. It will mean a lot to them. I'll probably be the only priest there, since they don't know priests in the parish too well. Go to the wake." (Conscience)

"Well, if I go, maybe no one will recognize me. I can sneak in, say a quiet prayer and sneak out, without declaring myself as a priest." (Superego making a concession, but hanging in there.)[4]

(As it turned out, the family asked Frank to come forward and lead the rosary.)

The development from the superego of the child to the personal value perception of the adult moral conscience does not take place automatically. One of the tasks of moral education and pastoral practice in moral matters is to reduce the influence of the superego and to allow a genuinely personal way of seeing and responding to grow. One of the great temptations of moral counseling is to "should" on the person seeking assistance. We can examine our pastoral practice on this score by asking, "Have I 'should' on anyone today? Or, have I drawn out of another what he or she perceives to be going on and wants to do?" The goal of adult moral education and adult moral development is to act more out of a personally appropriated vision and personally committed freedom and less out of superego.

Now that we have distinguished superego from the moral conscience, we can proceed with a more elaborate expression of the ways the Catholic moral tradition has understood the moral conscience.

## Moral Conscience in the Theological Tradition

The Catholic tradition has long attested to the primacy, dignity, and inviolability of the moral conscience. According to that tradition, no one is to be forced to act contrary to his or her conscience. The following two statements from the Second Vatican Council sum up the Catholic tradition's support of the dignity and inviolability of conscience:

> On his part, man perceives and acknowledges the imperatives of the divine law through the mediation of conscience. In all his activity a man is bound to follow his conscience faithfully, in order that he may come to God, for whom he was created. It follows that he is not to be forced to act in a manner contrary to his conscience. Nor, on the other hand, is he to be restrained from acting in accordance with his conscience, especially in matters religious (Declaration on Religious Freedom, n. 3).
>
> In the depths of his conscience, man detects a law which he does not impose upon himself, but which holds him to obedience. Always summoning him to love good and avoid evil, the voice of conscience can when necessary speak to his heart more specifically: do this, shun that. For man has in his heart a law written by God. To obey it is the very dignity of man; according to it he will be judged.
>
> Conscience is the most secret core and sanctuary of a man. There he is alone with God, whose voice echoes in his depths. (Pastoral Constitution on the Church in the Modern World, n. 16)

While the dignity and inviolability of conscience in our tradition is incontestably clear, the meaning of conscience in the minds of many is not so clear. What does the Church intend to uphold when speaking of the inviolable dignity and freedom of conscience? To what does the Church refer when speaking of conscience as our "most secret core and sanctuary"?

Whereas in the past we tried to restrict conscience to a function of the will or of the intellect, today we understand conscience as an expression of the whole person. Simply put, conscience is "me coming to a decision." It includes not only cognitive and volitional aspects, but also affective, intuitive, attitudinal, and somatic aspects as well. Ultimately, conscience is the whole person's commitment to values and the judgment one must make in light of that commitment to apply those values.

In light of this holistic sense of conscience we can appreciate the three dimensions of conscience to which the Roman Catholic tradition ascribes: (1) *synderesis*, the basic tendency or capacity within us to know and to do the good; (2) *moral science*, the process of discovering the particular good which ought to be done or the evil to be avoided; (3) *conscience*, the specific judgment of the good which "I must do" in this particular situation. To simplify matters, Timothy O'Connell refers to these dimensions as conscience/1, conscience/2, and conscience/3 respectively.[5] These are not three different realities, nor three distinct stages through which conscience moves in developing from infancy to adulthood, but simply the three senses in which we can understand the one reality of conscience.

The accompanying chart summarizes briefly the principal characteristics of each sense of conscience in our theological tradition.

As the chart indicates, conscience/1 (*synderesis*) is a given characteristic of being human. This is the capacity for knowing and doing what is good and avoiding what is evil. The very existence of this orientation to the good makes possible the lively disagreement over what is right or wrong in each instance of moral choice. The great array of moral disagreement which we experience in our lives does not negate the presence of conscience/1, but affirms it. Because we have *synderesis*, we share a general sense of moral value and the general sense that it makes a difference to do what is right and to avoid what is wrong. We cannot live morally without conscience/1, yet it is not sufficient in and of itself to enable us to choose what is right in each specific instance.

We also need conscience/2 (moral science). The force of conscience/1 empowers us to search out the objective moral values in each specific situation in order to discover the right thing to do. Discovering the operative moral values and the right thing to do is the work of conscience/2. Its primary tasks are accurate perception and right moral reasoning. For this reason, conscience/2 receives a great deal of attention in moral education and in moral debates. It is the realm of moral blindness and insight, moral disagreement and error. It needs to be educated, formed, informed, examined, and transformed. In a word, conscience/2 is subject to the process called "the forma-

# THREE SENSES OF CONSCIENCE

| Conscience/1 (Synderesis) | Conscience/2 (Moral Science) | Conscience/3 (Conscience) |
|---|---|---|
| A Capacity | A Process | A Judgment |
| The sense of the fundamental characteristic of being human which makes it possible to know and do the good. | The sense of our way of seeing and thinking. | The concrete judgment of what I must do in the situation based on my personal perception and grasp of values. |
| Our general sense of value and fundamental sense of responsibility which makes it possible for us to engage in moral discussions to determine the particular moral good. | The realm of moral disagreement and error, blindness and insight. | The primary object of this judgment is not simply this or that object of choice, but being this or that sort of person through what I choose. |
| The fundamental condition which serves as the presupposition to moral agreement or disagreement on a particular issue. | The proper realm of the formation and examination of conscience. | This act of conscience makes a moral decision "my own" and the moral action expressive of "me" by realizing and expressing my fundamental stance. |
| | Follows moral truth which it seeks to grasp by making use of sources of moral wisdom wherever they may be found. | This is the conscience which I must obey to be true to myself. |
| | The goal of its tasks is to reach "evaluative knowledge," personally appropriated, interiorized knowledge. | This is the "secret core and sanctuary" of our self which must not be violated (G.S. #16). Each "is bound to follow his conscience faithfully in all his activity so that he may come to God, who is his last end. Therefore he must not be forced to act contrary to his conscience" (D.H. #3). |
| | Searches for what is right through accurate perception, and a process of reflection and analysis. | |

tion of conscience." The goals of this process are correct seeing and right thinking. In its accountability to moral truth, conscience/2 is illumined and assisted in many ways to perceive and appropriate this truth. This means that conscience/2 is formed in community and draws upon many sources of moral wisdom in order to know what it means to be human in a truly moral way.

Conscience/3 (conscience, in the more narrow sense) moves us from perception and reasoning to action. The general orientation to the good (conscience/1) and the process of considering the relevant moral factors (conscience/2) converge to produce the judgment of what I must now do and the commitment to do it (conscience/3). In coming to make this judgment, many can help but no one can substitute for making the judgment which only I can make. The characteristic of the judgment of conscience/3 is that it is always a judgment for me. It is never a judgment of what someone else must do, but only what I must do. The quintessence of the dignity and freedom of conscience is to be found in conscience/3: I must always do what I believe to be right and avoid what I believe to be wrong. If a person truly believes in his or her heart (i.e., with one's whole person) that one line of action rather than another is God's objective call, then that line of action is no longer simply one option among many. It becomes the morally required line of action for that person to take, which is what we mean by being "bound to follow one's conscience." Conscience/3 cannot be violated. It is what the Vatican Council called our "most secret core and sanctuary" (G.S. n. 16) where we are alone with God.

A good illustration of conscience/3 at work is Sir Thomas More as portrayed by Robert Bolt in *A Man for All Seasons*. This play can be read as a portrayal of the conflicts which arise between one who answers to conscience and those who choose to follow what is convenient. Thomas More faces up to his conscience above the prestige of his service to the king. In so doing, he creates a conflict between what is expedient or popular and what he holds so strongly that it is inseparable from his very self. This makes the play a vivid portrayal of exercising the freedom of conscience, i.e., the freedom to think only what we believe to be true and to do only what we believe to be right.

Two short excerpts illustrate dramatically the power and dignity of the judgment of conscience/3. The first is a scene in which Thomas More defends his loyalty to the pope against the charges of the Duke of Norfolk:

NORFOLK: All right—we're at war with the Pope! The Pope's a Prince, isn't he?

MORE: He is.

NORFOLK: And a bad one?

MORE: Bad enough. But the theory is that he's also the Vicar of God, the descendant of St. Peter, our only link with Christ.

NORFOLK: (*Sneering*) A tenuous link.

MORE: Oh, tenuous indeed.

NORFOLK: (*To the others*) Does this make sense? (*No reply; they look at MORE*) You'll forfeit all you've got—which includes the respect of your country—for a theory?

MORE: (*Hotly*) The Apostolic succession of the Pope is—(*Stops; interested*) . . . Why, it's a theory, yes; you can't see it; can't touch it; it's a theory. (*To NORFOLK, very rapidly but calmly*) But what matters to me is not whether it's true or not but that I believe it to be true, or rather, not that I *believe* it, but that *I* believe it. . . . [6]

In another place Thomas More demonstrates that the freedom and judgment of conscience/3 do not extend to anyone else. In conscience/3 one stands alone with God.

NORFOLK: I'm not a scholar, as master Cromwell [the prosecutor] never tires of pointing out, and frankly I don't know whether the [King's] marriage was lawful or not. But damn it, Thomas, look at those names. . . . You know those men! Can't you do what I did, and come with us, for fellowship?

MORE: (*Moved*) And when we stand before God, and you are sent to Paradise for doing according to your conscience, and I am damned for not doing according to mine, will you come with me, for fellowship?

CRANMER: So those of us whose names are there are damned, Sir Thomas?

MORE: I don't know, Your Grace. I have no window to look into another man's conscience. I condemn no one.[7]

This same idea is expressed as poignantly by Martin Buber's tale of Rabbi Zusya who illustrates the integrity of conscience to be true to itself, for out of our loyalty to conscience will we be judged by God.

The Rabbi Zusya said a short time before his death, "In the world to come, I shall not be asked, 'Why were you not Moses?' Instead, I shall be asked, 'Why were you not Zusya?' "[8]

In light of this understanding of conscience, we can now appreciate the truth of the maxim, "Let your conscience be your guide." To follow this maxim uncritically would be to inject the personal nature of conscience with a strong dose of individualism and effectively cut off conscience/3 from being informed by other sources of moral wisdom. Yet genuine conscience is formed in dialogue, not in isolation. The work of conscience/2 is to carry on this dialogue with the sources of moral widsom. As Daniel C. Maguire explains it, "The individual and supremely personal nature of conscience does not mean *me* against *them*; it means *me* distinct from *them* but intrinsically *with them*."⁹

The proper interpretation of "Let your conscience be your guide" follows upon understanding it as referring to conscience/3. When conscience/2 has done its moral homework well, it yields to conscience/3. Its judgment in each case will be trustworthy in proportion to the thoroughness of the homework one does in forming one's conscience. In the last analysis, conscience/3 is the only sure guide for action by a free and knowing person. Violating conscience/3 would be violating our integrity. If we have done all we could possibly do to inform ourselves of what would be the most responsible thing to do, then we will not be entering the realm of sin even if we do something which we later discover was the objectively wrong thing to do. We need to consider, then, what the formation of conscience entails.

## Notes

1. Allport, *Becoming* (New Haven: Yale University Press, 1955), pp. 70–71.

2. In C. Ellis Nelson, ed., *Conscience: Theological and Psychological Perspectives* (New York: Newman Press, 1973), pp. 167–188.

3. *Ibid.*, p. 182.

4. Frank J. McNulty and Edward Watkin, *Should You Ever Feel Guilty?* (Ramsey: Paulist Press, 1978), pp. 53–54.

5. O'Connell, *Principles for a Catholic Morality* (New York: Seabury Press, 1978), pp. 88–93.

6. Bolt, *A Man for All Seasons* (New York: Random House, Inc., Vintage Books, 1962), pp. 52–53.

7. *Ibid.*, pp. 76–77.

8. Martin Buber, *The Way of Man According to the Teaching of Hasidism* (New York: Citadel Press, 1966), p. 17.

9. Maguire, *The Moral Choice* (Garden City: Doubleday & Company, Inc., 1978), p. 379.

# 10 The Formation of Conscience

*I*n the moral education of adults, the pastoral priority is to enable people to make their own moral decisions in light of the guidance of scripture and the teaching of the church. This means not so much providing answers to moral questions as encouraging the process of arriving at a moral decision. This brings us squarely into the domain of the formation of conscience.

## The Range of Interest in Forming Conscience

Often, discussions about the formation of conscience are preoccupied with answering the practical moral question, "What ought I to do?" The emphasis then is necessarily placed on what we need in order to make a particular moral choice (conscience/3). However, when the right "choice" becomes of primary interest, the formation of conscience becomes a matter of acquiring the necessary skills for making right judgments. These are such skills as the ability to assess morally relevant factors, such as the action itself, intention, circumstances, consequences, values, and norms; the ability to consider all sides of an issue; the ability to provide sound reasons for a moral judgment; and the ability to have a decisive will to execute a judgment. This is the process of deliberation proper to conscience/2. Certainly, the natural law tradition of Catholic moral theology encourages this kind of thinking. According to the natural law tradition, to be moral is to be reasonable. The Catholic tradition of natural law has been very optimistic about reason and has placed a premium in the moral life on developing the capacities for exercising reason rightly.

Our approaches to moral education and the moral development of conscience in recent years have been dominated by such a point of view. Craig

Dykstra rightly calls it "juridical ethics."[1] A prime example of this point of view, with its implications for moral education and the development of the moral conscience, can be found in the theories of Lawrence Kohlberg. According to his theories, the moral life is primarily a matter of making choices on the basis of reason. Moral development is a matter of acquiring the ability to provide increasingly more principled reasons to justify those choices.

One of the dangers of this approach is that it can too easily split the intimate connection between religion and morality in our lives. Religious beliefs, for example, too easily become dispensable baggage in the moral life, since moral choices can be defended on grounds other than religious ones. Another danger with Kohlberg's approach is that, if we limit the formation of conscience to the development of moral reasoning for making a decision, we severely restrict what is involved in morality and in the Christian conscience, and we oversimplify both.

While making a reasoned choice is indeed an important interest in the moral life, it is not the whole of morality. We have already seen in the first chapter that the twofold range of interest of moral theology includes not only making moral decisions but also forming moral character. The interest in character appeared again under the considerations for determining sin. There I indicated that determining sin is not a matter of examining isolated actions against a set of moral rules, but involves discerning the orientation and commitment of the person. We can expect, therefore, that the formation of conscience will involve more than simply answering the practical moral question, "What ought I to do?" It must also address the prior moral question, "What sort of person ought I to become?" This means the aim of the formation of conscience is not simply to increase a person's knowledge of facts and values, or skills for resolving a moral dilemma. It must also include the fuller texture of the person's moral character. As long as we can remember that morality is interested in *who we are*, as well as in *what* and *how we choose*, then we will not eliminate character from our consideration of the formation of conscience.

Conscience is properly formed in dialogue with several sources of moral wisdom. As *humans* we consult our own experience as well as the experience of family, friends, colleagues, and experts in the field which pertains to the area of judgment at hand. We analyze and test the stories, images, language, rituals, and actions by which the various communities in which we participate live the moral life. As *Christians* we turn to the testimony of scripture, the religious convictions of our creeds, the lives of moral virtuosos, and the informed judgment of theologians past and present who help interpret the traditions of Christian life. *Christian communities* have access to a rich heritage of stories, images, language, rituals, devotional practices, and spiritual disciplines which nurture one's moral vision and practice. These communities have also official statements of moral teaching from its leaders to give guidance in areas of specific moral concern. As *Catholics* we pay attention to our rich heritage of stories, images, and practices as well as to the official teachings of the magisterium which are pertinent to our areas of concern.

The proper formation of conscience uses these sources of moral wisdom to inform the four points of moral analysis which we took from James Gustafson and introduced in Chapter 1 under the consideration of the practical level of moral theology. Those four points are: the agent; beliefs; situational analysis; and moral norms. Although all work together in the formation and functioning of conscience, for purposes of analysis here we will correlate what pertains to the agent and beliefs with conscience and character, and correlate what pertains to situational analysis and moral norms with conscience and decision making.

## Conscience and Character

Perhaps the most serious danger in concentrating merely on choosing and acquiring more principled reasons for the choices we make is that we fail to deal adequately with the formation of *character*. Attention to character has been the sorely neglected side of the formation of conscience. Some theologians today are encouraging greater attention to character as the more important side of the moral life.[2] These theologians are saying that who we are matters morally. If a judgment of conscience is to be a response from the heart, then much depends on character, or virtue. We need to explore the moral import of "who we are" and to give full weight to all the factors which influence the formation of character.

Moral choices are not made in a vacuum. They are made by people who see the world in a certain way because they have become particular sorts of people. The very way we describe a situation and the kinds of choices we make follow from the kind of character we have. Character gives rise to choice. Choices in turn confirm or qualify character, for choices are self-determining. In choosing to adopt one or another course of action, we make ourselves into certain sorts of persons. Heroes, heroines, and saints illustrate this most vividly when they refuse to compromise on matters which seem to others of little practical importance. Once again, Thomas More portrays this well in Robert Bolt's drama. The following scene takes place in the jail cell when Thomas More's daughter, Margaret, comes to persuade him to swear to the Act of Succession:

MORE: You want me to swear to the Act of Succession?

MARGARET: "God more regards the thoughts of the heart than the words of the mouth." Or so you've always told me.

MORE: Yes.

MARGARET: Then say the words of the oath and in your heart think otherwise.

MORE: What is an oath then but words we say to God?

MARGARET: That's very neat.

MORE: Do you mean, it isn't true?

MARGARET: No, it's true.

MORE: Then it's a poor argument to call it "neat," Meg. When a man takes an oath, Meg, he's holding his own self in his own hands. Like water. (*He cups his hands*) And if he opens his fingers *then*—he needn't hope to find himself again. Some men aren't capable of this, but I'd be loath to think your father one of them.[3]

This scene emphasizes that any choice which really involves free self-determination includes one's whole self with it. Thomas More shows that when we do not act according to our character, our very self can be lost. Moral choices are fundamentally matters of integrity: we act in character or out of character.

What is this "character" which is so important in the moral life? When we "size people up" to get a glimpse of their character, what do we attend to? We pay attention to patterns of actions which reflect attitudes, dispositions, the readiness to look on things in certain ways and to choose in certain ways. These are indices of character, since character shows itself in its fruits. Character identifies the responsive orientation of a person: seeing the world as a hostile or friendly place, or being a person who loves and helps or one who is fearful and selfish.

We acquire character by directing our freedom to loyalties outside ourselves. Christian character, for example, is formed by directing our freedom to the person and message of Jesus as the ultimate center of our loyalty. Character is what results from the values we make our own. When a value has woven its way into the fabric of our being, we delight in doing what pertains to that value. The just person "justices" and the loving person loves with such ease that we say such actions are "second nature" to these people. Character predisposes us to choose in certain ways, even though it does not predetermine every choice. We can act against character, and by making new choices we can change our character.

## Conscience, Character, and Vision

*Vision* and *choice* are two key concepts which pertain to conscience and character. Clearly, vision is prior to choice in the moral life. After all, we choose what we do on the basis of what we see, and we see what we see because of who we are, our character. Think for a moment: What really makes us morally different? Is it the specific choices we make? Many of us make the same choices: to pay taxes, to resist violence, to visit the sick. We are morally different because of the underlying vision which provides the foundation for attitudes and choices.

Philosopher Iris Murdoch, who has contributed some foundational ideas to today's interest in vision and character, explains that we differ not because we choose differently, but because we see differently:

> When we apprehend and assess other people we do not consider only their solutions to specifiable practical problems, we consider something more elusive which may be called their total vision of life, as shown in their mode of speech or silence, their choice of words, their assessments of others, their conception of their own lives, what they think attractive or praise-worthy, what they think funny: in short, the configurations of their thought which show continually in their reactions and conversation. These things, which may be overtly and comprehensibly displayed or inwardly elaborated and guessed at, constitute what, making different points in the two metaphors, one may call the texture of a man's being or the nature of his personal vision.[4]

From this we can conclude that the first task of the formation of conscience is the attempt to help us see.

The model of responsibility for the moral life indicates that we respond to what we see. Before we can answer the question, "What ought I to do?" we need to ask, "What is going on?" This is the question of vision. In fact, most of what appears in our decisions and actions is the result of what we see going on, rather than the result of conscious rational choices. For example, if we look on our children as a burden, we refuse to carry them; if we look on our colleagues as competitors, we refuse to cooperate with them.

The "seeing" which is an expression of our character is more than taking a look. Seeing is interpreting and valuing as well. What we regard as worthy of our response depends on how we "view" it. For example, "My wife is a nag," "My employer is bossy," "My students are eager" are ways of seeing which profoundly influence our choices. But these ways of seeing have nothing directly to do with the logical application of rules. They have to do with the images through which we grasp what we see. What we see sets the direction and limits of what we do; it generates certain choices rather than others; and it disposes us to respond in one way rather than another. What is a choice for someone else may never occur to us as a choice at all, for we simply do not see the world that way.

## Conscience, Vision, and Story

The importance of vision and character for understanding the moral judgments of conscience cannot be emphasized enough. Most people most of the time do not make moral choices in the first instance on the basis of impersonal rules, rational abstractions, or logical procedures. Many of our moral decisions do not call for the leisure to sit down and ponder the rational dimensions, general principles, and logical procedures which go into every choice. More often than not, the analysis which discovers such dimensions and procedures comes after the fact of the decision. The real world of our moral choices includes imagination, vision, habits, affections, dispositions, somatic reactions, and countless non-rational factors which logical generalizations never account for in the immediate moment of making a decision. We make our decisions more out of the beliefs we live by and the habits we have formed than out of the principles we have learned. Linus is a prime example of this in his response to Lucy in this excerpt from a *Peanuts* comic strip which has Linus preparing a snowball to toss at Lucy:

LUCY: "Life is full of choices.
   You may choose, if you wish,
   not to throw that snowball at me.
   Now, if you choose to throw that snowball at me
   I will pound you right into the ground.
   If you choose not to throw that snowball at me,
   your head will be spared."

LINUS: (Throwing the snowball to the ground)
   "Life is full of choices,
   but you never get any."

This illustrates how much character (which includes the beliefs we live by as well as the habits we have formed), rather than rational principles, determines a decision or even whether a decision should be made at all. In this case, Linus' fear of Lucy, his belief that she will do what she says and his habitual experience of her habitual way of responding, makes up his mind for him, so to speak. Given what he sees and believes, he has no need to ponder any further.

Properly to understand moral behavior, then, we need to pay attention first to the images shaping the imagination, and the stories giving rise to these images, before we consider moral rules. We live more by stories than we do by rules. All of this tells us that learning moral rules is not the first task in the formation of conscience. We first need to learn *how* to see.

To a great extent, our vision is not something we provide for ourselves by ourselves. A moral vision is not so much chosen as it is inherited from our social worlds. Vision is a community achievement. Social scientists tell us that as we grow, the vision we acquire is in part the result of internalizing the beliefs and values, causes and loyalties of the community which make up our environment. Our vision is almost wholly dependent on our relationships, on the worlds in which we live, and on the commitments we have made. As a result, the morality into which we are socialized is not a set of rules but a collection of stories and images of what makes life worth living.

James Gustafson cites a personal experience which illustrates well how his participation in a religious family and a church community which lived by the religious belief "God is love" shaped his character and vision. He says that the church building of his childhood had across its front a painting of the Gethsemane scene, and above it was printed, "God is love." The juxtaposition of the anguish and suffering of Gethsemane with the affirmation "God is love" made an indelible impression on him. This visual image, together with exposure to preaching on 1 John 4 by his pastor (who also happened to be his father), as well as the experience of human relationships in which the affirmation of God's love was embodied, came together to shape his character and his awareness of being loved by God even in moments of his spiritual suffering of uncertainty and doubt.[5] Gustafson's experience shows how both the historical experience of the community of the church which gave formal expression to the conviction "God is love," and his lived personal experience of human relationships which affirmed that conviction, entered into the formation of his awareness and helped sustain him even when circumstances might have led him to object to such a conviction.

Yet the world of family and church are not the only worlds we live in. Religious beliefs and stories are not the only ones shaping our lives. Each of us inhabits many overlapping worlds at the same time. The formation of conscience takes place in these communities so that one's conscience reflects in many ways the values and loyalties of the most influential communities. For example, why do parents worry about where their children go to school, about the friends they make, about what they do in their free time, about the television shows they watch? They worry because the inner spirit, or the conscience, is shaped and developed by the structures within which we live, by what we see, and by what we do. To speak only moral rules to our children and to expect that this will make them virtuous is to miss the mark of forming conscience. We must also pay attention to their schools, their friends, the books they read, the television programs they watch, and so on.

If one is deeply involved in the Christian community, its beliefs and stories will highly influence one's moral conscience. From the perspective of "reason informed by faith," Christian beliefs have a great deal to do with shaping what we see.[6] But intense competition exists between the Christian community and the many others which vie for our attention. Each of these communities competes for our loyalty but often with contradictory beliefs, images, and norms.

In addition to family and church, we also live in the worlds of our ethnic community, school, profession, sports, politics, commerce, advertising, and entertainment, to name a few. To become aware of the strong impact these worlds have on us, try this little exercise. Place yourself in the center of a series of concentric circles.

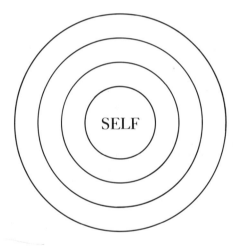

In each circle, beginning with the one nearest you, place the name of the world which you think has had the greatest influence on shaping your character and vision. Name some of the concrete particulars of these worlds which have had a significant influence on you. To extend this exercise, arrange the worlds in the order of their greatest influence on your present attitudes toward these moral issues: divorce, homosexuality, pre-marital sex, the arms race, the use of drugs, euthanasia, and a moral issue of your choice. Do the worlds of family and church come close to you in each instance? An exercise like this may not help us become totally conscious of our vision, but it at least helps us to see the ways our vision is shaped by participating in communities.

Each world we enter makes demands on our loyalty and is alive with many forms of communicating that loyalty. Rules and regulations try to do it, but stories, images, rituals do it better. Through these latter means, we come to see what life centered around the convictions of these communities is about, and how life is to be lived. The more we participate in the stories, rituals, images, and language of a community which has a great influence on us, the more we begin to take on its way of seeing.

Take the "community" or world of college and professional football, for example. The weekly exposure to the annual fall ritual of the quest to be "No. 1" has an unmistakable impact on our imaginations. Without this fall ritual and image, as well as the stories which go with it, football season would be less exciting. But once we get immersed in the world of sports with its stories and images, we have a hard time seeing what is going on anywhere else in any other way. For example, we may even find ourselves talking about having "to gain yardage" on a deal, or "to run interference" for a colleague, or "to punt" in order to get out of a jam. We may even begin to approach all forms of human interaction with the image of "No. 1." It tells us someone must win and someone must lose. When everyone is out to be victoriously undefeated, aggressive competition, not harmony, reigns supreme. When everyone is out to be "No. 1," then our lives become filled with competition and conflict, and our styles of interaction become a mixture of aggressively offensive and staunchly defensive behavior.

The worldview presented by the entertainment community competes most intensely with the Christian community's. Willam F. Fore's book, *Television and Religion: The Shaping of Faith, Values, and Culture*, maintains that television is usurping the role of the church in shaping the imagination and our system of values. He says,

> Television, rather than the churches, is becoming the place where
> people find a worldview which reflects what to them is of ultimate
> value, and which justifies their behavior and way of life.[7]

Few television viewers are so firmly established in their value commitments as to go untouched by the persistent promotion of the values and behavioral patterns which television programs transmit. For example, consider the number of "family" programs which do not prize marital fidelity, or which portray their central characters as single and free to explore a wide range of interpersonal dynamics, or whose humor is carried by sexual innuendo. Television is a powerful source of influence on attitudes and behaviors in the areas of violence and sexuality.[8] For children, it is in cartoons. For adults, it comes through situation comedies, soap operas, and police dramas. Such programs portray violence and coercion as natural parts of sexuality and tell us that the young, the strong, and the beautiful are the ones who are sexual and need loving. These programs transmit many images of what makes life worthwhile which stand in direct conflict with the images of the gospel and rob religious stories and images of their power to move people.[9]

In addition to the television programs themselves, consider how many of our preferences and ways of evaluating what is worthwhile in persons and in life are shaped by the powerful images communicated through the clever world of advertising. Recall the number of television commercials which tell us that enough is not enough, "You need more . . ."; "Get more out of life by. . . ." The advertising world's pursuit of "more" communicates a vision about life and how to live it meaningfully. We can soon take this vision of consumerism and use it to interpret the whole of our lives and our relationships. When we begin to look upon all our activities and people with a sense of insufficiency and know that whatever we have is not enough, the newest, or the most improved, then we have been converted by the images of the world of advertising. The rest of our lives will soon follow in kind.

The strong influence of the business world on moral vision and moral character was graphically brought home to me while I was watching the Oregon Shakespearean Festival's production of Arthur Miller's *Death of a Salesman*. This play is a strong indictment of society for its failure to provide its members with a worthy vision of life. The vision which ultimately destroys Willy Loman is born out of his belief in unrestrained individualism and his worship of success. Willy could not make this vision of life work. The competition of the business world, and the pressures of a success-oriented world in which respect is earned by achievement, eventually drives him mad. In a world which looked upon love, acceptance, and respect as something to be earned by achievement, failure was unbearable. The "successful" vision of Willy Loman's world finally led him to suicide. Part of his tragedy is that he had no other story to replace the vision his business world had given him.

These examples of the religious world of James Gustafson and the non-religious worlds of sports, television, advertising, and business give us a sense of ways our vision is shaped by the multiple worlds in which we live. Each world communicates what is "good" and how life ought to be lived. These examples show clearly that most of what we see does not lie in front of our eyes but behind them in the images which make up our imaginations. Images and the imagination, then, are extremely important for the moral life.

## Conscience, Imagination, and Christian Stories

The imagination is a powerful moral resource, not to be equated with mere fantasy or make-believe. As we saw in Chapter 5 on the human person, the imagination is our capacity to construct our worlds. By means of the imaginative process, we bring together diverse experiences into a meaningful whole. When we "get the picture" we have come to an image which helps us put all the diverse parts together so that we can understand what is going on and so relate to it appropriately. Human behavior is a function not so much of the moral propositions one holds as true, but of the imagination holding the images which give us a "picture" of the world. In forming our consciences for the sake of making a moral judgment, then, we need to be critically alert to images at play in our imaginations.

Our imaginations determine what we see and so influence how we respond. Every teacher knows the power of apt examples, and every preacher knows the effect of a story well told. Frequently, our students or congregations do not understand a simple point, not because they lack intelligence, but because their frame of vision has them looking in the wrong direction. A good example, or a well-told story, allows the listener to suspend prior judgment about the nature of reality and it frees one to let images play together in a new way. Suddenly all is clear: "Oh, I get the picture! I've just never seen it like that before!" From the point of view of the imagination, moral conversion is a matter of repatterning the imagination so as to see dimensions of reality which were not available to us before. When we begin to see differently, we will begin to respond differently. The challenge to pastoral ministry is to feed the imagination with the Christian stories and images through which we can see the world in depth and respond appropriately.

Christian morality believes that the stories and images which come to us in the Christian story portray and describe goodness in the moral life, and they provide truthful ways of seeing the world. Undoubtedly, these stories and images will be in competition with others coming to us from the various worlds in which we live. Each world tries to tell us something about what is good, and how life ought to be lived. The important question before us, then, is how decisive our Christian believing and beliefs ought to be for shaping our moral awareness. As James Gustafson would have it, "[they] ought to be the most decisive, most informing, most influencing beliefs and experiences in the lives of people."[10] However, how decisive they actually are will depend on how deeply one has appropriated them in becoming a Christian. The incorporation of these stories into our own way of seeing, feeling, thinking, judging, and acting will help us to engage the world as a people formed by Christian faith. Chapter 4 showed that the distinctively Christian aspect of morality is very much a function of the images of faith shaping one's vision and character. Chapters 12, 13, and 14 will treat more completely some of the ways which scripture, Jesus, and the church function in the moral life to influence moral character through the images of the good life which they provide.

## Conscience and Choice

From vision comes choice. We respond to what we see. The response we make is shaped, too, by the sort of persons we have become. In fact, being a good person has a greater influence on the choices we make than any system of principles or methods of making a decision. Since we choose on the basis of what we see and who we are, we need some way to check our vision and character. As we said above, the properly informed conscience sees rightly. Do we see what is really there? Or do we see just what we want to see? To answer these questions we need to have an accurate grasp of the situation and to make a proper use of moral norms.

A fundamental axiom of Catholic morality is that morality is based on reality. Asking the right questions to analyze the situation is the way to move toward seeing reality rightly. The reality-revealing questions of situational analysis can help us to test our vision, character, and conscience. Daniel Maguire offers several which we can use for this test. He asks: What? Who? When? Why? How? What if? What else?[11] We will examine these simple questions briefly to see how they help us set our sights on what is real in our human situations.

*What* is the human situation of this moral reality? *What* may seem too large as a question since it can stretch over all others. However, it does fix our attention on the primary data (physical, psychological, systemic) through which we first meet our world. Good moral judgments are those which fit the situation as it really is. *What* helps us to see what is really there. *What* presses us to make distinctions where there are true differences. Unless we see the differences we will not respond to what is really there. Many, if not most, moral disagreements result from the ignorance of what is really the case. Whether war is justified, for example, depends on what war is, what nuclear weapons do. In medical matters, we need to know what chemotherapy does, what death is, what abortions do. In sexual matters, we need to know what masturbation does, what contraceptive pills do, what sexual intercourse is. For everyday morality, we need to know what smoking does, what car pooling does, what overworking and overeating do.

Next is *who*. We have already explored some of the *who* dimension in our discussion of character. There we saw that character brings important dispositions to bear on our actions. For example, if I am more like Gandhi than Hitler, that will alter the reality of any situation of conflict. Whether I am an authentic conscientious objector or a coward alters the reality of my draft registration. Whether I am a diabetic or not affects the morality of my eating habits. The *who* also includes the other persons involved in the decision. The moral reality of sexual intercourse, for example, is different when my partner is my spouse or my neighbor.

The third and fourth questions are *when* and *where*. Driving 55 mph has different moral meaning when it is done in a school zone at three o'clock than when it is done on Interstate 80. And we all know the difference between yelling "fire" on a rifle range or in a crowded movie theater.

*Why* and *How* are the next two questions. They also have something to do with character. *Why* is the critical question of motivation that sends us back to clarify our values. What looks like love at the *what* level might truly be manipulation at the *why* level. For example, why do I care for my ailing parents? Is this an expression of love and sincere care on my part, or do I intend to guarantee a substantial cut of the inheritance? Why do I give such large donations to St. Jude's Hospital? To promote the efforts of health care and research carried on there, or to qualify for a sizable tax deduction? "The last temptation is the greatest treason: to do the right deed for the wrong reason," as Thomas a Becket puts it in T.S. Eliot's play, *Murder in the Cathedral*.

But we never do anything for only one reason. We are a mixed bag of motives and conditioning factors, some of which are conscious and some are not. A description of only conscious motives does not adequately account for the complex causes of our behavior. Answering the *why* question well, then, demands a great deal of personal honesty and integrity. Sometimes it may require psychological or psychoanalytic help.

The ethical challenge of *why* is to reach the highest possible level of honesty with ourselves so as to be as clear as we can be about what moves us. Our real enemy is rationalization. We can con ourselves so easily. But wholehearted wanting is the only sound basis for our *why*. The greater the impact an act will have, the more critical it becomes to know why we are doing it. Beneath our mix of motives and conditioning factors, then, we must try to discover what we really want to put forth and to express for ourselves and for others by our behavior.

But good motivation is not all that matters. The purest of motives can have catastrophic consequences. So, no matter how noble the motive, *how*, *what if*, and *what else* must also be taken into account. *How* can even tell us much about our *why*. *How* is a matter of style; it gives expression to our true convictions and real character. Our real *why* often sneaks through to show itself in our *how* all too easily. For example, today we hear some assert that while the *why* of saving many American lives in World War II was a good one, the *how* of atomic bombing Nagasaki and Hiroshima did not justify the killing and maiming of thousands of Japanese civilians. Or while the *why* of bringing on emotional calm is a good one, the *how* of taking drugs may not justify the physical and psychological dependency that results.

Overlapping the *how* question are the *what if* and *what else* questions. *What if* probes foreseeable effects. To act is to choose something, but not everything here and now. Hence the ethical necessity to ask *what if*: If I choose this, what will result? What are the foreseen consequences for myself and others in the short run and in the long run? The full moral reality of our actions is not limited to the immediate present, but extends into the future as well. Moral responsibility requires that we foresee the impact of our behavior as far as is possible. A morality based on love wants to do the least amount of harm possible. Therefore, it demands a prudent judgment well informed by predictable consequences.

Exploring *what if* is not making consequences alone determine whether our actions are right or wrong. This is excessive. The reality-revealing questions point to other factors as well. But because consequences are so often the focal point of moral meaning, foreseeable effects demand our serious attention. The great moral enemy is short-sightedness, the failure to look beyond the immediate good we seek to the evil effects we cause along with it. In asking *what if*, then, we look not only for the results in the short run and in individual dimensions, but we also look at the effects in the long run and in its social dimensions. Our moral universe is not limited to our contemporaries, nor to the immediate moment. Moral responsibility, which is always interpersonal responsibility with a history, has swollen to planetary size and extends through the generations. Discussions surrounding the arms race confirm this. Also, we have learned this lesson all too well in our fight with ecological balance.

*What if* cautions us from making decisions based on one or two effects, or of extending consequences only into tomorrow but not to the day after. While the short term and individual dimensions of an act can have beneficial effects, the long term and social dimensions of it can have catastrophic effects. For instance, euthanasia relieves the suffering of a dying patient in the short run, but what will result from the practice of euthanasia in the long run and from a social point of view? It threatens the trust upon which the physician-patient relationship depends, and it can devalue human life as well as the quality and attitude of mercy among health-care providers. Also, we need reflection on the foreseeable effects of marijuana. Its immediate consequences seem harmless enough, a mild high and no hangover. But what of the possible long range consequences of genetic deformation and brain damage? We also need reflection on the use of prescription drugs to settle tension caused by work. For many people, solving these tensions on the level of biological calm is to ignore the real source of tension which is often interpersonal, not biological, in the first place. As a result of taking the drugs, the effect is not only physical calm but also physical and psychological dependence on the drug, as well as ignoring the needed changes in one's interpersonal relationships. (Incidently, here we see that *why* we take drugs is as serious as the *what if*.) We also need to ask about the foreseeable effects of surrogate motherhood, of adopting children by single persons, of using pesticides on our lawns, farms, golf courses, and of shoplifting even if it is "nickel-and-dime" stuff.

One thing is for sure when we begin to explore *what if*. We face head-on the stark reality that a totally private moral act is pure illusion. "It won't affect anyone but me" is an impossibility when we take the relational dimension of our lives seriously and the consequences of our actions just as seriously. The *what if* question refuses to let us escape the fact that we belong to others.

Following closely behind the *what if* question is *what else*. *What else* can be done? What are the possible alternatives? If we think we are forced into an either/or choice, we ought to look again. We generally have more alternatives open to us than we think. What alternatives do we have to abortion for the unwanted pregnancy, to oil as our primary source of energy, to driving alone to work, to working overtime five days a week, to television as our primary source of family entertainment? The point is that, since every moral choice inevitably has some good and some bad outcomes, we need to explore alternatives. If there were no alternatives, there would be no moral problems. Too often we make the wrong moral choice not because we are bad people, but because we are just too unimaginative. We are not able to see the rich potential for good which lies within us and in our situation. Asking *what else* keeps us open and challenges us to be creative and to consult a wide base of moral wisdom and moral vision.

This, then, briefly sketches the reality-revealing questions which help us to see the reality of our human situation for what it truly is. But beyond asking these questions, the mature moral conscience also consults a wide base of moral wisdon to highlight values of our human situation which might otherwise go unnoticed if we were left on our own. Part Three of this book will discuss sources of moral wisdom to which we might appeal in making a moral judgment. For the Catholic, the moral teaching of the magisterium has a special place in the formation of conscience. In the Catholic view, a properly informed conscience is inescapably ecclesial. What is the relation, then, of personal moral conscience to the authoritative teaching of the church? This is the focus of our next chapter.

## Notes

1. *Vision and Character* (Ramsey: Paulist Press, 1981), p. 1. This book offers a careful criticism of Kohlberg as well as a proposal for an alternative to moral education based on a "visional ethics" rather than the standard "juridical ethics" promoted by Kohlberg.

2. Recent years have shown an increasing interest in character in moral

theology. This interest in ethics has developed along with the increasing interest in story, or narrative, in other areas of theology. Stanley Hauerwas has been a consistent advocate of an "ethics of character." See, for example, his major work, *Character and the Christian Life: A Study of Theological Ethics* (San Antonio: Trinity University Press, 1975); also, his collections of essays: *Vision and Virtue* (Notre Dame: Fides Publishers, Inc., 1974); with Richard Bondi and David Burrell, *Truthfulness and Tragedy* (Notre Dame: University of Notre Dame Press, 1977); also, *A Community of Character* (Notre Dame: University of Notre Dame Press, 1981); also, *The Peaceable Kingdom* (Notre Dame: University of Notre Dame Press, 1983); and *Suffering Presence* (Notre Dame: University of Notre Dame Press, 1986).

3. Bolt, *A Man for All Seasons* (New York: Random House, Inc., Vintage Books, 1962), p. 81.

4. "Vision and Choice in Morality," in Ian T. Ramsey, ed., *Christian Ethics and Contemporary Philosophy* (New York: The Macmillan Co., 1966), p. 200.

5. *Can Ethics Be Christian?* (Chicago: University of Chicago Press, 1975), p. 69.

6. See, for example, Donald Evans, "Does Religious Faith Conflict with Moral Freedom," *Faith, Authenticity, and Morality* (Toronto: University of Toronto Press, 1980), pp. 197–246.

7. Fore, *Television and Religion: The Shaping of Faith, Values, and Culture* (Minneapolis: Augsburg Publishing House, 1987), p. 24.

8. On media violence, see *ibid.*, pp. 131–158.

9. For a brief report of a study on the significance of television in attempts at moral education, see Thomas M. Martin, "Television and the Teaching of Christian Morality," *The Living Light* 18 (Fall 1981): 234–241.

10. Gustafson, *Can Ethics Be Christian?* p. 65.

11. Maguire, *The Moral Choice* (Garden City: Doubleday & Company, Inc., 1978), pp. 128–188.

# 11    Conscience and Church
## Authority

*T*he tension between conscience and church authority may be compared to what is portrayed in a scene from Herman Wouk's *The Caine Mutiny.* We pick up on the action in the terrifying typhoon at the point where Captain Queeg is thought to be too ill to command the ship responsibly. The executive officer goes to relieve Queeg of his duties, but Queeg sends him away and orders the helmsman to "come left to 180 degrees." But the executive officer yells to the helmsman, "Steady as you go!" The helmsman hears both commands: to turn left 180 degrees and to go straight ahead. Confused, he yells out, "What the hell should I do?"[1] The helmsman is a man trained to follow orders of those he respects, but he is now getting conflicting orders from two respectable sources. To whom does he listen? What weight is he to give to each voice?

The church found itself in a similar situation after *Humanae Vitae* in 1968. The encyclical provoked qualification throughout the world. Different episcopal conferences said different things about the way we ought to read and apply this normative teaching.[2] At other times, groups of theologians and bishops said different things on the same issue. To whom should we listen? What weight are we to give to each voice?

Likewise, in 1975 the Congregation for the Doctrine of the Faith issued *Persona Humana*, the Declaration on Certain Questions Concerning Sexual Ethics. In 1977 the Catholic Theological Society of America published its report, *Human Sexuality: New Directions in American Catholic Thought*,[3] to offer guidelines to religious teachers and pastoral ministers. But many of the conclusions in that book were not in accord with the teaching of the church as stated in *Persona Humana*. So the questions arise: To whom do we listen? Can we use the guidelines of the CTSA report or only those of the Congregation for the Doctrine of the Faith? What weight do we give each in the formation of conscience?

Conscience, as we have seen, is the whole person's commitment to values and the considered judgment of what "I must do" in light of that commitment to apply those values. Conscience has been traditionally regarded as the ultimate subjective norm of morality in contrast to the objective norm of the moral order which reason apprehends through nature and revelation. One is always bound to follow the judgment of a properly informed conscience. The informing takes place in community by appealing to various sources of moral wisdom. In the church, the magisterium is a source of moral authority. Its teaching is a very important, though not exclusive, factor in the formation of conscience and in one's moral judgment.

This chapter focuses specifically on the relation of conscience to the teaching authority of the magisterium. Its guiding question is "What is the normative character of the official teaching of the church in arriving at a judgment of conscience?"

## The Magisterium: Official Teaching Authority

In every area of life we rely on the experience and advice of knowledgeable persons. We allow ourselves to be influenced by them as an authority. This means that we treat them as presumptively right and we follow their lead even if we do not fully understand their reasons.[4] To appeal to authority is part of responsible living. It does not mean becoming passive or abandoning reason. We appeal to authority when we recognize that our knowledge and experience are too limited to settle a question satisfactorily. If we already have some knowledge of our question, then we hope the authority will affirm what we know and challenge us with what we do not yet know. When we do not have adequate knowledge, we hope the authority will provide us better evidence than we can get on our own. In appealing to an authority, we believe that it will be more correct about this question than we will, or than anyone else to whom we might appeal.

So the relationship between conscience and authority is inseparable. In most instances, they are not opposed since both seek the truth. But in some instances, tension between the two is likely to arise whenever authority asserts itself with the obligation to assent—for example, in the child's relationship to parents, or in a soldier's relationship to the commanding officer, or in a citizen's relationship to political authority, or in a Catholic's relationship to magisterial authority.

Since the early part of the nineteenth century, "magisterium" has been used almost exclusively with reference to the hierarchy (the pope, the bishops, and the Roman congregations who represent the pope) and its exercise of official teaching authority in the church. Only the teaching of the magisterium is the church's "official" teaching. It has special significance because it is proposed by the bishops who have the authority to teach by virtue of their inheriting the apostolic mandate to teach in the name of Christ.[5] The official teaching is the one to which we appeal in order to answer the question, "What does the Church say about . . . ?"

In the Roman Catholic Church, the magisterium is an institutionalized authority in matters of faith and morals. The great disadvantage of having an institutionalized authority in the church is that, if it does not function well in a cooperative and collaborative fashion, it can obscure the human character of the process of formulating a moral teaching. The guidance of the Holy Spirit does not exempt the magisterium from the human process of gathering data, consulting, reflecting on the data, making a proposal, entertaining counterproposals, doing more research, and so on. Rather, the Spirit guides the learning-teaching process in the church in and through these fallible human efforts. To obscure this process can result in creating an "extrinsic" authority for teachings. "Extrinsic" authority fails to recognize that a teaching is as strong as the thoroughness of the homework which produced it and the cogency of the arguments which support it.

However, the great advantage of having an "institutionalized" authority in the magisterium is that it provides a structure which can bring together, in a cooperative and complementary way, the experience and insights of various perspectives so as to reach as complete an expression of truth about the moral life as possible. When the collaborative function of teaching is working well in the church, we reap the fruits of this advantage. We have known this in the documents of Vatican II and in the wide acclaim given to the American bishops' pastoral letters in the 1980s.

Moreover, in the midst of so many conflicting voices telling us what to do, and so many diverse communities projecting images of what makes life worthwhile, we are fortunate to have the magisterium to teach in moral matters. The primary responsibility of the magisterium is to help us to understand the gospel for our times and to foster our assimilation of its basic values. By attending to the teaching of the magisterium, we may be able to cut through the conflicting voices, competing images, and even our personal bias and rationalizations in order to hear the call of the gospel more clearly.

Since the encyclical letter *Humanae Vitae* of Pope Paul VI in 1968, we have had extensive discussions of the normative character of non-infallible teaching in moral matters. These discussions have shown that while a moral teaching may not be defined as infallible, this does not mean that such a teaching is up for grabs, or that it is meaningless, useless, or irrational. It means that even though these teachings remain subject to reevaluation and the possiblity of revision, the Catholic must still take them into account in the formation of conscience. The formula, "no infallible decision—conscience decides," is a complete distortion of the real function of conscience. Conscience needs to be informed. For a Catholic to make a decision of conscience with indifference to, or in spite of, the magisterium would be forfeiting one's claim to be acting as a loyal Catholic and according to a properly informed conscience.

## Response Due Official Teaching

We can find some guidance for a loyal response to official church teaching from official documents themselves. The following statement from *Gaudium et Spes* gives us our basic orientation:

> Let the layman not imagine that his pastors are always such experts, that to every problem which arises, however complicated, they can readily give him a concrete solution, or even that such is their mission. Rather, enlightened by Christian widsom and giving close attention to the teaching authority of the Church, let the layman take on his own distinctive role (n. 43).

This statement marks a clear shift from parentalism to responsibility. The council affirms that the judgment of a well-informed conscience cannot be pre-directed by moral principles alone. The changing circumstances and complex character of a moral problem require that the conscience prudently assess everything at stake in light of moral principles. In order to act responsibly in making a moral judgment, we need the knowledge appropriate to the decision we have to make; hence, we often need to consult before making personal decisions. The judgment of conscience properly formed takes seriously that we are limited in our personal experience and vision of what is good but that we can learn from the broader experience and vision of the community to which we belong. The official teaching of the magisterium can open us to that broader experience and provide that broader vision.

The key text for understanding a loyal response to magisterial teaching is n. 25 of *Lumen Gentium:*

> In matters of faith and morals, the bishops speak in the name of Christ and the faithful are to accept their teaching and adhere to it with a religious assent of soul. This religious submission of will and of mind must be shown in a special way to the authentic teaching authority of the Roman Pontiff, even when he is not speaking ex cathedra.

What does "religious assent" or "submission of will and of mind" mean in moral matters?

"Submission of will and of mind" is something more than either respectful silence or external conformity to the teaching and something less than the
full commitment of faith. It calls for a serious effort to reach intellectual
agreement that what is taught is an expression of truth. Also, it means that
we must strive for a personal appropriation of the teaching so as to live by it
out of personal conviction. But submission of this nature applies in other
relationships to authority as well. It is not unique to our relationship to
church authority. What is unique is the grounds for such submission. The
grounds are religious ones.[6] "Religious" assent or submission means that such
effort and appropriation are motivated by the conviction that Jesus has com-
missioned the church to teach and that the Spirit guides the church in truth.
Francis A. Sullivan, an ecclesiologist from the Gregorian University in
Rome, has analyzed this expression in his masterful work, *Magisterium: Teaching Authority in The Catholic Church*, and offers this summary statement of its
meaning;

> As I understand it, then, to give the required *obsequium religiosum* to
> the teaching of the ordinary magisterium means to make an honest
> and sustained effort to overcome any contrary opinion I might have,
> and to achieve a sincere assent of my mind to this teaching.[7]

What does such a loyal response to magisterial teaching involve? It
involves responding to the teaching in a way which avoids two extremes.
On the one hand, we want to avoid regarding the official teaching as being
only as good as the arguments which support it. Such regard treats magisterial teaching as one more theological opinion alongside others. It fails to
recognize in the magisterium both the divine commission to teach and the
promise that the Spirit will guide its teaching. Together these give magisterial teaching an "authoritative" (or "official") status which no other religious
teacher has. On the other hand, we want to avoid treating magisterial
teaching as though it were totally independent of its supporting arguments.
Such regard easily opens the magisterial office to arbitrariness and replaces
teaching with dictating. If its teaching were accepted independently of its
reasons, then we would have no grounds for critical obedience, but merely
for blind obedience.

A middle position has been expressed in the official text of the 1978
National Catechetical Directory, *Sharing the Light of Faith*. It recognizes the
significant place that the teaching of the magisterium ought to have in the
formation of the Catholic conscience when it says,

> Catholics should always measure their moral judgments by the
> magisterium, given by Christ and the Holy Spirit to express

Christ's teaching on moral questions and matters of belief and so enlighten personal conscience (n. 190).

At the same time, however, the Directory goes on to recognize implicitly the limitations of the binding power of this teaching:

> It is the task of catechesis to elicit assent to all that the Church teaches, for the Church is the indispensable guide to the complete richness of what Jesus teaches. When faced with questions which pertain to dissent from non-infallible teaching of the Church, it is important for catechists to keep in mind that the presumption is always in favor of the magisterium. (n. 190)

With these statements the Directory suggests the kind of respect due the teaching authority of the church. This respect demands that we give serious attention to the teaching, and that we receive the teaching with an openness which is ready and willing to make the teaching our own.[8] In this way, when we act upon it, we will do so because we are personally convinced of the teaching. That is to say, we would be acting from evaluative knowledge.

The Directory also says that our primary disposition toward official teaching is "that the presumption is always in favor of the magisterium." What does this mean? To give the presumption in favor of a teaching is a rule of prudence for dealing with moral questions marked by great ambiguity and whose complexity reaches beyond our own resources to resolve. J. Philip Wogaman's notion of *methodological presumption* is illuminating for use with magisterial statements, though he did not develop this procedure with those statements expressly in mind:

> It is the method of arriving at a judgment despite uncertainties by making an initial presumption of the superiority of one set of conclusions and then testing that presumption by examining contradictory evidence. If, after examining the contradictory evidence, substantial doubt or uncertainty remains we decide the matter on the basis of the initial presumption.[9]

This means that to give the presumption in favor of magisterial teaching is to give a strong initial preference for what the teaching prescribes. If no weighty considerations were to intervene, the decision prescribed by the teaching would be the best guarantee of the values upheld by the teaching. By giving the teaching presumptive authority, we can proceed with confidence toward one way of resolving a moral conflict while at the same time remaining open to the possibility of setting aside our presumption if the evidence so warrants.

This means that the magisterial teaching is a co-determining factor in making a decision, though it may not ultimately be the decisive factor. The burden of proof lies on the side of one who would challenge the presumption. By giving the presumption in favor of a teaching, a Catholic ought to be willing to reassess one's own position and to rise above the limitations of one's own experience and insight in order to benefit from the broader experience, consultation, and accumulated wisdom made available through the official teaching.

Several reasons support presuming in favor of official church teaching on moral matters. One is that we trust that Christ will not abandon his church to error. Catholics believe that the Holy Spirit dwells within the whole church to guide and illumine its actions. This trust grounds our expectation that those appointed to guide the church can discern the Spirit and, when faithfully following the Spirit, do not lead the church astray. Another reason is that the sources of moral wisdom through which the Spirit assists the church (such as scripture, the teaching of theologians past and present, scientific information, broad human experience, and the witness of moral lives, to name but a few) are too many and too complex for any one person to understand and use well in making a decision. Furthermore, the magisterium of the church approaches moral issues with a concern to protect and to improve human dignity. It can draw upon worldwide resources to overcome the biases of a particular culture when putting a moral perspective together and taking a moral stand.

For reasons such as these, an attitude of openness of mind that desires to learn from this teaching and a readiness of will to assimilate the teaching and make it one's own are the proper and first responses due the official teaching of the church. Beyond this, the magisterium can impose no further obligation on personal conscience.[10] Such a response respects the normative teaching of the magisterium in a way that is proportionate to its pastoral mission.

But since magisterial teachings are presented with different degrees of authority, the "presumption" in their favor is necessarily more or less weighty. Extraordinary teachings articulate what is Catholic belief "everywhere and always" and so deserve the assent of faith. Such teachings would include the central articles of the creed and the basic moral teachings, such as God's unconditional love for us and the twofold commandment of love. These deserve more than the presumption in their favor.[11] Ordinary teachings, however, would receive the presumption correlative to their relationship to the core of faith. This would apply to moral teachings such as prohibiting the use of artificial means of contraception and advocating nuclear deterrence.[12] We would give moral teachings such as these the presumption in their favor until we come to clear evidence that overrides the presumption.

The exercise of prudence determines whether the presumption in favor of a teaching prevails in a particular situation of conflict. The prudential judgment of whether the presumption ought to prevail in making the practical application of a teaching must not be confused with dissent. Dissent does not pertain to prudential judgments applying a teaching in a particular situation of conflict. Dissent, rather, pertains to the critical disagreement on some aspect of official teaching. We will take up this issue in Chapter 14 on the church as a moral teacher. Here we are interested not in dissent, but in the relationship of the practical judgment of conscience to the normative character of magisterial teaching.

Vatican II taught us the proper relationship of conscience to magisterial authority in moral matters in the way it affirmed the primacy of conscience. A particularly significant position is found in the Declaration on Religious Freedom, n. 14, where we read, "In the formation of their consciences, the Christian faithful ought carefully to attend to the sacred and certain doctrine of the church." An earlier rendering of this text read "ought to form their consciences according to the teaching of the church." The rendering "according to" was rejected for being overly restrictive.[13] By accepting the less restrictive reading "attend to," the council affirms that the obligation binding on the faithful to follow the teaching of the church does not make the teaching the exclusive basis of a moral judgment. The less restrictive reading means that while Catholics must pay attention to the teaching of the church and give it presumptive authority, the magisterial teaching alone cannot settle a concrete case of conflicting values. Other circumstantial and personal factors also must be considered in trying to resolve a conflict of values.

The West German bishops followed this line of thinking when responding to *Humanae Vitae*. The first draft of their document read, "The choice of contraceptive methods must be found in accordance with the norms proposed by the church's teaching office." If this statement were accepted, it would make magisterial teaching exclusively the basis of any judgment about contraceptive methods. But this statement was not accepted. The revised statement reads, "The judgment about the contraceptive method must include in the conscientious examination the objective norms proposed by the church's teaching office." Here the phrase "must include" replaces the stricter reading "in accordance with" and falls in line with the Vatican document's notion of "attend to."[14]

These examples give us a sense of how to interpret official teaching as normative. To say that official teaching on moral matters is normative for the Catholic conscience does not mean that it is the exclusive basis of a moral judgment. What it does mean is that the Catholic ought to give a strong initial preference to what is being taught by the magisterium over other options. It also means that the Catholic ought to treat the teaching as a co-determining factor in making the decision, even though it may not be the decisive factor when all things are considered. Furthermore, a Catholic ought to make a sincere effort to overcome any contrary opinions in order to achieve sincere assent to the official teaching. In making a practical application of the teaching to a situation of conflict, however, other factors must also be considered along with the person's subjective capacity both to appropriate the basic values being safeguarded by the teaching and to measure up to the specific behavior prescribed by the teaching.

Pastoral moral guidance looks to what is a possible achievement for the person in conflict. A proper pastoral procedure assesses a person's moral capacity and attempts both to expand a person's perspective through a proper interpretation of biblical images and magisterial teaching and to maximize a person's strengths by encouraging a person to act in the light of those images and official teachings. But pastoral sensitivity knows the difference between the good that ought to be (which a normative judgment in the official teaching expresses) and the good that can only be for now (which a prudential, pastoral judgment expresses). If we keep this distinction clear, we may avoid concluding that the official teaching must be erroneous simply because some people have a limited capacity to measure up to the teaching in this particular situation.[15]

Perhaps an example can illuminate this point. A Catholic married couple, who give the presumptive authority to the church's teaching on marriage and want to live by it, know that for now they can best preserve their marriage and family life by using artificial means of birth control. Given their limited moral capacity, and the limiting factors of their marital and familial situation, they are unable to live by what the church prescribes in its official teaching for marriage. Their choice to use artificial contraception is a prudential judgment. It should not be confused with dissent.

Cardinal Carter of Toronto affirmed as much in an interview prior to the 1980 synod on the family and its consideration of the teaching on contraception. He said,

> The Synod . . . won't even recommend a change. People will have to realize there is a difference between saying, "I know this is what the church says but I can't practice it for practical reasons," and saying, "The church has no right to tell me this, so I quit."
>
> If a person studies the ruling and can't obey it, then he or she will have to say that for them it is a matter of conscience. A good Roman Catholic should want to obey, but if they can't, they have to resolve it as best they can. This is not dissent from the Church in my view.[16]

Cardinal Carter has it exactly right. His response respects the good which the couple is able to achieve for now without denying the validity of the teaching of the church. In this instance, the official teaching points out the good toward which we ought to strive through ongoing personal and social conversion oriented toward making the use of artificial contraception unnecessary.

## Conclusion

The Catholic preference in wanting to be guided by an expert, or a voice of authority, is to turn to the magisterium. The strong preference for the magisterial teaching guards against following cultural trends or special interest groups. It favors relying on the accumulated wisdom which the magisterium is able to articulate by drawing upon the expertise of a broad base of experience. Although no external authority can ever replace conscience, conscience cannot be properly formed without the help of authority. The tension between conscience and authority will always be with us. Because we know how easy it is to deceive ourselves, and because we give at least a presumption in favor of authority, we sometimes take for granted that the authority is automatically right and any contrary opinion is automatically wrong. This need not be so. Both authority and conscience are complementary aspects of the search for what is morally true, right, and good.

This chapter has focused on the relation of conscience to official teaching of the church. Other sources of moral wisdom also inform conscience. The third section of this book, which treats the third formal element of ethics, the criteria of judgment, will focus on these other sources. All of these act as co-informing sources of moral wisdom in the conscientious judgment of the Christian.

## Notes

1. Herman Wouk, *The Caine Mutiny* (New York: Doubleday & Company, Inc., 1951), Pocket Books edition, pp. 435–436.

2. For a collection of responses from different episcopal conferences, see William H. Shannon, *The Lively Debate: Response to Humanae Vitae* (New York: Sheed and Ward, 1970).

3. Anthony Kosnik, *et al.*, *Human Sexuality* (New York: Paulist Press, 1977).

4. On the notion of a presumptive authority, see J. Philip Wogaman, *A Christian Method of Moral Judgment* (Philadelphia: The Westminster Press, 1976), pp. 152–181.

5. Francis A. Sullivan, *Magisterium: Teaching Authority in the Catholic Church* (Ramsey: Paulist Press, 1983), pp. 26–28.

6. On this view, see Joseph Komonchak, "Authority and Magister-

ium," *Vatican Authority and American Catholic Dissent*, edited by William W. May (New York: Crossroad Publishing Company, 1987), pp. 110–111.

7. *Ibid.*, p. 164.

8. Richard A. McCormick has already outlined a mediating position of a loyal response to magisterial teaching in his "Moral Notes," *Theological Studies* 29 (December 1968): 715–716.

9. Wogaman, *A Christian Method of Moral Judgment*, p. 40.

10. See Richard A. McCormick, "Personal Conscience," *An American Catholic Catechism*, edited by George J. Dyer (New York: Seabury Press, 1978), p. 185.

11. The relation of the magisterium to matters of faith is different from its relation to moral matters. As Norbert Rigali explains, the sole source of Christian faith is revelation deposited in the Church. Therefore, the magisterium stands in direct relation to the entirety of faith. Morality, however, does not have its sole source in revelation. It is borne by everyone in whom conscience has been awakened and so is a shared responsibility of the human family, not an exclusive responsibility of the Church. Since the magisterium does not have a direct relation to morals in their entirety, it does not have the competence to answer all moral question. See Rigali, "Moral Theology and the Magisterium," *Horizons* 15 (Spring 1988): 116–124; distinction of the relation of the magisterium to faith and to morals at pp. 121–122.

12. One aspect of the debate over birth control is whether the magisterial opposition is infallible or not. Paul VI did not declare *Humanae Vitae* to be infallible. However, those who think that the opposition to birth control ought to be held infallibly assert that the opposition to birth control has been a consistent teaching of the magisterium for centuries. For this position, see John C. Ford and Germain Grisez, "Contraception and the Infallibility of the Ordinary Magisterium," *Theological Studies* 39 (June 1978): 258–312. For Sullivan's critical response to this position, see *Magisterium*, pp. 142–148.

13. Sullivan, *Magisterium*, pp. 169–170.

14. This reference to the German bishops is from Franz Böckle, *Fundamental Moral Theology*, translated by N.D. Smith (New York: Pueblo Publishing Company, 1980), pp. 253–254.

15. For a good example of using official teaching in a pastoral setting and respecting the moral capacities of individuals in light of official teaching, see Robert M. Friday, "Adults Making Responsible Moral Decisions," *The Living Light* 16 (Fall 1979): 358–362.

16. "The Examined Life—The Morality of Birth Control: Unfinished Business?" *U.S. Catholic* 46 (January 1981), p. 3.

# PART THREE: CRITERIA OF JUDGMENT

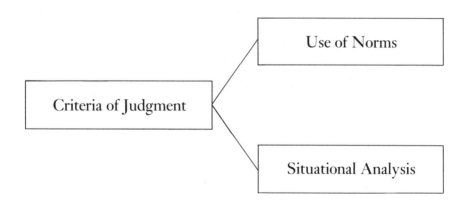

# 12  Scripture in Moral Theology

$T$he mandate of Vatican II on the renewal of moral theology is that it be "more thoroughly nourished by scriptural teaching" (O.T., n. 16), the "soul of all theology" (D.V., n. 24). Scripture is a normative criterion of judgment in Christian morality because Christians believe that in the events recounted there, pre-eminently in the life of Jesus, God's intentions for human living are revealed. Hence, the authority of the Bible for morality is that it is the word of God, the privileged, though not exclusive, source of our knowledge of God and of God's intentions for us. That scripture ought to inform and shape the Christian moral life, then, follows from its authority. But just how it does so is a difficult and complex matter.

The renewal of moral theology which began in the 1940s and 1950s sought to make morality biblical through and through. Since then many efforts have been made by Catholic and Protestant scholars to sort out the process of integrating scripture more critically into moral reflection.[1] The increased attention to this issue has not yet produced a consensus on how to relate scripture and moral theology. However, it has increased an appreciation for the complexity of the process involved.

This chapter will try to give an appreciation for that complexity without proposing a super-theory for relating scripture to moral theology. I will first assess the pre-critical use of scripture which was so prevalent in much of Roman Catholic morality. Then I will explain the four tasks of the critical integration of scripture into moral reflection—the exegetical, the hermeneutical, the methodological, and the theological tasks. From a particular methodological and theological perspective, I will show briefly how scripture functions in both an illuminative and prescriptive way to influence the twofold range of interest in moral theology: character and action.

## Pre-Critical Use of Scripture

The Catholic moral tradition has laid claim to two sources for acquiring moral knowledge: scripture and natural law. Because it has been so concerned with finding a common ground for the moral life which all peoples could endorse, Catholic tradition has given prominence to the natural law as the primary source of moral knowledge. Prior to the renewal of moral theology and the adoption of critical approaches to the biblical text, moral theology did not integrate the biblical material into its moral reasoning.

The pre-critical way of using scripture was in the form of the proof-text method—a form of corroboration whereby scripture enters indirectly and largely as an afterthought to support conclusions reached through natural law reasoning.[2] While it gives the appearance of a biblical grounding to moral theology, proof-texting really does not allow scripture to enter the fabric of moral theological reflection. A very clear example of it is in Gerald Kelly's significant *Medico-Moral Problems* from the 1950s. In his treatment of contraception, for example, he develops the Catholic opposition to it first on the basis of natural law and then by appealing to the teachings of recent popes. Only after those forms of argument have been used does he turn uncritically to the evidence of scripture in the Onan story of Genesis 38:8–10 to give biblical warrant for the prohibition.[3] Even Bernard Häring's *The Law of Christ*, for example, which is monumental as a breakthrough in the renewal of moral theology, largely uses the proof-text method.[4]

The biblical view of revelation from a critical perspective is that God reveals divine love through human words and historical experiences of people, pre-eminently through Jesus. Historical experience implies limitedness—chronological, geographical, linguistic, cultural, socio-economic, philosophical, religious, etc. The Bible is subject to these limitations in the way that all of experience is.[5] Because of their being subject to historical conditioning, biblical texts must be interpreted in order to be applied to a contemporary situation. Proof-texting, however, does not respect this principle. It conceives scripture as a collection of discrete texts which are essentially unconditioned by history, which can be completely separated from their historical and literary context, which are equally authoritative in their moral significance, and which are immediately relevant to a contemporary issue without any need to consider other criteria. These critical errors seriously undercut proof-texting as a valid use of scripture in moral theology.

## Critical Use of Scripture in Moral Theology

The critical use of scripture in moral theology is a complex process. In a fine review article, Kenneth R. Himes identifies four related tasks which the theologian must face to relate scripture and moral theology in a critical fashion:[6] (1) the exegetical task: determining the meaning of the text in its original context; (2) the hermeneutical task: determining the meaning of the text for today; (3) the methodological task: using scripture in moral reflection; (4) the theological task: explaining the relationship of scripture to other sources of moral wisdom.

## Exegetical Task

The exegetical task seeks to determine what the text meant in its original setting. The normative character of the Bible as the authoritative book to guide the lives of Christian believers requires serious attention to the original meaning of the text. What the text meant then has a controlling influence on what it means now.

Because the biblical text is the result of human expressions of faith, the word of God cannot come to us apart from time-bound, cultural categories. The biblical text is like any human composition in being subject to linguistic, literary, cultural, and historical influences. The controlling, objective kernel of moral teaching in the texts cannot be easily shelled out. For example, the problem of the meaning of "porneia" (Mt. 19:9) in the "exception clause" of Matthew's teaching on divorce is always with us. Even if we use the same terms as the Bible we are not always referring to the same reality. For example, the 1986 letter "On the Pastoral Care of Homosexual Persons" from the Congregation for the Doctrine of the Faith has been criticized for using doubtful exegesis in its condemnation of homosexuality. Does St. Paul have the same reality in mind when he condemns homosexuality as we have in mind when we use the term in light of our understanding of psychology and anthropology? We could ask similar questions about divorce since our understanding and expression of marriage is quite different from that of first-century Palestine. To know what the text meant in its historical time and for its particular audience, then, we must understand the historical circumstances surrounding the text, the presuppositions of the author and audience, the socio-economic and intellectual environment, the language, literary structure and context of the text, and so on.

Ultimately, our understanding of what the text meant is limited not only by the evidence we can acquire to disclose the full context in which the text was expressed, but also by the capacity of our language accurately to express what the original language meant. Since we are so far removed from the context of the original texts, we cannot be entirely confident that we have understood them correctly. As a result, we need to be modest about the claims we make when appealing to the Bible in moral reflection.

Even if we could achieve a proper, objective meaning of the text, we would still be limited in our appeals to the Bible in moral reflection. The Bible does not address many of the problems we have to face today (such as the use of nuclear power, or the distribution of medical resources). Moreover, the Bible does not tell us specifically how to resolve some of the issues we do share in common, such as the need to feed the poor. Limited though it may be, careful exegetical work is the crucial first step leading to the satisfactory fulfillment of the other tasks in using scripture in moral theology.

## Hermeneutical Task

With historical-critical exegesis establishing the original meaning of the text as the baseline of any valid interpretation, hermeneutics seeks to establish the meaning of the text for today. The cultural and historical limitations of a biblical text prevent it from being taken out of its context and applied directly without distortion to a new and different cultural and historical situation. This is precisely what proof-texting tried to do. But an historically conditioned text requires interpretation.

The task of hermeneutics is to get us from the biblical text to our present experience by bringing together the Bible's world of meaning and ours. In the process of interpretation, a conversation must go back and forth between the Bible and our present reality.[8] In order for this to happen, we must look on the text not as a collection of words with a fixed meaning limited by its own historical context, but as having the power to speak to us who have new questions and a new context of understanding. To understand the text for today, then, we need not only to discover the world lying behind the text with its particular cultural horizon and the presuppositions which influenced the author, but also to be critically aware of our own horizon and the new questions and presuppositions of a social, economic, political, or sexual nature which we bring to the text. Therefore, any use of the Bible is uncritical which ignores the cultural horizons and presuppositions both "behind" the text and "in front of" the text.

Any use of scripture which does take seriously the reality of two different worlds coming together in the interpretation of a text opens every biblical imperative to reexamination. For example, we do not live consciously waiting for an imminent end to the world as the New Testament period did. This eschatalogical view influences the way we interpret the radical demands of Jesus' proclamation of the reign of God. Also, attention to our different sociocultural environments has given rise to liberation theologians (Latin Americans and feminists) challenging any reading of the text which would claim the theological authority of revelation to support oppressive traditions. For them, the hermeneutical key which unlocks the true meaning of the text for today is the presupposition of liberation.

As these examples show, the task of hermeneutics does not allow us to be satisfied with just a critical examination of the context of the text; we must be critical of all that we bring to the text as well. Since presuppositions are always at work in our interpretations of a text, we cannot claim any purely objective interpretation. The knotty problem of the hermeneutical task is one of control. Whose presuppositions are to be determinative in our use of scripture? William Spohn advocates a mutually corrective hermeneutic in which the Bible shapes our presuppositions while at the same time we admit that our presuppositions shape our understanding of the Bible. Not to allow this to happen is to deny that the Bible is a two-edged sword.[9] The issue of control brings us to the methodological and theological tasks of using scripture in moral reflection.

## Methodological Task

The methodological task seeks to determine the use of scripture within the various levels of moral reflection. How one understands the nature of moral theology will influence the role of scripture in moral reflection. If moral theology is primarily about actions and making a decision, then the moral imperatives spoken in the Bible will get the most attention. But if moral character is central, then the literary forms such as narratives and parables get emphasized because they influence dispositions.

James M. Gustafson has sketched a typology of the ways in which the Bible has been used in moral theology.[10] He recognizes that some view scripture as "revealed *morality*" which serves a prescriptive function by offering authoritative guidance for judgments and behavior. Others view scripture as "revealed *reality*" which serves an illuminative function. As such, it offers a theological framework which informs the moral life by helping us to interpret the presence and action of God and thus gives us a clue as to what we are to do. Since Gustafson's schema is such a useful map of the territory, I will follow it in this section even though individual theologians may fit more than one ideal type.

Gustafson separates the uses of scripture as "revealed morality" into four subtypes, each distinguished by its own principle of ethical interpretation: law, ideals, analogies, and "great variety" (which includes values and norms through a great variety of biblical literature). Critical questions can be raised about each of these subtypes. The primary difficulties with law and ideals are determining precisely the content and mode of application of each. In the Catholic tradition, many documents on sexual ethics (e.g., *Humanae Vitae* and *Persona Humana*) use scripture as revealed morality by making explicit reference to absolute and immutable laws which serve as a primary or corroborative source of its moral positions. For analogies and "great variety" the difficulties are with control. To use these subtypes, some theological judgment must be introduced to determine the extent to which the circumstances of today are truly similar to those about which the biblical authors wrote, or to determine which ethical or theological principles will be the central ones for ordering the significance of various aspects of the Bible.

Even with its limitations, the "great variety" use still seems to be the most promising in light of the complexity of the biblical witness and the moral life itself. It avoids reductionism by respecting the diverse literary forms and historical circumstances which witness to a great variety of ethical material in the Bible, and it honestly respects the ambiguity surrounding all attempts to relate the moral witness of the Bible to contemporary events. William Spohn's fair-minded book, *What Are They Saying About Scripture and Ethics?*[11] shows how the Bible itself supports a variety of uses of scripture in moral theology. According to Gustafson's "great variety" use, scripture is one informing source for a moral judgment, but it is not sufficient in itself. Non-scriptural views and experiences are also relevant. Actions are judged wrong on the basis of reflecting about them in light of the variety of biblical materials as well as in light of other principles and experiences.

This "great variety" use of scripture leads into Gustafson's second focus on scripture as "revealed reality." While he does not want to draw a sharp line between the primarily moral and theological uses of scripture (since the four moral uses can be given theological justification), he does want to include the basically theological use of scripture within the range of possibilities. The theological use regards the Bible as the record of the relationship between God and human persons and so conceives the moral life as the believing person's response to what God enables and requires.

Scripture as "revealed reality" informs but does not determine the specific content of our moral judgments. Its bearing on morality is through images which inform a moral judgment. The images provide a framework which helps us to recognize divine action and to judge our lives in relationship to it. But how we are to respond to God in every instance is not precisely determined by the biblical images. We know what we are to do through the art of applying to a specific problem not only a critical understanding of the biblical text but also other principles and experiences of Christian life.

This method of using scripture is attracting attention from an increasing number of theologians today who are listening to the Bible contextually rather than as a collection of isolated and detachable citations. Robert J. Daly and the other members of the Catholic Biblical Association's task force on biblical ethics can be situated within this approach with their attention to the role of biblical images.[12] Also, this method is the favored one of the American bishops' letter on the economy. The introductory paragraphs of the second chapter, "The Christian Vision of Economic Life," give the hermeneutical key to the letter's use of scripture. The letter's basic criterion of "the dignity of the human person, realized in community with others" is grounded not in biblical citations which speak directly of economic life, but in "the Bible's deeper vision of God, of the purpose of creation, and of the dignity of human life in society" (n. 29). The bishops then elaborate the biblical vision by a summary of the biblical images of creation, covenant, and community. This approach to using the Bible in moral matters corresponds to the moral method advocated by *Gaudium et Spes*, which recommends scrutinizing the signs of the times and interpreting them "in the light of the gospel" (n. 4).

## Theological Task

The theological task of relating scripture to moral theology seeks to determine ways to combine the Bible with other sources of moral wisdom. Often in Catholic circles, the biblical foundations and theological presuppositions of a moral position have gone unexpressed in favor of a natural law argument. The absence of biblical and theological foundations for moral positions raises the question of the real difference the Bible makes in the moral life and in a moral tradition which relies almost exclusively on natural law thinking. This concern occupied a great deal of attention in the debate on the distinctiveness of Christian morality during the 1970s. This debate has forced a clarification of the relationship between the Bible and other sources of moral wisdom, such as personal experience, the example of moral virtuosos, reason, and magisterial teaching. One extreme would make scripture the sole source of moral wisdom and discount any other. The Catholic tradition has never endorsed this position. The other extreme would use scripture in a peripheral way to corroborate positions on other grounds. The Catholic tradition has found some affinity with this extreme in its proof-texting approach of the pre-critical use of scripture. Most theologians today reside in the expansive middle between these two extremes.

In my treatment of the role of vision in the formation of conscience, I pointed out that moral judgments are made by people who see the world in a particular way. The responsibility one has in a situation depends a great deal on the sort of person one is. One's character in turn depends a great deal on the images which shape one's imagination. Images from the Bible have the potential to influence a particular kind of character and so to evoke certain kinds of awareness and sensitivity which affect one's moral judgments. Vincent MacNamara speaks for most theologians today when he summarizes the theological task of using scripture in moral theology this way:

We depend on the bible for the great formative stories that tell us who we are and what the world and the human community are about, that these stories have a bearing on moral judgment, and that we find clues to that judgment in the ethical material of the bible.[13]

The second half of this chapter will look briefly at the use of scripture in moral theology which lies in the expansive middle between *sola scriptura* and proof-texting. The middle position correlates with Gustafson's method of the "great variety" use of scripture as both revealed reality (God's action on our behalf) and revealed morality (the human response to God). Revealed reality and morality, however, must not be separated too sharply, since the religious message of the Bible cannot really be divorced from its moral elements. The Bible is filled with stories expressing the imaginations of believers who experienced revealed reality and put their faith into practice. Revealed reality and morality are linked together by a moral vision which expresses the coherence and consistency of the life of faith. The section on revealed reality will focus on the images of covenant and God's reign. The section on revealed morality will focus on the radical sayings of Jesus and the great commandment. The entire next chapter will be devoted to Jesus and the image of discipleship.

## Revealed Reality

### Covenant

The covenant is a major, formative image of the moral life. It expresses God's action of reaching out to us with faithful and steadfast love in the covenant, pre-eminently fulfilled in Jesus. God's covenant with us is summed up in the Old Testament by the often repeated refrain which the prophets attribute to God, "I will be your God, and you will be my people." In the New Testament, Jesus' paschal mystery sums up the covenantal faithfulness and love of God for us and of our response to God.

In treating sin, I gave attention to the covenantal structure of the moral life: God calls—we respond. This structure makes the whole of the moral life an expression of our relationship to God in and through our relationship to everyone else. Furthermore, the covenant gives us our basic identity as the people of God and it affirms that out of our identity we are to decide and act. The basic requirement of covenantal existence is to respond to God's offer of love by living with God as the center of our heart's desire. The covenant discloses the truly objective ground of morality to be the word or deed of God's love—the only moral absolute in our lives. Every other authority is subordinate to God's word. The actions we perform ought to be in response to the experience of being loved and motivated by gratitude, faithfulness, and love—the primary motives for being moral at all.

In this light we can appreciate the place of the ten commandments in the moral life.[14] The commandments express, in a kind of shorthand, the meaning of being a people covenanted to God and to one another. They are no mere code of laws placing arbitrary restrictions on the life of the people; rather, they are laws which make life in the community possible. The decalogue considers first the nature of a covenanted people with God before it treats those responsibilities which pertain to living with one another as a covenanted people. In this way, the commandments proclaim that respect for others is entailed in a grateful and faithful response to God.

The context of the commandments gives a clue to their meaning. The context is God, through Moses, making Israel a people not on the basis of their prior virtues or obedience, but simply on the basis of the divine, gracious act of liberating them from Egyptian bondage. Three moments in the book of Exodus make up this context. Exodus 3 reveals God sharing the fate of Israel. Exodus 14–15 accounts God liberating Israel from oppression as an act of amazing grace. After grace comes the law. Exodus 20 reveals the law which expresses God's special relationship to Israel and Israel's relationship to God and to one another. In this context, the commandments are not the way of winning God's love but the way of responding with gratitude to a love already freely offered.

Situated in the context of covenant, the commandments show the close link between revealed reality and revealed morality. Like much of the ethical material in St. Paul, the commandments represent that aspect of scripture which is prescriptive for the moral life and, as such, co-determines the making of a moral decision. James Childress has cautioned against ignoring such material in favor of that which illuminates the moral life but does not specifically prescribe actions. He suggests that we think about the moral prescriptions found in scripture, such as the ten commandments, "in terms of principles and rules, especially in terms of principles that establish presumptions and burdens of proof for the moral life."[15] To give the commandment a "presumption" means that it is always relevant to moral deliberation as a co-determining criterion, though it may not be decisive by itself. So, the commandment "You shall not kill" establishes a presumption against death-dealing behavior. Anyone who lays claim to the biblical message and kills would have to be able to account for what makes the presumption against killing indecisive in a given case.

From the covenantal perspective, any other form of law, moral norms, or human authority must be seen as an aid in helping us to respond to what God is requiring and enabling us to be and to do, but it must never be taken as the ultimate object of our loyalty. A law, a norm, or an authority derives its value for the moral life from the extent to which it is an authentic expression of the call of God. To determine how much this is so requires the ongoing discernment of a heart attentive to what God is requiring and enabling us to be and to do.

## Reign of God

The reign of God is another major image of revealed reality. The moral teaching of Jesus is clearly aligned with his proclamation of God's reign, or rule, begun in his presence but not yet fulfilled. The proclamation of the reign of God is significant for the moral life because it stresses the urgency of conversion and engenders the virtue of hope.

The urgency of conversion and the importance of hope make sense if we realize that the reign of God does not refer to a static, geographical place but to a relational reality. The expression "kingdom of God" too easily suggests a geographical place of patriarchal domination. "Reign" or "rule of God" more adequately expresses the verbal quality of *basileia tou theou* as a dynamic, relational reality. God's reign is not a place, but a community-creating activity whereby each person experiences a strong sense of solidarity with others. For this reason, when we pray "Your kingdom come . . . " we are not praying to go somewhere, but that our world will exist in a certain way. In particular, we are praying that all peoples will be so caught up in the love of God that a state of affairs marked by the Spirit's activity will come about.

One sign of the Spirit's rule is that *God will be the ultimate authority* over our lives and that all other authorities will be seen in their proper relation to God. This state of affairs will require ongoing discernment so that we are sure to be led by God's word and are thus obedient to God. Another sign of the Spirit's rule is *justice*. In this state of affairs our relationships to one another and the material world do not destroy and oppress, but are marked instead by a strong sense of social belongingness so that we are living in solidarity with all according to our gifts. A third sign is that unconditional love and *peace* will prevail. Peace is not simply the absence of conflict; it is more fullness of life as God's people, living in covenantal unity in freedom from fear. In such a state of affairs, forgiveness and reconciliation are never out of reach. Reconciliation puts into practice the desire to dissolve enmity by making it possible for the one who is disturbing the peace to stop doing evil without the fear of being destroyed. The fact of the arms race between superpowers is a clear sign that the community of peace of God's reign has not yet come. A community of peace can only be created by forgiveness, not by evening the score. In peace, we live trusting in the goodness of one another and creating hospitable space where the gifts of others may flourish to nourish the life of all.

The parables of Jesus express most forcefully what the reign of God is like. In the parables, revealed reality and revealed morality converge in a subtle but radical way. One of the striking features of the parables is that they contrast the ordinary, everyday world with the extraordinary world of the reign of God. They are not stories of moral giants doing heroic deeds. Because they are stories of ordinary people and events, they call us ordinary people to conversion, they engender hope, and they direct us to social action.

The parables readily invite us into their world and urge us to feel its problems and possibilities as our own. We can identify with the characters and imagine ourselves in the places where we can easily be at home—dinner parties and judicial hearings, baking bread and sowing seed, losing money and finding it again, passing a helpless victim on the road and welcoming wayward children home again. Once we get drawn into the story, we get surprised by the extraordinary reversals which shock us out of our taken-for-granted world. When we return to our actual world, we see a new and different picture of the world and new possibilities for living because of the new eyes which the stories give us. For example, who would expect the owner of a vineyard to pay the same wage to laborers who have worked all day and to those who have worked only a few hours? When we hear what the owner does, our ordinary sense of justice is enraged. We see also that the reign of God does not run by our rules. This parable challenges our assumption about what it means to live in a world of grace. Consider other examples. Who would ever expect strangers and bums to be the favored guests at the wedding feast over the social elite; or the last to become the first and the first last; or those who make themselves great to become humbled and the humble great; or the prodigal to be the celebrated and the dutiful offended; or the Samaritan to be held up as an example of neighborly love and the priest and Levite as negligent? The everyday, humanly acceptable way of looking at life is shattered. The movement of reversal runs deep in the parables of Jesus and challenges us to picture the world differently and so to live differently.

As a narrative form which has the power to immerse us in a new way of seeing, the ethical power of parables depends on the whole story and not upon a single line commending or rejecting behavior. The parables do not tell us what we should do to be good by providing one-line statements of ethical principles. Their power for the moral life lies in their showing us that the reign of God is ready to erupt across a wide spectrum of everyday situations. They allow us to ponder our motives and actions within situations where the perspective of God reigning and the Spirit ruling is part of the context. They force us to be self-conscious and self-critical of the way we have created our lives and are looking on the world. They rock the status quo of our lives, take aim at our presuppositions, break down our narrow-mindedness, and challenge us to change the way things are. This unity of vision and action found in the parables is expressed well in the parable of the talents (Mt 25:14–30). There we see that the servant with one talent who maintained the status quo is rejected as being out of step with the demands of living under the reign of God.

Taken as a whole the parables disclose the profile of the sort of person, or character, one ought to be if one lives under the rule of God. John Dominic Crossan contends that the parables of the hidden treasure and the pearl of great price (Mt 13:44–46) are the key to understanding all the parables.[16] These parables contain a threefold pattern of advent, reversal, and action (in these parables the pattern appears as finding, selling, and buying) which enacts the basic structure of life under God's reign. We can find in this threefold pattern a profile of the moral character of one who is caught up in the reign of God. The character of such a person would be marked by reverence, conversion, and responsibility.

As we have seen, the parables turn our taken-for-granted world on its head. Anyone who is to live under the rule of God must be open to surprises. To be open to the unexpected, we first need to be *reverent.* The disposition of reverence keeps us from pre-judging what occurs so that we remain open to new possibilities of divine love breaking into our world. The parables teach us that divine love is at work in the seemingly insignificant, taken-for-granted parts of our lives. Reverence keeps us open to the unexpected newness in life.

As reverence welcomes the unexpected, *conversion* reorients our way of seeing, thinking, feeling, judging, and acting. The proclamation of the reign of God is inseparable from the call to conversion: "The time has come . . . the reign of God is at hand. Be converted and believe in the good news" (Mk 1:15). The Old Testament notion, *shuv,* implied a physical "about face" in order to achieve one's goal. The New Testament notion, *metanoia,* suggests an interior renewal which must accompany the physical "about face." In short, conversion is a profound transformation of the whole person. It is basically a letting go of a world in which we think we are in control and an opening of ourselves to a world over which divine love is the rule of our lives. Such conversion is only possible because God loves us. The change in awareness, attitude, and conduct which we undergo through conversion is our response to accepting the offer of divine love. The ongoing conversion which marks a person caught up in divine love means that we take seriously and reject the reality of sin and renounce it in our personal lives and in society. It also means that we can never rest content with what we have achieved as though we have reached the fullness of the reign of God.

As conversion reorients our way of seeing and leads to reforming our attitudes and actions, so *responsibility* is directed toward acting under the rule of God where love knows no limits. But our actions do not build up the reign of God as though the final in-breaking of God's reign were going to be the result of our moral efforts. When we act responsibly we are cooperating with divine love. To the extent that we cooperate, our actions by God's grace contribute to all people living under the ultimate authority of God in justice, love, and peace. Cooperating with divine love entails that we continually criticize and reform sinful structures of human existence so that everyone may live as brothers and sisters in a community of mutuality. Cooperating with divine love also means that we never absolutize any one of our achievements as the ultimate expression of the reign of God.

To the extent that we are irresponsible and do not cooperate with divine love, the reign of God is a judgment against our small-mindedness and hard-heartedness. But even those are not the final statements about human history. The fullness of God's reign is God's doing, not ours. The reign of God is not only about cooperation, it is also about grace—amazing grace. God's reign in its fullness will be a community of people gathered together into a new reality through the gracious action of God which surpasses any human achievement.

Hope is the central virtue of the reign of God. Hope is rooted in the confidence that all possibilities for life and its future are under the care and goodness of God. The good news of Christian faith is that God's love for us is undefeatable. This is most evident in Jesus' being raised from the dead. Our ultimate warrant for hope is the resurrection of Jesus, the best of all possible futures. Hope is not a passive virtue. Founded on the love of God and the resurrection of Jesus, hope frees us to live with confidence in the power of good to break into each particular place. Hope is confidence in the possibility that those things which are now destructive of human well-being and fellowship can be restrained so that the possibilities for new achievements can be realized. Hope allows us to avoid despair when we come face to face with our sinfulness. In hope we can lean on the future trustingly with the expectation that something good will happen. Since it always points to the love of God as the basis for the fulfillment of new possibilities of human well-being, hope is the source of our energy to respond creatively to new possibilities for re-creating society.

## Revealed Morality

### *The Radical Sayings*

The effect of the reversal of values and perspective in the reign of God is summed up in the sermon on the mount (Mt 5–7), the inaugural address of Jesus' ministry and the charter document of Christian morality.[17] The sermon on the mount together with related radical sayings of Jesus demonstrates scripture as revealed morality.

In the course of time, the radical demands of Jesus have been subjected to a variety of interpretations which have been tested and found wanting. For example, they are not to be read as counsels of perfection which apply only to the moral and religious elite who want to live the Christian life in an extraordinary way. According to the Second Vatican Council, all are called to "the one and same holiness" (L.G., n. 41) and so all must come to grips with the radical teachings of Jesus. Nor are these sayings to be read as another legal code demanding literal fulfillment at all times, or at least during the interim period of crisis waiting for the imminent ending of the world. The sayings are not a set of impossible ideals which, since they will always be out of reach of human fulfillment, make us recognize our ultimate dependence on God for salvation, but which can too easily be dismissed as irrelevant. [18]

Theologians today recognize the particular context of these sayings of Jesus to be the eschatological tension of the reign of God already begun but not yet fulfilled. The sermon is directed toward those who have already heard the proclamation of the reign of God and want to make this offer of divine love the total basis of their lives. In this context, the radical teachings of Jesus are expressions of the absolute claim which God has on anyone who hears God's word and lives under God's reign. The absolute claim of God is expressed through the sayings in the literary form of hyperbolic metaphors, something like parables. The forceful, imaginative language of these sayings makes us stop and consider whether we are truly living by the power of divine love or not.

As figures of speech, the radical sayings of Jesus dramatize the quality and direction which ought to characterize the Christian moral life under the absolute claim of the reign of God. As metaphors, these sayings are hardly reconcilable with human prudence. The sayings are, by and large, not for literal imitation but for imaginative inspiration. For example, "If your right eye causes you to sin, take it out and throw it away," is not an imperative for self-inflicted blindness. Rather, it is a dramatic way of saying that everything we have, even something as precious to us as our eyes, must be in service of cooperating with divine love to realize a community of faith, hope, and love. [19]

To be sure, not all the radical sayings of Jesus are figures of speech. "Love your enemies," for example, is not the same linguistically as "Pluck out your eye." John Gallagher offers a guide to distinguish what may be taken figuratively from what remains a literal command. He suggests that we apply the age-old principle of interpretation which says that individual passages of scripture are to be intrepreted by the rest of scripture. This means that a saying ought to be read for its figurative qualities if it goes against some other teaching of scripture when taken literally, or if it does not fit what the rest of scripture says about the same issue. [20] The saying "Love your enemies" fits the larger biblical teaching on love and so ought to be read literally.

However, as soon as we admit that many of the radical sayings of Jesus are not to be taken literally, fear arises that we have weakened the message of Jesus to make it suit the mood of the moment. On the contrary. The imaginative shock caused by these sayings enhances their power of calling us to conversion. As metaphors rather than as literal rules for moral living, the radical sayings of Jesus give a dynamic character to the moral life which reflects the nature of the reign of God. The literal application of moral rules does not express the dynamism of the Spirit. Rules specify customary behavior rather precisely. Once satisfied, they reinforce conventional living and no longer bear any moral bite. Living the moral life under the power of the Spirit in our complex world, however, requires creativity and imagination.

Like the parables, the radical sayings of Jesus as figures of speech cannot be reduced to a single, precise moral rule. Thus, they are not to be applied through the process of logical deduction. Rather, they are applied when their shock effect arouses the moral imagination and inspires creativity. Figures of speech prod us to see ourselves critically and differently, and they challenge us to creative expressions of conversion which will break through our conventional ways of living. They never let us rest content with where we are in our moral growth. Figures of speech take away our false securities about being morally upright and leave us unsettled in ways that precise rules of behavior never can. For example, "Anyone who looks at a woman and wants to possess her is guilty of committing adultery with her in his heart" more easily arouses the conscience about the quality of our vulnerability in interpersonal relationships than does the command, "Do not commit adultery." The hyperbolic metaphor gets us to see human relationships in a new way. It points far beyond the commandment to a whole array of possibilities for relating to another with reverence and respect.

## The Great Commandment

Whereas the sermon on the mount is like a series of parables, the great commandment (Mt 22:37–38, par.) is a formal moral imperative.[21] In Matthew's version, the emphasis on the inseparability of the love of God and love of neighbor is the key to making love the right interpretation of the law and the prophets. But what kind of love is commanded?

The New Testament word for the love which is commanded is *agape*.[22] The Greek word, however, does not seem to work for most people today. "Hospitality" works. Everyone seems to have some idea of what it demands. I believe that much can be gained by looking at the great commandment within the framework of hospitality.[23]

Love that expresses hospitality certainly cannot be equated with the warm glow of affection which we associate with falling in love. Such love is too self-centered. Nor is the commanded love the same as benevolence, or wishing another well. That kind of love remains too detached. Rather, the love which is commanded requires responding to another out of being caught up in the feelings and the meaning of what the other person is experiencing. Not until the other becomes incorporated into my self am I able to "love God and my neighbor as I love myself."

The key to hospitality is "paying attention," and the high price of attentiveness is what makes the command to be loving so difficult to fulfill. Paying attention costs us time and deliberate, conscious effort. When we pay attention, we divest ourselves of self-preoccupation. To be hospitable we have to get out of ourselves and become interested in the other. Hospitable love cares enough to create space in one's own life in order to welcome another in. The key to this space is that it be not merely an empty place, but an environment wherein others can be at home, hear some good news, experience new bonds of communion, feel the gentle touch of one who cares, and rejoice because someone has finally made room for them and accepts them.

In the gospel of John, especially chapters 13 and 15, we find the Johannine version of the love which is commanded. In the foot washing scene in John 13, Jesus demonstrates the distinctive characteristic of this love as the mutual self-giving which breaks down relationships marked by the superiority/inferiority structure. Jesus establishes a relationship built on equality.[24] In the great discourse of chapter 15, Jesus no longer calls his disciples servants but friends because he has abolished their inferiority to him and shares with them everything he has received from his Father (Jn 15:12–17). He commands them to love one another as he loves them, that is, with a love that has no room for one to be superior while another remains inferior. This Johannine "friendship" is what it means to create hospitable space to receive another on equal grounds. The most radical expression of creating hospitable space is to lay down one's life for those one loves, as Jesus laid down his life for us (Jn 15:12–13). To love as Jesus loved is to choose the other's life over our own if the choice comes to that. No one ever remains a "stranger" or an "enemy" for one who lives by the love which Jesus commanded.

The great parable of the love commandment in the synoptic gospels is the good Samaritan (Lk 10:30–37). It teaches not only the universality of love by showing that our neighbor is anyone in need, but it also portrays especially well both the kind of love which is commanded and the sort of person, or character, which the parables when taken as a whole desire. In this parable, three people notice the victim in the ditch. The priest and Levite look at him and pass on. When the Samaritan looks in the ditch and sees the victim, he is moved with compassion. We ask, "Did not all three see the same thing?" When we realize that the parable is set within the framework of explaining the meaning of "love your neighbor as yourself," we can understand that they obviously did not see the same reality. Whatever the priest and Levite saw when they looked in the ditch was clearly not themselves. So they continued on. The Samaritan, however, stops to help because he sees himself beaten and lying there wounded. He treats the victim as though he were caring for himself. Jesus holds up the Samaritan as an example of being neighbor and fulfilling the love which is commanded.

In acting so hospitably, the Samaritan also portrays the sort of moral character which the reign of God requires. He displays *reverence* in seeing the man in the ditch from the inside of his feelings and experience. He knows what it is like to be a victim. He has been there himself. Because of reverence, the Samaritan sees through the superiority/inferiority relationship to one of mutuality. When two people reach the level of equality of power, then all life is holy and no needs can ever be overlooked. Also, the Samaritan expresses *conversion* when he is moved by what he sees. The sight shocks his imagination with a fresh image of what being neighbor means. His conversion is heart deep, for out of the depths of his feeling comes healing action. The Samaritan then acts *responsibly* when he sees his assistance through to the victim's healing. His work of mercy establishes a bond with the victim but not an exclusive dependency which has no room for others to be involved in the work of mercy. Hospitality is like that. The healing space which hospitality creates is wide enough to invite others in to use their gifts while leaving oneself free enough to move on to something new. The love of hospitality does not try to absorb all other gifts into oneself in order to make oneself great. It accepts our mutual dependence so as to live with what others can contribute without the need to have to do or possess the same for oneself.

Selfishness, by contrast, does not let the inner eye of love ever look out. In selfishness, dominating power replaces reverence by wanting to make oneself great at the expense of the freedom and identity of the other. Jealousy takes over in place of conversion to resent the opportunities and gifts of the other and to take them over for one's own greatness. Betrayal replaces responsibility because the selfish person is unable to be committed to what the other is committed without losing one's own identity or freedom. The selfish person is an all or nothing person unable to share in the mutuality which makes the community a hospitable place in which to find healing, life, and peace.

## Conclusion

Is recourse to the Bible in the moral life possible? Yes. But it is very difficult. Is it necessary? Absolutely. It is the primary source for the stories and images which fashion a Christian imagination and so have an influence on character and action. Also, it is the context within which the concepts we use to talk about the moral life make sense. Of the many ways which the Bible may function in moral theology, I have given preference to Gustafson's "great variety." This seems most faithful to the diverse ways in which ethical material appears in the Bible. The Bible says what it has to say about the moral life in the forms and genres of laws and imperatives, to be sure, but also in narratives, parables, sayings, and other literary forms. The Bible is far from a handbook of ready-made judgments which we can immediately apply to current situations. Its ethical material both illumines the moral life with images to help us interpret what is going on and, in some instances, it prescribes behavior, such as in the ten commandments, the great command-ment, and the instructions of St. Paul. The proper use of the Bible in either instance involves an ongoing dialogue between the faith experiences of the biblical community and those of today.

Discipleship, however, begins by entering into the world of meaning of the Bible in order to let its moral vision become our own. This is to use the Bible the way that contemplative prayer savors it.[25] It is also a point of convergence for the moral life and spiritual life. The imaginative entry into biblical stories opens to us the world of religious and moral meaning arising out of the experiences of God becoming human in Jesus the Christ. Through the imagination, we almost forget that we are reading the Bible and we begin to live in the characters and events as if they were really part of what is happening to us now. We listen closely to the words of Jesus, to the charac-ters in his stories, and to the reaction of the people to whom the stories are addressed. We ask why Jesus said and did what he does, and why the people react the way they do. We ask what would the story affirm and challenge in its hearers, and what does it affirm and challenge in us. Without such an imaginative entry into the biblical story, we remain spectators of other peo-ple's experiences of God, but we never have the experience ourselves. Only when we have the experience of God for ourselves will we be able to grasp that morality which holds God as the center of value and only then will our hearts be able to live by it.

In the Bible Jesus portrays most clearly what it means to have one's heart centered on God and to be obedient to God alone. The words and deeds of Jesus ought to have an impact on what we see and what we value. We need to turn, then, in the next chapter to the role of Jesus in the moral life and to give special attention to the call to be disciples.

## Notes

1. A good sample of these efforts can be found in Charles E. Curran and Richard A. McCormick, eds., *Readings in Moral Theology IV: The Use of Scripture in Moral Theology* (Ramsey: Paulist Press, 1984). Also, a fair-minded exposition of various approaches of relating scripture and ethics can be found in William C. Spohn, *What Are They Saying About Scripture and Ethics?* (Ram-sey: Paulist Press, 1984). The interest in this topic by both Protestant and Catholic authors indicates one more aspect of the possibility of a truly ecu-menical dialogue on ethical issues.

2. A succinct description and evaluation of the proof-text method to which I am indebted is given by Sandra M. Schneiders, "From Exegesis to Hermeneutics: The Problem of the Contemporary Meaning of Scripture," *Horizons* 8 (Spring 1981): 29–30.

3. Gerald Kelly, *Medico-Moral Problems* (St. Louis: Catholic Hospital Association, 1958), p. 159.

4. See, for example, an assessment of the use of scripture in this early work of Häring by Vincent MacNamara, *Faith and Ethics* (Washington: Georgetown University Press, 1985), pp. 33–35.

5. See Raymond E. Brown, "The Human Word of Almighty God," *The Critical Meaning of the Bible* (Ramsey: Paulist Press, 1981), pp. 1–22.

6. Kenneth R. Himes, "Scripture and Ethics: A Review Essay," *Biblical Theology Bulletin* 15 (April 1985): 65–73.

7. For a review of the discussion of pertinent biblical texts, see Vincent Genovesi, *In Pursuit of Love: Catholic Morality and Human Sexuality* (Wilmington: Michael Glazier, Inc., 1987), pp. 262–273. The letter of 1986 from the CDF, "On the Pastoral Care of Homosexual Persons," for example, openly acknowledges the limitations of the biblical authors by their own cultural horizons, but it seems to dismiss these limitations in taking its own positions (see nn. 4–5). Gerald D. Coleman has introduced some necessary cautions on using scripture in the argument on homosexuality. See his "The Vatican Statement on Homosexuality," *Theological Studies* 48 (December 1987): 727–734.

8. For this understanding of hermeneutics I am following Sandra M. Schneiders, "From Exegesis to Hermeneutics," pp. 32–37.

9. Spohn, *What Are They Saying About Scripture and Ethics?* pp. 54–55.

10. James M. Gustafson, "The Place of Scripture in Christian Ethics: A Methodological Study," *Theology and Christian Ethics* (Philadelphia: United Church Press, 1974), pp. 121–145; see especially, pp. 129–138. In this article, Gustafson applies his approach to the issue of the U.S. invasion of Cambodia. But this topic need not be reviewed for our purposes here.

11. Spohn, *What Are They Saying About Scripture and Ethics?* (Ramsey: Paulist Press, 1984).

12. Robert J. Daly, James A. Fischer, Terence J. Keegan, Anthony J. Tombasco, et al., *Christian Biblical Ethics* (Ramsey: Paulist Press, 1984); see especially their Appendix, "A Methodology for Applying Biblical Texts to Ethical Decisions," pp. 289–295.

13. Vincent MacNamara, "The Use of the Bible in Moral Theology," *The Month* 248 (March 1987): 105.

14. John Gallagher, *The Basis for Christian Ethics* (Mahwah: Paulist Press, 1985), pp. 68–72. Also, for a contemporary critical interpretation of the ten commandments by a biblical scholar, see Raymond F. Collins, *Christian*

*Morality: Biblical Foundations* (Notre Dame: University of Notre Dame Press, 1986), pp. 49–63.

15. James F. Childress, "Scripture and Ethics," *Interpretation* 34 (October 1980): 378.

16. Crossan, *In Parables* (New York: Harper and Row, 1973), pp. 37–120.

17. For a recent study of the Sermon on the Mount, see Jan Lambrecht, *The Sermon on the Mount* (Wilmington: Michael Glazier, 1985).

18. John Gallagher, *The Basis For Christian Ethics*, pp. 106–107; see also Joachim Jeremias, *The Sermon on the Mount*, translated by Norman Perrin (Minneapolis: Fortress Press, 1963), pp. 1–12.

19. Here I am following the interpretation of John Gallagher, *The Basis for Christian Ethics*, pp. 107–112.

20. Gallagher, *The Basis For Christian Ethics*, p. 108.

21. For some recent interpretations of the great commandment, see Victor Paul Furnish, *The Love Command in the New Testament* (Nashville: Abingdon Press, 1972); also, Pheme Perkins, *Love Commands in the New Testament* (Ramsey: Paulist Press, 1982).

22. For a lengthy analysis of *agape*, see Gene Outka, *Agape: An Ethical Analysis* (New Haven: Yale University Press, 1972); for a more succinct treatment, see John Gallagher, *The Basis for Christian Ethics*, pp. 90–96.

23. My inspiration for approaching the great commandment within the framework of hospitality comes from my former teacher, Eugene Walsh, S.S., who has explored this notion as it pertains to the kind of love we would hope to find in Christian communities in order to enable good liturgical celebrations to happen. See his *The Ministry of the Celebrating Community* (Glendale: Pastoral Arts Associates of North America, 1977), pp. 14ff. The notion of hospitality has also been made popular by Henri Nouwen, *Reaching Out* (Garden City: Doubleday & Co., Inc., 1975), pp. 45–78. See also John Keonig, *New Testament Hospitality* (Philadelphia: Fortress Press, 1985).

24. For this interpretation I am following Sandra Schneiders, "The Foot Washing (John 13:1–20): An Experiment in Hermeneutics," *Catholic Biblical Quarterly* 43 (January 1981): 76–92, see esp. pp. 80–88.

25. Such prayerful entry into the biblical world as part of the relation of scripture to moral theology is encouraged by William Spohn, *What Are They Saying About Scripture and Ethics?* pp. 119–121. For a method of imaginative entry into the text, see Gerard W. Hughes, *God of Surprises* (Mahwah: Paulist Press, 1985), pp. 40–54. See also Richard M. Gula, "Using Scripture in Prayer and Spiritual Direction," *Spirituality Today* 36 (Winter 1984): 292–306.

# 13   Jesus and Discipleship

*T*he last chapter pointed in the direction of the normative role of Jesus Christ for the moral life. When we explore the normative role of Jesus in the moral life, we are calling on the full force of our faith in Jesus to inform our moral reasoning. This informing puts moral theology in dialogue not only with scripture but also with the systematic discipline of christology.

In this chapter we explore how our answer to the fundamental question of christology, "Who do you say I am?" informs the moral life. We focus first on the basis for claiming Jesus as the norm of the moral life. Then we see how an appeal to Jesus as normative for the moral life bears upon the twofold range of interest in morality: character and action. Finally we sketch a portrait of discipleship since each person's experience of Jesus ought to be the interpretive framework for his or her moral discernment.

## Jesus as the Norm of the Moral Life

The Christian community claims to experience the presence of a loving God reaching out to us with compelling clarity in Jesus of Nazareth. Jesus is God-with-a-face. Jesus Christ is normative for the Christian moral life not on the basis of any explicit teaching he may have given, but on the basis of who he was and is. From a moral point of view, we can answer "Who do you say I am?" by saying, "You are God's fullest revelation of the invitation of divine love to us, and you are the fullest human response to God." In other words, Jesus the Christ sums up the divine invitation and the human response in a way which makes him the new covenant, the fullness of what the Christian moral life ought to be. We look to Christ, then, as the model of the sort of persons we ought to become and the sort of actions we ought to perform as a full response of faith. For James M. Gustafson, who has written eloquently of the meaning of Jesus the Christ as moral norm, this means

. . . to assume that what he means and symbolizes has authority for me, for example, that I am obliged to consider him both when there is a conformity of my own desire and preference with what he represents, and when he is abrasive to my "natural" tendency on a particular occasion. . . . He is a standard by which my purposes are judged, he is an authority that ought to direct and inform my activity, if I acknowledge him to be my Lord.[1]

To say, then, that Jesus is normative for the Christian moral life is to claim that Christian morality is not in the first place a matter of principles, laws, or strategies for resolving a moral dilemma. Rather, it is first a matter of attending to the life of Jesus of Nazareth so as to exhibit in one's own life the virtues which Jesus had and to allow what Jesus has revealed about God and human life to inform moral discernment.

## Jesus and the Moral Life

### *Jesus and Moral Character*

When we call on Jesus the Christ to inform moral character, we are following the conviction that the moral life is influenced more by significant persons in our lives and how closely we identify with them than it is influenced by explicit moral instruction. Jesus is the paradigmatic figure for informing Christian moral character.

In my treatment of the formation of conscience, I pointed out that character is formed in community by committing our freedom to a particular object of loyalty and then by internalizing the images, rituals, traditions, etc. which the community has fashioned in order to carry the meaning attached to that object of loyalty. The sorts of persons we are as a result of the way we have committed ourselves determines to a great extent the way we see the world, think about it, and respond to it. Herein lies the moral significance of Christian believing and beliefs for moral character. Christian moral character is formed by committing our freedom to Jesus and internalizing the images, stories, and traditions which communicate his cause—to proclaim the nearness of God's reign. The stories of Jesus and about Jesus portray most explicitly what life looks like for one who is wholeheartedly committed to God. These stories show how the whole of one's life can become a response to the gift of divine love.

Our commitment to Jesus as Lord can and ought to have an influence on moral character. However, the extent to which our commitment actually does influence character is subject to the depth of our commitment, to forces of conflicting loyalties, as well as to social, psychological, and cultural conditioning. Some elements of character informed by our commitment to Jesus are our *perspectives, dispositions, affections,* and *intentions.* Since James Gustafson has elaborated quite effectively these aspects of character and the influence which one's commitment to Jesus as Lord can and ought to have on them, I will summarize his major points.[2]

*Perspective* represents the point of view from which we look on our experiences and evaluate them. Interpretations are always made in the light of something. When we say that we interpret our lives "in the light of Christ," we refer to the influence of our commitment to Christ for shaping our perspective. For example, the American bishops advocate an economic vision that shows a preference for the poor. This perspective is informed by the stories of Jesus' reaching out to the marginalized of his society. Without Christ as the reference point for our interpretations of life, we would have no basis for calling moral actions "Christian." Jesus lived his life caught up in the experience of divine love. His miracles, for example, are signs of the power of divine love to break in and shatter the powers of evil. Jesus lived with confidence that God was on his side. He trusted that life was not a bad joke, and he believed that upon his death his life would not echo into an empty future. The general perspective, then, which one can acquire in the light of the stories of Jesus supports the confidence that goodness ultimately sustains life and that goodness can break through even in moments of adversity.

The attitudinal expressions of our perceptions, called *dispositions,* ready us to act in certain ways. Dispositions are attitudes which carry over from experience to experience so that we acquire a relatively consistent way of acting. The traditional language of virtue speaks of dispositions. For example, "hope" is a disposition, or manner of life, grounded in the perspective that life is sustained by a fundamental goodness. Hope enables us to keep from falling into utter despair, for it lives with a confidence that something new is always possible. As an active virtue, hope seeks ways to actualize the goodness which is already present in all human life.

*Intentions* are the whole purpose for acting and *affections* are what move us to act in a certain way. Our loyalty to Christ informs our intentions and affections so as to influence our actions. For example, the intention to seek our neighbor's good or to seek the non-violent resolution of conflict can receive its energy from the affection of love which is aroused by seeing Jesus have compassion on the outcasts or by watching him submit to the crucifixion. The intention to do all for the glory of God can be evoked by the affection of gratitude for the experience of God's love aroused by meeting Jesus healing and forgiving the sinner.

When we put these aspects of character together under the influence of a collage of biblical stories, what might the character of one committed to Jesus look like? According to Bruce C. Birch and Larry L. Rasmussen, it is this:

Her general way of seeing life might become characterized by a set of acquired and nurtured moral sensitivities that search out those often invisible to many in society—the poor, the outcast, the ill, and infirm. She might come to possess a basic posture toward life that is more sensitive than most to human suffering and is at the same time unconcerned with her own needs. She might have a "feel" for where people hurt and be able to empathize deeply. She might acquire certain specific dispositions, such as an attitude of initial strong trust in people and a lack of suspicion and fear of strangers, an underlying hopefulness about improvement of the human lot, a deep appreciation for non-human life in the world of nature, and a severe impatience with people's claims to high and enduring achievement. There may be particular intentions present as well, all of them with plausible ties to the reigning example of Jesus in her life: to always seek non-violent resolution to conflict; to champion the causes of the oppressed; to see the kingdom of God before all else.[3]

As we have seen earlier in the discussion of faith and morality in Chapter 4, Christian morality can be distinguished, at one level, by the images, beliefs, or stories which inform moral character and provide reasons for moral action. More specifically, informing one's moral character by stories and beliefs about Jesus distinguishes the moral life as "Christian." The actions which flow from one's character, then, can be qualified as "Christian" as well. Of course, the non-Christian may do the same actions as a Christian. That is why the distinctive qualification of "Christian" refers to the fact that the person's moral character and actions are informed by the Christian beliefs and stories of Jesus.

## Jesus and Action

The role of Jesus in determining what one ought to do is mediated through the influence of Jesus on moral character. The stories and images of Jesus necessarily help to interpret one's experience. Jesus illumines a Christian interpretation of what is and what ought to be occurring. But this interpretation made "in Christ" is not sufficient in itself to determine precisely what one ought to do at some particular moment. When we follow the four points of moral analysis outlined in Chapter 1, we see that moral decisions do not have a simple religious resolution. More than religious beliefs must go into deciding what one ought to do. Jesus illumines one's options and conditions one's choices for the kinds of actions we ought to perform (e.g., loving, forgiving, healing, etc.), but our loyalty to him does not determine precisely what shape that action will take in specific circumstances. Even the commands of Jesus such as the great commandment of love, as well as the radical commands such as "turn the other cheek," "go the extra mile," "give to everyone who asks," and the like, do not tell us precisely what to do. They do, however, provoke the imagination and challenge us to grow from where we are now in our customary ways of behaving.

If the significance of the words and deeds of Jesus is part of making moral decisions in the Christian life, how does Jesus function in this process? James Gustafson puts the matter about as well as it can be put in the present state of the discussion. To turn to Jesus in making a moral decision means:

> . . . to recall him, and to think with reference to his deeds (including his death) and his words what trust in God's care and goodness, and love for man required. It is sometimes to have the imagination provoked by the parable, with the concreteness that that form of discourse has, and to exercise one's imagination in discerning what is concretely required in the moment. It is sometimes to think analogically about the deeds we are given opportunity to do in relation to the deeds Christ did under somewhat similar circumstances. It is sometimes to think very clearly about what the command to love requires, what an "in-principled love," or love in dialectic with equity, directs us to do in a given ambiguous instance. It is to be conformed to what one discerns about Jesus' own attitude and bearing toward others, about the intentions that express and are shaped by his trust in God.[4]

Turning to Jesus in making moral decisions in no way guarantees moral superiority, but it can help us to see the kind of life which is in accord with trusting in the goodness of God who sustains life and acts to redeem it.

## A Portrait of Discipleship

While we cannot come into physical contact with Jesus the way his disciples did, we can, through an imaginative entry into the gospels, encounter him and be present to him as he is to us. Discipleship is a matter of answering the invitation of Jesus to take an adventure to live under the reign of God as he did. To regard Jesus Christ as the norm of the moral life is to enter the way of discipleship. Living as a disciple necessarily entails forming a Christian imagination and converting our loyalty to God in Christ into a way of life.

Attention to the way of discipleship and its implications for understanding the moral life follows the shift in contemporary theology from a christology "from above" to a christology "from below."[5] The two types of christology are not mutually exclusive, and we need both for the full confession of our faith in Jesus as the Christ. They are distinct, however, and have different points of emphasis. Christology "from above," for example, begins its reflection in heaven and concentrates on the divinity of Christ in the mystery of the incarnation. This type has dominated traditional Catholic christology. Simply put, it maintains that God enriches us with divinity by the eternal Word descending into human existence and restoring us to our likeness to God which was disfigured by sin. It focuses on the identity or "being" of Jesus and therefore on the union of the divine and human natures in one person. The identity of Jesus as the eternal Word of God, the Second Person of the Trinity, is the foundation of his redeeming the human race and all creation. It finds its scriptural paradigm in the prologue of John's gospel: "In the beginning was the Word, and the Word was with God, and the Word was God . . . and the Word was made flesh" (1:1, 14).

The relevance of such a high christology for morality lies in the theological significance of God taking on human form. The ministry of Jesus is almost incidental to the theological point that the "Word was made flesh." Because the Word has descended into human existence, every human being bears a dignity beyond compare. The moral implication of this christology is to do whatever promotes human dignity and serves human well-being. In his first encyclical, *Redemptor Hominis*, John Paul II reflects this type of christology and its implications for discipleship when he supports incorporating a concern for social justice into the church's mission in the world.[6]

Christology "from below" begins its reflection on earth. It pays greater attention to the humanity of Jesus than was the case in the high, or more traditional descending christology. This low, or ascending christology attends to Jesus' moving toward God rather than moving from God. For this reason, it is greatly concerned with the life, ministry, death, and resurrection of the man Jesus of Nazareth. The pattern of this type of christology finds its scriptural paradigm in the synoptic gospels. It is developed in theology by attending to the ministry of Jesus and to the impact he had on those around him.

According to this christology, the moral significance of Jesus derives from his ministry announcing in word and deed the nearness of the reign of God. In and through his life, Jesus reveals the power of divine love to free everyone from bondage, especially from the bonds of sin and death. Discipleship is the operative moral category for one who lives in the power of Jesus' Spirit and continues in one's own time the mission of proclaiming the nearness of the reign of God. The sign of the reign of God present in the world is people being set free from powers keeping them from accepting the offer of divine love and living by it. The American bishops have drawn upon the moral implications of this line of thinking to advocate peace and justice in their pastoral letters on nuclear war and the economy.[7]

The way of discipleship is the way of the imitation of Christ. But to imitate is not to mimic Jesus. Mimicry forgets that the strategies and responses of Jesus were based on the developmental influences of his own life and the resources he had available to address the conflicts he faced as a first-century Palestinean Jew. For example, just because Jesus died at the hands of the political and religious leaders of his day does not mean that we ought to be similarly martyred in imitation of him. Or because Jesus drove the money changers out of the temple does not mean that the church ought to have no dealings with money in the imitation of Jesus. Mimicry is another form of fundamentalism. It tries to copy Jesus point by point. To take mimicry for imitation would be the death of any creative response to new issues and a new era. Imitation is to have his "attitude" as St. Paul says (Phil 2:4)—to let our imaginations be stirred by his words and deeds and to appropriate his message and style.

When we turn to Jesus to know what discipleship requires for the sort of persons we ought to be and the sort of actions we ought to perform, we meet a man whose whole life was caught up in the "Abba" experience of divine love. To be caught up in divine love, after all, is what the mystery of the reign of God is all about. Jesus lived with his heart set on one thing—the reign of God's love—and he knew himself to be special in God's sight. This, I believe, is the significance of his Jordan experience: "You are my own dear Son. I am pleased with you" (Mt 3:17; Mk 1:11; Lk 3:22). The rest of the gospel demonstrates the practical effect of holding fast to these words of worth received out of the waters of baptism. Because Jesus knew himself to be special in God's sight, he did not have to strive for greatness by abusing his capacity to influence change in others and in situations—that is, his power; rather, he was free enough to embrace the whole world in love.

We can live out of the power of divine love as Jesus did only when we divest ourselves of surrogate loves, everything else that presently holds sway over our lives. The call to be a disciple, quite simply, is the call to radical dispossession. We become disciples by following the way of renunciation (Mk 8:34). This means that we must be as Jesus was—dispossessed of all that we think can ensure greatness by our own efforts. Unless we learn to give up the presumption that we can ensure the significance of our lives by creating surrogate loves, and that we need to take control of history in order for everything to turn out right, we are not ready for discipleship. Not until we surrender to the gracious offer of divine love will we be able to experience the fullness of life under the reign of God.

To be a disciple, then, demands letting go of whatever occupies our hearts so that we may have room for divine love. When Jesus called his first disciples, he called them to make a radical break from what the world says gives us power over ourselves and over others. The call to be a disciple is a call to leave all and to follow Jesus. It includes giving up family and its affection (Mt 10:37), property (Mk 10:21), ambition (Mk 10:43), and even life itself (Mk 10:45). In sum, the disciple is to let go of all forms of self-made securities in order to be secured in divine love. Stanley Hauerwas, who has explored the meaning of discipleship as the call to dispossession, points out that the more we possess the more violent we have to become to protect what we have.[8] The non-violence of Jesus is rooted in the freedom of his being dispossessed and filled with divine love.

Perhaps the most challenging of gospel stories calling to dispossession is the story of the rich young man in the gospel of Mark (10:17–27). The young man asks Jesus what he must do to share in everlasting life. Jesus tells him to keep the commandments. The young man says he has kept them all his life. But being a law-abiding citizen does not make for discipleship. Something more is required. Jesus looks at the young man with love and invites him to give up all those things upon which he has come to rely for status, security, worth, and well-being, and to follow Jesus. At that, the young man's face fell. He went away sad, for he relied on much.

What is it about the rich young man that makes it impossible for him to share fully in divine love? We get a hint from a Peanuts cartoon which finds Linus sharing his hopes with Charlie Brown:

> LINUS: So I've decided to be a very rich and famous person who doesn't really care about money, and who is very humble but who still makes a lot of money and is very famous, but is very humble and rich and famous.
>
> CHARLIE: Good luck!

Charlie has it exactly right. "Good luck" if you try to manage a heart set on more than one thing. The challenge of discipleship is to make God the focus of our loyalty and hope, so that everything else will fall into proper perspective. What makes sharing in the reign of God difficult for the rich young man is his hanging on to home-made securities as the source of his worth and lovableness. The call to discipleship challenges us to make our hearts free to be filled with divine love.

The issue for discipleship which comes out of the call to dispossession and which is lived out in the ministry of Jesus is not one of power versus powerlessness. It is, rather, always a question of what kind of power to use. The power Jesus exercised in his life is the power expressive of the heart which treasures God. As the gospels have it, when our hearts treasure God, all other treasures will be treasured rightly (Mt 6:21; Lk 12:34). The Lukan Jesus aptly summarizes the implications of a heart so filled with divine love: "Of what the heart is full, the mouth will speak" (Lk 6:45). Words and deeds are but the heart in paraphrase. A heart full of divine love is a heart which exercises nurturing, liberating power in imitation of God's ways with us.

So, the gospels do not portray Jesus as powerless. In fact, the gospel of Mark opens with the crowds marveling at his power (Mk 1:22, 27). Matthew and Luke portray Jesus at the start of his public ministry being tempted to use demonic power. The temptation scene (Mt 4:1–11; Lk 4:1–13) can be read as a conflict over power: demonic power would use force in the name of doing good; Jesus insists that such power corrupts and will only defeat the good in the long run. In each temptation, Jesus refuses to prove that God reigns in any way but through the power of love. For example, when Jesus is tempted with dominion, he rejects it for the worship of God who rules by love. In doing so, Jesus rejects structures of domination based on the superiority of some and the inferiority of all the rest. Structures of domination thrive on the never-ending competition for the place at the top. They are supported by manipulation, coercion, and violence, and they in turn support the belief that one more act of power—one more person out of the way, one more weapon, one more war, one more corporate merger, one more gadget of technological genius—will make everything turn out right. Structures of domination sustained by demonic styles of power are still at work not only in the arms race between the two superpowers but also in wider dimensions of human oppression. We find this especially in the racism at work in the apartheid of South Africa as well as in the classism and sexism at work in the patriarchal oppression of women in the church and in society.

Jesus' message and use of power call for something radically different. Jesus constantly challenged any use of power that promoted superiority/inferiority as the paradigm of human relationships. His miracles, for example, are signs of liberating power. His parables are judgments about reversals in power relationships: the first become last; the last, first. Those who make themselves great will be humbled; the humbled, great. Jesus rebuked his disciples for striving for superiority over one another, over those who did not accept him, over the disabled, over women, and over children. He told them, in short, that they must become like children if they wished to share in the reign of God.

What is it that makes the child such an apt image of living under the reign of God? For one thing, the child holds the lowest possible status in relationships based on the superiority/inferiority structure. Moreover, the child's worth and security are constituted not by its status or achievements, but simply by the generous love of the parents. Jesus is saying that this is what we are like before God. We are grounded in a love which desires us out of the abundance of love itself and not because of anything we may have achieved by our own power.

In the life of Jesus we see what power looks like for one who is caught up in the abundance of divine love and takes it to heart. We learn from the actions of Jesus that our power, our capacity to influence change in others and in situations, is for mediating divine love and not for pre-empting it. Jesus' own disciples, as well as the political and religious leaders of his day, often served as foils of Jesus' loving use of power.

Consider, for example, the conflict between Jesus and his disciples who return to him after meeting a man casting out demons in Jesus' name (Mk 9:38–40; Lk 9:49–50). The disciples want to stop this man. Why? He is not one of them. Jesus, however, does not want to stop him. "Whoever is not against us is for us," says Jesus. The disciples want to use their power to control the good and to make themselves superior to another who is not one of their company. The fact that a man now lives free of demons is insignificant to them. What matters is that they did not work the wonder. The power directed by divine love does not want to usurp the good; the arrogant power which seeks to remain superior does.[9]

We can also see this liberating power at work in the scene of healing the bent-over woman in Luke 13:10–17. In this scene Jesus calls to a woman who has been bent over by an evil spirit for eighteen years. He places his hands on her and she stands up straight. She who was once weak is now strong. Friends of Jesus rejoice over her liberation, but the officials of the synagogue who observe this are angry over what was done and when it was done. The power which liberates by making the weak strong is too challenging to the community. Arrogant power of superiority wants to control the good by keeping some weak while others remain strong. The power which Jesus expresses is the power which transforms the structures of domination in the community.[10]

The great reversal of structures of power which Jesus reveals is especially evident in the famous conflict between Jesus and Peter in the foot-washing scene in the gospel of John (Jn 13:6–10). When Peter sees Jesus, the master, acting like the servant, he knows that something is wrong. It is not the picture he has in his imagination of the structure of power in the community. So Peter resists being washed. He realizes that if he complies with this washing, he would be accepting a radical reversal of the very structures of domination upon which he depends for his power. Such a conversion, both in his imagination and in his life, is more than he is willing to undergo. When Jesus deliberately reverses social positions by becoming the servant, he witnesses to a new order of human relationships in the community whereby the desire to dominate and establish superiority has no place.[11]

In the same vein, Jesus as seen by Matthew's community instructed his disciples to avoid all known techniques which would secure positions of superiority in their social structure. They were not to use religious dress (to broaden their phylacteries or to lengthen their tassels) in order to attract attention. Nor were they to take the reserved seats in religious assemblies which symbolized superior roles in the community. They were not to use titles, such as "rabbi," "father," or "master," which require others to recognize one's superior status (Mt 23:5–10). In short, they were not to dominate in the name of service.

Another example of Jesus refashioning the imagination of the disciples with new images of power and human relationships comes in the conflict between Peter and Jesus over forgiveness (Mt 18:21–35). "How many times must I forgive?" Peter asks Jesus. The contrast of Peter's "seven times" with Jesus' answer of "seventy times seven times" is more than a contrast between a definite number and an infinite capacity. It is a reversal in an image of power and superiority. Peter has the keys. So when he asks about the number of times he has to forgive, he is subtly asking Jesus when he can exercise his power to lock some out and others in. Jesus challenges his understanding of power and human relationships with an image of inclusion. Power which flows from the experience of divine love is not for keeping people inferior and distant but for creating a hospitable space where others can come in and be friends.[12]

Not to forgive is to assume some kind of superiority over another which says, "You owe me." The unforgiving person has a strong need to control the other. Forgiveness breaks down any kind of superiority and allows the other to be on equal footing. We fear the loss of control involved in forgiving and in accepting forgiveness. To live caught up in the reign of God, however, is to reject as a given the superiority/inferiority structure for human relationships and the distance its creates. The reign of God ushers in a new way of life whereby power is not for cruel exclusion, but for hospitable inclusion.

The passion story ultimately brings the issue of power and the reversal of the superiority/inferiority paradigm to a climax.[13] In Gethsemane Jesus' opponents come with familiar instruments of the power which guarantees superiority: betrayal, arrest, swords, and clubs. Jesus has no such weapons. Those who hold positions of superiority according to the social structure of that day, the Sanhedrin and Roman procurator, abuse him. Roman soliders torture him with the very symbols of superiority—a purple robe, a crown (of thorns), and homage (of spittle and blows). The ultimate weapon of the power of superiority inflicted on Jesus is public execution on the cross. In the crucifixion, the power which sustains the superiority/inferiority paradigm of human relationships is raging out of control.

Yet the very success of this power is its own subversion. In dying on the cross, Jesus does not resort to legions of angels to destroy the evil of those who appear to be in power. If he did, then his kind of power and theirs would be the same. The only difference would be in the size of the muscle. Jesus resorts to the only kind of power he knows—divine love—and offers forgiveness. The cross ultimately reveals the emptiness of all oppressive power. It puts to shame any pride in human power. As in his ministry so in his death, Jesus exercises a power that gives life: "Just as Moses lifted up the serpent in the desert, so must the Son of Man be lifted up, that all who believe may have eternal life in him" (Jn 3:14–15). The passion and death of Jesus reveal the steadfast love of God unmasking the arrogance of power which nailed him up. That same steadfast love invites us to become followers of Jesus and to live as he did—trusting in the power of divine love to sustain us.

The life of Jesus shows us that all those things which we think are necessary to guarantee our love and our lovableness really count for nothing. The cross witnesses to that. The cross stands as the central symbol of the Christian life not because it is a symbol of self-sacrifice, but because it is the summary of the whole of Jesus' life. Up to the cross, Jesus emptied himself of all he could give. On the cross, he is most empty of what he could humanly do for himself. The cross expresses his ultimate dispossession into the arms of God whose love has already conquered the powers of this world. Once Jesus accepted his death, he transformed the meaning of the cross. What is weakness and foolish to the world is strength and wisdom to faith. The cross is not a dead-end, but a break-through. Jesus died believing that we are made for life and that only through death will we find it.

If the cross is the presence of the reign of God where divine love rules, then the resurrection affirms that the way of Jesus is a truthful expression of life under the reign of God. The resurrection tells us that we abide in him and he in us because he has given us his own Spirit (1 Jn 4:13). When Jesus died, he did so as head of his body, the church. Where Jesus has gone, we are bound to follow if we catch something of his example and his Spirit. Because of the resurrection, we can take the risk to love as Jesus did. The love which is characteristic of the reign of God is the hospitable love of the unrestricted love of God and neighbor. The love of hospitality is possible only for those who have learned to live as friends and not to fear each other.

## Conclusion

To many of us, the call to dispossession and the renunciation of superiority/inferiority as the paradigm of human relations is a call to a radical way of life. It seems so far out of reach. Sin runs deep in us, for it is proud of its power. The seemingly unattainable life of the reign of God only reminds us that to be a disciple is to be on the way to full conversion. We are always letting go, learning to understand new experiences in the light of Christ, and learning to love with hospitable love. While each of us will live as a disciple in a way which corresponds to our openness to the Holy Spirit, the call to discipleship invites us to go beyond where we are now, to open ourselves to divine love, and to live as friends.

The challenge of discipleship is to make Jesus' way of life our own. The bad news is that disenchanted Christians believe we can do this by ourselves. They advocate a "me and Jesus" spirituality and morality which has no place for the church. The good news is that were it not for a "community of disciples"[14] we would have no access to Jesus at all. We learn discipleship by being initiated into it by others. Discipleship, like character, is a community achievement. To be like Jesus requires that we become part of a community pledged to be faithful to him. Avery Dulles suggests that unless we are able to develop strong affective bonds of solidarity with exemplary Christians who represent the way of the Lord in our own time, we will not be able to stand against the forces of the world and remain committed disciples.[15] This is what makes the nature and form of the church central to the moral life of discipleship. We turn next, then, to the role of the church in the moral life.

## Notes

1. Gustafson, *Christ and the Moral Life* (New York: Harper and Row, 1968), pp. 264–265.

2. His most extensive treatment of these aspects of character is in *Christ and the Moral Life*, pp. 240–264. A briefer treatment is in his *Can Ethics Be Christian?* (Chicago: University of Chicago Press, 1975), pp. 38–47.

3. Birch and Rasmussen, *Bible and Ethics in the Christian Life* (Minneapolis: Augsburg Publishing Co., 1976), p. 106.

4. Gustafson, *Christ and the Moral Life*, p. 269.

5. This nomenclature has reached official levels of the Church as it is used to describe the major approaches in christology in the 1984 document of the Pontifical Biblical Commission, *Bible et Christologie*. See the English translation by Joseph A. Fitzmyer, with commentary, "The Biblical Commission and Christology," *Theological Studies* 46 (September 1985): 407–479.

6. For an analysis of the christology in this encyclical along the lines suggested here, see Elizabeth Johnson, "Christology and Social Justice: John Paul II and the American Bishops," *Chicago Studies* 26 (August 1987): 155–160.

7. *Ibid.*, pp. 160–164.

8. Hauerwas, *The Peaceable Kindgom: A Primer in Christian Ethics* (Notre Dame: University of Notre Dame Press, 1983), pp. 86–87.

9. For this interpretation of liberating power in the ministry of Jesus, see John Shea, "Jesus' Response to God as Abba: Prayer and Service," in *Contemporary Spirituality: Responding to the Divine Initiative*, edited by Francis A. Eigo (Villanova: The Villanova University Press, 1983), p. 54.

10. For this interpretation, see Mary Daniel Turner, "Woman and Power," *The Way Supplement* 53 (Summer 1985): 113–114.

11. For this interpretation of the foot washing scene, see Sandra Schneiders, "The Foot Washing (John 13:1–20): An Experiment in Hermeneutics," *Catholic Biblical Quarterly* 43 (January 1981): 76–92; see esp. pp. 80–88.

12. On this interpretation, I am following the rendition of this story from John Shea, "Jesus' Response to God as Abba," in Eigo, ed., *Contemporary Spirituality*, p. 53.

13. For this interpretation of the passion from the perspective of power, see Donald Senior, "Passion and Resurrection in the Gospel of Mark," *Chicago Studies* 25 (April 1986): 21–34, esp. pp. 25–27.

14. The church as a "community of disciples" is a new image of the church used by Pope John Paul II in his first encyclical, *Redemptor Hominis* (n. 21), and which has been explored for its theological significance by Avery Dulles in *A Church to Believe In: Discipleship and the Dynamics of Freedom* (New York: Crossroad Publishing Company, 1982); see esp. pp. 1–18.

15. *Ibid.*, p.11.

# 14 The Church and the Moral Life

*M*ost of the attention given to the role of the church in the moral life focuses on the magisterium providing moral instruction on specific issues in the form of norms or laws in order to inform consciences and to guide the process of making a decision. The central concerns in those instances have been on the stance which the church officially takes ("What does the church say about . . . ?") and on the weight which ought to be given to official teaching in forming conscience and in making a decision. Chapter 11 explored these issues. But to limit the role of the church in the moral life to the relationship between conscience and the official teachings of the magisterium would be overly restrictive. We need to consider more broadly the role of the church in the moral life.

As we have seen, discipleship requires a personal response to Jesus. But how is it possible to encounter Jesus the Christ today? After Jesus died and rose from the dead, he disappeared from our sight so that we could no longer see him, hear him, or touch him. So, to keep in touch with us and to keep us in touch with him, he took us on as his body. Jesus the Christ is embodied in the community of his disciples through the Spirit. When the community tells the stories of Jesus and embodies them in sacramental ritual and in social action, Jesus is present so that others may encounter him and commit themselves in a free, self-conscious way. For that reason, the church is the place where discipleship remains a possibility.

How does the church fulfill its mission to make known the apostolic truth of the gospel and its moral implications? Bruce C. Birch and Larry L. Rasmussen have identified three ways in which the church functions in the moral life. Even though they do not use them as expressions of the Catholic church, I find these ways perfectly compatible with the role of the Catholic Church in the moral life. They are the church as shaper of Christian moral character, the church as bearer of moral tradition, and the church as a community of moral deliberation.[1]

## The Church as Shaper of Moral Character

We have seen that for the formation of conscience, explicit moral instructions are necessary but they are far less influential than the images or paradigmatic figures which influence our imaginations. The ways we see, judge, and act are all tied to the imagination, which is influenced by the communities to which we belong and to the images by which our communities live. More likely than not, then, only a small part of the moral life is influenced by the specific, conscious instruction which the church provides on moral issues. A considerably larger part is influenced by the church's effect on the imagination. With its heritage of ritual and religious images—such as creation, covenant, sin, incarnation, redemption, resurrection, reign of God—the church is an indispensable point of reference for acquiring a Christian moral character and making moral decisions. In fact, the church is the only community directly and uniquely responsible for communicating the stories of Christian faith and for relating the moral life to them in order to shape and to nurture Christian character and action. Herein lies the challenge to the pastoral ministry of preaching, teaching, celebrating, organizing, and individual pastoral care.

The challenge to pastoral ministry is to retell the stories of faith in order to fashion a Christian imagination. Through the images of our religious heritage, the church can focus our vision on realities we might not otherwise see, and it can also help us to see more deeply into those realities we have begun to take for granted. Because stories shape our interpretations of what is going on, they help us to determine in part what is of moral significance to us. They help us to see and to clarify what we are up against—what values are at stake, what attitudes are fitting, what principles ought to govern our actions on particular occasions, and what means of action are appropriate. Discipleship today requires the commitment to listen constantly to the Christian story in the depths of our hearts and to allow our vision and choices to be shaped by what we hear. By allowing our imaginations to be transformed by these stories, we discover the truly redemptive responses to life. Moreover, the church also serves as an integrating community by enabling us to order competing claims on our loyalty in relation to our most basic loyalty to God in Christ.

One of the places in the church where we are put in touch with Christian images is the liturgy—that activity of the community which presents the images of the Christian life which ought to form a Christian moral imagination.[2] Central to the Christian moral life is an understanding of God and what

God is enabling and requiring us to be and to do in Christ and through the Spirit. In the liturgy we acknowledge the sovereignty of God and so become a people according to the pattern of Jesus Christ. By remembering and retelling in word and sacrament the story and events of Jesus Christ, the liturgy reveals the meaning and direction of discipleship. For example, the stories of God's unconditional love for us can generate in us a disposition to take risks we might not otherwise take for fear of being rejected. Also, the liturgical reenactment of the death and resurrection of Jesus can influence our perspective to see that life, though tragic at times, is not beyond hope and renewal.

The church's influence on the moral imagination through the liturgy will depend a great deal both on how well the stories of faith are told and on how well the rituals are structured and performed. Herein lies a great challenge to pastoral ministry. The liturgical renewal has tried to reform our liturgical expression so that the images of God's revelation of divine love show clearly through our liturgical forms. However, even with the reforms thus far in place, many people experience the liturgy as deadening and impoverishing rather than as empowering or enriching their commitment to discipleship. The causes for this are many.

One cause, for sure, is the excessive reliance on verbal forms of communicating the mystery of divine love. We read the scripture, preach a homily, recite the creed and eucharistic prayer, sing hymns, etc. The rich sacramental and liturgical traditions of Roman Catholicism, however, can make a strong appeal to the moral imagination by expressing experiences of faith in non-verbal ways through artistic forms—dance, drama, visual arts, music, etc. The lack of sensitivity to beauty and to symbolic forms of communicating a religious experience is one of the great weaknesses in so much of Roman Catholic liturgical life. Yet symbolic forms, because they engage the whole person and not just the mind, can contribute much to moral perception and judgment. The sensitivity to beauty and to symbolic forms needs a vigorous, creative development in our time.

Another cause we cannot ignore is the very structure of the Catholic liturgy itself. It incorporates a division of the sexes which violates our deepest convictions about who we ought to be as a covenantal community of disciples who reject superiority/inferiority as the paradigm of human relationships. We find this division of the sexes not only in the sex-exclusive male language of our official rites, but also in the fact that women do not have access to all the significant roles in the liturgy. Language has power. It has the capacity to shape one's imagination and so to influence one's perception, attitudes, emotions, and values. Sex-exclusive male language abuses the humanity of women who share equally in the call to be disciples and to share in the covenantal community of mutual interdependence which is to enhance the dignity of each without debasing any. Similarly, the exclusively male structural features of the liturgy undermine the evangelical equality of women and create a disparity between word and reality in the church. Images of an ecclesially sanctioned inequality which come to us through the liturgy divide the church and perpetuate injustice by contributing to a negative image of the dignity and value of women. If the church is to use its rich liturgical tradition as a vital resource for influencing the moral life, then, the liturgy needs to be developed and engaged with greater sensitivity in our times.

## The Church as the Bearer of Moral Tradition

The church is also involved in the moral life as the bearer of moral tradition. This is perhaps most easily recognized in the form of a body of official moral teaching. Official documents on moral issues provide normative guidance to inform conscience for making a moral decision. The church as bearer of moral tradition also influences moral character. It enables a person to locate oneself within a history of value and along a continuum of development. Without a point of reference in the tradition, one would lack a sense of direction for moral growth. The moral tradition also provides a framework of accountability wherein we can assess what sort of character and what conduct is truly expressive of the tradition.[3]

Everyone shares in bearing the moral tradition in the church in different ways and with different kinds of responsibilities. We may be able to appreciate the different ways the moral tradition is carried on in the church by considering the teaching aspects of three different groups within the church: the faithful, theologians and pastoral ministers, and the hierarchy.[4]

### The Faithful

The impact of lay commitment in the church as a means of bearing the moral tradition is expanding all the time. Perhaps the most common Catholic expression of this is through the school system and catechetical programs. Perhaps we can safely say that, at the grass roots, the real teachers in the church are not the bishops but first the family and then the catechists. Our religious education programs are carried out largely by the commitment of catechists who bear the moral tradition not only in the content of their teaching but also in the witness of their lives.

In addition to our formal education programs, there are an increasing number of laity in the administration of church-sponsored institutions (hospitals, orphanages, social service agencies) or even the departments of civil government. Also, the laity animate our parishes and parish counsels so that policies and programs of local churches are being shaped by their interpreta-

*Lay ministers "put money where mouth is"*

tion of the moral demands of the apostolic tradition. Less formal structures in the church, such as cursillo, engaged and marriage encounter programs, and the charismatic movement, are also sustained predominantly by lay commitments and play an increasingly larger role in handing on the tradition.

The moral tradition is also embodied through social witness. According to the often quoted statement of the 1972 document, "Justice in the World," "Action on behalf of justice is a constitutive dimension of the preaching of the Gospel." This document confirms the role of social witness as bearer of the moral tradition. We are a church of martyrs. We attach great value to what Christians can declare by their behavior when they risk their peace, and even life itself, in order to testify to the gospel.

A particular form of public witness is the way we use our institutions and the property of the church. The world sees the way we put our resources to use and is influenced by that for good or ill. In fact, more people will experience the church's commitment to values through these public means than through any formal documents on moral issues we might provide. Our schools and hospitals, for example, already speak in a Catholic voice not only by where they are located and the populations they are willing to serve, but also in the policies they are committed to follow. The presence of a Catholic school in the inner city will encourage a disposition toward the poor more than the American bishops' letter on the economy. Likewise, Mother Teresa's hospice for persons with AIDS bears our moral tradition in a concrete fashion. It has the power to influence one's intentionality toward the victimized and one's perspective on the hopelessly ill. The sanctuary movement, which has committed some segments of church property as a refuge to promote liberation, is another example of using our institutions in a way that influences one's intentionality toward justice. In the seminary where I work, the student-sponsored "Freedom from Hunger" run involves hundreds of young people in raising not only social consciousness but also funds to support soup kitchens which serve the poor in the San Francisco Bay area. This 120-mile relay race bears the moral tradition in a practical way and does more to fashion one's imagination about the poor and the hungry than any discussions or debates we might have in our social ethics class. Public witness such as these give body to the intellectual content of the moral tradition. Without such experiential expressions of the values of our moral tradition, the generalized statements of formal teaching would remain quite empty.

## Theologians and Pastoral Ministers

Theologians and pastoral ministers are another group who share in the church's role to bear the moral tradition. They share an interpretive function but practice it at different levels.

At a basic level, the theologian interprets the givens of the apostolic faith: scripture, the witness of the tradtion, and the ongoing formulations of the magisterium. The task of theologians has been difficult in our time because of the different conceptions of what theologians are supposed to be doing. Some want theologians to stay with the task Pius XII stressed in *Humani Generis* in 1950: to justify the official statements of the magisterium from the sources of scripture and tradition. As such, the theologian's role is derived from the hierarchical teaching office and is dependent upon it. Others see the task of theology not as proving but as understanding (in the tradition of *fides quaerens intellectum*). As such, the theologian's role is cooperative but somewhat independent in relation to the hierarchical teaching office. "Somewhat" is an important qualifier of "independent" since the theologian gives due assent to the teaching role of the hierarchy. Theologians are not the official teachers of the church. Bishops are. To treat theologians as though they spoke officially for the church paralyzes not only their interpretative function but also the critical and creative work they are supposed to be doing. Since the fundamental documents of the faith are expressed in a language reflecting a particular cultural setting with its historical and social context, they need interpretation. Theologians interpret these documents and translate their substance into terms which make sense for the contemporary world. Theologians, then, suggest to the magisterium more adequate conceptualizations and formulations of the apostolic witness in order to make it accessible to our times. Theologians, therefore, exercise their cooperative and somewhat independent role not only by explaining doctrine, but also by raising critical questions about it, by probing the tradition for new possibilities of interpretation, and by offering a critical understanding of the apostolic faith in a way which meets the needs of a contemporary and educated world.[5]

In order to do their work well, theologians must have the ecclesial and academic space to question critically what is handed on as a given as well as to explore creatively the uncharted territory of what is possible. The very task of interpretation implies that the theologian cannot be content to gloss and justify what has already been stated as official teaching. Since the church is still on the way in its understanding of the gospel, theologians must continue to test the given teaching of the church against scripture and tradition as well as to use critically the human sciences in order to keep the teaching sound and applicable to contemporary living. The issue here is clearly the freedom of research and expression for theologians. The principle is unarguable; its application, however, is not easy.[6]

Pastoral ministers participate in this interpretative task at a different level. They bring the teaching from its general and abstract plane into contact with the specific lives of the people. The pastoral task is to apply the teaching. Pastoral ministers must communicate the substance of scripture and the teaching of the church realistically to those trying to live the apostolic faith in concrete circumstances affected by diverse cultural, social, and personal needs. To do this, the pastoral minister needs to be aware not only of the work that theologians are doing and of what the official teaching of the church is saying but also of what the particular context of the people is demanding.

Since pastoral ministers are often perceived as speaking for the church, especially in instances of preaching, teaching, or individual consultation, they must be careful not to give the impression that their private views are official church teaching. Pastoral ministers need to be careful to distinguish which elements of their teaching are official teaching and which are their own views, carrying only the authority of their own limited perspective and their limited ability to marshal the evidence. Pastoral ministers participate in bearing the moral tradition at the grass roots by remaining linked to what the church teaches and by being open to what still has to be done.

## Hierarchy

The special ministry of the hierarchy, or magisterium, is to provide a structure which helps to unite the church in its search for truth and discovery of it. Whereas the characteristic task of theological work is to question, to interpret, and to explore the apostolic faith, the fundamental responsibility of the ministry of the hierarchy is to affirm, to protect, and to promote the testimony of the apostles. The primary task of the bishops is to proclaim the apostolic faith and to enable all in the church to assimilate the values of the tradition so that these may be creatively present in our world in word and deed. Only secondarily does the responsibility of the hierarchy include the juridical function of determining when error and heresy are present.

While the magisterium needs the experience of the faithful and the reflection of theologians to fulfill its mission, the role of the magisterium in bearing the moral tradition differs from that of committed lay persons, theologians, or pastoral ministers in a significant way. The key difference is that the magisterium is the only official teaching body in the church. While others can repeat the official teaching of the church, no one else can designate a certain teaching of the church as the "official" teaching. Only the pope and the bishops speak *for* the church. Only they can designate certain interpretations of the apostolic faith as the official interpretations of the Catholic Church which are to guide pastoral practice. We speak of this as the function of the "authoritative magisterium." We can liken this function to that of the Supreme Court in relation to the Constitution and civil life in this country. The Supreme Court provides the official interpretations of the Constitution which direct the legislative efforts at every other level in this country.

The hierarchy exercises its responsibility to affirm, to protect, and to promote the moral implications of the apostolic faith in primarily three ways.[7] One way is by seeing that proper teaching of the church is provided by others. The bishops themselves cannot possibly do all the teaching which needs to be done, so they must see that teaching is done by others. They can do this by establishing commissions, by making experts available, or by setting up schools, such as pontifical academies or universities.

The hierarchy also teaches by deciding which teachers or what teachings are in conformity with the accepted teaching of the church through the use of the canonical mission to teach and by granting imprimaturs to certain books.

Third, the hierarchy teaches by instruction. These instructions can take various forms such as a formal definition of faith, decrees of an ecumenical council, encyclicals, apostolic exhortations, congregational declarations, pastoral letters, and the like. These official pronouncements of the magisterium serve different purposes and carry different weight.

The special ministry of the teaching office may not always function perfectly. Yet, it provides the great advantage of a structure which preserves and promotes the apostolic faith for the general membership of the church. It also provides a means by which to marshal the breadth of experience and expertise on the subject at hand so that all may benefit from a broader perspective. This leads to the third role of the church in the moral life—to be a community of moral deliberation.

## The Church as a Community of Moral Deliberation

If the church is to pass on the moral tradition in a reliable and accurate way, it must necessarily be a community of debate and deliberation. In this way the church contributes to the moral maturity of its members by identifying the underlying reasons and convictions which support its moral positions. It challenges the faithful to move beyond an emotive response to an ethical issue and to identify and to assimilate the fundamental convictions which underlie the position taken by the church. Also, by bringing deliberations into the public arena and by allowing the reasons for a position to be subject to scrutiny, the church contributes toward everyone's being able to make a more fully informed choice in the moral life.

We have a good example of the church's exercising its role as a community of deliberation in the way the American bishops conducted the drafting of their pastorals on nuclear war, the economy, and women's concerns. These documents were written in full public view as the bishops listened and learned from experts representing different persuasions. These pastorals encourage dialogue. They do not claim to have the last word on such complex issues as war and the economy. Rather, they invite others who have their own specific contributions, creativity, and wisdom to join in the search for truth.[8]

The American bishops have shown in their process that for the church to be an effective community of deliberation open dialogue must be maintained. They also showed that expressions of dissent are a necessary part of the learning-teaching process and of helping the church come to a clearer expression of moral truth. For the learning-teaching process, all must have guaranteed room in which to speak and to express the insight of their experience, research, and judgment. All must be willing to listen and to learn. An attitude of mutual criticism must prevail in order to prevent the absolutizing of one perspective or the domination of a peculiar theological or cultural idiosyncrasy. At all times, the point of reference for such deliberations must be the world, since the church does not exist for its own sake but to proclaim the apostolic faith for the life of the world.

## The Reality of Dissent

In this context of the church as a community of moral deliberation, we can best appreciate the role of responsible dissent in the church. "Dissent," however, is an unhappy expression. It is more a conversation stopper than it is a stimulus for open deliberation. It too readily connotes the reaction of a destructive rebel rather than the participation of one who wants to be critically loyal. Also, it is too sweeping in its meaning to be helpful in dialogue. For example, it could mean no more than intellectual disagreement on a particular point in an argument. Or it could be radical opposition which breaks the bonds of unity. For the most part, dissent pertains to critical disagreement with some aspect of a moral teaching, such as the accuracy and completeness of the evidence marshaled to make up the teaching, or the cogency of the argument made to support the teaching, or the formulation of the moral position based on the evidence and the argument. But dissent, in its proper sense, does not pertain to the prudential judgment of applying a teaching in a particular situation of conflict. (See Chapter 11 above on the relation of conscience and authority for the discussion of this matter.) Properly understood and exercised, dissent is an indispensable part of the learning-teaching process of the church involved in public discourse on moral issues.

The reality of dissent has been present throughout church history and has played an important part in the development of church teaching. From Paul's struggle with Peter over the law versus the freedom of the gospel (Gal 2:11–21) to Vatican II's affirmation of the presence of saving truth in the world's religions (N.A. #2), and of "the right of the person and of communities to social and civil freedom in matters religious" (the subtitle of the Declaration on Religious Freedom), the church's teaching has been revised and developed in light of ongoing experience and critical reflection. At one time, slavery was morally permitted and taking interest on a loan was forbidden by natural law. Biblical scholars were once prohibited from using critical methods for interpreting the biblical text, and religious discrimination was once acceptable. *Communicatio in sacris* was strictly forbidden until the ecumenical breakthrough permitted sharing with other Christians in joint prayer and worship. In each of these instances and others, official teaching changed due in part to the moral sensibilities of the faithful, to critical reflection of theologians, and to the attentive listening and discerning judgment of the magisterium, all occurring within the context of cultural changes.

The tradition of the moral manuals affirmed internal and private dissent. For the manuals, the assent given to non-infallible teaching is the conditional assent of moral certitude. Such assent recognizes that the position presently held is not necessarily free from error, but that error is not likely in the present situation. However, the church may change its position at another time when the evidence changes. Although the manuals support internal and private dissent, they do not support the freedom to voice this dissent publicly.[9]

Vatican II admitted to loyal dissent not specifically in any of its decrees but implicitly in the very process by which it adopted its decrees. For example, it employed as prominent experts those whose views were once held suspect. Some of the positions of the one-time dissenting theologians, such as Yves Congar, Henri de Lubac, and John Courtney Murray, became officially endorsed to correct positions which had been taught previously as official teachings. We can say that by its own practice of revising Catholic positions, the council taught the legitimacy and value of dissent as a way of purifying the development of the tradition of the church.

Cognizant of the possibility of dissent by those duly competent to assess official teaching in a critical manner, the Catholic bishops of the United States in their 1968 pastoral letter, "Human Life in Our Day," laid down three criteria for responsible dissent. These are: (1) the reasons for dissent must be serious and well-founded; (2) the manner in which one dissents must not impugn the teaching authority of the church; (3) the dissent must be such as not to give scandal.[10]

In view of the reformable nature of non-definitive teaching, the experience of the development of doctrine, and long-standing practice in the church, the possibility that someone truly competent in the appropriate field may have sufficient reason to disagree with certain aspects of the teaching is accepted Catholic practice and teaching.

## *Criteria for Dissent*

While responsible dissent remains a possibility in the church, perhaps it would be a less volatile issue, less divisive, and less frequent if it stayed within the boundaries of clear criteria. In the midst of the controversy over *Humanae Vitae*, Richard McCormick proposed criteria and a model of dissent which are still valid.[11] More recently, John Gallagher has provided an extensive treatment of criteria for dissent in his book, *The Basis for Christian Ethics*.[12] Only a synthesis of the major points of these proposals is necessary here, though a qualifying word is important. These criteria are intended for people trained in making sophisticated theological distinctions; they would not be of much use for others. As John Gallagher concludes, "Perhaps there are no criteria for dissent which can be applied easily by the non-specialist."[13] In the matter of morals, as in other professional matters, the non-specialist acts responsibly by following a trusted expert. Trusting an expert is something everyone recognizes from daily living. Karl Rahner has given a good analogy in this regard. In caring for our health, he says, we ordinarily follow the considered judgment of the medical expert not on the basis of the arguments put forth, but on the doctor's authority, even though we know the doctor's judgment may be wrong and that it is subject to revision. Similarly, the Catholic must normally adopt an analogous attitude in theory and practice toward the moral teaching of the church put forward authoritatively by its official teachers.[14]

*(1)Responsible dissent distinguishes between the degrees of authority of different teachings.*

The false notion that every magisterial statement deserves the same kind of response has already caused enough confusion in the church. *Lumen Gentium* n. 25 and canons 749–753 of the 1983 Code of Canon Law affirm the traditional teaching that the magisterium commits itself to a teaching in different degrees so that various levels of assent to those teachings are required of believers. The most important distinction of degrees of authority is, on the one hand, between teaching which deals with the core of faith and is proposed definitively as a non-reformable matter of divine revelation (infallible teaching), and, on the other hand, teaching which is more removed from the centrality of faith and is proposed authoritatively but in principle is reformable (non-infallible teaching). Dissent from teaching which expresses the core of faith would put one outside the communion of faith. Occasional responsible dissent from certain aspects of authoritative but non-definitive teaching, however, is one of the ways doctrine develops.

Likewise, not all authoritative teaching has the same weight. Just because a teaching is non-infallible does not make it an easy or ready object of dissent.

For example, a teaching of a general moral principle has more weight than a proposal for its practical application. On this score, we can recall the American bishops' pastorals on nuclear war and the economy. They distinguished between universally binding moral principles and their concrete applications to specific cases.[15] These letters recognize that in making an application of principles, a prudential judgment is involved based on specific circumstances. This means that a certain diversity of views will result even though all hold the same general principles. While the application of general principles calls for serious consideration by Catholics, these do not bind in conscience. Some of our most controversial moral questions fall in the category of practical application of principles. If we fail to distinguish a basic principle from its application, then we overly commit the magisterium in a harmful and embarrassing way, we risk damaging the credibility of the magisterium, and we confuse the sensitive pastoral use of moral teaching with dissent.

Also, the weight of a teaching is relative to the kind of document in which it appears and to the level of the magisterial source from which it comes. Each kind of statement occupies its own identifiable place and ought to be interpreted accordingly.[16] This point is summarized well in the address, "The Magisterium and Theological Dissent," given by Archbishop Roger Mahoney when he said:

> To assess the obligatory force of a teaching one would have to consider carefully who issued it, in what kind of pronouncement, how emphatically, how frequently, for how long a period, on what grounds and with what kind of support or reception from other authorities.[17]

In short, the greater the degree of authority, the stronger the presumption of truth which it carries, and the more serious the reasons one needs to dissent.

Unfortunately, reporters of religious news show little awareness of the subtle distinctions among church documents and their relative authoritative weights. When the headlines in the papers read "The Vatican declares . . ." or "The Catholic bishops say . . ." we can be sure that the fine distinctions which identify the authoritative weight of the document as a whole, as well as statements within it, will be lost on the public. The popular media generally treat all magisterial documents, and statements within documents, with the same authority.

*(2)Responsible dissent follows when the only remaining reason left for holding a position is that it is being taught by the magisterium though not adequately supported by convincing reasons.*
    The point of this criterion is that, after a duly competent person has examined the evidence and the arguments and found certain aspects of the

teaching wanting, such a person would not be inclined to accept the teaching except for the fact that the magisterium holds it to be true. To apply this criterion, one must first take adequate account of the episcopal and papal authority behind the teaching. Such consideration gives the presumption in its favor and a willingness to examine the limitations of one's personal experience and perspective. This response respects the magisterial position as being of a status higher than just one more theological opinion among others. If one were to reach a tentative judgment that a certain aspect of the magisterial position is positively doubtful, this judgment ought to be supported by a considerable number of "experts" in the field. The tradition of probabilism has always demanded as much.[18] Asking for a "considerable number" is a way of assuring that dissent is not based on the eccentricities of a single theologian or some isolated theological camp. However, determining who are the true experts in the field relative to an issue can be difficult to do, especially for the non-specialist.

> *(3) Responsible dissent is proportionate to the competence of the person to make an assessment of the teaching at stake.*

The force of "proportionate competence" can be appreciated when we qualify or distinguish between different classes of dissent. Avery Dulles has distinguished between internal, private, public, and organized dissent.[19] The further one moves from internal to public, organized dissent the greater the competence required.

Internal dissent comes when someone, in spite of sincere efforts to give assent, is unable to accept certain aspects of a teaching as being true. In internal dissent, the person keeps this disagreement to himself or herself.

Private dissent is an external expression of internal dissent, but to a very private audience. For example, it may take the form of sharing one's disagreement in a letter to one's bishop or to one's professional colleagues. Greater competence is needed to move from internal dissent to the overt expression of private dissent. Internal and private dissent are fairly readily tolerated in the church.

Public and organized dissent are more volatile expressions of dissent and many aspects of them have been at the center of controversy in light of the attention brought to the case of Charles Curran.[20] Public dissent is a quantum leap beyond internal and private dissent. Reasons which justify internal and private dissent do not necessarily justify public dissent. Public dissent refers to open disagreement with official church teaching. It is communicated publicly through the mass media, and through popular and professional journals. Dissent in this public way requires a significant degree of competence since the person dissenting is making a public case for the dissenting position and risks misleading the faithful. Yet, in the course of carrying out their professional duty to serve the truth of the gospel and the good of the church, theologians may have to dissent in a public way. For example, if some of the professional theologians who shaped the teachings of the Second Vatican Council had not previously published their dissenting views in a scholarly way to invite critical dialogue, the council may never have given them serious consideration. The crucial issue with public dissent, however, is the manner of expressing it. I will take up the issue of "the manner of dissent" under the next section on guidelines.

Organized dissent is even more serious. Organized scholarly dissent must be distinguished from organized popular dissent. For example, scholars may convene a professional conference in order to examine a teaching and to propose a critical response to the magisterium for the purpose of further refining or possibly revising the teaching. Organized dissent of this nature is indispensable to the learning-teaching process in the church. It clearly respects the special status of the magisterium.

Organized popular dissent, however, is quite another matter. It is an effort to influence public opinion toward official teaching and to call for the official recognition of an alternative position. In its extreme form, organized popular dissent actively promotes its own judgments as an alternative pastoral norm which can replace the official teaching of the church. The great danger of dissent of this nature is that it usurps the role of the official magisterium by setting up a rival magisterium. The official magisterium cannot tolerate this form of dissent in the ways it tolerates the other forms, not so much for the sake of truth, but for the sake of the public order in the church which is threatened. For the sake of order, we need a clear expression of who the official teacher is and what the official teachings are.

## Guidelines for Dissent

Granted that dissent is possible in the church for those who are competent, are there any guidelines to direct a responsible expression of it? From what has transpired since the reaction to *Humanae Vitae* in 1968, we have learned some of the special features of responsible private and public dissent. Organized popular dissent, however, is a breed apart. We have no clear indications that it will be accepted as a tolerable form of dissent in the church. Since Richard A. McCormick has succinctly outlined guidelines for private and public dissent, I only need to summarize them here.[21]

### (i) Affirm the teaching authority of the church
In dissenting from one or another authoritative formulation of the magisterium, one must not be denying the authority of the church to teach in moral matters. Indeed, the very manner by which one dissents and the anguish and prayerfulness of the dissenter would assert the opposite. Dissent

is not done so as to overthrow the structures of teaching authority in the church or to embarrass the official teachers. Dissent, rather, is oriented toward purifying the formulations of Catholic teaching so that the authoritative structures of teaching can communicate the substance of Catholic convictions more clearly to a contemporary world.

### (ii) Be concerned for the means

One of the chief concerns which public dissent raises is the possibility of scandal. The theological meaning of scandal is that it provides others an occasion of sin. But the sin likely to be caused by dissent is hard to determine. Perhaps the real concern with scandal is not personal sin but social sin, or the objective harm that could be brought to the church through a social evil. This may be something such as the polarization of the church which results in serious disunity. Or it may be the evil of short-circuiting the critical process of dialogue and assessment which are integral to the learning-teaching process.

Moreover, the fear of scandal is often directed toward protecting those whose faith is weak, or whose critical ability to assess pluralism in the church is weak. However, as Charles Curran has insisted, scandal of the strong also needs attention.[22] Many of those who do have a critical ability to assess magisterial teaching could be scandalized if theologians were not searching for better understandings of church teaching and proposing new ways of expressing the meaning of our basic teachings. The risks involved in dissent may be ones we cannot afford not to take if we are to protect the overall good of the church and the credibility of the magisterium. The Gallup-Castelli report of 1987 shows that the church's credibility on matters of sexuality is already severely damaged.[23] Francis Sullivan suggests that a community of people who vote "no confidence" in the magisterium could be an even more serious matter than dissent.[24] The credibility of the magisterium and the overall good of the development of Catholic teaching needs those who are capable of searching for better understandings and meaningful ways of presenting Catholic convictions. Perhaps the substance of the concern about scandal is to encourage prudent expressions of dissent.

In this age of multi-media and rapid communication, public dissent can no longer be held within a closed group of experts. Summaries of provocative essays in sophisticated and sometimes obscure theological journals can show up in the *New York Times* or in the "Religion" section of *Time* magazine. Theologians and bishops have, at times, appeared on a nationally televised news broadcast to represent opposing opinions. With media coverage such as that, the public awareness of dissent within the church is inevitable. Therefore, care must be taken that the means of dissent show deference for the teaching authority in the church and not be disrespectful of it, or that the dissenter not claim to replace magisterial teaching with his or her own. These means of expressing dissent also ought to respect the intelligence of the faithful and not undermine their confidence in the hierarchy to teach.

### (iii) Contribute toward reformulating the teaching

Dissent that is an integral part of the learning-teaching process does not stop with making a public display of disagreement. Dissent is not an end-product. It is part of the process of growth in understanding. Therefore, responsible public dissent works to contribute toward an improvement in the formulation of the teaching by submitting to public discussion and criticism suggested ways of revising a present formulation. The aim of dissent is to try to convince the magisterium that a present formulation of a teaching is inadequate or erroneous. The development of moral teaching happens through a public process of critical review by other competent theologians, by the general assimilation of a teaching by the faithful, and by the discerning listening and judgment of the magisterium.

### (iv) Count the cost

The one who dissents publicly must be willing to pay the price which may come with the dissent. Counting the cost is another way of affirming authority in the church and showing respect for it. In some cases, the cost may mean being removed from a teaching position, or not being allowed to publish as a Catholic theologian. It may incur other disciplinary measures restricting one's behavior in the church or in society when acting as an official representative of the church. Anyone who risks public dissent must be convinced that the harm done to oneself by dissenting would be less than the harm caused by not dissenting.

Responsible dissent, then, remains a real possibility and a necessary part of the learning-teaching process. It is not an act of destructive disobedience. Rather, dissent can be a service to the church when it recognizes that a teaching is incomplete and inaccurate as it stands. If the formulation of the substance of the teaching is not revised, then the teaching may lead to personal harm for some and to possible disillusionment for others that the church is a reliable teacher. For the church to continue promoting a truly defective teaching would ultimately be detrimental to its mission of proclaiming the apostolic faith in the contemporary world.

Responsible dissent in the church rests upon the conviction that the achievement of truth in the church is a process in which we all have a responsibility. Teaching and learning are a communal experience. Dissent is part of the process by which we learn. When it comes at the end of the process of respectful and docile reflection, it plays a significant part in the purification and development of the church's understanding of its apostolic inheritance. If we serve the church well by receiving its teaching with a thoughtful and critical spirit, the church will be a more effective community of moral deliberation.

## Conclusion

This chapter has tried to show only some aspects of the role of the church in the moral life, which extends beyond simply providing official documents to address moral issues in order to provide guidance in the form of moral norms. The ultimate concern of the church as a moral teacher is to keep discipleship alive by giving faithful witness to the gospel of Jesus Christ. The responsibility for this witness belongs to the whole church, not just to the hierarchy. Everyone who professes faith in the Lordship of Jesus Christ is enlivened by the Holy Spirit to share in celebrating and living the truth received from the apostles. The basic sentiment of the Second Vatican Council toward the responsibility to witness to the gospel is, "We're in this together." Everyone shares full ecclesial status and responsibility for the gospel by virtue of baptism, not ordination. Therefore, serving the gospel is not just the business of the hierarchy and the clergy. Everyone is called to discipleship and to participate in the church as a moral teacher, though clearly in different ways according to each one's competence and office.

This treatment of the role of the church in the moral life confirms the four aspects identified by Lukas Vischer for the faithful and effective exercise of the church's teaching authority.[25] They provide a convenient conclusion to this chapter.

### Change

Everyone is aware that changes which occur in society have their effect on the life in the church. The reality of change makes imperative the need to adapt to shifting times. Faithfulness to the apostolic tradition is not the mere repetition of the past. Fundamentalism is not faithfulness; neither is blind obedience. Faithfulness demands a new presentation of the gospel in a way appropriate to different historical and cultural situations. Teaching must take place in constant interaction with the world in order for the church to fulfill its mission of speaking to the world about those apostolic values which it holds dear.

### Pluralism

Closely related to change is the plurality of situations which need to be addressed, the diversity of experiences and perspectives which need to be respected, and the subsequent variety of positions which may be taken as an expression of the one gospel. John Mahoney identifies the recognition of diversity as one of the characteristics of modern moral theology.[26] By that he means using different lenses through which to view moral experiences. Feminism, ecumenism, and liberation theology would be examples.

Recognizing diversity leads to appreciating pluralism as a positive good. As simply a descriptive term, pluralism can refer to a variety of values as espoused by different individuals or groups and operating simultaneously in society without evaluating them or their relationship to the total moral reality. Pluralism in that sense can lead to chaos. But when used in theology as Karl Rahner uses it, pluralism has a positive sense. Mahoney follows Rahner to show that pluralism considers the claim that

> several varying approaches may all contain some measure of truth, or may be considered as equally valid expressions of Revelation, and may together provide complementary aspects of the many facets of God and his activities. What theological pluralism claims as a matter of principle is that, not simply because of cultural and other differences in the perceiving subject, but also because of the inexhaustible nature of the divine "object," it is impossible to comprehend God from only one viewpoint or to express that comprehension in only one manner.[27]

Just as we can appreciate the richness of various aspects in the Bible and the variety of interpretations which flow from them, so we need to appreciate the various perspectives on moral experience and the various ways we can make prudential, practical application of various aspects of our moral tradition. While admitting to the validity of the general moral principles which command assent, we must expect a certain diversity of views when making prudential, practical application of these principles. A plurality of concrete expressions of a general principle need not diffuse the visible unity of the church. The unity of the church has its roots in the apostolic faith. Authoritative teaching should seek to maintain this unity without denying creative differences of expression in the concrete. But the church, through its official teachers, must also know how to say "no." The line between truth and error, faithfulness and unfaithfulness must be drawn. While forms of discipline in matters of faith and morals are necessary in the church, these must be used to maintain the clarity of the church's message and not to deny freedom of conscience or to halt the development of a theological discussion in the process of maturing.

## Participation

Today more and more people are participating in the full life of the church. The pastoral letters on peace, the economy, and women's concerns, for example, drew upon the experience and expertise of a wide range of people, not just the bishops, theologians, or even just Catholics. Also, local communities participated in shaping catechetical materials (as we experienced in the writing of the National Catechetical Directory), and experiences of the local church are being brought to the universal level (as we are finding to be the case with the increasing interest in the role of women in the church and the subsequent discussions at the synod of 1987). Structures to promote such participation need further development as a sign of respecting the faith as it is being lived among the faithful. The sense of the faithful is an important theological source for understanding the witness of the gospel, so we must find the best ways to tap this resource.

## Reception

Reception is part of participation.[28] It indicates the process of assimilating a teaching, decision, or liturgical practice into the life of the community. Reception does not suggest passive endorsement, but the gradual assimilation of the values of the tradition being embodied in diverse ways through time.

Structures by which the whole community participates in the mission of the church prepare the way for receiving the insights and teaching of the leadership. Through structures of participation, such as local councils, diocesan pastoral councils, study groups, faith-sharing groups, commissions, and synods, as well as through the public witness of the faithful, we can see which insights of the leadership are digested and which are not. For such participation to be effective, we need to communicate more clearly and encourage more strongly the different levels of responsibility by which the church is involved in the moral life.

These four features spell out something of the rich texture of the church's role in the moral life. However, the explicit moral teaching of the church in the form of normative moral statements about morally right and wrong behavior is still the center of attention and controversy. In order to understand this controversy and to appreciate the role of the church as a moral teacher through its explicit statements, we need to have some understanding of the tradition of natural law which lies behind its teaching. Also, we need to understand the meaning and use of moral norms expressed in the teaching so that we can interpret and use these official church documents appropriately. Explaining the meaning and use of natural law, positive law, and moral norms will be the focus of the following chapters.

## Notes

1. Birch and Rasmussen, *Bible and Ethics in the Christian Life* (Minneapolis: Augsburg Publishing House, 1976), p. 127.

2. The literature on the relation of the moral life to liturgy is still young and relatively sparse. For a collection of seminal essays, see the *Journal of Religious Ethics* 7 (Fall 1979).

3. *Ibid.*, pp. 132–134.

4. For the responsibilities of these groups, see Yves Congar, "Towards a Catholic Synthesis," translated by John Maxwell in *Who Has the Say in the Church?* edited by J. Moltmann and Hans Küng, *Concilium* 148, *Religion in the Eighties* (New York: Seabury Press, 1981), pp. 72–77.

5. Jon Nilson, "The Rights and Responsibilities of Theologians: A Theological Perspective," in Leo O'Donovan, ed., *Cooperation Between Theologians and the Ecclesiastical Magisterium: A Report of the Joint Committee of the Canon Law Society of America and the Catholic Theological Society of America* (Washington: Canon Law Society of America, 1982), pp. 53–75.

6. The issue of the theologian's freedom of research and expression converges with the issue of faith and freedom for theologians teaching at Catholic colleges and universities. See Joseph A. O'Hare, "Faith and Freedom in Catholic Universities," in William W. May, ed., *Vatican Authority and American Catholic Dissent* (New York: Crossroad Publishing Co., 1987), pp. 160–167. Also, Ladislas Orsy, *The Church: Learning and Teaching* (Wilmington: Michael Glazier, Inc., 1987), pp. 109–160.

7. John Gallagher has provided a sufficiently thorough treatment of the role of the hierarchy in the teaching function of the church in his *The Basis for Christian Ethics* (Mahwah: Paulist Press, 1985), pp. 194–200. For these three ways the hierarchy exercises its responsibility to teach the apostolic faith, see pp. 199–200.

8. For an assessment of the manner in which the peace pastoral was written, see Edward Vacek, "Authority and the Peace Pastoral," *America* 149 (October 22, 1983): 225–228.

9. See for example, my review of the manualist positions in Gula, "The Right to Private and Public Dissent from Specific Pronouncements of the Ordinary Magisterium," *Eglise et Théologie* 9 (May 1978): 319–348.

10. *The Pope Speaks* 13 (1968): 386, n. 51.

11. McCormick, "Notes on Moral Theology," *Theological Studies* 29 (December 1968): 716–718; also, 30 (December 1969): 651–653.

12. Gallagher, *The Basis for Christian Ethics* (Mahwah: Paulist Press, 1985), pp. 212–237.

13. *Ibid.*, p. 236.

14. For Rahner's use of this analogy, see *The Christian of the Future* (New York: Herder and Herder, 1967), p. 30; also, "The Dispute Concerning the Church's Teaching Office," *Theological Investigations*, Vol. XIV, translated by David Bourke (London: Darton, Longman & Todd, 1976), p. 90.

15. In the pastoral, *The Challenge of Peace*, see par. 9–10. In the pastoral, *Economic Justice for All*, see par. 135.

16. I am following the pamphlet by Francis G. Morrisey, *The Canonical Significance of Papal and Curial Pronouncements*, published by the Canon Law Society of America, n.d. See also Piet Fransen, "The Exercise of Authority in the Church Today: Its Concrete Forms," *Louvain Studies* 9 (Spring 1982): 1–25, see esp. pp. 20–23.

17. The address was given on October 16, 1986 at the University of Southern California. The full text is in *Origins* 16 (Nov. 6, 1986): 372–375; quotation on p. 373.

18. For a manualist view of probabilism, see H. Noldin, A. Schmitt, G. Heinzel, *Summa Theologiae Moralis*, Vol. 1 *De Principiis*, thirtieth edition (Innsbruck: Felizian Rauch, 1952), p. 218; also, Henry Davis, *Moral and Pastoral Theology*, Vol. 1 *Human Acts, Law, Sin, Virtue* (London: Sheed and Ward, 1945), p. 95. For more recent views, see Bernard Häring, *Free and Faithful in Christ*, Vol. 1, *General Moral Theology* (New York: Seabury Press, 1978), pp. 284–294; also, Philip S. Kaufman, "An Immoral Morality?" *Commonweal*, 107 (September 12, 1980): 493–497; John Mahoney, *The Making of Moral Theology* (Oxford: The Clarendon Press, 1987), pp. 135–143.

19. Dulles, "Authority and Conscience," *Church* 2 (Fall 1986), p. 14.

20. For Curran's account of his controversy with the Congregation for the Doctrine of the Faith, see his *Faithful Dissent* (Kansas City: Sheed and Ward, 1986).

21. McCormick, "Moral Notes," *Theological Studies* 29 (December 1968): 716–718; also, 30 (December 1969): 651–653.

22. Curran, "Heresy and Error," *America* 142 (March 1, 1980): 165.

23. George Gallup, Jr., and Jim Castelli, *The American Catholic People: Their Beliefs, Practices, and Values* (Garden City: Doubleday and Company, Inc., 1987), p. 51.

24. Sullivan, *Magisterium*, p. 168.

25. Lukas Vischer, "How Does the Church Teach Authoritatively Today?" in *Who Has the Say in the Church?* edited by Moltmann and Küng, pp. 6–7.

26. John Mahoney, *The Making of Moral Theology* (Oxford: Clarendon Press, 1987), pp. 321–337.

27. *Ibid.*, pp. 330–331. Mahoney draws on Karl Rahner, "Pluralism in Theology and the Unity of the Creed," *Theological Investigations*, Vol. V (London: Darton, Longman and Todd, 1966), pp. 3–23.

28. On "reception" see Joseph A. Komonchak, "*Humanae Vitae* and its Reception: Ecclesiological Reflections," *Theological Studies* 39 (June 1978): 221–257; also, Thomas P. Rausch, "Authority and Credibility," in *Vatican Authority and American Catholic Dissent*, edited by William W. May (New York: Crossroad Publishing Company, 1987), pp. 122–124.

# 15 The Natural Law in Tradition

*T*he natural law is central to Roman Catholic moral theology. It is the kind of "reasoning" which "faith" informs. Perhaps the single most characteristic feature of traditional Catholic morality is that the church can teach a morality which is applicable always, everywhere, and for everyone because it relies on the natural law as the basis for its teaching. In fact, the claim of the Roman Catholic natural law tradition is that moral knowledge is accessible not just to believers but to anyone who is willing to reflect critically on human experience. The advantage of using natural law is that the church shows great respect for human goodness and trusts the human capacity to know and choose what is right. Also, by means of appealing to natural law, the church can address its discussion and claims for the rightness or wrongness of particular actions to all persons of good will, not just to those who share its religious convictions. One of the great disadvantages of such an approach is that it can easily lead to handing Christian morality over to moral philosophy wherein religious beliefs do not really make a difference for moral claims.

The magisterium has appealed to the natural law as the basis for its teachings pertaining to a just society, sexual behavior, medical practice, human life, religious freedom, and the relationship between morality and civil law. But the appeal to natural law to support both the universal and absolute prohibitions of very specific behaviors, such as in sexual matters, as well as the openness and respect for ambiguity, such as in social matters, has occasioned considerable curiosity and confusion over the notion of "natural law" and its use.

Natural law is a highly ambiguous notion. In a sense, natural law is neither "natural" nor is it "law." It is not "natural" in the sense that the natural *moral* law cannot be identified with physical, chemical, or biological laws of nature which try to express the way the natural world works. It is not "law" in the sense that is not a written code of precepts which carry public sanctions from the legislator. Furthermore, historical surveys of the meaning and use of natural law quickly put to rest any notion that natural law is a single philosophical system which yields a clear and consistent code of conduct.[1]

In order to understand the church's moral teaching, we will need to examine the natural law tradition in its origins and its status today. The traditional Catholic point of reference has been the scholastic conception of natural law synthesized by Thomas Aquinas.

## Roots of Natural Law in Antiquity

### The Bible

The Bible offers some basis for appealing to human nature as a source of moral enlightenment. For example, the Wisdom literature of the Old Testament draws upon collective human experience to discover moral value. In the New Testament, the parables of Jesus use ordinary human experiences to light up basic human values. Paul, in particular, was explicit in his reference to "nature" as a source of moral knowledge for those who did not have access to the revelation of the God of Israel. Critical reflection on experience is sufficient for moral enlightenment (Rom 1:20).

In his major work, *Natural Law: A Theological Investigation*,[2] Josef Fuchs develops this line of thinking. He maintains that creation is intrinsically connected with redemptive incarnation so that revelation adds nothing new to what we can discover of the material content of morality through reason. Natural law itself is graced; therefore, the rational requirements of morality are the commandments of the creator. As a source of moral knowledge, scripture offers a new motivation for living the moral life. Bruno Schuller has explored the role of scripture in morality to a greater extent and maintains that, even though natural law is authorized by scripture, natural law is necessary in the first place if we are ever to hear and understand revealed morality. The revealed moral law in scripture is an expression of natural law; it does not establish a different morality.[3]

In any case, the development of a natural law tradition among Christian thinkers is due not so much to the scriptures as to the influence of Greek philosophy and Roman law.

### The Greek Influence

Among the Greeks, the Stoics were the earliest ones to develop a notion of natural law to a significant degree. They contributed to the natural law tradition by emphasizing "nature" and the moral requirement to "conform" to what is given in nature. For the Stoics the goal of philosophy was to achieve right moral conduct. As thorough-going materialists they believed that the world was an inter-connected series of events and that right moral living came with conforming to the given world order. "Don't fool with Mother Nature" may be taken as their basic moral imperative. Abiding by this maxim demands accepting what is given in nature as it is, cooperating with the inter-connected rhythms of life, and not attempting to control or shape nature to fit a personal goal. Any talk of self-direction would make no sense to the Stoics. Since the given order of events will ultimately assert themselves according to their own design anyway, the human task is simply to capitulate to what is given.

Aristotle influenced the natural law tradition, especially in St. Thomas, even though Aristotle did not develop a natural law theory as such. From within the framework of his hylomorphic theory of matter (a passive principle), he also emphasized "nature" but understood it as the cause or source of activity in a being. The "law" of nature is the orientation of all beings toward their perfection. Since the specific nature of humans is rationality, morally good actions would be those which are rationally directed toward the full actualization of human potential.

## The Roman Influence

Whereas the Greeks emphasized "nature," the Romans emphasized the "law" of the natural order. The Romans were interested in establishing political order not only within the Roman state itself but throughout the world by expanding the Roman empire. Cicero (d. 43 B.C.) spoke of natural law as the innate power of reason to direct action. To live according to the law given in nature is to live according to what reason commands. For Cicero, then, we ought to use prudential and thoughtful judgments in directing human behavior and establishing social order.

Another Roman, Gaius (d. 180 A.D.) distinguishes two kinds of law for regulating political order: *jus civile* regulates the civil rights within a legally autonomous society such as the Roman state itself; *jus gentium* regulates the relationships between legally autonomous territories. This kind of law is the work of reason and gets its name from the fact that all peoples could observe it since it is based on the common needs and concerns of all people. As such it is not distinguishable from the natural law, or that which is reasonable.

By the third century, however, the natural law becomes clearly distinguished from *jus gentium*. This is due to the influential work of the Roman jurist, Ulpian (d. 228 A.D.). To the two types of law distinguished by Gaius, Ulpian adds a third, *jus naturale*, what nature has taught all animals. This law is not peculiar to humans, but is the generic rule of action common to humans and to animals. In this sense, natural law comes close to the idea of animal instinct. Ulpian's understanding of "nature" leads to identifying the human with animal structures, tendencies, and behaviors. In this way, Ulpian was making humans more like animals than unlike them.

By adding this kind of law, Ulpian isolated natural law from the law proper to humans. In doing so, Ulpian opened up implications which have had unfortunate effects on much of the subsequent moral reflection based on natural law. For example, Ulpian's threefold division of law distinguished what is proper to humans (reflected in *jus civile* and *jus gentium*) and what is common to humans and animals (the domain of *jus naturale*). Unfortunately, each aspect gets treated as a separate layer retaining its own purpose without having any influence on the other. Natural law now takes on a physicalist cast whereby the natural moral order becomes identified with the properties, operations, and goals of the "natural" or given structures of physical, animal life. According to such a view, the moral act becomes identified with the physical act which corresponds to animal processes. Moral obligations arise from what is already prescribed in the physical structures of being human apart from their relation to the totality of the person, which includes such aspects as reason, freedom, affections, and relationships. Moral evaluations, as a result, become based on the integrity and purpose of physical actions taken apart from the totality of the person.

Ulpian's definition has had a lasting effect on subsequent developments of natural law theory. The influence of Ulpian on the natural law tradition has been long-lived due to his definition being adopted by the most influential and authoritative source of Roman law, the *Corpus Juris Civilis* of Justinian. Ulpian's definition passed on to St. Thomas through Roman law itself as well as through those who commented on it. By the time St. Thomas undertook his great synthesis, Ulpian's definition had been so firmly established in the tradition of law that St. Thomas could not ignore it. He had to deal with it.[4]

## Natural Law in Thomas Aquinas

By the high Middle Ages, two strains of interpretation dominated the natural law tradition. One, the "order of nature," identified with the Stoics and Ulpian, focused on the physical and biological structures given in nature as the source of morality. The other, the "order of reason," identified with Aristotle, Cicero, and Gaius, focused on the human capacity to discover in experience what befits human well-being. St. Thomas accepted both. Since his teaching is the seminal influence on the traditional Catholic use of natural law, subsequent Catholic theology has been influenced by both interpretations as well.[5]

The vacillation between the "order of nature" and the "order of reason" as the basis of moral teaching has caused great confusion in Catholic moral thought. We may better appreciate the confusion and vacillation of the use of natural law in present Catholic teaching if we understand the ways St. Thomas interpreted and used it.

In the *Summa*, natural law (I–II, q. 94) is set in the theological context of the *exitus et reditus principle:* all things come from God and return to God. The natural law is situated in the treatise on law (I–II, qq. 90–97) as a means of returning to God. It is linked with the notion of law in general as an ordinance of practical reason (q. 90) and with eternal law, which is the way of saying that God is the ultimate source of moral value and moral obligation (q. 93).

Everything created participates in the eternal law according to its nature. Insensible beings participate passively by following the direction of physical, chemical, and biological forces. The animal world participates by instinct. Humans participate in eternal law by reason. In this context we find the classic expression of the most fundamental understanding of natural law in St. Thomas: the human person's participation in eternal law through the use of reason (cf. I–II, q. 91, a. 2; and q. 93).

This definition of natural law has wide-ranging implications for morality. With eternal law as the primary point of reference, what God requires and enables becomes the ultimate norm of morality, the basis of objective morality, and the source of moral obligation. The proximate norm of morality is authentic human existence. The natural law is the human way of knowing the ultimate norm of morality—eternal law, or what God requires and enables. It knows this by reflecting critically on the proximate norm of morality—what it means to live a fully human life in community with others striving for human wholeness.[6]

An accurate appeal to this classic understanding of natural law, then, depends on discovering what being "human" really means. This is the work of reason reflecting on the totality of human experience and not only one aspect of it, such as the physical or biological. "Reason" is not to be construed here in the narrow sense of logic or analysis. "Reason," in the Thomistic sense of *recta ratio*, entails the totality of the human tendency to want to know the whole of reality and come to truth. This sense of "reason" includes observation and research, intuition, affection, common sense, and an aesthetic sense in an effort to know human reality in all its aspects. In short, whatever resources we can use to understand the meaning of being human will be appropriate for a natural law approach to morality.

This fundamental understanding of natural law shows St. Thomas' preference for the rational aspects of natural law, a view hardly reconcilable with the biological natural law of Ulpian's definition. If St. Thomas were consistent, the case against Ulpian's definition would then be closed and the Catholic tradition of natural law might well have followed the "order of reason" interpretation throughout its moral teaching.

But St. Thomas is not consistent. According to the historical analysis of Michael B. Crowe, St. Thomas was ready to welcome conceptions of natural law from his predecessors which had little in common with each other and which did not even fit the demands of his own basic thought.[7] As Crowe further observes, "Aquinas does appear to feel a need, not altogether explained by his habit of deference to authorities, to make provision for Ulpian."[8] Crowe concludes that St. Thomas' retention of Ulpian's definition remains "slightly puzzling."[9]

The influence of Ulpian's definition makes an unmistakable appearance in his key discussion of natural law in I–II, q. 94, a. 2. The question is whether the natural law has several precepts or only one. St. Thomas answers this question by first identifying the one fundamental norm of natural law: do good and avoid evil. In the Thomistic perspective, doing good is following reason's lead to actualize human potential. Evil is whatever frustrates or prohibits that full realization. This fundamental norm does not give content for action, but it does indicate a basic disposition we ought to have. As such, this basic norm pertains more to the ethics of being than to the ethics of doing. It encourages us to become who we are by acting in a way that would actualize our potential. This first principle of natural law underscores the dynamic character of the natural law as a tendency rather than a code ordering human persons toward being authentic persons.[10]

Aquinas then moves on to the specific norms of natural law based on the natural inclinations. The origin of our specific moral obligations lies in these natural inclinations which give content to the fundamental requirement to do good and avoid evil. The practical reason perceives the natural inclinations in human persons in the form of moral imperatives which become the concrete conclusions of natural law.

The first inclination to the good is common to all created reality. It is the tendency to persevere in being. Preserving and protecting life as a basic value belongs to the natural law on the basis of this inclination. St. Thomas appeals to this inclination in his argument against suicide (II–II, q. 64, a. 5) and in his argument for killing in self-defense (II–II, q. 64, a. 7).

The second inclination to the good is generic to animals. Insofar as humans are animals, what nature has taught all animals belongs to natural law. Included here is the tendency toward the procreation and education of offspring. This is the "order of nature" strain of interpretation of natural law in St. Thomas. The influence of Ulpian is quite evident here even though St. Thomas does not mention him by name. St. Thomas appeals to the order of nature of "generic natural law" in his discussion of sexual matters (cf. II–II, q. 154, aa. 11, 12).

The third inclination to the good is specific to humans. Insofar as humans are rational, whatever pertains to reason belongs to the natural law. This includes the tendency toward truth and cooperating with one another in a social existence. This is the "order of reason" strain of interpretation of natural law, which is consistent with St. Thomas' fundamental definition of natural law as the human participation in eternal law through the use of reason. He appeals to the order of reason of "specific natural law" when dealing with matters of justice (cf. II–II, q. 64).

The interpretation of natural law which corresponds to the "order of nature," or generic natural law, in St. Thomas is influenced by Ulpian's definition of *jus naturale:* what nature has taught all animals. This way of understanding natural law emphasizes human physical and biological nature in determining morality. It suggests a "blueprint" or "maker's instructions" theory of natural law which supports physicalism over personalism. "Personalism" is hard to define with precision. It is characterized by placing emphasis on dimensions of the human person and human actions which extend beyond the physical and biological to include the social, spiritual, and psychological dimensions as well. "Physicalism," on the other hand, refers to the tendency in moral analysis to emphasize, or even to absolutize, the physical and biological aspects of the human person and human actions independently of the function of reason and freedom.

Natural law physicalism is the guiding principle in the following analogy provided by Gerald A. Kelly, one of the leading Catholic moralists immediately prior to Vatican II, in his major medical-moral manual.

Suppose that an inventor-mechanic would construct a new type of machine, e.g., a special type of automobile; and suppose that he would then sell it to me and would present me with a book of instructions concerning its correct and incorrect use. Granted that the mechanic acted reasonably, these instructions would not be a merely arbitrary afterthought without any reference to the nature of the machine. Rather, they would be a written formulation of "dos and don'ts" based upon his own intimate knowledge of the machine. He planned it for a certain purpose; he chose the materials and arranged them according to a certain design; he knows what is in it; and his instructions express this knowledge in a practical way. · Another talented mechanic might examine this same machine and, by perceiving its materials, its arrangement, and its purpose, he could reach substantially the same conclusions as the inventor had expressed in his book of instructions. In other words, both the inventor and the examining mechanic would know that the very nature of the machine requires that it be operated in a certain way, or in certain ways, in order to accomplish its purpose.[11]

This analogy illustrates the "blueprint" or "maker's instructions" theory of natural law physicalism in bold terms. It understands nature as the viceroy of God. This turns the natural law theory into a kind of natural fundamentalism whereby the rule of God and the rule of nature are practically one. In nature, God speaks. The structures and functions found in nature are the expressions of God's actions on humankind. The human task is to examine the givens in nature in order to understand their arrangement and purpose. Moral obligation can be read off what nature requires in order to fulfill its inherent design.

Such an understanding of natural law has significant implications for morality. Physicalism discovers criteria for moral judgment by studying human structures and their functions in their natural (read: "God-given") state before any intervention by the human person. Moral norms, for example, are "written in nature." They can be "read off" the physical properties, operations, and goals of the human faculties (e.g., the faculty of speech is for truthtelling, the reproductive faculty is for producing life). Moral obligations are fulfilled by conforming human action to the detailed patterns found in nature. An action is immoral, or "intrinsically morally evil," because it is contrary to nature, i.e., it frustrates the finality of a natural (read: "God-given") faculty. For example, speaking falsely frustrates the faculty of speech which is oriented to telling the truth, and contraception or sterilization frustrates the reproductive faculty which is oriented to the giving of life.

The physicalist interpretation of natural law has dominated much of the Catholic moral tradition in sexual and medical matters pertaining to reproduction. It allows moral positions to be taken without ambiguity in every instance where the same kind of physical action occurs.[12] The Catholic tradition has regarded any violation of the natural order as a serious offense since violating the natural order is an affront against God, its author. This helps explain in part why our traditional morality maintained no "light matter" in the area of sexual morality.

Since the order of nature comes directly from God as its author, it assumes a priority and superiority over the order of reason which comes more immediately from the human person. St. Thomas maintained this position in the *Summa* when dealing with the morality of sexual matters:

Reason presupposes things as determined by nature . . . so in matters of action it is most grave and shameful to act against things as determined by nature (II–II, q. 154, a. 12).

This position establishes the superiority of the order of nature as coming from God (cf. II–II, q. 154, a. 12, ad. 1) and makes reason subject to it in a subordinate and passive way (ad. 2).

St. Thomas goes on to say in II–II, q. 154, a. 12 that in matters of chastity, the most serious offenses are those against the order of nature, i.e., those actions which do not fulfill the finality written by God into biological nature. Louis Janssens has studied this section of St. Thomas carefully to show where such a position leads.

> Sexual activities excluding procreation (Thomas classifies them in an order of ascendent gravity: masturbation, marital contraceptive intercourse, homosexuality, bestiality) are sins against biological nature (*contra naturam omnis animalis*). They are graver than the sins which do not exclude procreation (in ascendent degree of gravity: fornication, adultery, incest), because they go directly against God, the Creator who expresses his will in the biological nature. Therefore, in a certain sense they are even graver than sacrilege.[13]

Following St. Thomas' principle that the most serious actions are those which go against nature, we would have to conclude that masturbation is a more serious violation of chastity than incest, adultery, rape, or fornication (II–II, q. 154, aa. 11, 12). Janssens shows that contemporary moralists would not draw such conclusions. A different understanding of "nature" and "natural law" explains the different conclusions.

The modern worldview of contemporary morality does not look on nature as a finished product prescribing God's moral will and commanding a fixed moral response. Rather, it looks on nature as evolving. For example, the laws and properties of the given world can and do combine with unexpected circumstances to give us something new. Within the limits set by necessary physical laws which already determine reality somewhat, human reason and freedom can intervene to bring about something new. In this view, "nature" provides the material with which we have to deal in a human way to promote the well-being of human life. We are not subjected in a fated way to the inner finality of nature. We discover what natural law requires by reason reflecting on what is given in human experience to lead to authentic human life and the full actualization of human potential.[14]

With this brief overview of the understanding of natural law in tradition, we are in a better position to appreciate the use of natural law in ecclesiastical documents and to identify the characteristic features of the status of natural law today. Such will be the focus of the next chapter.

## *Notes*

1. Heinrich A. Rommen, *The Natural Law* (St. Louis: B. Herder, 1947); Yves R. Simon, *The Tradition of Natural Law* (New York: Fordham University Press, 1965), pp. 16–40

2. Fuchs, *Natural Law: A Theological Investigation*, translated by Helmut Reckter and John A. Dowling (New York: Sheed and Ward, 1965). See also his "Is There a Specifically Christian Morality?" in Charles E. Curran and Richard A. McCormick, eds., *The Distinctiveness of Christian Ethics: Readings in Moral Theology No. 2* (Ramsey: Paulist Press, 1980), pp. 3–19.

3. "Zur theologischen Diskussion über die lex naturalis," *Theologie und Philosophie* 41 (1966): 481–503. See also his "The Debate on the Specific Character of Christian Ethics: Some Remarks," in Curran and McCormick, eds., *The Distinctiveness of Christian Ethics*, pp. 207–233.

4. For the legal and theological uses of natural law and its influence on St. Thomas, see Michael B. Crowe, "St. Thomas and Ulpian's Natural Law," *St. Thomas Aquinas 1274–1974: Commemorative Studies*, ed. Armand A. Maurer, 2 vols. (Toronto: Pontifical Institute of Mediaeval Studies, 1974), Vol. 1, pp. 261–282; see especially 267–272.

5. Even brief historical sketches of the natural law help to identify these two strains. See, for example, Charles E. Curran, "Natural Law," *Directions in Fundamental Moral Theology* (Notre Dame: University of Notre Dame Press, 1985), pp. 119–172; Timothy O'Connell, *Principles for a Catholic Morality* (New York: Seabury Press, 1978), pp. 134–144; Columba Ryan, "The Traditional Concept of Natural Law: An Interpretation," *Light on the Natural Law, An Interpretation*, ed. I. Evans (Baltimore: Helicon Press, 1965), pp. 13–37.

6. I am following here the insights of Columba Ryan, "The Traditional Concept of Natural Law: An Interpretation," in Illtud Evans, ed., *Light on the Natural Law* (Baltimore: Helicon Press, 1965), pp. 22–24, 32.

7. See especially the thorough analysis of natural law in St. Thomas by Michael B. Crowe, *The Changing Profile of Natural Law* (The Hague: Martinus Nihoff, 1977); see especially Chapter VI, "Aquinas Faces the Natural Law Tradition," pp. 136–165, and Chapter VII, "Aquinas Makes Up His Mind," pp. 166–191. See also Crowe's study, "St. Thomas and Ulpian's Natural Law," in *St. Thomas Aquinas 1274–1974: Commemorative Studies*, pp. 261–282.

8. Crowe, "St. Thomas and Ulpian's Natural Law," in *St. Thomas Aquinas 1274–1974: Commemorative Studies*, p. 278.

9. *Ibid.*, p. 282.

10. I am following here the insights of Louis Monden, *Sin, Liberty and*

*Law*, translated by Joseph Donceel (New York: Sheed and Ward, 1965), pp. 88–89.

11.  Gerald A. Kelly, *Medico-Moral Problems* (St. Louis: Catholic Hospital Association, 1958), pp. 28–29.

12.  An excellent book which traces the physicalist interpretation of natural law through Catholic medical ethics in North America is David F. Kelly, *The Emergence of Roman Catholic Medical Ethics in North America* (New York: The Edwin Mellen Press, 1979).

13.  "Norms and Priorities in a Love Ethics," *Louvain Studies* 4 (Spring 1977): 234–235. References to St. Thomas in this quotation are II–II, q. 154, aa. 11, 12 ad. 4; *De Malo* q. 15, a. 1, ad. 7; II–II, q. 154, a. 12 and 12 ad. 2.

14.  *Ibid.*, p. 236.

# 16 Natural Law Today

$S$ince the tension between the "order of nature" and the "order of reason" approaches to natural law has been so paramount in subsequent Catholic theology, we need to give more attention to the meaning and implications of each and show examples of their use in official Catholic teaching.[1]

## Natural Law in Magisterial Documents

The manner of deriving a moral position on the basis of the "order of nature" over the "order of reason" and pronouncing specific moral judgments on acts in themselves has found its way into the documents of the magisterium on sexual and medical moral matters pertaining to reproduction. For example, Pius XI in *Casti Connubii* (1930) says this:

> But no reason, however grave, may be put forward by which anything intrinsically against nature may become conformable to nature and morally good. Since, therefore, the conjugal act is destined primarily by nature for the begetting of children, those who in exercising it deliberately frustrate its natural power and purpose sin against nature and commit a deed which is shameful and intrinsically vicious.[2]

This same understanding of natural law appears again in Pius XII's *Address to Midwives* in 1951:

> Nature places at man's disposal the whole chain of the causes which give rise to new human life; it is man's part to release the living force, and to nature pertains the development of that force, leading to its completion. . . . Thus the part played by nature and the part played by man are precisely determined.[3]

Paul VI carried this understanding of natural law forward in *Humanae Vitae* in 1968 by maintaining:

> Nonetheless the Church, calling men back to the observance of the norms of the natural law, as interpreted by the constant doctrine, teaches that each and every marriage act (*quilibet matrimonii usus*) must remain open to the transmission of life. . . .

> To make use of the gift of conjugal love while respecting the laws of the generative process means to acknowledge oneself not to be the arbiter of the sources of human life, but rather the minister of the design established by the Creator. In fact, just as man does not have unlimited dominion over his body in general, so also, with particular reason, he has no such dominion over his generative faculties as such, because of their intrinsic ordination toward raising up life, of which God is the principle.[4]

Paul VI also reflects St. Thomas in making the order of nature superior to the order of reason in sexual matters by claiming:

> The church is the first to praise and recommend the intervention of intelligence in a function which so closely associates the rational creature with his Creator; but she affirms that this must be done with respect for the order established by God.[5]

In 1975 the Sacred Congregation issued *Persona Humana*, the Declaration on Certain Questions Concerning Sexual Ethics, which repeats the perspective of *Humanae Vitae*, as can be seen from this excerpt:

> The main reason [that masturbation is an intrinsically and seriously disordered act] is that, whatever the motive for acting in this way, the deliberate use of the sexual faculty outside normal conjugal relations essentially contradicts the finality of the faculty.[6]

The same understanding of natural law is used again by the Congregation in its 1986 letter to bishops, "The Pastoral Care of Homosexual Persons." It points out that homosexual acts are deprived of their essential finality and are intrinsically disordered (n. 3). While this letter does appeal to personalism by claiming to base its teaching on the reality of the human person in one's spiritual and physical dimensions (n. 2), the personalist perspective is not carried through consistently. The method of the document is ultimately based on the essential nature of the sexual faculty which is taken to be the same as the whole personality.

Similarly, the 1987 document on bioethics, "Instruction on Respect for Human Life in its Origin and on the Dignity of Procreation," of the same Congregation is mixed in its natural law perspective. Even though it uses more personalistic terms and admits in the Introduction to a preference for the rational and not the biological emphasis of natural law, it falls back on natural law physicalism in treating some specific issues. For example, in the Introduction we read:

> Therefore this law [the natural moral law] cannot be thought of as simply a set of norms on the biological level; rather it must be defined as the rational order whereby man is called by the Creator to direct and regulate his life and actions and in particular to make use of his own body. . . .

> [Artificial interventions regarding procreation and the origin of life] must be given a moral evaluation in reference to the dignity of the human person, who is called to realize his vocation from God to the gift of love and the gift of life.[7]

Yet behind these personalistic terms and openness to the rational order lie the framework and conclusions of physicalism regarding the morality of reproductive interventions. For example,

> Homologous artificial insemination within marriage cannot be admitted except for those cases in which the technical means is not a substitute for the conjugal act but serves to facilitate and to help so that the act attains its natural purpose.[8]

Physicalism, however, does light up some truth. Part of being human is to have a body whose structure and functions cannot be arbitrarily treated. So the strength of the physicalist approach to natural law is that it clearly recognizes the "givenness" of human nature. Human effort must indeed cooperate with the fixed character of human existence in promoting the well-being of human life. The weakness of this approach, however, is to mistake the "givens" of human nature as the whole of human nature, or to take the fixed character of human existence as being closed and beyond the control of human creative development. The danger of physicalism is to derive moral imperatives from bodily structure and functions and to exclude the totality of the person and his or her relational context in making a moral assessment.

Karl Rahner has captured well the tension between the givenness of nature and human creative capacities in this statement:

> For contemporary man, nature is no longer the lofty viceroy of God, one which lies beyond man's control, but instead has become the material which he needs so as to experience himself in his *own role of free creator* and so as to build *his* own world for himself according to his own laws. Of course, it is true that this material of human creativeness has laws proper to itself which will weigh heavily on man. It is true that this human creativeness consequently subjects itself, whether it likes it or not, to what is alien and given to it; it is not pure creativeness as we acknowledge it of God; it does not come completely from within and it is not simply a law unto itself; it does not evoke matter and form out of nothing, and hence this creativeness of man, which has to deal with the laws of matter, is naturally also in every case a growth in obedience and "servitude" in the face of an alien law . . . but it is creation in knowing, willing and mastering sense, a creativeness which forces nature into its own service.[9]

The physicalist approach to natural law has been criticized on many counts.[10] Typical of the critical reactions to this approach to natural law and the conclusions it yields is this one by the Georgetown philosopher, Louis Dupre, made during the birth control debates of the 1960s:

> Such a way of reasoning about nature contains, I feel, two basic flaws. It confuses man's biological structure with his human nature. And it takes human nature as a static, unchangeable thing, rather than as a principle of development. Man's biological life and its intrinsic laws are but one aspect of human existence.[11]

Charles E. Curran has been consistent in his criticism of the physicalist approach to natural law. His criticisms run along several lines. He finds physicalism to reflect the naive realism of the classicist worldview. This means that physicalism is based on an essentialist definition of human nature which has no room for change; it views nature as a finished product so that change and historical process are incidental; also, it depends on a moral order that is fixed and undeveloping. Physicalism gives exaggerated importance to the human physical and biological nature in determining morality and puts these on a par with the whole personality. It also separates the action from the totality of the person and the full moral context. Physicalism claims too many negative moral absolutes based on the action taken in itself, and it does not make room for historical development and the creative intervention of reason to humanize the given patterns of nature.[12]

Catholic theology today is trying to revise the physicalist approach to natural law which dominated the manuals and the magisterial decrees on sexual ethics and medical moral matters pertaining to reproduction. Many theologians today are saying that natural law is not necessarily tied to physicalism and the classicist worldview; it belongs also in a worldview that takes experience, history, change, and development seriously. Contemporary theology's use of natural law is more historically conscious and taps into the second strain of interpretation of natural law, the order of reason.

The trend in Roman Catholic moral theology today is to develop more and more the rational aspect of the natural law tradition. In this use, reason, and not the physical structure of human faculties or actions taken by themselves, becomes the standard of natural law. Building on Thomistic foundations, this approach understands reason (*recta ratio*) in the broad sense of the dynamic tendency in the human person to come to truth, to grasp the whole of reality as it is. A morality that has reason as its basic standard, then, is a morality based on reality. The work of reason is to discover moral value in the experience of the reality of being human. This seems to be the fundamental direction which recent trends in interpreting the natural law are taking. Much more attention is being given today to the total complexity of reality experienced in its historically particular ways.[13]

In a natural law approach which emphasizes the rational aspects, the human person is not subject to the God-given order of nature in the same way the animals are. The human person does not have to conform to natural patterns as a matter of fate. Rather, nature provides the possibilities and potentialities which the human person can use to make human life truly human. The given physical and biological orders do not dictate moral obligations; rather, they provide the data and the possibilities for the human person to use in order to achieve human goals.

The natural order remains an important factor to consider if the human person is to base moral norms on reality. But the natural order is not to be taken as the moral order. The human person can creatively intervene to direct the natural order in a way that is properly proportionate to full human development. The "nature" which reason explores is no longer separated from the total complexity of personal, human life taken in all its relationships.[14]

This understanding of natural law has important implications for morality. Natural law morality is objective morality insofar as it is based, not on selfish interest, but on a critical effort to grasp the whole of human reality in all its relationships. Insofar as reality continues to change, moral positions must be open to revision. Inasmuch as we can grasp only a part of the whole at any one time, specific moral conclusions based on natural law will necessarily be limited and tentative. These conclusions are reliable insofar as they reflect as accurate a grasp of human reality as is possible at one time. But such conclusions must necessarily be open to revision since more of the meaning of being human is yet to be discovered.

While right reason is the full exercise of our capacity to grasp the whole of reality, the full exercise of reason is limited by individual capacities, emotional involvements which bias the interpretation of data, and cultural conditions which influence one's perspective on reality (cf. I–II, q. 94, a. 6). All of these factors necessarily place limitations on moral judgments, contribute to moral differences, and lead to more modest claims of certitude than did the order of nature approach to natural law.

The order of reason approach to natural law is used in magisterial documents on social ethics.[15] Even though the great social encyclicals *Rerum Novarum*, *Quadragesimo Anno*, and *Pacem in Terris* reflect something of a static social order, they do move away from the order of nature interpretation of natural law evident in decrees on sexual and medical moral matters to an interpretation of natural law which is based on the prudential use of reason. Consider this brief excerpt from *Pacem in Terris* (1963) as a point of illustration for this shift:

> But the Creator of the world has imprinted in man's heart an order which his conscience reveals to him and enjoins him to obey: *This shows that the obligations of the law are written in their hearts: their conscience utters its own testimony. . . .* But fickleness of opinion often produces this error, that many think that the relationships between men and states can be governed by the same laws as the forces and irrational elements of the universe, whereas the laws governing them are of quite a different kind and are to be sought elsewhere, namely, where the Father of all things wrote them, that is, in the nature of man.[16]

In that encyclical John XXIII could address all persons of good will, not just Catholics specifically or Christians in general, because he emphasized that reason can discover the demands of human dignity placed in creatures by the creator.

Paul VI reflects a dynamic view of natural law in his great social encyclical *Populorum Progressio* (1967). He appeals to the creative intervention of the human person and the community to direct natural processes toward fulfillment:

> In the design of God, every man is called upon to develop and fulfill himself, for every life is a vocation. At birth, everyone is granted, in

germ, a set of aptitudes and qualities for him to bring to fruition. Their coming to maturity, which will be the result of education received from the environment and personal efforts, will allow each man to direct himself toward the destiny intended for him by his Creator. Endowed with intelligence and freedom, he is responsible for his fulfillment as he is for his salvation. He is aided, or sometimes impeded, by those who educate him and those with whom he lives, but each one remains, whatever be these influences affecting him, the principal agent of his own success or failure. By the unaided effort of his own intelligence and his will, each man can grow in humanity, can enhance his personal worth, can become more a person.[17]

In his apostolic letter of 1971, *Octogesima Adveniens* (more popularly known as "A Call to Action"), Paul VI also expressed a dynamic view of natural law. It is based on the order of reason which grounds morality in reality and yields tentative moral positions open to development.

In the face of such widely varying situations it is difficult for us to utter a unified message and to put forward a solution which has universal validity. Such is not our ambition, nor is it our mission. It is up to the Christian communities to analyze with objectivity the situation which is proper to their own country, to shed on it the light of the Gospel's unalterable words, and to draw principles of reflection, norms of judgment and directives for action from the social teaching of the Church.[18]

A comparison of documents representing the order of nature approach to natural law with those representing the order of reason approach shows the two different methods which have been operating in Catholic moral theology side by side to give us our moral norms and moral positions.[19] The clear distinctions and definitions which were possible by using the order of nature approach in sexual and medical moral matters are not present in the areas of social ethics. On the basis of the order of nature criteria, Catholic sexual ethics and medical ethics pertaining to reproduction have achieved a degree of certainty, precision, and consistency of moral judgment which we do not find in the documents on social ethics. The order of reason approach to understanding natural law does not yield the clear unambiguous positions which the order of nature approach does.

The church's epistemological claims in regard to natural law in social matters are more modest, more cautious, and more nuanced than those in sexual ethics and medical moral reproductive matters. In social ethics, the church readily accepts the inevitability of conflict on the philosophical level as well as in social life. The above excerpt from *Octogesima Adveniens* acknowledges this and the American bishops openly acknowledge inevitable diversity in their recent pastoral letters on war and peace and the economy. In *The Challenge of Peace* (1983) we read:

> When making applications of these principles we realize—and we wish readers to recognize—that prudential judgments are involved based on specific circumstances which can change or which can be interpreted differently by people of good will.
>
> . . .On complex social questions, the Church expects a certain diversity of views even though all hold the same universal moral principles.[20]

From such a perspective, the church accepts conclusions of the application of general principles which are limited, tentative, and open to revision—all of which are characteristic of the order of reason strain in the tradition of natural law.

A review of what we have seen thus far will prepare us for a synthetic view of the profile of natural law in contemporary Catholic moral theology. For this review, see the accompanying chart which contrasts the salient features of both approaches to the natural law. The examples under the order of nature approach actually show a mix in their use of natural law. However, the order of nature interpretation of natural law does dominate to control the moral method and conclusions of these documents.

## Synthetic Description of Natural Law

In light of the tradition of natural law just considered, we can bring together a synthetic description of natural law which highlights its salient features.

### *The Meaning of "Natural"*

As it is used in natural law theory, "natural" is not opposed to "artificial," nor does it refer to the well-defined given structures and functions of the body or of any created reality. To equate "natural" with well-defined patterns in creation leads to a natural fundamentalism and yields a "blueprint" of "maker's instructions" theory of the natural moral law. Such an approach has no room for the distinctively human, creative aspects of moral knowledge and freedom. Moral knowledge would be simply the matter of

# TWO STRAINS OF INTERPRETATION
# OF NATURAL LAW
# AND IMPLICATIONS FOR MORAL NORMS

| FEATURES | "THE ORDER OF NATURE" | "THE ORDER OF REASON" |
|---|---|---|
| 1. Designation of Moral Norms | "According to Nature" | "According to (right) Reason" |
| 2. Source of Moral Norms | "Written in Nature" <br><br> God is the author of nature. <br> God-given structures take priority over anything derived from human reflection. | "Human Experience" taken in all its complexity and in its relationships <br><br> Norms express the prudent use of reason in the human, rational effort to grasp moral obligation grounded in human experience. |
| 3. Knowledge of Moral Norms | Observe the way nature works. | Rational grasp of human experience. <br><br> Reason is expressed through whatever means would help us grasp the meaning of being human in all its fullness. |
| 4. Violation | Any interference with the order designed by God is gravely serious. No "light matter" here. | Acting against what you know to be a true expression of what most fulfills human potential as this can be known through reason's reflection on human experience. |

| FEATURES | "THE ORDER OF NATURE" | "THE ORDER OF REASON" |
|----------|----------------------|------------------------|
| 5. Examples | *Casti Connubii* (1930) | *Rerum Novarum* (1891) |
| | Pius XII's *Address to Mid-wives* (1951) | *Quadragesimo Anno* (1931) |
| | *Humanae Vitae* (1968) | *Pacem in Terris* (1963) |
| | *Persona Humana* (1975) | *Gaudium et Spes* (1965) |
| | *Letter on the Pastoral Care of Homosexual Persons* (1986) | *Populorum Progressio* (1967) |
| | *Instruction on Bioethics* (1987) | *Octogesima Adveniens* (1971) |
| | | *The Challenge of Peace* (1983) |
| | | *Economic Justice for All* (1986) |

discovering the given patterns in the world, and freedom would be reduced to a matter of abiding by or violating what is given.

Rather, the notion "natural" in natural moral law theory is more accurately construed as shorthand for the total complexity of human reality taken in all its relationships and with all its potential. What pertains to "nature" is accessible to all and provides the potential with which human creativity must deal in order to achieve human wholeness. Since "nature" is constantly changing, it continues to make new demands on us. As a result, change, revision, and development would be constitutive of the natural moral law.

The force of "natural," then, is not to oppose what is artificial or to point to a fixed pattern in the world. Rather, it is to ground morality in reality lest moral obligations become the product of self-interest groups or subjective whim. "Natural" is what is in reality providing the potential which would make it possible for each person to come to wholeness in community with others seeking wholeness.

## *The Meaning of "Law"*

The notion of "law" in natural moral law theory is "law" only in a secondary sense. It is "law" in the sense of disclosing moral obligation. But it does not have the meaning of a codified system of rights or regulations prescribed by a legislator, such as the Bill of Rights or the Nuremberg Code. Nor does it have the sense of a scientific law of uniform behavior, such as the law of gravity or the law of thermodynamics. While uniformity is indeed an important aspect of law in the regulation of elements and organisms, human moral behavior is not regulated in the same way as animate or inanimate objects are. Human moral behavior respects the creative human capacity for knowledge and freedom.

The force of "law" in natural moral law theory is the force of reason in the Thomistic sense of *recta ratio*—the inclination to grasp the whole of reality and come to moral truth. "Law" then means that reason is the basic standard by which we discern moral obligation in the total complex of human relationships. As we discover more and more what contributes to human well-being and personal wholeness in community, we can formulate with confidence these discoveries of value into guiding norms, such as respect human life, treat others as you would wish to be treated. Insofar as these norms reflect truly human values, they can be invoked as guiding principles for all peoples.

From these understandings of "natural" and "law" we can put together a synthetic definition which reflects the core of the Catholic natural law tradition: natural law is reason reflecting on human experience discovering moral value.

## The Function and Value of Natural Law

Natural law functions in the Catholic moral tradition more as an approach to discovering moral value than as a body of established content. As an approach to moral value, it yields three basic convictions which are hallmarks of Catholic morality.[21]

*1. Natural law claims the existence of an objective moral order.*

This claim follows from the conviction that morality is grounded in reality. On this basis Catholic morality claims some actions as right and some as wrong since moral obligation is not something which can be made up at will, nor is it dependent on a single individual's or group's interest. This conviction places natural law morality in strict opposition to the extreme forms of situation ethics which emphasize the uniqueness of each moment of moral choice and an unpredictably changing moral order. It also puts natural law morality in strict opposition to voluntarism (or legal positivism) which makes the will of the legislator the determiner of the morally right or wrong.

*2. Natural law morality is accessible to anyone independently of one's religious commitment.*

This conviction claims that our knowledge of moral value and moral obligation is available to anyone who is able to do the critical work of reflecting on human experience with an interest in discovering moral truth. It enables the Catholic tradition to argue for the rightness of particular actions without recourse to religious insight or motivation. As such, this puts Catholic natural law morality in strict opposition to a divine command theory of ethics, such as that of Karl Barth, which requires access to divine revelation to know what is morally required. It enables Catholic morality to engage in ecumenical dialogue on moral issues not only with other Christian traditions, but also with non-Christian religions as well as with non-religious persons.

The claim that the natural law is accessible to everyone does not mean that everyone actually knows what is morally required or is equally committed to it. This does not change the fact that morality has an objective ground. It may, however, render a person less culpable of immorality. For example, not every murder is committed by a morally culpable person, but that does not lessen the immorality of murder. This conviction is the basis in natural law for the requirement of a keen pastoral sensitivity when dealing with others who may not be culpable in some moral matters. The traditional Catholic distinction between the objectively immoral action and the subjectively non-culpable person derives from this conviction.

*3. The knowledge of moral value can be universalized.*

The Catholic moral tradition has addressed its teaching to all people of good will in the belief that it is teaching the truth about being human generally. To discover an objective moral value which renders some actions right and some wrong is to discover something which would apply wherever that value is at stake or those particular actions are done.

These are three hallmarks of Catholic morality rooted in its natural law tradition and still viable today. From these we can move on to sketch the characteristic features of a contemporary profile of natural law which represents the dominant tendency of a significant number of contemporary Catholic theologians.

## Contemporary Profile of Natural Law

While no totally systematic treatment of a revised theory of natural law has yet been made, at least certain key features which would make up the profile of such a theory have emerged. Timothy E. O'Connell has outlined them well as real, experiential, historical, and proportional.[22] I will summarize his presentation here and add the component of "personal" which, though implicit and running through all his other features, he does not identify specifically.

### Real

Natural law asserts that morality is based on reality. Realism stands, on the one hand, in opposition to legal positivism which makes something right merely because it is commanded. On the other hand, realism stands against a morality based on personal whim whereby one can arbitrarily decide what is right and wrong. The dimension of realism in a natural law theory means that the moral life, ultimately, is not merely a matter of obedience to positive law, nor is it a matter of doing whatever you want. The moral life is a matter of doing the good. The moral person and the moral community must discover what is morally good by critically reflecting on the total complexity of human reality in all its relationships. The more we discover what it means to be human the more we may have to revise our previously accepted conclusions in morality. Our views of what is moral may change as our knowledge of what it means to be authentically human develops. This is the fundamental direction of a contemporary natural law approach to morality. A moral position based on natural law, then, would be an expression of what the moral community discovers in its experience to be most contributing to the full actualization of human potential to attain human wholeness.[23]

## Experiential

If morality is based on realilty, we come to know morality through experience. The experience of what helps or hinders human well-being precedes and directs the course of a moral argument. For example, we see what lying does to people before we put together arguments about what makes lying wrong. This suggests an inductive method for moral theology and an appeal to empirical evidence in our process of deriving moral norms and carrying on moral evaluations.[24] We discover moral value through our experience of living in relationship with self, others, God, and the world. A moral position of the community ought to reflect its collective experience of what it means to live this relational life. The inherited formulations of a moral position are tested by continued experiences of what builds up and promotes the dignity of human life. All this means that our moral theology must pay close attention to human experience, past and present, in telling us what it means to be human.

## Consequential

Closely related to the experiential is the consequential. With the feature of "consequential" we are entering an arena of much controversy, especially because "consequences" are often intrepreted too narrowly to mean the short-run, immediate consequences.[25] Consequences are an important part of moral meaning, but consequences *alone* do not tell us what is right or wrong. The totality of moral reality includes more than consequences. Yet consequences are important if we are going to pay attention to the accumulation of human experience. The moral community's ongoing experience of what helps and hinders the well-being of human life gives rise to a moral position. These positions are retained within the community as a way of passing on to the next generation the accumulated wisdom of the moral community's experience of moral value.[26]

## Historical

One of the most frequent criticisms made of traditional natural law theory, especially of the order of nature strain of interpretation, is that it fails to account for the possibility of change and development. Its static view of the moral order produced universal and immutable positions. In contrast, the historically conscious worldview of contemporary theology has as a central characteristic the reality of change and development. Contemporary theology asks whether we can continue to presume that moral conclusions drawn on the basis of historically conditioned experience and a limited perspective can be equally valid for all times, places, and peoples. Whereas traditional moral theology grounded natural law norms in the abstract, ahistorical, metaphysical nature of the human person which it held to be unchanging through the ages, contemporary natural law theory grounds its position in the human person concretely realized in various stages and situations of history. But nothing is more damaging to natural law than to absolutize what is, in fact, relative to history and to culture. Contemporary theology recognizes that it cannot ignore the unfinished, evolutionary character of human nature and the human world. Historical changes cannot be dismissed as accidental to what it means to be human. The evidence of experience and the verification by data of the historical sciences are too strong to support such a position.

The influence of historical consciousness on morality today is great. Moral teaching today must be able to take into account our fundamental capacity for change and development. What has built up human well-being in the past may, or may not, continue to do so in the present or future.[27] This historical component of natural law leaves room for change and development. A moral position developed from this approach will reflect the tentativeness of historical consciousness and the provisional character of moral knowledge.[28]

## Proportional

O'Connell's last component is introduced to help us answer the practical moral question, "What ought we to do?" At the most fundamental level, we ought to do what is genuinely good, what is most loving, what truly contributes to the well-being of persons and community. Yet we know that we are limited in so many ways—such as our personal capacities and skills, our time, and our freedom. The good we do comes mixed with some bad. Our moral efforts are directed toward trying to achieve the greatest proportion of good to evil. The component of proportionality in natural law tells us that we are doing the morally right thing when we achieve the greatest possible proportion of good over evil.[29] This, in fact, gets to the heart of the Christian virtue of prudence as it comes to us through St. Thomas (I–II, q. 61, a. 2). It tells us that moral persons must be able to guide us in our prudential judgments, i.e., in our judgments of proportionality.

## Personal

*Gaudium et Spes* (1965) is a landmark document for the shift from "nature" to "person" in an official Church document.[30] This historically conscious, empirically oriented, personally focused document of the Second Vatican Council introduced new considerations into natural law by the attention it calls not to human nature as such, but to the human person. Part I of that document lays the groundwork for this shift, and Part II addresses specific problems in light of a personalistic perspective. We have already explored the implications of the shift from nature to person under the analysis of Louis Janssens' version of the personalistic criterion of "the human person adequately considered." Again in brief summary, they are: (1) to be a moral subject, i.e., to act with knowledge and in freedom; (2) to be an embodied subject; (3) to be an historical subject with continuing new possibilities; (4) to be an embodied subject who is part of the material world; (5) to be related to others; (6) to be in a social group with structures and institutions worthy of persons; (7) to be called to know and worship God; (8) to be unique yet fundamentally equal (cf. Chapter 5).

A person-based morality avoids the fragmenting of human nature into distinct faculties each having its own inherent purpose and morality independently of other aspects of the person and of the totality of the person's relationships. The shift from "nature" to "person" acknowledges not only what all persons have in common, but also their differences as unique individuals with a distinct origin, history, cultural environment, and personal vocation from God. The focus on the person in natural law theory can move us closer to realizing that our vocation as persons is to image the divine community of persons.

These in brief are the salient features of a contemporary profile of natural law. It is rooted in the order of reason strain of the natural law tradition, and it is consistent with the historically conscious worldview of contemporary theology. This approach to natural law calls for an inductive method of moral argument which takes historical human experience seriously. It is sensitive to the ambiguity of moral experience and to the limitations of formulating absolute, universal, concrete moral norms. The use of natural law in Catholic morality today is becoming more open to the great complexity and ambiguity of human, personal reality. Its conclusions, while as accurate as the evidence will allow, are accurate enough to be reliable but must necessarily be tentative and open to revision.

With this overview of the tradition and use of natural law in Catholic moral theology, we are ready to explore in the following chapters the particular applications of natural law in the form of human, positive law, and moral norms.

## Notes

1. For a comparison of the natural law approaches in sexual and social ethical documents, see Christopher Mooney, "Natural Law: A Case Study," in *Public Virtue: Law and the Social Character of Religion* (Notre Dame: University of Notre Dame Press, 1986), pp. 140–150. See also Charles E. Curran, "Catholic Social and Sexual Teaching: A Methodological Comparison," *Theology Today* 44 (January 1988): 425–440.

2. Unless otherwise indicated, all excerpts from official ecclesiastical documents in this section are taken from the handy resource book, *Official Catholic Teachings: Love and Sexuality*, ed. Odile M. Liebard (Wilmington, N.C.: McGrath Publishing Company, 1978). This quote is on p. 41.

3. *Ibid.*, p. 102.

4. *Ibid.*, pp. 336–337.

5. *Ibid.*, p. 339.

6. *Ibid.*, p. 436.

7. Congregation for the Doctrine of the Faith, "Instruction on Respect for Human Life in its Origins and on the Dignity of Procreation," St. Paul Editions (Boston: Daughters of St. Paul, 1987), pp. 8–9.

8. *Ibid.*, p. 31.

9. "The Man of Today and Religion," *Theological Investigations*, Vol. 6, translated by Karl-H. and Boniface Kruger (New York: Seabury Press, 1974), p. 8.

10. See, for example, the excellent article by Edward A. Malloy, "Natural Law Theory and Catholic Moral Theology," *American Ecclesiastical Review* 169 (September 1975): 456–469, especially pp. 457–461.

11. Dupre, *Contraception and Catholics: A New Appraisal* (Baltimore: Helicon Press, 1964), pp. 43–44.

12. See Curran's "Absolute Norms in Moral Theology," *Norm and Context in Christian Ethics*, edited by Gene Outka and Paul Ramsey (New York: Charles Scribner's Sons, 1968), pp. 139–173; also "Absolute Norms and Medical Ethics," in Curran's edited collection *Absolutes in Moral Theology?* (Washington: Corpus Books, 1968), pp. 108–153; and his "Natural Law," in *Directions*, pp. 119–172.

13. Summaries of trends in natural law thinking can be found in Richard A. McCormick, "Moral Notes," *Theological Studies* 28 (December 1967): 760–769; also, George M. Regan, *New Trends in Moral Theology* (New York: Newman Press, 1971) pp. 115–144. For a Protestant view of trends in Catholic natural law thinking, see James M. Gustafson, *Protestant and Roman Catholic Ethics: Prospects for Rapprochement* (Chicago: University of Chicago Press, 1978), pp. 80–94. For some creative articles on natural law, see those by Curran in the note above; also Bernard Häring, "Dynamism and Continuity in a Personalistic Approach to Natural Law," *Norm and Context*, Outka and Ramsey, eds., pp. 199–218; Michael B. Crowe, "Natural Law Theory Today," *The Future of Ethics and Moral Theology*, Richard A. McCormick, *et al.* (Chicago: Argus Communications Co., 1968), pp. 78–105.

14. This is a point clearly made by Josef Fuchs; see especially "Human, Humanist and Christian Morality," *Human Values and Christian Morality* (London: Gill and Macmillan Ltd., 1970), pp. 140–147, especially at p. 143.

15. For a study of natural law in the social encyclicals, see Charles E. Curran, "Dialogue with Social Ethics: Roman Catholic Ethics—Past, Present, Future," *Catholic Moral Theology in Dialogue* (Notre Dame: Fides Publishers, 1972), pp. 111–149.

16. Unless otherwise indicated, the excerpts from ecclesiastical documents on social ethics are taken from the convenient resource, *Official Church Teaching: Social Justice*, ed. Vincent P. Mainelli (Wilmington, N.C.: McGrath Publishing Co., 1978). For this first excerpt, see p. 64. For an interpretation of "imprinted in man's heart" that follows the order of reason approach to natural law, see Fuchs, "Human, Humanist and Christian Morality," *Human Values*, pp. 144–147.

17. Mainelli, ed., *Social Justice*, p. 210.

18. *Ibid.*, p. 255. This excerpt also shows the elements of a moral method for reflecting on a social issue: namely, situational analysis, religious convictions, and moral norms. Not included is a consideration of the "agent," which is often hard to identify in a social issue.

19. Such a comparison is astutely made by Charles E. Curran in "Catholic Social and Sexual Teaching: A Methodological Comparison," *Theology Today* 44 (January 1988): 425-440.

20. *The Challenge of Peace* (Washington: USCC, 1983), paragraphs 10–12, pp. 4–5. The bishops make a similar claim in their letter, *Economic Justice for All* (1986), paragraphs 20–22.

21. What follows is a summary of the key themes of the section "Basic Catholic Principles" concerning moral objectivity in Philip S. Keane, "The Objective Moral Order: Reflections on Recent Research," *Theological Studies* 43 (June 1982): 260–262.

22. O'Connell, *Principles for a Catholic Morality* (New York: Seabury Press, 1978), pp. 144–154.

23. Daniel C. Maguire confirms "realism" in his approach to morality. See *The Moral Choice* (Garden City: Doubleday & Co., 1978), p. 220.

24. This has been a consistent theme of John G. Milhaven. See his "Toward an Epistemology of Ethics," *Theological Studies* 27 (June 1966): 228–241; also, "Objective Moral Evaluation of Consequences," *Theological Studies* 32 (September 1971): 407–430; and "The Voice of Lay Experience in Christian Ethics," *CTSA Proceedings* 33 (1978): 35–53. See also Maguire, *The Moral Choice*, pp. 221–222. Robert H. Springer is another Catholic theologian who has appealed to the empirical grounding for morality in his "Conscience, Behavioral Science and Absolutes," in Charles E. Curran, ed., *Absolutes in Moral Theology?* pp. 19–56. Charles E. Curran has written a valuable article identifying some of the difficulties involved in moral theology's efforts to dialogue with empirical science. See his essay "Dialogue with Science: Scientific Data, Scientific Possibilities and the Moral Judgment," *Catholic Moral Theology in Dialogue*, pp. 65–110.

25. Richard A. McCormick, "Moral Notes," *Theological Studies* 36 (March 1975): 93–100, reviews pertinent literature on the interpretation of "consequences."

26. The issue of how to regard consequences is receiving a great deal of attention in the moral literature. In addition to McCormick's "Notes" above, see the balanced treatment of Maguire, *The Moral Choice*, pp. 150–170. For two essays negatively critical of consequences, see John R. Connery, "Morality of Consequences: A Critical Appraisal," *Readings in Moral Theology No. 1: Moral Norms and Catholic Tradition*, edited by Charles E. Curran and Richard A. McCormick (Ramsey: Paulist Press, 1979), pp. 244–266. In the same collection, see also Paul M. Quay, "Morality by Calculation of Values," pp. 267–293.

27. John Noonan's work, *Contraception* (Cambridge: Harvard University Press, 1965), shows how historical factors influence the weight given to competing values in different historical periods. Natural law theory that is historically conscious will be cautious about issuing single, unambiguous answers for all times.

28. This has been a consistent theme of Charles E. Curran in his analysis of natural law. See for example his "Natural Law" in *Directions in Fundamental Moral Theology* (Notre Dame: University of Notre Dame Press, 1985), pp. 119–172.

29. The idea of proportionality has been receiving a great deal of attention in recent years. For some seminal works on this notion in the collection edited by Curran and McCormick, *Readings in Moral Theology No. 1*, see Peter Knauer, "The Hermeneutic Function of the Principle of Double Effect," pp.

1–39; Louis Janssens, "Ontic Evil and Moral Evil," pp. 40–93; Richard A. McCormick, "Reflections on the Literature," pp. 294–340. Also see the collection of essays responding to Richard A. McCormick's major contribution to this discussion, *Ambiguity in Moral Choice*, which is the first chapter in the collection, *Doing Evil to Achieve Good*, edited by Richard A. McCormick and Paul Ramsey (Chicago: Loyola University Press, 1978).

30. David F. Kelly has traced the methodological development of Catholic teaching on medical ethics in America from natural law physicalism (1900–1940) to empirical personalism (1965 and beyond). "Empirical personalism" is a shorthand formula for the contemporary understanding of natural law. Kelly shows it emerges with the impetus of the shift made at the Second Vatican Council. See his *The Emergence of Roman Catholic Medical Ethics in North America* (New York: Edwin Mellen Press, 1979), pp. 416–436 and 449–454.

# 17  Law and Obedience

*I*n the last chapter we looked at a general overview of the tradition of natural law and its application in contemporary theology. Now we are ready to sketch particular applications of natural law in the forms of positive law (ecclesiastical and civil) and moral norms. This chapter looks briefly at some of the issues pertaining to positive law—a rule of behavior enacted by lawful authority for a particular community. The following three chapters will treat at greater length the issues pertaining to moral norms, a center of great controversy in moral theology since the Second Vatican Council.

This chapter focuses on some of the elements common to civil laws and ecclesiastical laws (such as canon law and liturgical rubrics). Though these kinds of laws share much in common, they are not the same in every way. For example, ecclesiastical laws try to give expression to the inner reality of the church as a community of love empowered by the Spirit. Civil law makes no such claim. Ecclesiastical law tries to create an order and climate within the ecclesial community which expresses the presence and action of the Spirit while enabling everyone to respond to his or her unique call of the Spirit. Civil law is oriented toward protecting the freedom of all and upholding public order so that everyone may contribute to the common good. Whether the forum is the state or the church, however, the Christian's primary law remains "the law of the Spirit, which brings us life in union with Christ Jesus" (Rom 8:2). All other laws remain subordinate to that.

Today we need an appreciation of law and its place in the moral life combined with a critical awareness of the limitations of law. Legalistic mentalities which equate moral goodness with obeying the letter of the law are still with us. For example, confession of sins is often made in light of the disciplinary laws of the church rather than the gospel call to love, justice, and forgiveness. Legalism stifles creativity, initiative, and conversion. Where legalism abounds, moral minimalism and spiritual laziness are not far behind. Asking "How far can I go?" for example reflects such a posture. It looks for a rule to define the scope of personal responsibility rather than exercising moral muscle to engage in moral discernment.

Similarly, imposing obedience to disciplinary laws (such as eucharistic and Lenten fasts or Sunday Mass attendance) "under the pain of mortal sin" abuses moral and legal authority and distorts the notions of sin and obedience as well as the purpose of law in the Christian life. As we have seen, sin makes sense in the context of covenant where it refers primarily to a break in the relationship of love for God, not to a breaking of the law. Such a theological understanding of sin does not support treating sin as a penalty attached to actions proscribed by law or as a threat to ensure obedience of the law. Bernard Häring has assessed such a practice and has offered his personal opinion of it:

> In a critical age, the laws of the Church become more effective through convincing arguments that show their necessity or genuine utility rather than through sanction. Not only can obligation under sin, and especially under pain of mortal sin, arise only from the urgency and importance of the law itself and never from the mere will of the legislator, but this urgency and relevance must be made clear not so much by sanction as by insight. Exaggerated sanctions and threats of punishment appeal merely to the superego and pervert its dynamics.

> In my opinion, the Church should never impose any man-made law under threat of mortal sin, which means threat of eternal condemnation. The reason is that I cannot think of any positive disposition that is neither part of the Gospel nor of natural law yet could be so important as to be proportionate to the threat of eternal punishment.[1]

At this time in our history, we are still adjusting our mentality and our actions after a long period in our history wherein we practically equated the fullness of the Christian moral and spiritual life with observing the law. This chapter hopes to point out the prevailing understandings of law and obedience which are helping the Catholic community make this adjustment.

## The Nature of Positive Law

### The Purpose of Law

No society can survive without some organization. The social dimension of being human is the very reason for having laws, and it is the proper context for understanding them. Therefore, laws well formulated will always have a place in any human community. They function primarily in two interrelated ways: to identify basic values and to safeguard the public order.

First of all, laws spring from the experience of value.[2] Legalism forgets that. Legalism wants to make an end of the law rather than to see the law as pointing to a value. Laws identify certain values and challenge us to promote them. Laws protect values by commanding us to pursue certain ones and by forbidding us to jeopardize others. Because we value freedom or bodily health, for example, we enact and accept laws to protect these values. So we have laws which support our freedom to speak and to assemble, and we have laws which prohibit smoking in certain areas or require the use of seat belts while driving. In approaching laws, then, we ought to understand and appropriate the values which the laws are trying to protect and promote. Values are primary; laws are secondary.

As expressions of the experience of values, laws are products of the accumulative wisdom of the community's experience of what helps or hinders life together. As such, laws also function to open us to the wisdom of the ages. Since laws serve as repositories of moral wisdom, we ought to approach them as reliable guides with the presumption in their favor. In this way laws function like a road map helping us to find our way through the often confusing and conflicting pathways of life. Moreover, because of our sinfulness, individual and social, we need laws to protect us from our sinful inclinations and to challenge us to foster the good of all.

Yet laws by themselves never satisfy the full measure of moral responsibility. While laws do identify basic values and point to corresponding beneficial courses of action, laws set the lower limits of protecting values. Each person must choose and act in light of the laws to realize the fullness of the values at stake. Without laws each person would have to discover the best course of action in every instance on his or her own. But no one alone has the energy, capacity, or vantage point for such a task. We need to rely on the wisdom and perspective of other people around us as well as those who have gone before us. With laws based on the wisdom of a broader experience of value, everyone is freed from the necessity of deciding at every step what is the best thing to do. By having laws, therefore, everyone is freer to go about the business of living together in an orderly way.

The second function of laws based on the accumulative experience of value is to safeguard the public order by regulating relationships within the community, and by protecting basic rights and freedoms. Laws do this not by directing every facet of life within community, but by providing the framework within which individuals and institutions can exercise their freedom. According to John Courtney Murray, the chief architect of the *Declaration on Religious Freedom* of the Second Vatican Council, the public order protected by law includes an order of peace to enable individuals to live in harmony, an order of public morality which is the minimum moral consensus necessary to enable people to live together, and an order of justice to secure what is due to the people, particularly their freedom.[3]

In what may be considered the most significant statement of the principle of a "free society," the *Declaration* circumscribes the role of law and emphasizes human freedom in this statement:

> For the rest, the usages of society are to be the usages of freedom in their full range. These require that the freedom of human beings be respected as far as possible and curtailed only when and insofar as necessary. (n. 7)

This official position of the church, which maintains that protecting the freedom of individuals is the political means by which to attain social goals, has significant implications for understanding the relationship of law and morality.

## Law and Morality

The order of law and the order of morality are frequently confused. The mentality which is quick to assert "There ought to be a law!" wants whatever is good to be enforced by law and whatever is evil to be prohibited by law. However, such a mentality too easily confuses the legal and the moral orders so that whatever is not against the law is thought to be morally acceptable. But the moral order and the legal order do not completely coincide. John Courtney Murray distinguishes them this way:

> The moral law governs the entire order of human conduct, personal and social; it extends even to motivations and interior acts. Law, on the other hand, looks only to the public order of human society; it touches only external acts, and regards only values that are formally social.[4]

Murray's distinction shows the limited scope to the law and its minimal moral aspirations. The law ought to enforce only what is minimally acceptable and necessary.

Similarly, Peter Chirico has argued convincingly on the basis of the distinction between private moral values (what pertains to personal growth) and public moral values (what benefits society as a whole) that the latter is the proper realm of legislation.[5] Therefore, to say "the state ought not to legislate morality" is false. The state is legislating morality all the time when it comes to public moral values. Since the purpose of law is to promote public order, the state can and does use law to enforce moral standards which affect the public order. For example, homicide, rape, and theft are immoral actions which also bear legal sanction. But doing bodily harm to oneself or lying to a friend in a private conversation does not carry legal sanction. The difference is that the former actions undermine the public order whereas the latter do not.

Granting the distinction between the moral order and the legal order, how ought they to be related? Roman Catholic thought supports two approaches, both of which appear in official documents of the magisterium. Charles Curran has carefully delineated the structure of each.[6] In brief, his analysis runs as follows.

One approach is based on the theory that positive law is derived directly from natural law. Since the natural law defines the moral order which is prior to the legal order and superior to it, political authority must look to the natural law in forming its laws. The laws of the state ought to direct human beings to do what nature dictates.

This approach is taken in the 1974 *Declaration on Abortion* from the Congregation for the Doctrine of the Faith: positive law "cannot act contrary to a law which is deeper and more majestic than any human law: the natural law. . ." (n. 21). Since this approach maintains that the law is to reflect what nature demands, it supports translating a moral teaching into a matter of law. The practical consequence is that a Christian can never "conform" to a law which supports abortion, "campaign in favor of such a law, or vote for it" (n. 22).

The second approach finds its guiding criterion on the relation of law and morality in the statement quoted above from Paragraph 7 of the *Declaration on Religious Freedom*. The context of this statement is the freedom of personal conscience and the freedom of individuals within a limited form of constitutional government. According to Curran's analysis of this view, morality can be translated into law only if four criteria are met. The first is that law ought to protect the freedom of individuals as far as possible. Second, the law ought to interfere in this freedom only when public order requires it. Third, the law must be equitable and enforceable. The fourth criterion is that the law must satisfy the prudential judgment of feasibility which depends on a broad consensus about the moral character of an action. The prudential aspect of this criterion argues against any necessary translation of a moral position into a legal one.[7]

This second approach has also been employed in official magisterial documents, but with differing conclusions. On the one hand, the 1987 *Instruction on Bioethics* uses Paragraph #7 of the *Declaration on Religious Freedom* as its point of departure in its section on morality and law. While it acknowledges that law "must sometimes tolerate, for the sake of public order, things which it cannot forbid without a greater evil resulting,"[8] nevertheless it advocates translating into law its moral teaching on the rights which pertain to human nature. As such it comes to the same conclusion about laws regulating the use of reproductive technology as the *Declaration on Abortion* does about laws pertaining to abortion.

On the other hand, the American bishops write from this perspective by acknowledging that the application of their moral principles to public policies regarding nuclear war and the economy involve different prudential judgments which can be interpreted differently by people of good will. While asking that their moral judgments be given serious attention and consideration by Catholics, the bishops realize that these judgments applied to specific cases are not binding in conscience and do not lead to necessary translations into law. For example, in *Economic Justice for All* we read:

> We are aware that the movement from principle to policy is complex and difficult and that although moral values are essential in determining public policies, they do not dictate specific solutions. (n. 134)

Where does all this leave us? We are left with two different, officially endorsed approaches to the relationship of morality and law. But we need not reduce them to an either/or alternative. The approach which looks for civil law to back up moral teaching challenges the Catholic community to work to bring civil law in line with Catholic morality. The other approach, which accepts a limited role for law in a pluralistic society, challenges the Catholic community to create a climate through example, education, and service where Roman Catholic moral values will be effectively mediated to the community. While both approaches leave room for Catholic participation in public debate, they support different strategies and goals for such participation. With both approaches being part of Catholic practice, we need to help one another in deciding which of our moral convictions we should try to legislate for the sake of public order, and which we should try to advance by persuasion but not necessarily by legislation. Disagreement on this score will inevitably arise. But in disagreement and in cooperation we can help each other contribute to what befits human well-being.

## The Nature of Obedience

### Binding Power of Law

However one might articulate the relationship of law and morality, everyone must deal with laws once promulgated. What is the binding power of law?

The Roman Catholic moral traditon has supported a common under-standing of positive law, but has approached the binding power of law from two different perspectives: the rationalist and the voluntarist. The common understanding of law is defined by St. Thomas as: "an ordinance of reason promulgated by competent authority for the sake of the common good" (I–II, q. 90. a. 4).

For the rationalist, something is commanded because it is good. The rationalist perspective, commonly identified with Thomas Aquinas, has inter-preted strictly the elements pertaining to law ("reason" and "common good"), whereas it has interpreted broadly the elements pertaining to the lawgiver ("promulgated" and "competent authority"). As an ordinance of reason, posi-tive laws are specific expressions of natural law and participate in eternal law. This makes God the ultimate source of obligation, the one to whom we are finally obedient. Good law ought to enable one to respond to the call of God in the concrete situation. The task of the competent authority is to bring laws in line with the good which public order demands, and to provide valid reasons for them. The binding power of laws for the rational-ist is proportionate to the persuasiveness of the reasons which ground them in natural law. A practical implication of this view is that laws must be forsaken which are unreasonable and do not serve the good. Anyone who is willing and able to make a critical assessment of the reasonableness of the law in serving the good can make this judgment. With reason as the basic criterion for good law, blind obedience to the lawgiver has no place in the rationalist's perspective.

However, for the voluntarist, something is good because it is com-manded. The voluntarist's perspective, commonly identified with Francis Suarez (d. 1617), interprets strictly the two elements, "promulgated" and "competent authority," which pertain to the legislator in the definition of law. Since the will of the legislator determines what is good, blind obedience is in order for those subject to authority.[9]. By focusing on the one who has authority to determine what is good, voluntarism gives all the power to the legislator and none to the individual. It presumes that by birth, election, or appointment such a person is truly capable of prescribing the conduct which will safeguard public order.

These few characteristics of voluntarism sound familiar to those who lived in religious communities prior to the Second Vatican Council. Since then, religious communities have been revising their structures of gover-nance. They are making a transition from a predominantly voluntaristic form of government which was based on the commands and prohibitions coming from the absolute will of the superior to rationalistic forms of government which are based on respecting human potentiality and on having rational discussions through dialogue with the community to attain consensus.

## The Virtue of Epikeia

Both the rationalistic and the voluntaristic perspectives have influenced an understanding of the limitations of law. Laws are limited expressions of value. Since laws are based on what public order demands, they are inevitably historically conditioned and will lag behind the developments of the community's life. Since a limited formulation of value cannot possibly foresee all possible combinations of circumstances which affect public order, the law will not serve the demands of justice in every particular instance. The Roman Catholic tradition of law has dealt with the inherent limitation of laws in various ways. For example, it has recognized certain conditions under which laws cease to bind, such as invincible ignorance, physical impossibility, grave inconvenience, and dispensations, to name a few. The Catholic tradition has also advocated one other built-in safeguard for properly applying a limited law to a changing human reality. It is called *epikeia*. It is a part of the Catholic tradition on law which we could do well to retrieve in our day when contemporary theology is putting such a stress on individual responsibility.

The voluntarist's interpretation of epikeia requires recourse to the actual or presumed will of the legislator. As such, it has many difficulties. It is pessimistic about the individual's ability to make a personal decision. In this way, it denies a basic component of human dignity. Moreover, it makes moral duty extrinsic to the situation at hand by locating it in the will of the legislator. What is right or wrong depends on the determination of the one with authority. According to such a view, we have no basis for moral obligation apart from what the one with authority determines it to be. Moral goodness becomes equivalent to blind obedience. Voluntarism, in short, prepares fertile ground for tyranny.

Difficulties such as these make the voluntaristic interpretation of epikeia inadequate and dangerous. Moreover, it is an obsolete view since laws today (civil laws, at least) are not made by one single person as the legislator. Josef Fuchs advocates that we pay more attention to the spirit of the law and not to the will of the legislator.[10] Doing so situates us squarely within a rationalistic perspective.

The rationalistic perspective of St. Thomas treats epikeia as an expression of justice (II–II q. 120, a. 2). According to Josef Fuchs, situating epikeia within justice shows that it is not a dispensation from the law but that it is the correct application of an inherently limited law oriented toward serving the public good.[11] Timothy O'Connell provides a definition of epikeia which adequately captures the Thomistic sense:

Epikeia is the virtue (power, skill, habit) by which Christian persons discern the inner meaning of any human law so as to intelligently obey it in the majority of cases and to reasonably violate it in the properly exceptional case.[12]

Exercising the virtue of epikeia is morally superior to the mere observance of the letter of the law. It is realistic about the inability of law both to cover every contingency and to define the full measure of moral responsibility. Epikeia enables each person to respond to the demands of the Spirit by discerning the inner meaning, or spirit, of the law before making the final decision in a concrete situation.

The rationalistic perspective separates the law from the legislator. The authority of the law lies in its reasonableness to serve the public order, not in the fact that it has been promulgated by one with authority. The force of law lies not in the power of its legislator, but in the law being able to achieve its end of safeguarding public order. In this way, one does not have to turn to the legislator for an interpretation in order to apply the law rightly. Rather, the individual can interpret the law on the basis of its reasonableness for achieving the value which it is trying to protect.

Charles Curran's interpretation of epikeia in St. Thomas affirms that St. Thomas himself did require recourse to the legislator in doubtful cases. However, the Thomistic notion of epikeia does not strictly require this. Curran maintains that since today's society is not structured in the hierarchical fashion which St. Thomas knew, we do not need to have recourse to the will of the legislator to make a proper use of epikeia. The situation today depends much more on the creative freedom and responsibility of individuals and institutions within society to safeguard the public order. For this reason, Curran urges that an appropriate application of epikeia rests with the individual who must determine whether the law will best safeguard the public order in this instance.[13] Such a position is optimistic about the human person's ability to choose the good. The danger of such a position is that it can lead to the disorder of anarchy.

However, Curran's analysis of epikeia in St. Thomas shows that, while the ultimate responsibility for interpreting the law lies with the individual, epikeia does not lead to anarchy when properly exercised. First, as an expression of justice, epikeia is not a license to follow personal whims. Second, epikeia is connected to prudence. Since prudence is an art which does not operate with absolute certainty, a certain element of risk remains. Third, epikeia does not try to escape from the law but tries to seek the higher law of the Spirit which calls for careful discernment to choose rightly. Fourth, epikeia must always be informed by *agape*, the kind of love which is willing to make personal sacrifices for the good of others. Curran believes that these four aspects of the proper exercise of epikeia will lessen its abuse. Yet even abuses do not negate the proper use of epikeia as a virtue enhancing freedom and responsibility.[14]

## Civil Disobedience

The rationalistic perspective on law in the Catholic tradition, together with its long-standing endorsement of epikeia as a way of dealing with the limitations of law, attests that blind obedience to law is not a virtue. Laws, while necessary for civil order, must be evaluated in relation to their reasonableness for attaining their end of protecting public order, and lawmakers must be assessed in light of their due competence to use their authority to serve the community, not to dominate it. For the sake of civil order and with good faith in the political processes which produce laws, we ought to approach laws and the human authorities responsible for interpreting them with the presumption in their favor. Our first response ought to be to want to cooperate. Sometimes, however, this presumption gives way to the weight of new evidence. Some laws are not serving justice; some authorities are not servants, but tyrants. In such instances, responsible participation in the community requires criticism and the courageous refusal to cooperate. When this happens we cross the line into civil (or ecclesiastical) disobedience.

The grounds for civil disobedience lie in the fundamental moral obligation of natural law: to seek and to do the good and to avoid evil. If a law does not serve the good, then we are morally obliged (not just permitted) to violate the law. Moreover, as we saw above in the Thomistic tradition, the law is separate from the lawgiver so that we live with the law, not because it is commanded, but only insofar as it serves public order. Citizens are to judge for themselves whether this is the case. The "burden" of cooperating with the law and human authority or of acting with civil disobedience ultimately falls on the person who claims that the law is justifiable or not.

Morally responsible civil disobedience, however, must not be confused with mere law-breaking activity. Briefly put, the difference is that civil disobedience is done publicly for the purpose of reforming the law and promoting public order. Mere law-breaking activity is not. Daniel Stevick has summarized the characteristics of civil disobedience in his set of criteria necessary to justify an act of law-breaking as civil disobedience.[15] We only need to review them here to get a fuller picture of what is at stake in an act of civil disobedience.

### 1. Counts the Cost
A civil disobedient pursues a law-breaking activity fully aware and ready to assume the penalty which accompanies it. The civil disobedient must be

convinced that the harm brought to oneself is less than the harm being perpetrated by following the law. The willingness to accept the penalty for breaking the law is a strong statement against the wrong being protested and the sort of witness which may cause others to rethink their position on the issue being brought to public attention.

### 2. Affirms the Law

While civil disobedience is clearly law-breaking activity, it does not disregard the law but is done in the name of the law. It is oriented toward reforming the law in order to protect the public order.

### 3. Is a Last Resort

Civil disobedience comes only after other ways of bringing the wrong to public attention have been tried and found ineffective. Some of these other means are petitions, boycotts, legislative activity, letter-writing campaigns, and the like. Since publicly violating the law can be so threatening to the order of the community, the civil disobedient would not choose it when the same objective can be achieved by less disruptive means.

### 4. Identifies a Specific Aim

Civil disobedience is not just a negative reaction to the established order, but has some cause or principle in mind. Civil disobedience grows out of an analysis of some specific wrong and acts in a way to make clear what the wrong is.

### 5. Is Concerned for the Means

The most difficult aspect of civil disobedience is deciding the appropriate means. The Christian bias is in favor of non-violence. Since violent means are so destructive and so difficult to control, they can too easily go beyond the intended objectives and undermine the values being upheld.

### 6. Respects the Structures of the Community

Civil disobedience does not seek to overthrow the government. It is not revolution. It works within the structures in order to reform them. Accepting the appropriate penalty for violating the law is an example of respecting the structures of the community.

### 7. Contributes Toward Reordering the Community

The civil disobedient does not end his or her relationship to the community once the penalty is paid. Rather, now that a serious wrong has been brought to the attention of the community, the civil disobedient must work to heal the disruption in the community and help to create the structures which will correct the wrong.

At times, responsible citizenship calls for responsible civil disobedience. Civil disobedience is morally responsible when it is done as a last resort and in hope that a better future can be had through non-violent protest.

From a theological point of view, civil disobedience participates in the "already but not yet" tension of the reign of God. The "not yet" fullness of the reign of God relativizes everything existing at the present time and stands in criticism of our tendency to absolutize historically conditioned structures of society. Such a false conservatism easily arises out of a strict law-and-order mentality and fails to notice the sinfulness existing in social structures. It wants to identify the existing order as the perfect reflection of the reign of God.

The Christian living with hope in the coming fullness of God's reign can never be satisfied with the present order. Rather, the hopeful Christian must realize not only personal sinfulness and the need for ongoing conversion, but also social sinfulness and the need for changes in social structures as well. In light of the pull into the future of the reign of God, working to improve social structures is an imperative for Christians. Responsible civil disobedience reminds us that the fullness of the reign of God has not yet arrived and will not come easily or quickly. Moreover, the hope for the Christian living in an imperfect world with ongoing renewal lies not in accomplishments already achieved, as important as these are, but ultimately in the promise God has made through Jesus in the resurrection. The paschal mystery of Jesus is the paradigm not only of personal growth in the Christian life but also of social progress. It reminds the Christian civil disobedient that only through suffering and death comes the fullness of life.

## The Virtue of Obedience

The theological perspective on civil disobedience brings us to the heart of obedience as a virtue for social life. Faith informs reason's reflection on law most significantly in the area of obedience. Christian faith tells us that God alone, as the author and sustainer of life, sets the direction of our freedom and our love. Moreover, it tells us that all law is relative to the great commandment of the absolute call to love God with our whole heart, and to love our neighbor as we love ourselves.

Obedience is the virtue which enables us to direct our freedom and neighbor-love in ways which are responsive to what God requires and enables. The true object of obedience is not laws, human authorities, or social structures. The true object of obedience is God. No human word or institution can take the place of what God requires. To respond to any human agency as though it were equal to God is idolatry, not obedience. Obedience, in its deepest sense, involves the word of God and the human hearing of that word as a personal call.

The religious understanding of obedience as the wholehearted response to the word of God raises two critical issues. Sandra Schneiders has identified and analyzed them well in her treatment of obedience in religious life.[16] Her analysis serves us well here. She identifies mediation as the fundamental difficulty in understanding obedience in a religious context, and discernment as the fundamental challenge a believer has to face who wants to be obedient.

Mediation refers to the "in and through" approach to God. In the Judaeo-Christian tradition, the God who is with us (immanence) is also the God who is totally other (transcendence). When we accept the total otherness of God, we admit that we cannot know God immediately, but only in a mediated way. The theology of the "in and through" approach tells us that every human experience, if given a chance, can disclose God. The way of mediation begins with the presupposition of universal divine presence. We really have nothing to do with God's being there. We cannot induce it, conjure it, or create it. God's presence to us is always a gift of God's loving and free action. The question for us is not how to make God present. Our question is, "How can we allow God, who is already present to us, to enter our minds and hearts?"

To be obedient to God requires that we develop a sense of the presence of God and a loving union with God. This demands, above all, a disciplined life of prayer. If we were consciously united to God, we would be able to exercise our freedom and love in making our social judgments and choices out of this union with God. Nothing can quite substitute for a nurtured sensitivity to divine presence and to divine promptings.

However, few of us live out of such an intense, mystical communion with God. We rely on the ordinary ways in and through which God speaks to us. These are thoroughly human ways, such as persons, customs, structures. The church has formalized some ways of mediating what God requires as revealed in Jesus. One of these is its system of laws as interpreted by properly appointed officials. The great danger of so formalizing an instrument of mediation is to turn it into an idol. Rather than the mediator serving as the means through which God is present to us, the mediator becomes the vicar of God, an idol, the one who takes the place of God. When this happens, we have a hard time hearing God's word in and through human words.

As Sandra Schneiders clearly explains, our surest protection against such idolatry is our personal religious experience of God. Only this can test the authenticity of the mediation. But a personal religious experience of God requires a disciplined, mature life of prayer. For one who has no access to God through mature prayer, avoiding idolatry is hard. The weaker a person's personal experience of God, the more dependent he or she is on the human mediations of God. Legalism results. It appears unobtrusively in the disguise of obedience.[17] What looks like obedience to God is actually conformity to the law, but without any of the tension or the ambiguity which is inevitably part of human moral living. In the end a person's sense of living free and faithful in response to God gets lost. It is replaced with the sense of being confined by laws and oppressed by structures or human authorities designated to interpret the laws.

Obedience as a religious virtue, however, means that God is the one who has our ear. A human command places an absolute claim on the moral conscience only to the extent that it actualizes the call of the gospel, i.e., when it is the word of salvation. But relatively few commands in our lives are laden with such authority. As Sandra Schneiders points out, even though we listen to privileged mediators of God's word with special deference, none of us is thereby dispensed from personal discernment about whether and to what extent one is hearing the word of God in this instance.[18] Since obedience is directed only to God, the challenge of living in society is to determine which claims coming from the wide range of legitimate authorities over us can be integrated into our obedience to God. This is the challenge of discernment. We really cannot talk about being obedient in a virtuous way as a believer until we have done the necessary discerning which enables us to give a somewhat confident yet modest answer to the question, "What is God requiring and enabling me to be and to do?"

The process of discernment is the point of convergence of the moral and the spiritual life. Discernment pertains not only to the role of laws in the moral life, but also to our use of moral norms. For this reason, I will take up the issue of discernment after the treatment of moral norms. The treatment of discernment at the end of the book will serve as a synthesis of the entire range of issues and considerations which go into living the moral life in response to the presence and action of God in our lives.

## Notes

1. *Free and Faithful in Christ*, Vol. 1: *General Moral Theology* (New York: Seabury Press, 1978), p. 413. Charles E. Curran takes a similar position in "Church Law," *Directions in Fundamental Moral Theology* (Notre Dame: University of Notre Dame Press, 1985), pp. 202–205. See also Sean Fagan, *Has Sin Changed?* (Wilmington: Michael Glazier, Inc., 1977), pp. 33–37.

2. For a clear, succinct expression of the relation of law to value, see Fagan, *Has Sin Changed?* pp. 43–47.

3. Murray, *The Problem of Religious Freedom* (Westminster: Newman

Press, 1965), pp. 29–30. See also the unofficial footnote #20 of the *Declaration on Religious Freedom* in *The Documents of Vatican II*, ed. Walter M. Abbott (New York: Guild Press, 1966), p. 686.

4. Murray, *We Hold These Truths* (New York: Sheed and Ward, 1960), p. 166.

5. Chirico, "Moral Values and Political Responsibilities," *Chicago Studies* 24 (April 1985): 97–110.

6. Curran's most extensive treatment of these two approaches is in "Civil Law and Christian Morality: Abortion and the Churches," *Ongoing Revision* (Notre Dame: Fides Publishers, Inc., 1975), pp. 107–143; see especially 110–134.

7. In *ibid.* Curran treats these as three criteria by combining the last two into one criterion. He treats them as four criteria in "The Difference Between Personal Morality and Public Policy," *Toward an American Catholic Moral Theology* (Notre Dame: University of Notre Dame Press, 1987), p. 198.

8. *Instruction on Bioethics* (Boston: Daughters of St. Paul, 1987), p. 36.

9. For these characteristics of the rationalist and voluntarist perspectives on law, I am following the analysis of Charles E. Curran, "Church Law," in *Directions*, pp. 205–214; also Josef Fuchs, "Epikeia Applied to Natural Law?" in *Personal Responsibility and Christian Morality*, trans. by William Cleves and others (Washington: Georgetown University Press, 1983), pp. 185–199; and Timothy E. O'Connell, *Principles for a Catholic Morality* (New York: Seabury Press, 1978), pp. 184–195.

10. Fuchs, "Epikeia Applied to Natural Law?" *Personal Responsibility*, p. 194.

11. *Ibid.*, p. 187.

12. O'Connell, *Principles*, p. 190.

13. Curran, "Church Law," in *Directions*, p. 210.

14. *Ibid.*, pp. 211–212.

15. Stevick, *Civil Disobedience and the Christian* (New York: Seabury Press, 1969), pp. 102–113. For a clear, succinct treatment of civil disobedience with particular application to tax resistance, see Gerald D. Coleman, "Civil Disobedience: A Moral Critique," *Theological Studies* 46 (March 1985): 21–37.

16. Schneiders, "Religious Obedience: Journey from Law to Love," *New Wineskins: Re-Imagining Religious Life Today* (Mahwah: Paulist Press, 1986), pp. 137–167.

17. *Ibid.*, pp. 145–146.

18. *Ibid.*, pp. 147–148.

# 18  The Morality of
# Human Action

As the first chapter of three on moral norms, this chapter takes up the fundamental issue of the structure and the morality of human action, the object of specific material norms. The next chapter will consider the meaning, types, and functions of moral norms. The chapter following will take up the issue of moral norms in moral decision making and pastoral moral guidance.

## The Three-Font Principle

Traditional moral theology has used the three-font principle for determining the morality of human action. This principle still serves us well. It is based on an understanding of the relationship of the three aspects of moral action—intention, the act-in-itself, and the circumstances.[1]

The intention (*finis operantis*) is the internal part, or the formal element of the moral action. It is also called the "end," or that which we are after in doing what we do, i.e., the whole purpose of our action. The intention gives personal meaning to the action. The act-in-itself (*finis operis*), or the means-to-an-end, is the external part, or the material element of the moral action. This aspect of the moral action is so easily observed that it could be photographed.

According to the theory of St. Thomas, the act-in-itself cannot be accurately evaluated as moral or immoral apart from considering the intention of the person acting (ST I–II, q. 20, a. 3, ad. 1). Louis Janssens' analysis of this text of St. Thomas concludes:

> For this reason [St. Thomas] reacts sharply against those who are of the opinion that the material event of an act can be evaluated morally without consideration of the subject, of the inner act of the will or of the end. As he sees it, an exterior action considered as nothing but the material event (*secundum speciem naturae*) is an abstraction to

which a moral evaluation cannot be applied. This object-event becomes a concrete *human* act only insofar as it is directed toward an
end within the inner act of the will. Only this concrete totality has a
moral meaning.[2]

On these grounds, actions which have the same material features can have
different moral meaning depending on the intention which directs the action.
The moral quality of an action comes from the intention, specifically, the
agent's intention to be loving or not. For example, Janssens says, making a
donation can be morally good when the intention is to bring relief to a person in
need, but morally bad if intended to satisfy one's vanity and to win praise.[3]
Josef Fuchs holds the same position and illustrates it with this example:

> One may not say, therefore, that killing as a realization of a human
> evil may be morally good or morally bad; for killing as such, since it
> implies nothing about the intention of the agent, cannot purely as
> such constitute a human act. On the other hand, "killing because of
> avarice" and "killing in self-defense" do imply something regarding
> the intention of the agent; the former cannot be morally good, the
> latter may be.[4]

The theory of St. Thomas, illustrated by these examples from Louis
Janssens and Josef Fuchs, tells us that different intentions constitute different
human actions. We cannot judge the morality of the physical action without
reference to the meaning of the whole action which includes the intention of
the agent. Intention is part of the objective act, or the act taken in its totality.
It is neither a mitigating factor nor an accidental extra; rather, it is constitutive of the meaning of the action. Unless we consider the intention and the
physical action together, we are not dealing properly with a human action as
a moral action.

But can a physical action embody any intention whatever? Or, to put it
another way, can the end justify any means? On the basis of the matter and
form theory (hylomorphism) which St. Thomas uses, an action can only
absorb that intention which is *adequately proportionate* to it (ST I–II, q. 6, a.
2); the material element must be adequate matter for realizing the form, or the
intention. Only an action congruent with the intention adequately expresses
the intention.

The act of self-defense serves to illustrate the relational tension between
end and means. In the case of self-defense, the use of violence (the material
element, or the means-to-an-end) which wounds or even kills the assailant is
justifiable when it falls within the limits of what is necessary to save one's
own life (the formal element, or the intention). However, violence which

exceeds the bounds necessary to save one's life is not justifiable because it is no longer properly proportionate to the intention of self-defense. Therefore, in one case the violence which inflicts harm or even death can be justified, but in the other case it cannot. The difference lies in the proportionality of the means to the end.[5]

We determine whether the physical action is properly proportionate to the intention by considering the action within its *circumstances*. The end and the means exist in relational tension to one another and to all the essential aspects which make up the circumstances. According to St. Thomas, "actions are good or bad according to circumstances" (ST I–II, q. 18, a. 3). Only by considering the action in reference to the intention within the total context of its qualifying circumstances can we determine the true moral meaning of the action. We can uncover the relevant circumstances by asking those reality-revealing questions (who, what, when, where, why, how, what else, and what if) which we have already explored above in our treatment of the formation of conscience.

The three points of reference for determining the morality of human action, then, are the physical act-in-itself (the object of the act, or the means), the intention (end), and the circumstances (which include the consequences). These three aspects of one composite human action make up the traditional three-font principle. A proper moral evaluation of a human action according to this principle must take all three of these aspects into consideration simultaneously. British moralist John Mahoney recognizes this "drive to totality" as a characteristic feature of contemporary moral theology.[6] By this he means "a refusal to ignore the relationships of the parts to each other and to the totality which is implied in their being 'parts' and within which alone their full significance can be recognized."[7] When we forget that the act-in-itself, the intention, and the circumstances are three aspects of *one* composite action, then we too easily make moral evaluations of any one part without considering the whole. This gives us either an "act-centered" morality which forgets the person acting in a context (intention and circumstances), or an "intentions only" morality which does not take seriously enough the act being done, or a "situationalism" which maintains that circumstances make all the difference. But the traditional Catholic morality of the three-font principle claims that we do not have a true moral evaluation of a human action until all aspects are taken together. Today theologians aligned with what is known as "proportionalism" (which we will explore later in this chapter) claim that the most we can say about any one of these elements taken apart from the other two is that it is *premoral*, since it is not yet fully morally qualified. The recent debates on "proportionalism" are trying to show that we must understand the relationship of the various aspects of an act in order to arrive at the total moral meaning of the act.

## Intrinsic Evil

The understanding of the three-font principle has significant implications for reevaluating "intrinsic evil" as a moral notion. Traditional moralists have claimed that certain actions (such as masturbation, contraception, sterilization, artificial insemination, direct killing of the innocent, divorce, and remarriage) were intrinsically morally evil in themselves. These actions were regarded as such either by being contrary to nature (following the "order of nature" interpretation of natural law discussed in the chapters on natural law) or by defect of right. This latter meant that in killing innocent life or in divorce, for example, the human agent was assuming the absolute dominion over life or marital union which belongs by right only to God. To qualify any action as intrinsically morally evil means that no intention or set of circumstances could ever justify it. Its moral quality is already determined before the person does it in whatever circumstances.

Josef Fuchs has been critical of such use of "intrinsic evil" from the perspective of the demands of the three-font principle. For Fuchs, to declare an action from the moral point of view as an "intrinsic evil"

> . . . would presuppose that those who arrive at it could know or foresee adequately *all the possible combinations* of the action concerned with circumstances and intentions, with (premoral) values and non-values (*bona* and *mala "physica"*).[8]

Therefore, the proper use of "intrinsic evil" as a moral category would come only after all the qualifications of the action have been considered. According to Fuchs, the most we can say about an action apart from its qualifying intention and circumstances is that this action is good or evil only in a *premoral* sense:

> For (1) a moral judgment of an action may not be made in anticipation of the agent's intention, since it would not be the judgment of a "human" act. (2) A moral judgment is legitimately formed only under a *simultaneous* consideration of the three elements (action, circumstances, purpose), premoral in themselves; for the actualization of the three elements (taking money from another, who is very poor, to be able to give pleasure to a friend) is not a combination of three human actions that are morally judged on an individual basis, but a single human action.[9]

This presentation of the three-font principle and its implications for reevaluating the notion of "intrinsically morally evil" leads us to clarify the distinction between a "premoral" evil and a "moral" evil, or a morally wrong action.

## Premoral/Ontic Evil and Moral Evil

The further refinement of the analysis of the moral act into its premoral/ontic features has been the center of much discussion and controversy. Part of the confusion is due to the variety of terms used to describe the same reality. For example, Peter Knauer's seminal article used the manualists' term of "physical evil."[10] Josef Fuchs carried the discussion further by using the term "premoral evil."[11] Richard McCormick has also adopted this term though at times he, along with Bruno Schuller, also uses "nonmoral evil" for the same reality.[12] Louis Janssens, who has contributed what many consider one of the principal moral reflections of our time in his article, "Ontic Evil and Moral Evil," prefers the term "ontic evil,"[13] although he has also used the term "premoral disvalue" to convey the same meaning.[14] But all of these terms—physical evil, premoral evil, nonmoral evil, ontic evil, and premoral disvalue—refer to the same reality, and they are used interchangeably in the discussion.

By using the notion of a premoral/ontic good or evil in human action, these authors are admitting to the inevitable ambiguity of human actions. This ambiguity, which is the result of human finitude, means that all human actions contain some features which enhance our humanity and some features which restrict it. To the extent that these features enhance the potential for human goodness and growth, they are premoral or ontic goods. To the extent that these features frustrate the full potential for promoting the well-being of persons and of their social relations, these features are premoral or ontic evils. As Janssens puts it, premoral/ontic evils are inevitable features of our actions "because we are *temporal* and *spatial*, live together *with others* in the same *material world*, are involved and act in a *common sinful* situation."[15] As a result, we are not able to realize all the values open to us in any one action without causing or tolerating some degree of premoral/ontic evil.

Because the authors who use this notion are interested in distinguishing premoral/ontic evil features in human action from a moral evil, they more often speak about premoral/ontic evil than they speak about premoral/ontic good. Premoral/ontic evil refers to the lack of perfection in anything whatsoever. As pertaining to human actions, it is that aspect which we experience as regrettable, harmful, or detrimental to the full actualization of the well-being of persons and of their social relations.[16] Since we will never get away from these features of our actions, we must learn to live in ways which will keep the premoral/ontic evil features to a minimum, even though we cannot completely eliminate them in all their forms.

But premoral/ontic evil is not the same as moral evil. We need to keep this distinction clear. If causing or permitting premoral/ontic evil were the same as causing or permitting a moral evil, then we could never act morally at all. How do we determine whether an action which contains some degree of premoral good and evil is morally right or wrong?

## The Principle of Double Effect

Theologians who accept the distinction between premoral/ontic evil and moral evil are addressing this question through a reevaluation of the principle of double effect.[17] The premises for this principle can be found in Thomas Aquinas' discussion of self-defense (ST II–II, q. 64, a. 7), but the four conditions of the principle were finally formulated by Jean Pierre Gury in the mid-nineteenth century.[18] The four conditions are expressed in a variety of ways, but are basically the following:

1. The action itself is good or indifferent.
2. The good effect is not produced by means of the evil effect.
3. The evil effect is not directly intended.
4. A proportionate reason supports causing or tolerating the evil effect.

The classic example used to illustrate this principle is the one of the pregnant woman with the cancerous uterus. If nothing is done, both the mother and fetus will die. If the uterus is removed, the fetus will die but the mother will live. The principle of double effect allows the uterus to be removed because:

1. Removing the uterus is a morally indifferent action.
2. Saving the life of the mother is not produced by means of the death of the fetus, but by removing the uterus.
3. The direct intention is to save the life of the mother.
4. The proportionate reason is the mother's life at stake.

The past two decades have witnessed a vigorous reevaluation not only of the conditions which make up the principle of double effect, but also the moral relevance of the principle itself. While I cannot do full justice to a complex discussion and to the nuances of individual authors who have assessed this principle, I may be able to identify predominant themes or basic trends.

The first condition presumes we can specify the act-in-itself as morally good, bad, or indifferent independently of other factors. It implies that certain actions in themselves are intrinsically evil and to do them would always be morally wrong. However, when we enter the realm of a "moral" action, we are speaking of an action qualified by intention and circumstances. So unqualified actions can only be properly called "premoral" actions. The first condition, then, points only to "premoral" features of an action.[19]

The second condition is no real advance over the first. It shares the same basic presupposition as the first regarding acts-in-themselves. It claims that we cannot do evil to achieve good, or that a good end does not justify an evil means. This condition does not allow the good effect to be linked in a direct causal relationship with the evil effect. The problem with this condition, like the first, is whether or not we are dealing with premoral evils or moral evils. If we are dealing with a moral evil, which presumes that the action is fully qualified, then the end (moral evil) does not justify the means. We cannot do moral evil to achieve good. But if we are dealing with premoral evils (which are inevitable in every human action), we must evaluate them in relation to the intention and circumstances. We can, and inevitably do, commit some premoral/ontic evil to achieve good.

Theoretically, the third condition can stand independently of the first two. It simply requires that the agent may not morally seek evil, premoral or moral, as an end. The difficulty with this condition is with determining what a person's intention really is and judging its moral relevance. Morally speaking an agent can only have one intention which gives meaning to the full human act. Traditionally the principle of double effect used the distinction of the direct and indirect intention because it regarded certain actions as intrinsically evil. We eventually formulated norms in these terms, such as "no direct killing of non-combatants in war" and "no direct sterilization." Formulations such as these show that actions were now defining the intention, rather than the intention defining the moral meaning and quality of the action. Consequently, directness and indirectness became all-important in determining morality. An increasing number of philosophers and theologians do not tie the moral quality of an action to the intention in the way the traditional use of this principle does. Rather, many contend that the moral agent is responsible for the full range of foreseeable consequences, directly intended or not. The critical variable in making a moral assessment is not the intention but the agent's foreknowledge of effects. The agent must be able to justify the risk of causing some undesirable effects in light of the undesirability of other options.[20]

According to the present state of the discussion, "direct" and "indirect" are no longer tied to physical actions in themselves nor to intentions in themselves. If we are going to use the distinction at all, we ought not to use it as designating a moral difference in actions themselves. Rather, the distinction designates a descriptive difference between actions involving premoral evils by showing what is being sought, by what means, and in what circumstances. Direct and indirect are morally relevant to disclose something about the agent rather than the moral quality of an action. They show the relationship of the agent's attitude of approval or disapproval to an action, but in themselves they do not designate the total moral significance of an action.[21]

The fourth condition remains as the master principle. It is ultimately concerned with the true moral meaning of an action. As such, it takes into consideration the relationship between the premoral good and evil aspects of an action, and the intention within the total configuration of circumstances. In other words, the fourth condition is concerned with the relationship of the various aspects of an act to the total moral meaning of the act. Moral actions are judged differently when taken in their totality rather than when certain aspects are treated in isolation.

The fourth condition of the traditional principle of double effect is known today as the principle of proportionality, proportionalism, or proportionate reason.[22] It recognizes that moral choices involve balancing premoral goods and premoral evils in an ambiguous world. We cannot make a judgment of the act-in-itself (the means) apart from its relation to the intention (the end) in the total configuration of essential circumstances. The moral judgment is a judgment of the proportion of the means to the end. The action which inevitably causes some premoral evil can be considered a moral action when "no intrinsic contradiction between the means and the end may be found in the total act when the act is placed in the light of reason."[23] In other words, the means do not directly contradict the end so that a proper proportion exists between them. This establishes a proportionate reason for allowing the premoral or ontic evil to happen. The key to determining the morality of an action, then, is the presence or absence of a proportionate reason. Proportionate reason is what distinguishes a premoral or ontic evil from a moral evil and a morally right from a morally wrong action.

## Proportionate Reason

The notion of a proportionate reason is key to an analysis of the morality of human action. It is a difficult notion to grasp and the discussion surrounding it is often confusing. James Walter has carefully identified the three levels of inquiry which operate in the discussions of proportionate reason but which are seldom distinguished. The three levels of inquiry are

(1) the *definition* of proportionate reason, (2) the *criteria* that guide and establish the assessment of proportionate reason, and (3) the *modes* by which we know that the criteria have been fulfilled and thus that a proportionate reason has been obtained.[24]

## Definition

Walter shows that when speaking of a proportionate reason, those who propose it as a way of determining the morality of an action do not mean merely any reason whatever. Rather, the "reason" for action refers to a specific value at stake. In social issues, for example, the value may be property, freedom, truth, or personal dignity. In medical matters, the value may be life, health, bodily integrity, or personal autonomy. In sexual matters, the value may be personal dignity, procreative capacity, unity, freedom, privacy, or the family as a stable institution for human flourishing.

The standard usage of "proportion" suggests a weighing notion such as in some mathematical calculation. When taken in this sense, the use of proportionate reason becomes a kind of cost/benefit analysis. This leads to a strict consequentialist or utilitarian interpretation of proportionality. For this reason, the mathematical notion is not the one meant by the proponents of this approach.[25]

The more adequate notion of "proportion" refers to what truly gives an action its moral meaning: the relation of the means to the end. More broadly speaking, "proportionate" refers to the relation between the specific value at stake and the premoral evils (the limitations, the harm, or the inconvenience) which will inevitably come about in trying to achieve that value. So a "proportionate reason" refers to both a specific value and its relation to all the elements (including the premoral evils) in the action.[26] From this perspective, proportionate reason truly defines what a person is doing in an action and not something merely added to the action already defined.

Perhaps an illustration can clarify the matter. In health care, for example, a surgeon may seek the value of saving the life of a patient by means of amputating a leg. If the premoral evil of losing the leg is properly related to saving the life of the patient, then we would define the surgeon's action as a life-saving act, since the surgeon has a proportionate reason for causing the harm. But if the patient's life could have been saved by injecting serum into the blood stream, then the amputation would be disproportionate to the value of saving life. We would then define the surgeon's action as mutilation, since no proportionate reason exists for such an act. Even so, the analysis of proportionalism makes no claims about the surgeon's being virtuous or sinful (morally good or bad). It only claims that an action is morally right or wrong.[27]

## Criteria

What criteria help us to decide whether a proper relation exists between the specific value and the other elements of an act? Establishing these criteria has been one of the most difficult parts of developing the proportionate reason approach to the morality of human action. Richard McCormick, whose criteria for a proportionate reason are clearest, first proposed them in the Pere Marquette Lecture of 1973, *Ambiguity in Moral Choice*,[28] and has subsequently reworked them in response to criticisms of his first effort.[29] The substance of his criteria are as follows:

*1. The means used will not cause more harm than necessary to achieve the value.*

In other words, the specific value being sought must be at least equal to the value being sacrificed. For example, in the illustration of self-defense, the values in conflict are equal: the defender's life is in conflict with the attacker's life. In medical practice the value being sought may be restoring the patient's well-being. The values sacrificed, such as comfort, bodily integrity (e.g., losing a limb), or full freedom or movement, are not equal to the patient's total well-being. The decision to have surgery or to use medications depends on which of these means would cause the least amount of harm to achieve the good of the patient's well-being. Or, if surgery had to be done, this criterion would demand that the surgeon not cut out more than is necessary to restore health and to save life. Of course, this criterion raises the difficult issue of the theory of value which underpins the proportionate reason approach in order to define a proper hierarchy of values and to determine which can be weighed one against another.

*2. No less harmful way exists at present to protect the value.*

This criterion demands that we choose the best means available to us at the time, even though this may have to change in the future. In medicine, for example, many people who suffer from cancer may have to experience the pains of chemotherapy or radiation treatment now until something is discovered which produces less pain or discomfort with equal or more effect.

*3. The means used to achieve the value will not undermine it.*

This criterion suggests that in the case of trying to protect innocent life, for example, we do not engage in indiscriminate killing. The American bishops reflect this criterion in their pastoral letter, *The Challenge of Peace*, when they call for non-combatant immunity in war. Their point is that we are not morally protecting the value of life when we attack life indiscriminately.

Perhaps we can appreciate these criteria for a proportionate reason if we see them at work in a more extended example. Do we have a proportionate reason to justify smoking? Does smoking cause more harm than necessary to achieve its values of relaxation and enjoyment? It appears so, given what we know about the risks of smoking to one's health. The physical harm one causes by smoking is not equal to the relaxation one achieves when we have other less risky ways to achieve the same relaxation. For example, a whole array of recreational activities, meditation techniques, or non-harmful oral compensations (such as chewing sugarless gum) are available. Smoking ultimately undermines the value it seeks since it causes so much harm to one's health. Proportionalism does not seem to support smoking as a moral action. However, due to the addictive quality of nicotine, we can understand how one who has formed the habit of smoking may have less culpability for smoking than one who is not addicted and starts to smoke on a regular basis.

This example shows that the way to reach a moral evaluation of an action is to consider the proportionate relationship of the material action and the intention in the total set of essential circumstances. If better ways presently exist by which to achieve the value, and the means chosen does not exclude as much premoral evil as possible without undermining the value intended, then we cannot say that a proper proportion of means to ends exists. That particular causing of premoral evil, then, would be a moral evil. The basic rule for an ethics based on love is that in every situation in which we have to choose between several possibilities, we ought to do what will contribute as much as possible to the well-being and development of persons and their social relations and to avoid as much as possible what harms or hinders this well-being.[30]

While the three criteria developed by McCormick may still need further refinement and development, they do provide some help for assessing the proper relationship between the specific value sought and the other aspects of the action. But how do we know that these criteria have been fulfilled and that a proportionate reason exists? This brings us to the third level of inquiry, the epistemological level.

## Modes of Knowing

Contemporary theology is increasingly more sensitive to the historically conditioned nature of all knowledge. No one enjoys an ahistorical vantage point which will give absolute certitude on moral matters. Therefore, anyone who would claim that a proportionate reason exists for doing a particular action is making a modest claim and realizes that this judgment remains open to further clarification and revision.

Richard McCormick has offered three modes of knowing whether we have a proportionate reason.[31] He suggests that one of the ways we know that a proper relation exists between a specific value and all other elements of an act is through *experience*. For example, experience tells us that private property contributes to the overall well-being of persons and their social relations. This makes robbery counterproductive, or disproportionate. With regards to war, we are now getting very close to the claim that waging war, especially nuclear war, is disproportionate to the value of protecting life, since in war we are all losers. Furthermore, experience teaches us that the meaning of family, sexuality, and procreation are best preserved within the context of permanent marriage. This would make actions which undermine the stability and permanence of marriage disproportionate. Among such actions would be adultery and the use of reproductive technologies employing an outside donor, such as artificial insemination by donor and surrogate motherhood.

A second way of knowing whether a proper relationship exists, suggests

McCormick, is through our own *sense of outrage* or *intuition* that some actions are disproportionate. Torture and forms of fanatical human experimentation fall under this category.

A third way of knowing is through the method of *trial and error.* This mode of knowing pertains especially to those areas where we have little experience as yet and would proceed cautiously to support technological advancement. Recombinant DNA research could be such an instance.

James Walter builds on McCormick's foundation to suggest three other ways of knowing whether a proper relationship exists.[32] He adds the mode of *rational analysis* and *argument.* By gathering evidence and formulating logical arguments, we try to give reasons to support our choice for certain values over others which we have already grasped prior to reasoning. This mode would be a necessary supplement to McCormick's mode of trial and error or to knowing through a sense of outrage or intuition.

Walter also appeals to McCormick's earlier claim that long-term *consequences* can illuminate proportionality.[33] This mode, however, seems to be almost the same as the mode of experience. Walter also follows Janssens' proposal that we can discover disproportion through *feelings of disunity* within the self, while we can discover proportionality through the *experience of unity.*[34] This mode of knowing is closely aligned to McCormick's sense of outrage or intuition and, like it, is difficult to use since distinguishing between authentic and inauthentic senses of guilt is not easy to do.

## *Proportionate Reason:*
## *An Assessment*

The understanding of the proportionate reason thought-pattern just presented is a relatively recent development in Catholic moral theology, though its roots are well established in the tradition. It began to receive critical attention shortly after the Second Vatican Council and has been the focus of ongoing development and criticism ever since. While it receives the active support of some of the most significant and influential moral theologians of the Church since Vatican II, such as those whose opinions make up the heart of this chapter, others have raised serious reservations about it.[35] In the final section of this chapter, I will risk oversimplification by identifying only some of the objections raised about this approach and then summarize the proportionalists' response.[36]

*Objection: Proportionalism denies the existence of intrinsic evil.*
*Response:* Proportionalists respond to this objection by appealing to the distinction between premoral/ontic evil and a moral evil. They are willing to qualify an action as intrinsically evil once the action in its totality has been deter-

mined as an objectively immoral action, or a moral evil. Proportionalists refuse, however, to use "intrinsic evil" for actions taken independently of the agent's intention and circumstances. Proportionalists insist that "intrinsic evil" does not properly apply to the premoral/ontic evil features of human action.

*Objection: Proportionalism is equivalent to consequentialism.*

*Response:* "Weighing the consequences" is a familiar expression among proportionalists. It is often taken to be some form of consequentialism which seeks as great a balance of good over evil as the available alternatives can offer. For proportionalists, consequences are indeed important in determining the morality of an action. But consequences alone are not sufficient. Proportionalists want to include everything which gives an action its meaning. So the utilitarian quest for maximizing pleasure or seeking the greatest good for the greatest number is not the goal of proportionalists. Utilitarianism, for example, runs roughshod over persons in order to further the welfare of the majority. Proportionalists, on the other hand, want to seek the well-being of persons and their social relations as a fitting goal, but they do not want to achieve this at the expense of respecting persons. Furthermore, proportionalists oppose utilitarian pragmatism by maintaining that a reason is not "proportionate" if the value sought is undermined by an action. For example, killing one innocent victim in order to protect the killing of five others would be unjustifiable since such a killing undermines both respect for life as well as for the law designed to protect life. Therefore, proportionalism takes consequences seriously as part of the total meaning of the action, but it avoids an overly exclusive emphasis on consequences.

*Objection: Proportionalism promotes relativism and subjectivism.*

*Response:* Since proportionalism respects the relational character of reality, it is a form of relativism. But it is not relative in the sense of being arbitrary. It is relative in the sense that intention and circumstances, or all the objectively given aspects which make up the total meaning of an action, are relevant to the morality of human action. To hold to such a relational character of moral reality is not equivalent to relativism. To know the context of an action before determining its morality is nothing new to Catholic moral thought. For example, the action of "taking money" begs for specification before we can evaluate it. Calling for the specification of the context does not make proportionalists relativists.

Another form of the objection of relativism is subjectivism. Subjectivism does not mean leaving the moral subject to make his or her own responsible judgments. That is quite ordinary. Only a system which advocates blind obedience would avoid that. Subjectivism as a danger to proportionalism takes the form of either claiming that an action can mean whatever we want it to mean, or that the community has no role in discerning and maintaining moral standards. Proportionalism is not so inherently subjective that an action becomes moral because someone thinks it is moral. On the basis of proportionalism's reliance on the matter/form theory underpinning the structure of the human action, the material element of the action must be apt matter to sustain its intention, or form. An action cannot mean just anything we want it to mean. For example, to batter a disobedient child in the name of love is a disproportionate act, and morally wrong.

Moreover, the demands for a proper consideration of proportionality require the person to be very much reliant on communal discernment. Determining the proper proportion of premoral goods and evils is not to be left to an individual's soul searching. Rather, it requires drawing upon the wisdom of past experience as it is embodied in the community's standards, and it demands broad consultation to seek the experience and reflection of others in order to prevent the influence of self-interest from biasing perception and judgment. Using proportionalism requires more moral consultation with the community than would ever be required if the morality of actions were based on only one aspect, such as the physical, apart from its relation to all the objective features of the action.

*Objection: Proportionalism quantifies values so as to measure one against another.*
*Response:* Proportionalism is frequently criticized for trying to weigh values which are of a different sort, such as putting on the same plane human life and human fertility, or economic justice and corporate profit, individual freedom and social responsibililty. Such a criticism points to the most underdeveloped aspect of the proportionate reason approach—its theory of value. It uses "calculating" metaphors which imply that values are quantitative entities which can be weighed and balanced, as though a moral judgment were just another form of cost-benefit analysis. But proportionalism requires not the shrewd computations of a calculating mind, but the well-ordered heart sensitive to the breadth and depth of value. Edward Vacek has it exactly right when he says that proportionalism could dispel its aura of calculation if love and wisdom received greater attention.[37]

*Objection: Proportionalism does not allow for specific universal norms.*
*Response:* Proportionalists maintain a significant place for specific norms in the moral life. These light up patterns of premoral goods and evils which accumulative communal experience has found helpful or harmful to human wellbeing. Because we have norms, we do not have to consider all possible combinations of values and conflicting premoral evils in each instance. But for proportionalism, morality is not co-extensive with norms, and moral reasoning can never be purely deductive. While norms may be a co-

determining factor in making a moral judgment, they do not replace the discerning judgment of conscience.

The issue of universal, specific, material norms raises the question not only of how we arrive at objectively evil moral actions but also of how we can know all possible combinations of relevant values in advance so that we can be certain that a given action is always wrong. Proportionalism holds that once an action is understood to be objectively immoral, it is always so. A norm prohibiting such an action would be universal. But proportionalists accept only an evaluation of an action totally considered. The epistemological issue, then, is whether we can ever foresee all possible combinations of premoral goods and evils involved in a concrete deed so as to be certain it is always wrong. Insofar as we do not have such an epistemological vantage point which would give us this certainty, proportionalism is reluctant to admit to universal, specific, material norms. The next chapter will take a closer look at the issue of norms to put this position in perspective.

Philip Keane's assessment of the criticisms of proportionalism finds that, as a developing thought-pattern, proportionate reason calls for ongoing analysis. The questions raised about it are serious enough to press for further refinements. But none of them have proven strong enough to reject proportionate reason as a tool of moral analysis.[38] Bernard Hoose wants to widen the debate on proportionalism beyond trying to convince its opponents of the validity of proportionalism. He wants to find ways to put it within the grasp of ordinary people who may then use it to find what is objectively right. In order to do this, Hoose raises some critical questions which yet need to be explored: How do we acquire knowledge about the accumulated wisdom of the community regarding premoral goods and evils and acts described generally as right or wrong? How does a person learn to appreciate moral rightness and moral values at various stages of moral growth? What processes are involved when a person begins to compare premoral goods and evils? These questions will lead us to understand how a person arrives at knowledge of objective rightness.[39]

The method of proportionalism leads to a rethinking of the meaning and function of moral norms. It lends a greater flexibility to their formulation than past approaches of a natural law method would allow. We turn in the next chapter, then, to the meaning and function of moral norms.

## Notes

1. Timothy E. O'Connell has given a fine summary of the major features of this principle in his *Principles for a Catholic Morality* (New York: Seabury Press, 1978), pp. 169–170.

2. Janssens, "Ontic Evil and Moral Evil," *Readings in Moral Theology No.*

*1: Moral Norms and Catholic Tradition*, edited by Charles E. Curran and Richard A. McCormick (Ramsey: Paulist Press, 1979), p. 49.

3. *Ibid.*, p. 51.

4. Fuchs, "The Absoluteness of Moral Terms," in *Readings in Moral Theology No. 1*, p. 119.

5. Janssens, "Ontic Evil and Moral Evil," *Readings in Moral Theology No. 1*, pp. 56–58.

6. John Mahoney, *The Making of Moral Theology* (Oxford: Clarendon Press, 1987), pp. 309–321.

7. *Ibid.*, p. 310.

8. Fuchs, "The Absoluteness of Moral Terms," *Readings in Moral Theology No. 1*, p. 124.

9. *Ibid.*, p. 121.

10. Knauer's seminal article on this issue is "The Hermeneutic Function of the Principle of Double Effect," in *Readings in Moral Theology No. 1*, pp. 1–39.

11. Fuchs, "The Absoluteness of Moral Terms," *Readings in Moral Theology No. 1*. pp. 94–137.

12. See, for example, the extensive coverage McCormick has given to the discussion on the morality of human action and the meaning of moral norms which employs these terms in his *Notes on Moral Theology: 1965 Through 1980* (Washington: University Press of America, 1981). See also his *Notes on Moral Theology: 1981 Through 1984* (Lanham, Md.: University Press of America, 1984). For Bruno Schuller's usage, see, for example, "Direct Killing/Indirect Killing," *Readings in Moral Theology No. 1*, pp. 138–157.

13. In *Readings in Moral Theology No. 1*, pp. 40–93. In another place, Janssens explains the Heideggerian influence on his use of "ontic": "The adjective ontic—as distinct from ontological which deals with being itself (*das Sein*)—applies to concrete things (*das Seienden*), to the limited, worldly realities." See "Ontic Good and Evil: Premoral Values and Disvalues," *Louvain Studies* 12 (1987): 80.

14. Janssens, "Norms and Priorities in a Love Ethics," *Louvain Studies* 4 (Spring 1977): 207–238. See also his more recent article, "Ontic Good and Evil: Premoral Values and Disvalues," pp., 62–82.

15. Janssens, "Ontic Evil and Moral Evil," *Readings in Moral Theology No. 1*, p. 61. For an elaboration of these conditions, see pp. 61–66; also, "Ontic Good and Evil: Premoral Values and Disvalues," pp. 62–76.

16. Janssens, "Ontic Evil and Moral Evil," *Readings in Moral Theology No. 1*, p. 60.

17. Much of the significant literature which has contributed to this reevaluation can be found in Curran and McCormick, eds., *Readings in Moral Theology No. 1*. See also, Charles E. Curran, "The Principle of Double Ef-

fect," *Ongoing Revision: Studies in Moral Theology* (Notre Dame: Fides Publishers, Inc., 1975), pp. 173–209; David F. Kelly, *The Emergence of Roman Catholic Medical Ethics in North America* (New York: Edwin Mellen Press, 1979), pp. 244–274; William E. May, "Double Effect," *Encyclopedia of Bioethics* 1 (New York: Macmillan and Free Press, 1978), pp. 316–320; also, Joseph A. Selling, "The Problem of Reinterpreting the Principle of Double Effect," *Louvain Studies* 8 (Spring 1980): 47–62.

18. Joseph T. Mangan, "An Historical Analysis of the Principle of Double Effect," *Theological Studies* 10 (March 1949): 41–61, at 58–61.

19. According to the interpretation of Joseph Selling, the meaning of the first condition is that the act should not contain *any* evil (even a premoral evil?) from the very beginning. But if we maintain that the premoral features are inevitable in every action, then the principle of double effect would never apply. According to Selling, the principle applies *only* to those cases where doing good results in a foreseeable evil. But whenever doing evil directly is involved, we need to appeal to another principle. See Joseph A. Selling, "The Problem of Reinterpreting the Principle of Double Effect," *Louvain Studies* 8 (Spring 1980): 59.

20. A good summary of recent discussion on the significance of intention leading to this conclusion can be found in the President's Commission for the Study of Ethical Problems in Medicine and Biomedical and Behavioral Research, *Deciding to Forego Life-Sustaining Treatment* (Washington: U.S. Government Printing Office, 1983), pp. 77–82. See also Bernard Hoose, *Proportionalism* (Washington: Georgetown University Press, 1987), pp. 113–121.

21. This interpretation is developed by Richard A. McCormick, "The Principle of Double Effect," *How Brave a New World?* (Garden City: Doubleday & Company, Inc., 1981), pp. 413–429.

22. For a study of the American debate on proportionalism and its European roots, see Bernard Hoose, *Proportionalism* (Washington: Georgetown University Press, 1987).

23. Janssens, "Ontic Evil and Moral Evil," *Readings in Moral Theology No. 1*, p. 71.

24. Walter, "Proportionate Reason and its Three Levels of Inquiry: Structuring the Ongoing Debate," *Louvain Studies* 10 (Spring 1984): 30.

25. For a good article which shows that proportionate reason is not utilitarian by nature, see Lisa S. Cahill, "Teleology, Utilitarianism, and Christian Ethics," *Theological Studies* 42 (December 1981): 601–629; also, on the same theme, see Charles E. Curran, "Utilitarianism and Contemporary Moral Theology: Situating the Debates," *Readings in Moral Theology No. 1*, pp. 341–362.

26. Walter, "Proportionate Reason and its Three Levels of Inquiry: Structuring the Ongoing Debate," p. 32.

27.  See Hoose, *Proportionalism,* Chapter Three, "The Moral Goodness/ Moral Rightness Distinction," pp. 41–67.

28.  McCormick, *Ambiguity in Moral Choice* (Milwaukee: Marquette University Press, 1973).

29.  See especially the responses to his lecture and then McCormick's response to his critics in *Doing Evil to Achieve Good,* edited by Richard A. McCormick and Paul Ramsey (Chicago: Loyola University Press, 1978).

30.  Janssens, "Norms and Priorities in a Love Ethics," *Louvain Studies* 4 (Spring 1977): 213–214.

31.  McCormick, "Notes on Moral Theology: 1980," *Theological Studies* 42 (March 1981): 74–90.

32.  Walter, "Proportionate Reason and its Three Levels of Inquiry: Structuring the Debate," pp. 38–40.

33.  McCormick first made this claim in *Ambiguity in Moral Choice,* p. 93, but has since revised his position in *Doing Evil to Achieve Good,* p. 265.

34.  For Janssens' position, see "Ontic Evil and Moral Evil," *Readings in Moral Theology No. 1,* p. 72.

35.  Prominent critics among Protestants are Paul Ramsey, "Incommensurability and Indeterminacy in Moral Choice," *Doing Evil to Achieve Good,* pp. 69–144; Frederick Carney, "On McCormick and Teleological Morality," *Journal of Religious Ethics* 6 (Spring 1978): 81–107; also his "McCormick and the Traditional Distinction," in *Doing Evil to Achieve Good,* pp. 145–164. Among Catholic critics, see especially John Connery, "Morality of Consequences: A Critical Appraisal," in *Readings in Moral Theology No. 1,* pp. 244–266; also his "Catholic Ethics: Has the Norm for Rule-Making Changed?" *Theological Studies* 42 (1981): 232–250; Germain Grisez, "Critique of the Proportionalist Method of Moral Judgment," in his *The Way of the Lord Jesus,* Vol. 1: *Christian Moral Principles* (Chicago: Franciscan Herald Press, 1983), pp. 141–171; William E. May, "The Moral Meaning of Human Acts," *Homiletic and Pastoral Review* 79 (1978): 10–21.

36.  Three important articles in the nature of commentaries on the discussion which are providing the focus for this assessment are Philip S. Keane, "The Objective Moral Order: Reflections on Recent Research," *Theological Studies* 43 (June 1982): 260–278; Paul E. McKeever, "Proportionalism as a Methodology in Catholic Moral Theology," in *Human Sexuality and Personhood* (St. Louis: Pope John XXIII Center, 1981), pp. 211–222; Edward V. Vacek, "Proportionalism: One View of the Debate," *Theological Studies* 46 (June 1985): 287–314.

37.  Vacek, "Proportionalism: One View of the Debate," p. 297.

38.  Keane, "The Objective Moral Order: Reflections on Recent Research," p. 273.

39.  Hoose, *Proportionalism,* p. 142.

# 19 $\mathrm{M}$oral Norms

$T$he last chapter examined the moral components of human action and the theory of proportionalism in Catholic moral theology for determining the objective morality of human action. This chapter will consider the meaning and limits of moral norms which, together with the discussion of the objective morality of human action, are at the center of much controversy in contemporary Catholic moral theology.

The discussion of moral norms turns frequently to the issue of the existence of permanent and enduring moral norms. Are there any moral absolutes? Yes, indeed there are. Official magisterial documents witness to them and the consensus of theologians endorses that witness. At times, however, affirming absolutes can have the unwanted side-effect of creating the impression that all norms are absolute. They are not. Yet showing that not all are absolute can often create the impression that none are. Simple alternatives—either all norms are absolute or none are—will not suffice. The discussion which tries to sort out the difference is complex. This chapter will try to focus on the directions of a complex and incomplete discussion of moral norms.

## The Meaning and Function of Moral Norms

Moral norms are the criteria for judging the sorts of persons we ought to be and the sorts of actions we ought to perform in faithful response to God's call to be loving. As such, norms are more or less adequate expressions of moral truth. They differ from positive laws in that norms do not carry any sanctions with them. Often what the community regards as a moral norm is also a positive law (such as the prohibitions of killing, rape, and stealing). But not everything which the community requires as minimal moral behavior is necessarily translated into positive laws (cf. the discussion on the relation of law and morality in Chapter 17).

The interpretation of natural law proposed at the end of Chapter 16 tells us that moral norms are derived from the experience of value, particularly the value of persons and their social relations. For example, out of the experience of the value of persons we discovered that killing destroys the basis of all humanizing values. As a result, the moral norm "do not kill" arose to express the experience that killing leads in a dehumanizing direction. Out of the experience of the value of social relations, we discovered that speaking an untruth leads to destroying the confidence between people which is necessary for social cohesion. The norm "do not speak an untruth" protects the value of inter-human confidence which is needed to live together effectively. With regard to absolute prohibitions, the judgment is that the objective direction of certain actions is always extremely dehumanizing (such as with acts of murder, torture, adultery, stealing, and the like).

From the perspective of natural law, moral norms are the moral memory of the community; they are the repository of its collective, experiential wisdom.[1] Through the ages and in a variety of circumstances, the human community has experienced that certain actions often have humanizing or dehumanizing effects which cannot be passed over. Moral norms preserve in propositional form the insights of the human experience of value—those experiences of what helps or hinders the well-being of persons and their social relations. As such, moral norms allow us to bring to our moral judgments a breadth and depth which we could not achieve if we were to rely on our limited personal experience alone. But they are not recipes for moral action, nor are they the blueprint for present or future moral structures. While never taking the place of the freedom of conscience, moral norms are an integral part of discerning what is good or bad, right or wrong.

Moral norms are rich with advantages to assist moral thinking and moral living. For example, they help to prevent moral paralysis by providing illuminating patterns of behavior and common denominators of value which help to inform our consciences as we make our way through potential or real moral dilemmas. We need moral norms since none of us has the time to be in touch with everything involved in a decision before we must act.

Moral norms also provide some consistency and stability in the moral life by identifying what is expected of us as participants in a shared moral community. Because moral norms take seriously the repetitive aspects of human experience, they provide a reliable point of reference and direction for moral living. We do not continuously have to question ourselves about what is right or to exercise our ethical creativity to "reinvent the wheel" every time we have to make a decision.

Moral norms also challenge our moral living by giving expression to the good toward which we ought to strive. Since they express experiential wisdom, moral norms reflect the capacity of certain practices to humanize or dehumanize life. As such they stretch us beyond our individual experiences and challenge us to look again at our immediate impressions of what most humanizes or dehumanizes. By representing a broader vision, they challenge us to take into account the accumulated experience of the community and to consider the collective consequences of our behavior as well. They also serve as a corrective to our behavior by calling us up short when we do not strive to express our humanity as authentically and completely as we can.

But moral norms do not tell the whole story when it comes to moral responsibility. While they have many advantages, such as those identified above, their great disadvantage is that they can circumscribe too narrowly the scope of moral responsibility. Life is too complex and changing for a few axioms to express the crucial dimensions of the moral life. The endless nuance which an unfolding and inter-related life demands cannot be captured in generalized formulas. While it would be foolish to reject the moral wisdom enshrined in norms, we do not want to idolize the experience of the past by raising norms to a status they cannot bear, or by treating them as the last word in a moral conversation which must listen to many voices in order to discern moral truth.

## Moral Norms and the Message of Jesus

A discussion of moral norms can easily get so philosophical that it seems far removed from the message of Jesus. We can too easily forget that the moral life is a response to God in Christ and through the Spirit. Moral norms participate in the effort to communicate the moral message of Jesus, particularly his commandment to be loving.

The core of Jesus' message and ministry is the call of the reign of God that requires a response. Though nowhere does Jesus, or the New Testament at large, provide a moral system as such, the message and ministry of Jesus nevertheless make demands on us which directly affect moral behavior. The reign of God exists in a tension between the present and future. That is, while the reign of God is present in the person of Jesus, and through his words and deeds (such as the healings and exorcisms), it is not yet fully present in all its peace, power, and glory. This tension between the present and future reign of God provides a fertile source of moral obligation. Jesus' parables, as we have already seen, challenge us to reexamine our accepted norms of behavior, our basic attitudes, values, and perspective on life. The fundamental demand made by Jesus on those who wish to share in the reign of God is repentance, or conversion. Conversion (*metanoia*) calls not just for an inner attitude of regret and sorrow, but also for turning away from a life not centered on responding to God's love and turning toward a new life marked by faithful love.

Discipleship is a life most fully turned around by conversion, focused on the reign of God's love, and lived in loving response to God's enabling love. Jesus showed us through his own life, and most especially by his death (1 Jn 3:16), what loving God and neighbor as the self can mean in specific ways. Jesus remains the model of love, the norm of Christian discipleship. Jesus taught us by his life and continues to teach us through his Spirit what love demands. But we still face a problem. How are we supposed to follow Jesus' example and live by his command of love in our vocations as wives and husbands, mothers and fathers, priests and religious, single women and men, young people and children? It is not easy to say.

We are helped in this effort not only by the testimony of moral witnesses (such as the saints), but also by the formulation of moral norms. While the Spirit continues to be the inner law enabling us to imitate and embody the love of Christ, the formulation of moral norms helps us to translate and transmit the Spirit's bidding through the ages. Following Jesus' example of love in the general orientation of our lives is hard enough; expressing that love in particular actions is even harder. We are helped to express this love by moral norms which have been discovered and formulated by those sensitive to the Spirit's lead through the ages. Moral norms participate in the effort to make meaningful the love which Jesus commanded.

## Types of Moral Norms

I indicated in Chapter 1 that moral theology has a twofold range of interest: character and action. Moral theology distinguishes two general categories of norms which correlate with this twofold range of interest. *Formal* norms (also called general norms) relate to character when they are expressed in the language of virtue or vice. *Material* norms (also called specific, particular, or behavioral norms) relate to action.

### Formal Norms

With formal norms we confidently enter the realm of moral absolutes. The Roman Catholic Church has frequently witnessed to these absolutes in official teaching. Of the many examples which can be given of this witness, a statement from *Persona Humana* of 1975 is typical:

> Now in fact the Church throughout her history has always considered a certain number of precepts of the natural law as having an absolute and immutable value, and in their transgression she has seen a contradiction of the teaching and spirit of the Gospel. (n. 4)

Many theologians today interpret the norms which fit this description as formal norms. These permanent and enduring norms reflect fixed points of divine revelation, such as Jesus, the reign of God, conversion, the commandment of love, or openness to the poor. They also reflect what is universal to humankind, such as basic needs of security, acceptance, and affection, as well as basic goods such as life and freedom. The origin of such norms reaches below the permutations of culture and different ages. As *Persona Humana* maintains:

> These principles and norms [which pertain to certain fundamental values of human and Christian life] in no way owe their origin to a certain type of culture, but rather to knowledge of the divine law and of human nature. (n. 5)

Timothy O'Connell explains this well when he says that formal norms express values which are universal among humankind. While the way of expressing these values may differ among persons and groups, the affirmation of them as constitutive of what it means to be human is universally accepted.[2] Louis Janssens explains the implications of the absolute character of formal norms in this way:

> For instance, it will remain true that, always and in all circumstances, we must be just: we ought to be so disposed as to be concerned with the growth of truly human social relationships and structures as well as with the promotion of the possibilities for that purpose.[3]

Yet the specific expressions of these fundamental values inevitably belong to particular cultures and historical epochs. What these theologians seem to be saying, then, is that while we can and must speak of some moral norms as absolute, these are nonetheless limited in their expression by nothing less than the cornerstone of Christian faith itself—the incarnational principle.

Many theologians further relate formal norms to the sorts of persons we ought to be, or, as Louis Janssens puts it, they "assert what our dispositions ought to be."[4] This means that formal norms point to what the animating force of the moral life ought to be. For Timothy O'Connell, formal norms "articulate the inner value-dynamic of the human person."[5] This means that formal norms do not tell us what we ought to do, but bring to a focus the sorts of persons we ought to become, and they exhort, challenge, and encourage us to become that way.[6]

What are some examples of formal norms? The great commandment:

love God and love your neighbor as yourself (Mt 22: 37–40; cf. Mk 12:29–34; Lk 10:27) and the golden rule: "Whatever you wish others to do to you, do so to them" (Mt 7:12; Lk 6:31) are formal norms. Other examples are the first principle of the natural law: do good and avoid evil. Formal norms are also expressed positively in the language of virtue: for example, be honest, be just, be chaste, be grateful, be humble, be prudent, be reasonable. They are expressed negatively in the language of vice: for example, do not be selfish, vain, promiscuous, proud, stingy, merciless, or foolish.

## Formal Norms in Synthetic Terms

Expressions of formal norms which refer to actions are a little more puzzling than those which explicitly use the language of virtue or vice. These formal norms refer to such actions as murder, lying, stealing, adultery, blasphemy, genocide, euthanasia, slavery, torture, and rape, and they are somewhat puzzling because they are expressed with "synthetic" terms.

What is the meaning of synthetic terms? According to Louis Janssens, synthetic terms are words "which refer to the material content of an action but at the same time formulate a moral judgment."[7] This means that synthetic terms are compact value terms, not simply descriptive terms; that is, they already bear a moral qualification as part of their meaning. For example, "murder" is a morally qualifying term affirming that a killing (a descriptive term) is unjust (an evaluative term); "lie" is a morally qualifying term affirming that a falsehood (a descriptive term) is immoral (an evaluative term); "adultery" is a morally qualifying term affirming that an act of sexual intercourse (a descriptive term) is with the wrong person and for the wrong reasons (evaluative terms).[8]

Therefore, formal norms which use synthetic terms *not only* identify material action *but also* bear moral evaluation of that action. When an action is finally designated as "murder," "adultery," or "genocide," for example, nothing can ever justify the action to make it morally right. Norms formulated in these terms are absolutes—norms such as "do not lie," "do not steal," "do not commit adultery." These are absolute because they are tautological; that is, they simply tell us that immoral behavior is immoral. Once an action is understood to be objectively immoral, it is always so and can never be justified.

The real issue pertaining to norms with synthetic terms is not whether murder, lying, stealing, adultery, blasphemy, or the like could ever be justified. They cannot be. The real issue is how intention and circumstances must be related in order to count this material action (killing) as immoral (murder). We cannot know which act of killing is murder until we have considered the whole action with all its qualifications. So, for an act of killing rightly to be defined by the synthetic term "murder," it must lack a proper proportion of the action, intention, and circumstances taken together.[9]

Formal norms, whether pointing to character in the language of virtue and vice or pointing to actions in the language of synthetic terms, are limited in that they do not determine the specific content of what we ought to do. The formal norm "be chaste," for example, describes an inner attitude of ordering our sexuality in such a way that we respect ourselves, others, and the demands of social life. This norm does not, however, tell us which actions embody a chaste disposition in every instance. In like manner, the formal norm "do not murder" does not give us new information about the action of killing. It simply reminds us of what we already know (an unjust killing is unjust) and urges us to act on it.

Even though formal norms do not tell us what to do, they are still quite useful. Timothy O'Connell and Louis Janssens have been emphatic on the importance of formal norms to provide motivation, exhortation, and challenge to do what we already know to be right.[10] Timothy O'Connell says it well:

> I do not need only the data, I also need encouragement. I need formulations of my own values, formulations which in their conciseness and directness help me remain faithful to those values. And here is the specific (and very important) function of formal norms. They take the meaning of humanity, with its challenge of intellect and freedom. They apply that meaning to a particular area of human life (for example, property rights). And they declare, in pithy form, what I already know but tend to forget or neglect: Do not steal. By presenting me with that challenge, almost in aphoristic style, formal norms serve me in those moments of human weakness and temptation which are so much a part of our sin-affected situation.[11]

Formal norms, then, are absolute in character and motivational in function. In the language of virtue and vice, they do not give us specific information to answer the practical moral question, "What ought I to do?" But they encourage us to be a certain sort of person. In the language of synthetic terms, they remind us of what we already know and encourage us to do what is right and to avoid what is wrong.

## Material Norms

Whereas formal norms pertain to the sorts of persons we ought to be, material norms relate to the sorts of actions we ought to perform. Material norms attempt to attach formal norms of virtue or vice to specific instances of behavior—to speech, to killing, to making promises, to sexual conduct, for example. Thus we have material norms like these: entrusted secrets ought to be kept, give to each what is due him or her, do not speak falsely, do not kill, do not use artificial means of contraception, do not use artificial insemination or in vitro fertilization. Material norms lead us closer to answering the practical moral question, "What should I do?"

Situations of conflict have forced moral theologians to look more closely at the meaning and limits of material norms. Consider these two examples which are typical of the kinds of moral dilemmas which have forced a great deal of rethinking about the meaning and limits of material norms. If a doctor tells the truth to her patient, she may harm the patient's emotional health. If the doctor speaks a falsehood, she may begin to damage the confidence the patient has in her, and she may begin to experience a loss of truthfulness in herself. How is the doctor to live with the material norm: Do not speak a falsehood?

Or take the case of the married couple who have all the children for whom they can care in a reasonable way. They cannot enlarge their family without compromising the well-being of their present children. At the same time, the couple feels that fairly regular sexual expression is necessary for the growth and development of their marriage. They do not feel that they can respond adequately to both values and follow the proscription of contraception in *Humanae Vitae*. What do they do?

Since material norms pertain to actions we ought to avoid or actions we ought to perform, the meaning and use of material norms is related to the way we determine the objective morality of human actions. We explored this issue in the last chapter. There we saw that every human action inevitably embodies premoral/ontic good and evil features. The key to the meaning and use of material norms rests on the distinction between premoral/ontic evils and moral evils.

Moreover, in the last chapter we saw that an action cannot be judged morally on the basis of its materiality. Rather, the action must be taken in its entirety with all parts in proper relationship. Thus the material aspect of the action must be taken in relation to the intention of its agent and to the circumstances which make up its context.

Against this background we can understand the two primary limitations of material norms. First, material norms are limited expressions of moral truth—of who we ought to be and what we ought to do in this instance as a faithful response to God's call to be loving. They do not provide a complete moral evaluation of actions because they do not take into account all aspects of the action in their proper relationship. This means that material norms do not treat the act-in-itself as equivalent to the objective moral order. They do not encompass the totality of the objective features which constitute the whole moral action. Material norms are limited descriptions of the features of premoral/ontic good when stated positively (such as in "entrusted secrets ought to be kept") or premoral/ontic evil when stated negatively (such as in "do no kill"). They implicitly demand a proportionate reason to cause or to tolerate premoral evils. Material norms, then, ought to be interpreted as containing the implied qualifiers "if there were no further intervening factors," or "unless there is a proportionate reason," or "all things being equal."

Second, material norms are also limited by historical conditions and linguistic forms. The formulation and interpretation of the significance of premoral/ontic evils is relative to cultural development. For example, different times have recognized different degrees of application for the norm "do not kill"—the Catholic tradition has justified killing in war or in capital punishment. Today we are rethinking the moral acceptability of both since cultural developments have opened new opportunities to protect the values of life, freedom, and justice which once were protected by means of just wars or capital punishment. Other norms have been dropped (e.g., the prohibition of usury) or modified as we recognize the significance of certain values worth realizing in the process of being human. For example, we no longer speak of the primary and secondary ends of marriage, but we put on the same level the unitive and procreative aspects of sexual intercourse.

Given these limitations, how do material norms function in a positive way? Even though by themselves they do not express the whole of moral truth guiding what we ought to do in order to live faithfully in response to God and so solve our moral dilemmas, material norms do express an aspect of moral truth. They help us to recognize premoral goods and evils and prepare us to exercise prudence in attaining what befits human well-being and avoiding what does not. As Richard McCormick interprets them, material norms help us to remember that when we are faced with a premoral evil, we must not simply settle for it as though it were not harmful to human well-being. Material norms keep us from growing comfortable with the presence and influence of premoral evils. Material norms, when stated negatively, point out the kind of conduct which ought to be avoided as far as possible, and they warn us never to choose premoral evils as ends in themselves. McCormick also maintains that material norms direct us toward the goal of bringing about relationships which would lessen the presence and significance of the premoral/ontic evil features which inhibit the full development of persons and their social relations. To recognize premoral evils in war, the economy, contraception, or sterilization, for example, is to imply that we ought to be moving steadily to the point where causing or permitting such premoral evils is no longer necessary.[12] Louis Janssens holds a similar position:

> Briefly, concrete material norms invite us to bring about the ideal
> relations which lessen more and more effectively all forms of ontic
> evil which by their definition hamper the development of human
> beings and communities. [13]

These theologians are saying that if there were no other intervening
circumstances, or if we lived in a world where all things were equal, we ought
not to cause or tolerate premoral evils. But since many circumstances intervene so that all things are not equal, we must strive to create a world where
we do not need to kill, speak falsely, or increase the population without
decreasing the quality of life. In our world where values inevitably conflict,
we may cause or permit premoral evils only if we have a proportionate reason
for doing so. The lack of proportionate reason is precisely what makes acting
contrary to a specific material norm, or causing a premoral evil, morally
wrong.

## Material Norms and Absolutes

In his treatment of natural law (ST I–II, q. 94), St. Thomas distinguished universal principles (formal norms), which are absolute, from secondary or concrete precepts (material norms), which are not always applicable
(*valent ut in pluribus*, St I–II, q. 94, a. 4). He explains that the more specific a
moral precept becomes, the more frequent and likely will be the cases when it
does not apply. The complexity of circumstances surrounding every act does
not allow a point-for-point correspondence between the norm and the
variabilities of the moral life. [14] St. Thomas demonstrates here a more flexible
conception of the practical precepts of the natural law than do some interpretations to which it has been subjected. His treatment of prudence affirms the
same limited or relative character of material norms when he emphasizes that
the considerations of prudence require us to examine each situation in light of
all the relevant factors, not only the material norms (ST II–II, q. 51, a. 4).

To raise material norms to the level of an "absolute" would mean that
they adequately and completely express the whole of moral truth for the
situations to which they pertain. As such, the action or class of actions
identified by the norm would always be objectively required or forbidden,
i.e., always, everywhere, in all circumstances, and for all persons without
exception. For a material norm to have such a status, it would have to include
all the possible combinations of premoral/ontic evils and goods involved in a
specific deed. But does anyone who participates in an interrelated and changing world have the epistemological vantage point which would give access to
such certain knowledge? Josef Fuchs, Louis Janssens, Richard McCormick,

and Edward Vacek, to name but a few, do not think so.[15] Edward Vacek covers the territory well and speaks for many with this observation:

> One can, and indeed must, strive for moral certainty. But *theoretically* one can never be sure that one has properly seen all the values resident in act. Hence one can never be theoretically certain that a given act is always wrong. Further, an "absolute" would have to be formulated in such a way as to ensure in advance that the uniqueness and development of individuals, the variations of cultures, the changes of history, and the involvement of God in the world will never introduce any significant differences. This seems impossible if one takes historicity seriously. New situations, conceivably, may appear which will introduce new values that would tip the balance or recharacterize, i.e., give a new *ratio* to, an action.[16]

Vacek goes on to say that even though material norms may not be absolute, this does not deny universally relevant values, such as life, love, or beauty. These values remain objectively valuable in themselves and can be recognized and respected as such even if they are not being realized at the moment.[17] To be open to these values is a way of expressing our openness to God. To realize these values is a way of expressing our love for God. But not to embrace them in their fullness at one particular moment, or to prefer one value to another in one's choice, is not to spurn the value not chosen as though it had no validity, or to turn one's back on God. Conversely, premoral evils, such as pain, hunger, or death, remain such even when they must be tolerated. These ought to be something we would want to avoid as far as possible, even though at times we must inevitably tolerate them.

If material norms are not absolute, then how are we to understand them as being open to exceptions? Cautions about making exceptions and criteria for doing so become most important for a theory in which morality is co-extensive with norms or in which norms are the sole factor in making a moral decision. Catholic casuistry of the manualist era, for example, tried to extend or multiply norms in order to cover every condition or exception. In the manuals, norms are given a priority in a deductive process which is identified with the judgment of conscience. Using norms in making a decision took something like the following form: The norm serves as the major premise of a syllogism, the minor premise is the situational analysis identifying the circumstances relevant to the norm, and the conclusion of the deductive process is the judgment of conscience, or what the person is morally obligated to do.

But if material norms do not embody in themselves the whole of moral truth (who we ought to be and what we ought to do in response to God's invitation to be loving), and if moral reasoning is not exclusively deductive, then we need to rethink our attitude toward the role of material norms in making a decision. Material norms always apply, but they do not always constrain. Material norms have limitations. They do not express the whole of moral truth and so cannot be the sole determination of what we ought to do in some particular instance bearing its own configuration of circumstances and intention. Complex moral reality cannot be captured adequately in the formulation of a norm. Material norms, for example, do not capture the unique, personal involvement of the moral agent which is also part of the whole moral reality and moral truth of it. We can never have moral truth independently of the moral agent and the complexity of human existence.

But if we did not treat norms as an integral part of moral analysis, we would risk eroding not only their general observance but also the general appreciation of the values which lie behind them. Dismissing norms altogether can lead to a kind of moral relativism or subjectivism which we saw in the last chapter as a possible objection to the approach employing proportionate reason. While we presume in favor of the norm as a reliable expression of premoral evils to avoid and premoral goods to embody, the proper use of the norms still needs to include the human agent adequately considered as well as the totality of the relational moral context. In short, using material norms in making a decision requires not only the cognitive skill of logical reasoning but also the prudence of a carefully discerning and well-ordered heart open to the action of the Holy Spirit.

## Virtually Exceptionless Material Norms

If we cannot claim specific norms as absolute *in theory*, we ought to hold some as such *in practice*. These kinds of material norms are called "practical absolutes" or "virtually exceptionless" material norms. This means that while we cannot theoretically demonstrate them as absolute, these norms highlight values which, in the general course of events, will take precedence and, for all practical purposes, should be preferred.

For example, Josef Fuchs cannot conceive of any kind of exception to the norm which would prohibit the "cruel treatment of a child which is of no benefit to the child."[18] Richard McCormick speaks of "the direct killing of non-combatants in warfare"[19] as a practical absolute. Louis Janssens identifies "You shall render help to a person in extreme distress" and the prohibition of rape as two examples of virtually exceptionless norms.[20] In *The Challenge of Peace* of the American bishops, the general principles of "non-combatant immunity" and "proportionality" in war fall under this type of norm, as do the general principles structuring their letter, *Economic Justice for All*.[21] Paul Ramsey includes rape along with "Never experiment medically on a human being without his informed consent," "Never punish a man whom one knows to be innocent of that for which he would be punished," and "No premarital intercourse" as being significantly closed to exceptions.[22] Thomas L. Beauchamp and James F. Childress place in the same category the norm, "Always obtain the informed consent of your competent patients except in emergency or low-risk situations."[23] As with defining Fuchs' "cruel treatment" and Ramsey's "pre-marital" (which for him is not the same as pre-ceremonial), considerable debate might surround what constitutes an "emergency" or "low-risk" in the Beauchamp-Childress example.[24] Nevertheless, what these examples show is that some material norms can and should be regarded as virtually exceptionless.

What is the force of saying "virtually" exceptionless? For McCormick, "virtually" indicates that we cannot prove with the sharpness of deductive syllogistic logic that no exception could ever occur. Yet these norms light up values which human experience tells us, in the general course of events and for all practical purposes, ought to take precedence even though their preference in every instance cannot be demonstrated absolutely.[25]

For Donald Evans, who coined the expression "virtually exceptionless," the point of saying "virtually" is to avoid a "creeping legalism" which tries to extend the range of moral absolutes farther than can be justified. Evans sees moral norms on a continuum. Some are open to extensive revision, some less so, and others are in varying degrees virtually exceptionless. "Virtually" respects the freedom and discretion of the moral agent, the ambiguity of moral action, the limitations of human knowing, and the limitations of any attempt to capture the experience of value in a pithy formula. The force of being "virtually" exceptionless also puts the burden of proof on those who would want to make an exception.[26]

For Albert DiIanni, the force of being "virtually" exceptionless means that while we cannot demonstrate their absoluteness theoretically, we ought to teach these norms and act on them *as if* they were absolute. To be virtually exceptionless for DiIanni means that there are no practical options to these norms. Since their exceptions are so unimaginable, we ought to live with them and regard them in our moral education as being absolute.[27]

But how do we come to know which norms ought to be regarded as practical absolutes? Exploring this epistemological issue will widen the debate on moral norms. We can make a beginning in this direction, however, by pursuing the modes of knowing introduced in the last chapter to help us to determine a proportionate reason.

## Moral Norms and the Moral Imagination

The understanding of the types, meaning, and limits of moral norms brings us to the challenge of making moral decisions which are both responsive to contemporary issues and responsible to the moral values grounded in the faith and life of the Christian community and in our common humanity. Yet, well-formulated moral norms, though necessary in the moral life, are not enough. Philip Keane has shown that moral norms need to be interrelated with the imagination if they are to function well in the moral life.[28] As an aspect of the uniqueness of the human person, the imagination draws together the concrete and universal elements of human experience to lead us toward a more appropriate grasp of our experience.[29] In the moral life, the imagination relates our moral experience to the abstract expression of moral meaning found in moral norms. By means of the imagination, we can see new aspects of our experience by using moral norms to inform our interpretations of moral reality, and we can use our experience both to stretch the meaning of moral norms and to disclose their limits. The constant interaction of these norms and the flow of new experiences gives us a deeper understanding of what we know about the moral life. The key to Keane's analysis is that we need both moral norms and the imagination to interact with each other in order to reach a proper moral judgment.

Keane offers three major reasons why norms must be interrelated with the imaginative process.[30]

First, our inherited norms will be more or less effective for us to the extent that we have a first-hand experience of living through the process which gives rise to norms in the first place, at least in some cases. When we can make for ourselves the appropriate connections between our moral experiences and the abstract ideas related to them, moral norms will make sense for us and we will be able to appropriate them more deeply. For example, norms regulating relationships in health care, such as the norms protecting patient autonomy, truth-telling, and confidentiality, may make more sense to us when we use our own experience of being subject to the health care system as the particular experience with which to understand the nature of these norms and the wisdom they enshrine.

Second, the imagination helps us to appreciate the limitations of moral norms. The formulations of all norms are of necessity historically and linguistically conditioned and are thus always open to further refinement. We must continue to reflect on our norms to discern their fuller meaning. The efforts of the American bishops to rethink or, better, to reimagine the norms of a just war tradition in a nuclear age are an example of using the imaginative process to deepen the meaning of accepted norms and to test the adequacy of their formulations.

Third, the imagination helps in applying moral norms. One of the benefits of the vigorous situation ethics debate is that it has made us aware that no moral case is exactly the same as the previous one. In each instance we need to verify the relationship of the specific case and the moral norm in order to be sure that it actually applies and how it applies. The imagination helps this process of verification through the images it provides. The images we acquire through our experiences in family, community, education, and church, for example, shape what we see in our moral norms and what ground we can cover with them. For example, how differently would we approach the hopelessly ill if we imagine death as ultimate catastrophe or as the final stage of growth? How differently would we attend to the dying if our image of medicine is to care rather than to cure? How differently would we look on marriage if we used the image of covenant rather than contract?

The church can be a rich resource for shaping the imagination by drawing upon its stories, metaphors, heroes, and heroines of faith to communicate the deeper meanings of its moral experience and moral norms. For example, the image of the reign of God can be a rich resource for approaching and understanding the norms of justice which apply to war and peace. The paschal mystery of Jesus and its story of suffering-death-resurrection can enliven and broaden the norms of care for the dying. A hero such as Thomas More can shape our vision of courage, loyalty, and sacrifice. The public celebrations of long-term wedding anniversaries can do much to enrich our understanding of norms oriented toward commitment and fidelity. The image of covenant with its stories of steadfast love and fidelity can become the context for understanding the norms of sexual morality. The image of children as gifts of wonder and mystery may enlighten the imaginative dimensions of our norms regulating the use of reproductive technology and for focusing our decisions around the care of handicapped newborns.[31]

Philip Keane shows by his analysis that moral norms cannot really do their work unless they spring from an ongoing imaginative process and move us toward it. Moral norms and the moral imagination are both necessary for the moral life. Our norms will continue to act in ways that discipline the pure fancy of imagination, while the imagination will continue to revitalize long-standing moral norms. The role of norms and the imagination in pastoral moral guidance and personal moral decision making remains the issue for the next chapter.

## Notes

1. This formulation is based on the analysis of Daniel C. Maguire, *The Moral Choice* (Garden City: Doubleday & Company, Inc., 1978), p. 220.

2. O'Connell, "The Question of Moral Norms," *American Ecclesiastical Review* 169 (June 1975): 383–386.

3. Janssens, "Norms and Priorities in a Love Ethics," *Louvain Studies* 4 (Spring 1977): 207.

4. *Ibid.*, p. 208.

5. O'Connell, "The Question of Moral Norms," p. 386.

6. O'Connell, *Principles for a Catholic Morality* (New York: Seabury Press, 1978), pp. 160–162.

7. Janssens, "Norms and Priorities in a Love Ethics," *Louvain Studies* 4 (Spring 1977): 216.

8. Traditionally, the kinds of actions to which these terms point are considered *secundum se* evils. This means that these actions carried their own absolute condemnation in their very name (*mox nominata sunt mala*). The very meaning of the name joins the material action to a sinful intention (*ex libidine*). *Secundum se* evil actions are immoral. Such actions can never be made good by any configuration of intention and circumstances. John Dedek has provided a series of valuable historical studies which explore this sense of "intrinsically evil acts" or moral absolutes in St. Thomas and his predecessors and the theologians who immediately followed him. The first study was "Moral Absolutes in the Predecessors of St. Thomas," *Theological Studies* 38 (December 1977): 654–680. The second was "Intrinsically Evil Acts: An Historical Study of the Mind of St. Thomas," *The Thomist* 43 (July 1979): 385–413. Next came "Premarital Sex: The Theological Argument from Peter Lombard to Durand," *Theological Studies* 41 (December 1980): 643–667. The last of the series was "Intrinsically Evil Acts: The Emergence of a Doctrine,"*Recherches de Théologie Ancienne et Médiévale* 50 (1983): 191–226. For another historical essay with similar findings, see Franz Scholz, "Problems on Norms Raised by Ethical Borderline Situations: Beginnings of a Solution in Thomas Aquinas and Bonaventure," *Readings in Moral Theology No. 1*, edited by Charles E. Curran and Richard A. McCormick (Ransey: Paulist Press, 1979). pp. 158–183.

9. Richard McCormick has explained these issues regarding synthetic terms well in his "Moral Notes," *Theological Studies* 37 (March 1976): 73–74, and again in 39 (March 1978): 93.

10. O'Connell, "The Question of Moral Norms," pp. 385–387; also, *Principles for a Catholic Morality*, pp. 161–162. Louis Janssens, "Norms and Priorities in a Love Ethics," p. 209.

11. O'Connell, *Principles for a Catholic Morality*, pp. 161–162.

12. McCormick, "Moral Norms and Their Meaning," *Lectureship*, edited by Mount Angel Abbey (St. Benedict, Oregon: Mount Angel Abbey, 1978), pp. 43–46.

13. Janssens, "Ontic Evil and Moral Evil," *Readings in Moral Theology No. 1*, p. 216.

14. For a commentary on the variability of natural law in its specific precepts according to St. Thomas, see Michael B. Crowe, *The Changing Profile of Natural Law* (The Hague: Martinus Nijhoff, 1977), pp. 184–191.

15. For Fuchs, see "Absoluteness of Moral Terms," in *Readings in Moral Theology No. 1*, pp. 125–126; for Janssens, see "Norms and Priorities in a Love Ethics," pp. 217–218; for McCormick, see "Ambiguity in Moral Choice," in *Doing Evil to Achieve Good*, edited by Richard A. McCormick and Paul Ramsey (Chicago: Loyola University Press, 1978), pp. 42–44; for Vacek, see "Proportionalism: One View of the Debate," *Theological Studies* 46 (June 1985): 294.

16. Vacek, "Proportionalism: One View of the Debate," *Theological Studies* 46 (June 1985): 294.

17. *Ibid.*, pp. 294–295.

18. Fuchs, "Absoluteness of Moral Terms," *Readings in Moral Theology No. 1*, p. 126.

19. McCormick, "Ambiguity in Moral Choice," *Doing Evil to Achieve Good*, pp. 42–44.

20. Janssens, "Norms and Priorities in a Love Ethics," p. 217. However, just how Janssens sees the norm prohibiting rape to differ from a synthetic, formal norm is not really evident.

21. *The Challenge of Peace* (Washington: United States Catholic Conference, 1983), n. 9, p. 4; *Economic Justice for All* (Washington: United States Catholic Conference, 1986), Chapter II–B.1, pp. 33–40.

22. Ramsey, "The Case of the Curious Exception," *Norm and Context in Christian Ethics*, edited by Gene Outka and Paul Ramsey (New York: Charles Scribner's Sons, 1968), pp. 67–135.

23. Beauchamp and Childress, *Principles of Biomedical Ethics* (New York: Oxford University Press, 1979), p. 43.

43. Donald Evans has made a good analysis of the significance of words with "elastic" meanings in norms such as these. See his study of Paul Ramsey in "Paul Ramsey on Exceptionless Moral Rules," *The American Journal of Jurisprudence* 16 (1971): 184–214, esp. 198 ff.

25. McCormick, "Ambiguity in Moral Choice," *Doing Evil to Achieve Good*, pp. 42–44.

26. Evans, "Paul Ramsey on Exceptionless Moral Rules," pp. 205–207. See also his article, "Love, Situations, and Rules," *Norm and Context in Christian Ethics*, pp. 367–414, esp. pp. 236–238.

27. DiIanni, "The Direct/Indirect Distinction in Morals," *Readings in Moral Theology No.1*, pp. 215–243, esp. 236–238.

28. This is a major theme in his work, *Christian Ethics and Imagination* (Ramsey: Paulist Press, 1984).

29. *Ibid.*, p. 81.

30. *Ibid.*, pp. 90–95.

31. Keane explores examples like these and more at greater length in *ibid.*, pp. 110–146.

# 20  Moral Decision Making and Pastoral Moral Guidance

W e began the study of moral norms with how to determine the objective morality of human action by means of the traditional three-font principle and the premoral/ontic evil and proportionate reason thought-pattern. Then, in light of that framework, we considered the meaning and limits of moral norms. We saw that, as short-hand summaries of moral wisdom inferred from a wide range of human experience, moral norms illumine and guide moral choices but do not definitively determine them. Situations of moral conflict are so complex that moral norms have to be applied imaginatively and wisely.

So far, we have looked at only the pre-responsible level of human action which must be considered in trying to determine morally right or wrong behavior. We have not yet studied the total moral reality, particularly the moral person acting or the particular context in which to place the action. We move, then, from asking "What is morally right?" in the abstract to asking "What ought I to do in this context?" To show how one might answer this question, this chapter will first sketch the three leading methods for making a moral decision and then propose a model of pastoral moral guidance.

## Methods of Decision Making

Now that we have considered a way of determining the objective morality of human action, we need a strategy of love which enables us to do something about what we believe to be right. How do we defend, or justify, our moral choices? This question leads to a method of making a moral decision. Chapter 2 already introduced, however briefly, the three principal strategies of love used in contemporary moral reflection—the deontological, the teleological, and the relational-responsibility methods of decision making. Now we can take a closer look at each.

In a systematic moral theory, one of these methods will be primary. However, these methods are not mutually exclusive. Even though one method may be primary, elements of the others may also be used. For example, the relational-responsibility method has a place for laws and norms even though these are not given as privileged a place for understanding experience and making a moral judgment as they are in the deontological method.

## Deontological Method

The deontological method is commonly associated today with Germain Grisez and William E. May on the Catholic side, and with Paul Ramsey on the Protestant side. While those who use this method differ somewhat, they share its general orientation.

The Catholic moral manuals in use prior to the Second Vatican Council also used the deontological method primarily for decision making, even while they favored the teleological method for finding the premises. For example, in the manuals the first ethical consideration is the final end of the human person (a teleological concern). Also, their approach to sexual morality is based on the finality, or end of the human reproductive capacity (showing a teleological orientation). Once the teleological orientation found the major premises, the decision making favored by the manuals was reduced to a law-oriented method in practice. Moral reasoning involved applying the general moral principles, or the moral law which ultimately comes from God (eternal law), to typical situations in a form of a practical syllogism. In more legal terms, divine law comes from God as author of revelation, and natural law is the rational creature's participation in eternal law. Civil law and ecclesiastical law are subordinate to the natural law and eternal law. Most of Catholic moral teaching from the manuals is based on the natural law which determines the basic rights and obligations fulfilling the moral order. The function of conscience is to draw the practical conclusion which follows from subordinating the situation to the particular moral principle.

Law, duty, and obligation are the points of reference in deciding what to do according to the deontological method. In other words, it approaches the practical moral question, "What ought I to do?" by first answering the question, "What does the law require?" or "What is my duty?" Also, this position holds that some actions, or classes of acts, are right or wrong by virtue of intrinsic features of the actions independently of consequences. For example, telling the truth and keeping promises are always right, and killing the innocent is always wrong. It is consistent with the deontological position to hold that certain actions are "intrinsically morally evil" in themselves and can never be done since no set of intention, circumstances, or consequences could ever justify the wrong-making characteristics inherent in certain actions (e.g., according to official Roman Catholic teaching, many sexual actions fall into this category). When such actions are the major moral term in the formulation of a moral norm, then these norms are treated as absolutes and they become the sole criterion for judging the morality of an action.

According to the deontological method, we make a decision by determining what duty or positive law applies to the situation, or by referring to whatever the authority (secular, ecclesial, divine) demands of the person. In situations where more than one norm applies, or where the voices of authority conflict, the decision must be made on the basis of the higher norm or authority.

One strength of the deontological method is that it preserves consistency and stability in the moral life and clearly supports the social fabric of the human community by giving such a prominent place to commonly shared norms, laws, or duties as its point of reference. Also, it shows that some aspects of actions cannot be sacrificed to consequences. For example, the deontologist would claim that entrusted secrets ought to be kept because confidentiality belongs to the dignity, privacy, and autonomy of the person who entrusts personal information to another. Disclosing private information creates a bond with another person which entails an obligation to respect confidence despite the consideration of consequences which might follow.

The weakness of this position is that it does not adequately account for the temporality and contextuality of moral living. It absolutizes the past and the present without considering the future, ongoing interaction as integral to the moral meaning of actions. Also, it does not adequately account for the complexity of circumstances which can change the moral reality of an action. No human action carries moral meaning outside its actual relationships. Since life is full of endless nuances which cannot be captured in abstract norms or laws, deontology suffers from failing to correlate and weigh numerous factors in order to discover the meaning, or value, of our actions. The choice one makes in light of norms or laws ought not to be made independently of the person adequately considered and the totality of the human relational context.

## Teleological Method

The teleological method appears in a variety of forms. For example, St. Thomas Aquinas, the most significant Roman Catholic teleologist, held that the ultimate end of the human person is the first ethical consideration. Since the fundamental drives or tendencies of the person are oriented toward the fulfillment of human potential, the morally good is whatever leads to that ultimate fulfillment—union with God. St. Thomas does have a treatise on law, but it comes at the end of his moral theory. Law serves the final end of being human.

Joseph Fuchs, Louis Janssens, Richard McCormick, and Bruno Schuller also use the teleological method. Their form of moderate teleology judges the proportion between premoral goods and evils which accompany every human action in light of the full range of relationships which constitute the moral meaning of the action. In Chapter 18 I discussed their form of teleology under proportionalism.

An extreme form of teleology has been made popular by Joseph Fletcher in his *Situation Ethics*.[1] He summarizes his approach well in these few sentences:

> *Christian* situation ethics has only one norm or principle or law (call it what you will) that is binding and unexceptional, always good and right regardless of the circumstances. That is "love"—the *agape* of the summary commandment to love God and the neighbor. Everything else without exception, all laws and rules and principles and ideals and norms, are only *contingent*, and only valid *if they happen* to serve love in any situation.[2]

Later Fletcher defines the "love" which is required as "the greatest amount of neighbor welfare for the largest number of neighbors possible."[3]

A strict teleological approach to the practical moral question, "What ought I to do?" first answers the question, "What is my goal?" The point of reference in making a moral decision is neither laws nor duties, but the consequences. In making a moral decision, the strict teleologist first determines possible alternatives for action and the consequences which each produces. The alternatives are then weighed against each other to determine which produces the greatest possible value in its consequences. For example, in trying to decide whether or not to keep an entrusted secret confidential, the teleologist would promote confidentiality insofar as it avoided the disruptive effects on society which would result if confidences were broken.

One of the advantages of this method is that it takes seriously the future implications of an action and regards them as part of the action's moral meaning. In this way, this method challenges us to look into the future as far as we can and to follow the impact of our actions as far as possible.

The great weakness of teleology is that it substitutes a part of morality (the consequences) for the whole. One form of teleology, utilitarianism, demonstrates this clearly when it claims that morality is determined by achieving the greatest good for the greatest number. By locating the good in the many (universalism), utilitarianism can easily overlook and sacrifice the individual for the sake of the many. Also, for a strict teleologist, only the future is morally relevant. Making consequences determine the full moral significance of an action runs roughshod over the present and over all the other aspects which make up the full determination of morality. While consequences do indeed have moral significance, so do the ways in which the agent brings about the consequences. Consequences must always be taken in relational tension with the many other elements which constitute the moral significance of the action taken in its totality.

Another weakness of the teleological method is that we often have no unanimity on the goal to be realized. Moreover, the goal upon which we finally do base our evaluation of an action is still in the future and not yet proven. Since no one is an expert on the future, this method is limited by our inabililty to predict what will happen.

## Relational-Responsibility Method

The relational-responsibility method is commonly identified with H. Richard Niebuhr and James M. Gustafson on the Protestant side, and with Bernard Häring and Charles E. Curran on the Catholic side. The relational-responsibility method answers the practical moral question, "What ought I to do?" by asking first, "What is happening?" In this method, one decides what to do by determining what action is most harmonious or proportionate to the meaning of the whole relational context. This method does not do away with laws or consequences since these help one to grasp what a harmonious relationship might be.

The relational-responsibility method sees the moral life primarily comprised of relationships held together by ongoing interaction with God, neighbor, world, and self instead of seeing each as standing alone and being subject to a pre-arranged system of laws or a plan in search of a goal. As a result, it requires a "sympathetic" sense or a "fine feeling" of what fits the relational context. This method recognizes that making a moral decision is more an art than a science. As such, it requires a mode of thinking which is grounded in a well-ordered heart. In coming to a decision, someone using this method tries to include all the factors in the relevant situation within a proper relationship. It also recognizes the uniqueness of all standpoints, considers an action as part of an ongoing set of interaction, and emphasizes the ongoing process of relationships which make up the context. On the issue of keeping confidences, this style of decision making would keep confidences which properly fit the network of relationships which evoke it.

The great strength of this method is that it realizes that all human behavior must be judged in the context of actual relationships. Better than the other methods, it accounts for the complexity and ambiguity of human reality. This method is so attractive because it highlights moral meaning from within the relational context, and it acknowledges the person's ability to discover that meaning. It does not accept imposing the meaning from some external authority, some prearranged pattern of rules, or some plan in search of a goal. The moral meaning of an action can be found only in the context of the person adequately considered and in the process of ongoing interaction. Since this method places the accent on the person's full relational context and the process of coming to self-realization through the exercise of personal acts of freedom, it puts a greater emphasis than the other methods do on character formation, virtue, and moral discernment.

Among the weakensses of this method is that its lines of moral analysis are not always that clear and so it relies on a refined moral sensitivity more than the other methods do. To caricature this method's weakness, one could say that it raises "muddling through" to the undeserved heights of ethical sophistication. Moral decisions in this model come with some degree of uncertainty and tentativeness. The goal of moral analysis is to reduce this uncertainty to a manageable size. It tries to ensure that consideration is given to at least the most obvious alternatives and outstanding consequences which can be determined on the basis of past experience, the guidance of moral norms, the insight gained from broad consultation, and the evidence of empirical investigation. But the very complexity of this method, and its efforts to be inclusive of everything in its proper relationship, makes it more difficult to use than the other two methods, and it leaves one with a much less settled conscience. Anyone who follows this method must learn to live with ambiguity and an uneasy conscience and be ready to revise one's judgment as the evidence changes.

Since each of these methods emphasizes something integral to moral experience, we would expect to find something of each always taken into consideration. Yet moralists, in fact, often prefer one method over another. James Gustafson's analysis of ethics has clearly shown that an adequate method for helping us love well must answer the practical question, "What ought I to do?" by addressing at least the four points which inform the moral level of thinking: the agent, the beliefs, the situation, and the appropriate norms.[4] These points can be used to test the comprehensiveness of any of these strategies. The process of using these four points in making a decision can be summarized as follows:

The answer to the practical moral question begins and ends with the *moral agent*, the "I" of "What ought I to do?" by attending to the features of the person adequately considered. For a decision to be a truly personal decision, it ought to arise out of the person's identity and intentions and be consistent with the person's integrity and capacities for certain moral action.

This requires attention to *beliefs*, or stable convictions, which shape the agent's self-understanding and ability to consider what is possible to do. Beliefs also challenge the agent to act in a way most consistent with his or her identity and integrity. Next, since morality is based on reality, moral analysis demands getting a clear lay of the moral land. This means *analyzing the situation* by exploring as thoroughly as possible the reality-revealing questions, such as the ones we asked in forming conscience for decision making. Moreover, the proper assessment of proportionate reason demands a clear knowledge of the circumstances which surround situations of conflict. Besides an analysis of the situation, practical moral thinking consults various sources of moral wisdom. Moral consultation appeals to *criteria of judgment*. Especially important at this level is to appeal to scripture, Jesus, human experience, and the moral wisdom communicated by the teaching of the church and through the witness of the lives of moral virtuosos. Moral norms help tremendously in this process of consultation, for they are the generalized expressions of inference from a broad experience of value. But appealing to moral norms does not end the process. The Christian moral person ought to bring the full force of Christian beliefs and commitments to bear on the moral analysis as well as on the evaluation and selection of alternatives for action. Exploring beliefs at this stage brings us back to the person who ultimately must decide and act. The process of addressing adequately the four points of moral analysis is demanding. It provides the framework for the model of pastoral moral guidance which follows.

## Pastoral Moral Guidance

### Moral Theology and Pastoral Moral Guidance

The Catholic moral tradition has distinguished the levels of moral theology and pastoral moral guidance. According to this distinction, moral theology is concerned with pursuing moral truth at the level of objective morality. It asks, "What sorts of persons ought we to be and what sorts of actions ought we to do in response to God's call to love?" Or, "What sorts of persons and actions best contribute to the well-being of persons and their social relationships?" Moral theology functions on the descriptive and evaluative levels of moral discourse. At the descriptive level, it points out the virtues and the premoral/ontic good and evil features of actions. At the evaluative level, it draws on communal discernment to determine the presence or absence of those virtues and a proportionate reason for judging whether an action is moral or immoral when taken in its totality. Pastoral moral guidance, on the other hand, is concerned with the person's moral capacities (which include the extent of one's knowledge and freedom) to act in accord with objective moral standards which lead one to the ultimate goal of fulfilling the twofold commandment of love.

Pastoral guidance addresses a particular person in an immediate dilemma. It assesses subjective culpability, or personal responsibility, by asking, "Given where you are, what is the next step you can take toward the ultimate good of living by God's call to be loving?" In this way, pastoral guidance is directed toward the best possible moral achievement of the person for now, while encouraging and supporting the person's openness and growth toward the ultimate goal of living the fullness of love. As such, pastoral guidance respects the principle of gradualness in the Christian life as the person strives to live the life of love through imperfect steps and stages. The call to conversion, on the one hand, is a challenge to move beyond the minimum requirements of objective standards. On the other hand, it is the pastoral moral counselor's basis for treating with compassion those who are unable to realize for now all that the objective standards or the twofold commandment of love may require.

Appropriate pastoral moral guidance does not abandon the community's accepted normative moral standards when a particular person cannot measure up to them for now. Nor does it want to fall prey to the fallacy of universalizing the particular by raising to the level of a general rule the experience and capacity of a single individual. As we saw in the treatment of norms in the last chapter, normative moral standards reflect the accumulated wisdom and experience of the moral community and not just the isolated experience of a single individual. Pastoral guidance holds in tension the objective norms of morality and the particular person's capacity for responsibility. In this way it relates moral judgments to pastoral judgments, but does not collapse one into the other. Both moral theology and pastoral guidance seek the same moral truth of who we are to become and what we are to do in response to God's call of love. But they differ by engaging different levels of discourse in the process.

From within this framework, the challenge to the pastoral person is to be true both to the objective norms of morality (such as we find expressed in the moral teaching of the magisterium) and at the same time to be respectful of the limited, subjective capacities of the person to embody the values upheld by these norms. A mark of pastoral sensitivity is to distinguish between the good which ought to be (a normative moral judgment based on the moral order) and the good which can only be achieved for now (a pastoral moral judgment based on subjective capacity). Although we are always required to do what we can, no one is ever morally obligated to do what is impossible. Not everyone can fulfill the objective moral standards to the same degree. Impediments to freedom and knowledge, together with what different stages of moral development allow a person to realize, influence what a person perceives to be morally required and the way a person relates to normative standards.

Catholic morality traditionally distinguished between objective moral judgment and subjective pastoral judgment; it also distinguished between the objective immorality of an action and the subjective non-culpability of the person performing the action. This means that even though certain actions are considered to be materially (or objectively) sinful or "intrinsically evil" in themselves at the evaluative level, a person may not necessarily be formally sinful or morally culpable for doing them. Traditional Catholic morality accounted for this non-culpability on the basis of excusing causes or impediments to knowledge and freedom which make it impossible for the person to satisfy the demands of objective morality in their fullness. *Humanae Vitae*, in fact, acknowledged as much in its "Pastoral Directives" which advise priests to proclaim the full Catholic teaching on marriage (n. 28) but also to show the same kind of compassion which the Lord himself had in being merciful to individuals while opposing evil in all its forms (n. 29). However, we must be cautious not to use this distinction to cover cases for which it does not apply. For example, if we accept the premoral/ontic evil features of actions and are more restrictive in what we consider to be intrinsically morally evil (a restriction which demands the full qualification of the act in its totality, not just the deed itself), then we should not appeal to this distinction for many of the cases it once satisfied.

The distinction, however, can help us to appreciate that the Catholic moral tradition does not condemn individuals who are unable to fulfill the moral imperatives of objective morality. It shows us how the Catholic tradition deals with them compassionately. In the tradition of conscience, for example, we have explained this incapacity as an expression of "invincible ignorance." Louis Monden, Bernard Häring, and Charles Curran still find this notion useful as long as it is not restricted to the person's lack of cognitive knowledge or rational grasp of objective morality. For them "invincible ignorance" more properly pertains to the person's inability to assimilate and to respond to all that a moral imperative demands.[5]

## A Model of Pastoral Moral Guidance

In light of this way of conceiving the relationship between moral theology and pastoral moral guidance, I will sketch a tentative model of pastoral moral guidance.[6] This model makes its way between two extreme approaches for determining what one ought to do. At one extreme is the approach of uncompromising enforcement of the normative standard. This extreme insists that objective moral standards capture the whole of moral truth and so dictate what must be done regardless of the person's capacities. The other extreme lets sentiment determine what ought to be done. According to this approach, doing whatever feels right is the way to moral truth regardless of whatever makes up the relational context. This approach insists that since subjective capacities entail the whole of moral truth, one can act as an isolated individual apart from the experience and standards of the moral community. Neither extreme adequately respects moral truth. Something in the middle is needed.

Sensitive pastoral people probably already intuitively do much of what appears in the following model of a mediating position. The purpose of spelling out what we already know and do by heart is to help us to be more critically aware of what we do or of what we are striving to do as pastoral ministers called to serve as moral guides. A model such as this, however, has limited value. First of all, it serves best for complex cases which need serious consultation and time for discernment. It is not necessary for less complex, daily moral living. Above all, having a "good nose" for what is right is the gift of wisdom, not the conclusion of a set of instructions. If we want to know the right thing to do, we ought to watch a wise person act. Such wisdom, unfortunately, is not something which can be captured and passed on through a set of instructions which will guarantee success if followed correctly. Also, in offering moral guidance, we may do well to keep in mind that most people, most of the time, ultimately choose largely on the basis of some combination of taste, a good hunch, and intuition arising out of their internalized value system and not so much on the basis of someone else's advice.

## Pastoral Posture

A pastoral posture is the stance, perspective, attitude, or disposition of the pastoral person involved in the helping relationship of pastoral moral guidance. That posture is positively disposed both toward the individual seeking guidance and toward the normative standards of the community.

Toward the person seeking guidance, the pastoral posture ought to be marked first by an *openness to understand* the other person's history and values before bringing to bear on it the imperatives of objective moral standards. Being open to understand enables the pastoral person to appreciate the limited capacity of the other. A person's evaluative knowledge and self-determining freedom are subject to many determining influences which need to be acknowledged as a real part of the person's total moral reality. Only by facing these influences as real limitations can the pastoral person *encourage* and *challenge* the other to capitalize on his or her strengths while living realistically within his or her given limits. Only after first acknowledging and accepting the limitations on one's moral capacity will anyone realistically be able to take the next step toward responding to God's call to be loving. A pastoral posture marked by an openness to understand and a willingness to encourage will invite critical reflection and moral growth much easier than will approaching the other in an authoritative manner armed with the answers of abstract, objective moral imperatives.

The pastoral posture must be critical as well. It expresses a critical aspect in its attitude toward normative standards. A critically liberating and humanizing attitude toward normative standards is to look on them as reflecting the *good toward which we ought to strive* in our effort to fulfill the great commandment. The pastoral person recognizes, however, that our evolving, interrelated world is marked by sinfulness and so is filled with ambiguity and conflict. Moral norms, in such a world, remain indispensable pole stars of moral guidance. The appropriate disposition toward them is to appreciate the values which these standards light up and aim to protect and to promote. Experiences of value gave rise to the norms in the first place. So, in using norms the values ought to remain primary. With an eye toward the values at stake, we can use normative standards as challenges to appropriate the values as best we can so that we might move toward living more humanly in a loving manner.

## Pastoral Procedure

The first task of proceeding pastorally is to clarify values. This phase considers Gustafson's first two points of moral analysis, the moral agent and the beliefs, in order to help the other name and own his or her moral character. Only in this way will the person ever be able to choose out of his or her own convictions and be able to act as his or her own person.

The pastoral person can help the other to come to this self-awareness by having him or her step back from the present situation in order to see it as part of the larger, unfolding story of one's life. Trying to understand oneself in the present situation is like trying to understand an important character in a novel. We do not discover the true identity of this character by starting in the middle of the story, or by reading only excerpts of the story. We need to get a sense of the unfolding drama and the development of the character from the beginning. For the moral agent seeking guidance, the present conflict is of a piece with other experiences, pressures, and choices which come together to give intelligibility to the present moment and to light up future possibilities.

Through this process of clarification, the one seeking guidance may come to recognize what he or she truly believes or cares about with heartfelt commitment. Since morality begins in the heart, we want to touch that which moves another at a heartfelt level. Through this process of clarification, we eventually disclose not only the structure of one's faith but also the make-up of the person's moral identity or character. Moral character reveals the strengths of a person's capacity for action. A sensitive pastoral response at this point aims to maximize the person's freedom by encouraging him or her to live out of his or her strengths while learning to live within the limits of his or her weaknesses.

After clarifying values we need to confront them. Moral guidance does not end with empathic understanding of the affective content of the moral subject's immediate experience of a moral conflict and commitment to value. Moral guidance also moves on to confront the moral subject with the somewhat predictable impact that various options can have on the individual and the wider community.

Beliefs is the point of moral analysis which links the task of clarifying values with confronting them. The phase of confrontation proceeds by appealing to beliefs, to situational analysis, and to norms. By appealing to these points of analysis, pastoral moral guidance aims to move the moral agent beyond his or her immediate vision and impressions of what is most humanizing in the short run and to take into account the long run and collective consequences of various options. Appropriate for this task are not only the images born out of one's religious convictions but also the experiential wisdom of the community as expressed in moral norms, such as those found in the moral teaching of the church. This task also includes drawing upon wide consultation and empirical evidence to get as accurate a map of the moral landscape as possible.

The way one views the situation affects the way one will analyze it and bring moral norms to bear on it. We respond to what we see. In turn, one's beliefs and life experiences affect what one sees. For example, the religious conviction that we are all made in God's image, or that God wills the well-being of all, or that we are all called to work to make enemies into friends, affects the way one would interpret a situation. So, as important as abstract norms are, we must not ignore the beliefs which help one to define a situation and to regard some aspects of it as more important than other.

Since we respond to what we see, the aim of this phase of the procedure is to challenge the other's moral vision. Since images shape the moral response best, confronting another's values happens most effectively at the level of the moral imagination. This is the way Jesus worked. His parables in word and deed shocked the assumptions of his followers to look on themselves, others, the world, and God differently. Images from the Bible or the Christian tradition can be a powerful source of moral conversion. For example, the covenant can be a powerful image to understand marriage or friendship and the responsibilities that go with them. Images of self-sacrifice from the Christian tradition's moral heroes and heroines (the saints) can also be a source of moral conversion. With new images we will interpret our relationships differently and so discover new moral demands.

After discerning the person's capacities, clarifying values toward which we ought to strive, and challenging the imagination with new images for the moral life, the procedure of pastoral moral guidance can begin to explore as many ways as possible to achieve the values which deserve priority. Again, engaging the moral imagination is crucial here. The "What else?" and "What if?" questions can open as many possible courses of action as would be fitting for the person and the total relational context in question. Through imaginatively picturing the future, and through consulting broadly the experience of the community and empirical science, the agent can identify which course of action would create the least amount of harm in trying to appropriate the value toward which he or she ought to strive.

Moreover, the imaginative process can visualize foreseeable consequences for each alternative and let the emotions which accompany each be experienced consciously. Imaginatively living inside each alternative is an integral part of discernment. The affective experiences of peace and joy are the gospel signs of following the call of God with a good moral decision. Through the imaginative exploring of alternatives and feeling the responses evoked in that process, the person can get a sense of which alternatives are most congruent with his or her authentic moral self. Paying attention to feelings helps one to recognize inner resources and ensures against unacknowledged feelings becoming the real "reasons" for acting in a certain way. The alternative one finally chooses ought to be the one which fits not only the context but also the agent's present sense of moral integrity and moral capacity. Ideally, the supportive context for engaging this imaginative process is leisure, a well-rested body, emotional balance, a discipline of listening prayer, and the sharing with a critical listener what one hears and feels in the process of engaging the imagination.

## Pastoral Judgment

The pastoral judgment of what one ought to do in this context aims to maximize the person's moral strengths to take the next step toward fulfilling God's call to be loving. A pastoral person knows that a judgment of what is the moral truth for one person may not be so for another. One person's capacity for action cannot be made into a moral imperative for all people. A pastoral person also knows that one may judge wrongly about the appropriateness or morality of an action, but still act in good faith. This is an example of acting in invincible ignorance. A pastoral person may have to leave such a person in good faith who is unable to appreciate everything that makes the action immoral. But a person who is capable of appreciating them and is failing to do so ought to be challenged in his or her assessment.

The pastoral judgment is determined above all by what God requires and enables a person to be and to do. All else is relative to that. The readiness to hear the call of God and to live the moral truth of responding to God is the most important attitude one can bring to making a moral decision. This is the challenge of being a disciple of Jesus and of being alive in the Spirit of God. The need to be open to the Spirit of God demands a prayerful discerning heart. For this reason, we need to turn in our final chapter to the insights of the spiritual tradition of the discernment of spirits.

## Notes

1. *Situation Ethics: The New Morality* (Philadelphia: Westminster Press, 1966).
2. *Ibid.*, p. 30.
3. *Ibid.*, p. 95.
4. James M. Gustafson has clearly shown the futility of extreme positions of deontology or teleology in his significant contribution to the "new morality" debates. See "Context Versus Principles: A Misplaced Debate in Christian Ethics," *Christian Ethics and the Community* (Philadelphia: United Church Press, 1971), pp. 101–126; see especially, pp. 101–117. On these four points, see pp. 117–125.
5. For the interpretation of "invincible ignorance" in Louis Monden, see *Sin, Liberty and Law*, translated by Joseph Donceel (New York: Sheed and Ward, 1965), p. 138; for Bernard Häring, see "A Theological Evaluation," in *The Morality of Abortion: Legal and Historical Perspectives*, ed. John T. Noonan, Jr. (Cambridge: Harvard University Press, 1970), pp. 139–140; for Charles E. Curran, see "The Pastoral Minister, the Moral Demands of Discipleship, and the Conscience of the Believer," in *Directions in Fundamental Moral Theology* (Notre Dame: University of Notre Dame Press, 1985), p. 265.
6. The approach presented here shares some affinity with, though it is not identical to, the approach of Roger Burggraeve, "Meaningful Living and Acting: An Ethical and Educational-Pastoral Model in Christian Perspective," *Louvain Studies* 13 (Spring 1988): 3–26.

# 21    Discernment of Spirits

*I*n the last chapter, we considered the leading methods of making a moral decision and sketched a model of pastoral moral guidance. Going hand-in-hand with that pastoral model is the process of the discernment of spirits. While the discernment of spirits cannot be separated from pastoral moral guidance in practice, I am separating it here for purposes of analysis. The importance of discernment appeared time and again throughout this book. With the discernment of spirits we reach the high point of faith informing reason. It is a fitting theme with which to bring this study of Catholic morality and the moral life to a close. I will try to give it due attention by exploring the meaning, the importance, the theological foundations, the process, and the limits of the discernment of spirits in the moral life.

## The Meaning of Discernment

The meaning and function of discernment of spirits may be seen by comparing our relationship to God to an ongoing conversation with a friend.[1] God speaks and we respond. In a conversation, no set rules of grammar tell us what to say next. The conversation progresses on the basis of fine feeling picking up the mood and attitude of the other as well as the meaning of the issue under discussion. The grammar which makes the language intelligible to the conversation partners is like the moral norms which make action intelligible within a community of shared moral values. If we speak according to proper grammar, we can understand each other. But grammar does not tell us what to say next in the conversation. Discernment does. In the moral life, a gap exists between moral norms and one's personal imperative in a situation. Norms can direct us toward what we ought to do, but discernment ultimately leads us to the action most expressive of ourselves and of our relationship with God.

Or consider another analogy. Virtuous moral living is like gourmet cooking. The gourmet has a recipe as a guide, but the gourmet cooks not by his or her head, but by taste. The decision of how much of what ingredient to add is led by a discerning taste rather than by a precisely defined recipe which can be followed blindly. Ordinary cooking follows the recipe exactly, even to the point of leveling the teaspoon with a scraper to make sure the measurement is exactly what the recipe prescribes. The resulting meals are adequate to keep one nourished, but they are not always exciting and they do not reflect the personal taste of the cook in the way a gourmet meal does. The gourmet version of the moral life does not dispense with the recipes of moral norms, but the moral gourmet is not so bound by the recipe that he or she would not adjust according to taste. Discernment is what helps the gourmet make the proper adjustments. So if the moral life is going to be a personal response to one's hearing the call of God in this instance, moral discernment of spirits is indispensable.

"Discernment," as we generally use the term, refers to the quality of perception and the capacity to discriminate degrees of importance among various features before making a judgment. The ability to discern involves a keenness of perception, sensitivities, affectivities, and capacities for empathy, subtlety, and imagination. For example, teachers can tell when research projects are produced by discerning students and when they are not. Undiscerning students may be generally exhaustive in their bibliographical preparations for the project. However, even though they gather all kinds of facts, they fail to show the proper relationship among them and the subtle distinctions which make certain facts relevant. The discerning students, on the other hand, make judicious use of research findings and show subtleties and proper relationships. Likewise, an employer can tell which letters of recommendation are written by discerning persons and which ones are not. Letters which come from a discerning person clearly isolate significant detail, draw attention to subtleties in a person's character, or make relationships between a person's character and performance which other persons generally miss. The common use of discernment, such as in these two examples, helps us to understand something of what is involved in the process of the discernment of spirits.

In our spiritual tradition, discernment of spirits is an ordinary practice for helping a person to determine his or her faithful response to God. It is the point of convergence of the moral life and the spiritual life, both of which share the common concern of living one's faith in response to hearing the word of God. "Discernment of spirits," according to our spiritual tradition, is carried out in faith by sifting through various interior stirrings or "spirits" (such as feelings, attractions, hungers, intuitions, impulses, resistances, or inclinations) which arise within us when we confront a situation calling for a decision. Discernment of spirits wants to know if God is the one leading me in my experiences and desires or not. So, discernment is not for determining right and wrong in the abstract. It is for determining which of the possible courses of action available would be most consistent with who I am and want to become in response to God's offer of love and call to be loving.[2]

Discernment is primarily a matter of the heart; it is an aesthetic judgment of affectivity and virtue. As such, it aligns the moral life and moral decision making closer to art than to science. The strict logic of a scientific nature is necessary in morality in order to defend publicly what we have decided. But we do not actually make our decisions in the same logical way that we try to justify them. Ordinarily in the moral life, we lead with the heart. Judgments of rationality follow in a complementary way. They set the outer limits of moral action and they provide reasons for action which are publicly intelligible.

As a matter of the reasoning heart, discernment requires the fuller use of the virtue of prudence and the theology of the moral conscience. Prudence, in the teaching of St. Thomas, is the virtue which enables a person to discover the best way to do the right action (ST II–II, q. 51). Prudence listens to experience, one's own and others, it seeks counsel, it looks into the future to anticipate difficulties and to size up consequences. It sifts through all these to come to a decision which fits the particular configuration of circumstances at hand. It chooses the best way to do the right action for now. The teaching of St. Thomas on prudence shows a particular respect for subjective sensing and grasping the invitation of God in a particular instance when material norms do not adequately take into account the complexity of the particular situation. His interpretation of prudence goes beyond the application of the objective criteria of moral norms and aligns the virtue of prudence more closely with discernment's attending to the internal stirrings of the heart.[3]

In our discussion of conscience, we saw the whole person, not just the intellect, is involved in the assessment and judgment of moral realities. The judgment of conscience is a personal response to one's experience of God mediated through the objective factors of a situation. In this way we can see that the exercise of prudence, the fully functioning conscience, and the discernment of spirits work together.

As a process of discovering the presence of God in one's inclinations and choices, discernment of spirits engages the whole network of human intelligence. This includes not only the conscious mind and its power of reason but also the unconscious as well as the whole body with its physical and emotional reactions to experience.[4] In fact, the unconscious and the body respond to human experiences more quickly and sensitively than does the reasoning mind. To follow the process of the discernment of spirits adequately, then, we need to read the signals of the whole network of intelligence. Our discernment will be as reliable as our ability to attend to this whole network and to read all the signs which point to God's presence.

## The Importance of Discernment

Discernment of spirits in the moral life is receiving more attention of late.[5] The moral maxim, "Keep the law and the law will keep you," which has served generations has been stretched now about as far as it can go. The assembly-line religion which it supports is being replaced with custom-made responses to God arising from deep within one's heart. Neither virtue alone nor norms alone satisfy as an adequate expression of the moral life. Pre-defined patterns of living, absolute certainty reached by strict deduction from a single moral principle, and settled answers applicable to all people every-where and for all time are increasingly suspect in a world marked by rapid change, pluralism, and personalism.

Moreover, if we are going to maintain that the basic structure of the Christian moral life is to respond to the initiative or call of God, then, with God as the center of value for us, we need to see all things in their relation to God and to integrate all things into our love of God. Discernment helps us to do that. It is an important part of our effort to make an authentically personal response to God.

Discernment gives a central place to the person over norms as the locus for discovering the call of God. While it recognizes that objective constraints and the accumulated wisdom of others are helpful aides for right moral living, discernment does not find that these express adequately the personal impera-tive of God's call here and now. As we become more serious about our relationship with God, we give more importance to discernment so that we can bring more and more of life under the influence of God.

## Theological Foundations of Discernment

Since moral discernment of spirits is carried out in faith, it presupposes some basic theological convictions. The stance one takes toward them will influence the context, process, and expectations of the discernment of spirits. Four theological foundations stand out for special consideration—faith, the will of God, Jesus, and the human person.

### Faith

Discernment of spirits is only possible for a person who looks on life from the perspective of one committed to God in Christ and through the Spirit. Faith that is foundational to discernment is not faith as a supplement to philosophy, or as intellectual loyalty to an institution, or even as a set of propositions about divine love. Faith, rather, is seeing more than meets the eye. Faith looks into the deepest dimensions of human experience and sees the presence and action of God.

For the person of faith, every human experience, if given a chance, could disclose God. For example, experiences of pain and frustration as well as of joy and compassion can be moments in and through which faith sees God reaching out with a summons calling us to freedom and to life. In such instances, faith is perceiving the paschal shape of life lived in conformation to the pattern of Jesus' faithful response to the call of God in his life. For the person of faith, our relationship with God and our responses to God are going on all the time, whether we want them to be or not. Without faith, we could not discern the presence and action of God and the choices which may lead to deepening a relationship with God.

## God

Closely related to the perspective of faith are our convictions about God. For discernment, the fundamental conviction about God is that God is always and everywhere redemptively present to us, calling us through our experiences to a deeper life of faithfulness and love. If God were not so present to us, then we would have no sure basis for trusting our experiences as a way of giving meaning and direction to our lives. We have already seen this in our treatment of natural law as grounded in eternal law. With God always and everywhere present to us, we can discern through our experiences the ultimate measure of meaning and direction for our lives.

Traditionally, we have called the measure of life which transcends us the "will of God"—the ultimate object of our obedience. The notion "will of God" comes with strong biblical warrants (Mk 14:36; Mt 6:10; 26:39; Jn 4:34; Col 1:9; Heb 10:5–7) and is well-founded in our theological vocabulary for understanding God and for relating to God. Yet "will of God" can be very misleading in the context of the discernment of spirits.

For example, if we understand the "will of God" to be a preconceived plan, already fixed from the beginning and existing in its fullness totally extrinsic to us, then human freedom and responsibility would not really matter in the moral life. All we would need to do then is to fit into the divine plan. In this scenario, God is a hard determinist who has already established the moral pattern for our lives and is now playing with us some version of the game, "Guess What Number I'm Thinking." If the mind of God or the divine plan has not already been revealed to us by persons in authority over us, then we would have to hunt it down like some bloodhounds sniffing out clues to the divine plan hidden somewhere out there in creation. Such an understanding of the "will of God" trivializes the process of discernment.

More viable interpretations of the notion "will of God" have been offered in spiritual literature. For example, John Futrell has interpreted the "will of God" according to the rich, dynamic notion of the "word of God" as something constantly spoken to us and calling for a response.[6] The richness of "word of God" is larger than the Bible as a fixed collection of books. It includes the "existential" word which pertains to all dimensions of the specific situation in which the discerning must take place. It also includes the "prophetic" word which is the revealed word of God in scripture, preeminently in the person of Jesus, as well as in the tradition of the teaching of the church, and in one's own personal history. It includes as well the "here and now" word of the call of God to each one, uniquely and individually, at this moment.[7] Discernment, according to such a view, attends to all that makes up the rich, dynamic character of the word of God.

John Wright has suggested interpreting the will of God as God's love for us.[8] According to this interpretation, doing God's will is allowing God's love to flow through us in our love for others. God's will, then, gives a general orientation for our lives, but the specifics are left to us. They depend on our own talents, temperaments, upbringing, social constraints, opportunities, and attractions. In other words, the will of God is not so fixed from the beginning that it excludes human involvement. Rather, if we can say that the ways we are gifted (graced) are expressions of God's love for us, then the will of God unfolds in its specificity as we accept the gifts of God and live out of them with gratitude.

Discernment, according to such a view, is the matter of determining how we might best express our freedom to live out of the gifts which are ours. We have Jesus as a model of the free and faithful response to God's giftedness, and we have the Spirit to empower us to make such a response. The dynamics of moral growth include both the humility to accept our gifts and the ambition to use them rather than to wrap them in a sock and to bury them for safe-keeping (cf. the parable of the talents, Mt 25:14–30).

These interpretations of God's will as "word of God" and as "God's love" take seriously the freedom of God's creative activity as well as human responsibility and initiative. According to these interpretations, the better question to guide discernment is not, "What is God's will for me?" but rather, "What is God requiring and enabling me to be and to do?" Putting the question this way admits to the dynamic character not only of the divine word and divine love but also of the human freedom which we must respect in the process of discernment.

## Jesus

Christian discernment of spirits presupposes that we have taken a stand
on the meaning and direction human life ought to take. Jesus is the one who
embodies better than anyone else the fundamental meaning and direction of
human life lived in response to the presence of God. For the Christian, Jesus
is God-with-a-face. He is the clearest expression of God revealing or speaking
a word to us, and he is the clearest expression of an authentic human response
to God. He provides for the Christian discerner, then, the normative point
for interpreting what God is enabling and requiring us to be and to do.

If we are going to profess Jesus as Lord, truly divine and truly human,
then our fundamental relation to Jesus ought to shape the framework for all
the decisions coming out of the discernment process. Discerning with reference to the words and deeds of Jesus sets us in the direction a disciple is to go
even if it does not quite yield the detailed knowledge for a decision which
fulfills the imperative of the moment. Along with contemplating Jesus, we
also need to consider the relational context of the moral situation as well as
the uniqueness of the individual and his or her capacity for action. But
contemplating the words and deeds of Jesus does light up the route of the
paschal mystery which we are all called to follow.

## The Human Person

Discernment is also founded on some basic convictions about the human
person which we have already explored in other parts of this book. In discernment, we assume that the human person is an embodied subject. Nature and
grace are so intertwined that we cannot separate them without destroying the
human person. A dualistic view of the human person with its dichotomous
thinking is reflected in the question, "Is this my idea or is it God speaking to
me?" Since God comes to us in and through human ways, the answer to the
question is "Both!" George Bernard Shaw's portrayal of Joan of Arc in his
play *Saint Joan* illustrates this well, especially in this short dialogue between
St. Joan and Captain Robert de Baudricourt, a military squire. As a warrant
for her mission to save France, Joan claims to have heard voices:

ROBERT: How do you mean? voices?

JOAN: I hear voices telling me what to do. They come from God.

ROBERT: They come from your imagination.

JOAN: Of course. That is how the messages of God come to us.[9]

St. Joan's response reflects both the anthropological conviction that the human person is an embodied subject and the theological conviction that God's way to us and our way to God is in and through the human.

In discernment we also assume that the structuring of the human person is multi-leveled. A level of subjectivity lies beneath the surface level of our various actions, roles, and experiences. The deepest level of ourselves, what biblical anthropology designates as the "heart," is the point of contact with the presence of God within us. At this level, God's Spirit joins with our spirit, to use the image of St. Paul (Rom 8:16).

This is the level of the human person which escapes clear conceptual knowledge. But we do have a felt awareness of this deepest level of ourselves so that we have an affective sense of experiencing God there. In the process of discernment we try to pay attention to the interior stirrings at this level. When we touch our heart's deepest desires, we touch God's word for us. On the basis of this anthropological feature, the tradition of discernment maintains that what we want in our heart of hearts will be consistent with whom God is enabling and requiring us to be and with what we are to do. Deep within ourselves we have a prevailing sense or a pervasive feeling that tells us "This is right for me. This fits." This is the moral and spiritual truth which we are called to embody. In short, being an authentic person and being the person God is calling us to be are one and the same. Through the process of discernment, then, we try to cut through all the "shoulds" amd "have-tos" which belong to someone else, and to cut through all the fantasies and passing fancies which are not of our wholehearted wanting so that we might follow our heart's deepest desires. Wholehearted wanting is the only sound basis for an authentic moral choice which is a response to the word of God at some particular moment.

These four theological foundations of the discernment of spirits lead us to consider the process of discernment itself. This process needs to be an integral part of the pastoral moral guidance introduced in the last chapter.

## The Process of Discernment

The process of discernment has three structural components: prayer, gathering information, and seeking confirmation. Isolating these features for the purpose of closer examination must not obscure the fact that in practice they are interrelated and move toward the judgment that God is present in one's inclinations.

### Prayer

In discernment, prayer holds a primary place since discernment begins with prayer, is sustained by prayer, and follows upon prayer. Prayer brings knowledge which comes from love. While prayer is the indispensable framework for discernment, being a prayerful person is even more important. The prayer for discernment, or being a prayerful person, is not the matter of repeating formula prayers which have little to do with one's personal experience and the specific circumstances which evoke the need for discernment in the first place. The frequent recourse to formula prayers in discernment can give the false sense of being a prayerful person. Prayer for discernment is prayer which remains in close contact with daily activities, personal experiences, feelings, and alternatives.

In his play *Saint Joan*, George Bernard Shaw illustrates the difference between prayer for discernment and merely saying prayers through a brief encounter between Joan and Charles, the new king of France. Joan has just been challenged by the archbishop to account for her claim that she always knows she is right when she speaks.

> JOAN: I always know. My voices—
>
> CHARLES: Oh, your voices, your voices. Why don't the voices come to me? I am king, not you.
>
> JOAN: They do come to you; but you do not hear them. You have not sat in the field in the evening listening for them. When the angelus rings you cross yourself and have done with it; but if you prayed from your heart, and listened to the trilling of the bells in the air after they stop ringing, you would hear the voices as well as I do.[10]

The prayer for discernment is some form of contemplative prayer which takes a long, loving look into one's own experiences, both internal and external, in order to see God there. Since the first steps for discerning are to identify, to clarify, and to express what is happening within us and around us as a manifestation of God's presence and action in our lives, prayer must be above all some form of listening prayer. By paying attention to what is happening to us in our experiences and to the feelings evoked in us by our experiences, we may begin to hear the here and now word of God for us. We can relate all that we hear (i.e., sense) to our awareness of God mediated through the Christian stories and in the community. Praying with scripture is an important part of discernment. In the conclusion of my discussion of scripture and moral theology, I suggested a method of praying with scripture which engages the moral imagination with the stories and images of scripture. The images of scripture function as prisms to refract personal and social experience in fresh ways for the imagination. Discernment uses these to discover the gracious mystery of God as a specific invitation to action. In this way our prayer brings together the existential word of God with the prophetic word of God to make clearer the word of God for us here and now.[11]

The goal of such a spiritual discipline is to reach that purity of heart wherein we experience God in Christ as being "God for me." For proper discernment, one should have known at least once the peace which comes from the experience of accepting God's love and giving oneself to God. Such is our equivalent of Jesus' own Jordan experience where he experienced himself as loved by God: "You are my own dear Son. I am pleased with you" (Mk 1:11). The Jordan experience was a turning point in the life of Jesus and the touchstone of his self-awareness of having a special, unique identity with God. Our own Jordan experience must be the keystone experience for measuring all other experiences as being experiences of God. To use the process of discernment well, then, requires the renewal in prayer of this fundamental experience of being loved by God.

The prayer which heightens our awareness of God's presence engenders spiritual liberty—the freedom from being fixed in advance on one alternative. With freedom gained through prayer, we can undertake discernment with an indifference which leaves us open to making a choice which is truly expressive of our gifts and responsive to the needs of the time.

Achieving spiritual liberty is not easy. It can easily be deflected or disrupted along the way by interior and exterior obstacles which take some form of enslavement or illusion. Some of the interior obstacles can be prideful desire for recognition, a crippling fear of rejection, a selfish attachment to a present position in life, or a lazy lack of self-knowledge. Exterior obstacles can be such things as desire for social status, blinding peer pressure, or attachment to money or power. To be spiritually free we need to purge ourselves as much as possible of these enslavements and illusions. The process of coming to spiritual liberty, however, is fostered by psychological and spiritual maturity. It requires such disciplines as a continuous rhythm of prayer, leisure, silence, exercise to nurture physical and emotional health, and other spiritual exercises, such as spiritual direction, dreamwork, fasting, and whatever else enables us to unlock our imaginations and to let go of those paralyzing attachments which prevent us from being aware of God's presence in our lives and from bringing our lives into the drift of our deepest desires. The judgment to which the process of discernment leads will be as true for us as the freedom with which we make it.

## Gathering Information

While prayer is absolutely essential for discernment, prayer alone is not sufficient. We also need the right information, which comes from knowing the territory about which our decisions will be made. Making decisions in a life which is becoming more and more complex demands careful investigation of the territory. We must make every effort to gather relevant information and to test its accuracy, since getting to know the lay of the land is one way to listen to the existential word of God. While discernment cannot be equated with the results of gathering data and making an objective analysis of them, discernment cannot ignore the data. Inadequate or mistaken information can lead to serious misjudgments. Gathering data and prayer must work together in order to determine which aspects of the information are relevant and how they fit together as an integrated whole.

Gathering information involves the discipline of research. In order to be properly informed, we need to use methods of investigation appropriate to the areas at issue. The variations and depth of the research we need to do will depend on the issue at hand and the time we have. For example, we need to turn to appropriate psychological methods and instruments in order to attain critical self-knowledge. We need to appeal to appropriate empirical studies in order to have accurate information about the social, political, medical, or economic realities which pertain to our decision. In other words, we need to use whatever methods and resources will help us to know the territory, and we need to ask good questions which will help us survey the territory. The reality-revealing questions which we explored in the chapter on the formation of conscience may be the kinds of questions we could use to start surveying the territory.

## Confirmation

The subjective factors attended to in prayer and the objective factors attended to in gathering evidence do not add up in a neat logical sum to a clear, unambiguous decision. Once we become attuned to the existential and prophetic word of God, we are ready to hear the here and now word. In order to hear this word, we need to let the various alternatives open to us resound within our already God-sensitive and God-focused subjectivity. For this to happen we must project ourselves imaginatively into the possible alternatives in order to size them up and to try them on so that we can know them through the whole network of human intelligence, not just our heads. The way in which these alternatives fit our God-heightened subjectivity gives an indication of what the here and now word of God is.

One suggestion for this process is to list our alternatives along with the advantages and disadvantages of each. Then we imaginatively walk around inside each alternative and pay attention to what stirs within us as we live inside the advantages and disadvantages of each. In order to know each alternative with our whole person, we pay attention to the emotional reso- nance which each evokes: what excites us, what makes us anxious, what gives us energy or drains us, and so forth. In this process, we are concerned not with which alternative has the longer list of advantages over disadvantages, but with the way each one fits and "rings true" inside us at a level deeper than what our head tells us is reasonable. The criteria we use are not ones of strict logic, but they are aesthetic ones. The signs of peace, delight, and harmony are signs which tell us which course of action is most consistent with the sort of persons we are and want to become.

At the end of a certain period of time, we make a tentative choice based not on how the facts line up, but on how true the choice "rings" within us. We feel a harmony within ourselves with it. We live with this decision for a while before finally committing ourselves to it. We ask, "Can I live with this decision? Does it 'ring true' for me? When I sit with this decision in prayer, does it please, delight, or bring me peace?"

But sometimes we mistake the relief we feel after struggling to make a hard decision with the peace and harmony of true discernment. Since we can easily be fooled in the area of being attuned to our heart of hearts, we need to apply certain criteria which help us assess whether the interior stirrings which we are following lead us to God or not. The tradition of discernment of spirits has given us internal and external criteria to confirm a decision as an authentic response to the here and now word of God.

## Internal Confirmation

The internal signs of confirmation are the affective experiences of consolation or desolation.[12] Consolations open us to greater spiritual freedom and enable us to love God more. Consolations are felt in experiences such as those described as fruits of the Spirit in Galatians 5:22—"love, joy, peace, patience, kindness, goodness, faithfulness, humility, and self-control." Consolations reflect a choice which harmonizes with the persons we know ourselves to be and/or are capable of becoming. The experience of consolation which confirms a choice does not mean that all ambiguity is gone and that everything will be rosy from that point on. In every choice some values remain unfulfilled to create ongoing tension. The consolations tell us that we are moving in the right direction and that we are acquiring the interior freedom we need in order to face whatever struggles and tensions lie ahead.

Desolations, on the other hand, pull us away from God. In desolation, gloominess replaces gladness, confusion replaces peace, coldness replaces warmth, and we tend to lose our confidence in God's love and care for us. During the experience of desolation, we should resist making a significant decision or reversing the direction of formerly well-made decisions. We act against desolations not only by praying for deliverance, but also by exploring the source of the desolation (What was I doing that brought me to this condition?) and by engaging in activities which enhance the commitments once made on the basis of a decision which was confirmed by consolation.

## External Confirmation

The external signs of confirmation fulfill the gospel criterion: "By their fruits you will know them" (Mt 12:33). The conviction behind this criterion is that choices and actions which lead to God ought to produce the effects of charity in the life of the discerning person. The way we enhance real communion and community among those with whom we live and work would be a positive sign of our openness and growth in God's love. Conversely, to close in on ourselves and to be more self-protective would be a negative sign.

James Fowler has offered a profile of the Christian view of the human vocation which fits the traditional external criteria well.[13] He suggests that when we are living the Christian vocation, we do not need to live in fierce competition with anyone else in a way which seeks to establish ourselves over and against others. We realize that a great diversity of ways exists to participate in divine love. As a result, we can live free of the anxiety that someone else will also do, and perhaps even do better, what is the uniquely honest expression of ourselves. Another sign is that we would be able to rejoice in the gifts of another, receive them as complementary to ours, and not be threatened by them. We would be able to accept our limits graciously and not try to inflate ourselves into omnicompetence and strive to be all things to all people. Also, we would not seek to ground our worth in work. Rather, we can achieve a balance of time and energy.

Another traditional external criterion is the confirmation by the community. Since we live with others, a choice which is of God will lead to building up the community—if not immediately, then, at least, in the long run. This criterion requires that our choice expresses not only our giftedness but also that it responds to the needs of the community. This criterion, however, must be used cautiously since someone may be called to stand against the community as the prophets were. For instance, what ultimately leads to greater love and unity may at first create division as a necessary step toward harmony. In such a case, the criterion can be applied by testing the quality of that person's relationship to the community over a long period of time.

## Limits on Discernment

Such, in brief, is the process of discernment. It demands living an examined life striving for awareness—a critical awareness of self and a faithful awareness of God. But being able to be so aware presupposes that we have created around us a climate for discernment and it presupposes a significant degree of maturity. For example, creating a climate for discernment would involve being able to identify for oneself what life is all about, especially as it relates to the life of Jesus. It also involves sufficient self-awareness and an acceptance of the ways we can be a blessing for others. It also demands actively participating in a community of faith in order to keep one's perspective of faith alive and to have one or more persons of faith with whom to review life and to test one's self-understanding. It also involves a life in which leisure is a significant reality and prayer has a place in which to hear and to feel God's love. It also demands a regular vehicle for reviewing life in a critical way, such as through journaling, the consciousness-examen, dreamwork, or spiritual direction.

After going through the process of discernment and applying the criteria to confirm a decision, we can still only make modest claims about discerning with certitude the word of God for us now. We must recognize the limits of this process as well as of ourselves. Only a system of tight syllogisms, which leave no room for the personal, affective element, would come near guaranteeing certitude about knowing and doing what God requires and enables. The process of discernment does not yield detailed directives of a technical sort. But it does indicate whether our hearts are centered on God and whether we are moving in the right direction with our lives.

The process of discernment is limited by many factors. The effectiveness of the process of discernment depends on one's psychological and spiritual maturity. If we are divided by chaotic emotions, mood swings, low self-esteem, or other inhibiting neurotic conditions, we will not be able to rely on our effective states for reliable guidance. Emphasizing a psychological perspective, Ernest Larkin summarizes this point well in this statement:

> Basically *the* difficulty in all discernment is personal authenticity. If you are not in touch with yourself, if you don't know what is going on, you cannot hear the "other," even when the Other is God.[14]

As we become psychologically and spiritually balanced, and as we acquire critical self-knowledge which can check our self-deception, the process of discernment will become more effective. To the extent that we touch the center of ourselves in truth, then to that extent we can touch the living word of God in us.

The quality of prayer is another factor which influences the process of discernment. Without prayer we are unable to keep our love of God foremost in our consciousness and so would-be discernment becomes nothing more than disciplined deliberation. Even with prayer we may not reach true spiritual liberty which sets us free of selfish preferences and external pressures.

Other factors putting limits on our discernment would be the clarity of our perception of the situation and the accuracy of the information we gather.

Because some factors quickly change, or we may have overlooked or not given sufficent attention to others, discernment can be mistaken. But even though we recognize that ongoing discernment is necessary, we must be ready to act on the best resoundings within us at the moment, and then remain open to change.

## Conclusion

Although discernment does not yield the certitude we may like to have in directing our lives through moral choices in complex circumstances, it does stimulate our desire to find God in all things and to be mindful of being subject to the presence and governing action of God. Discernment does not consign us to discontent or moral paralysis; instead, as faith increasingly informs reason, we live more consciously, freely, and faithfully in the service of God, treating all things as relative to God and choosing all our actions in response to God. This, in brief, is the culmination of the moral life lived according to reason informed by faith.

## Notes

1. The metaphor of conversation is taken from John Wright, *A Theology of Christian Prayer* (New York: Pueblo Publishing Company, 1979), p. 131. I have adapted it here to fit the relational model of the moral life.

2. For a thorough analysis of the discernment of spirits in the Ignatian tradition, see Jules J. Toner, *A Commentary on Saint Ignatius' Rules for the Discernment of Spirits: A Guide to the Principles and Practice* (St. Louis: Institute of Jesuit Sources, 1982). From within the same tradition, see Karl Rahner, *The Dynamic Element in the Church* (New York: Herder and Herder, 1964), especially chapter three, "The Logic of Concrete Individual Knowledge in Ignatius Loyola." Perhaps a more accessible interpretation of the Ignatian tradition is in John Haughey, *The Conspiracy of God* (Garden City: Doubleday & Co., 1973), pp. 118–154. Another brief interpretation of discernment which emphasizes a psychological approach is in Ernest E. Larkin, *Silent Presence: Discernment as Process and Problem* (Denville: Dimension Books Inc., 1981).

3. ST II–II, q. 51, a. 4, ad. 3. Another place where St. Thomas deals with the subjective aspects attended to in discernment is in his treatment of wisdom as a gift of the Holy Spirit which brings about right judgment from a connaturality with divine things. See ST II–II, q. 45, aa. 2, 4. For a recent interpretation of prudence which balances its objective and subjective dimensions and integrates this virtue with the tradition of the discernment of spirits,

see Bernard Häring, *The Law of Christ*, Vol. 1, translated by Edwin G. Kaiser (Paramus: Newman Press, 1966), pp. 498–513. For a fuller treatment of moral discernment in Aquinas, see John Mahoney, "The Spirit and Moral Discernment in Aquinas," *The Heythrop Journal*, 13 (July 1973): 282–297.

4. The need for an adequate anthropology with special attention to the importance of discovering and assessing unconscious forces as a necessary and appropriate feature of the discernment of spirits is well documented by Luigi Rulla, "The Discernment of Spirits and Christian Anthropology," *Gregorianum* 59 (1978): 537–567, especially at pp. 543–551.

5. James M. Gustafson has explained the moral life by construing it as a process of discernment in his "Moral Discernment in the Christian Life," *Theology and Christian Ethics* (Philadelphia: United Church Press, 1974), pp. 99–119. See also his *Ethics from a Theocentric Perspective*, Vol. 1: *Theology and Ethics* (Chicago: University of Chicago Press, 1981), pp. 327–342. Philip S. Keane has shown the relation of the moral life to the discernment of spirits in his "Discernment of Spirits: A Theological Reflection," *American Ecclesiastical Review* 168 (January 1974): 43–61. William C. Spohn has explored the meaning and dynamics of discernment for the moral life from within the perspective of American theologians in his "The Reasoning Heart: An American Approach to Christian Discernment," *Theological Studies* 44 (March 1983): 30–52.

6. Futrell, "Ignatian Discernment," *Studies in the Spirituality of Jesuits*, Vol. 2 (April 1970), p. 48.

7. For Futrell's expanded interpretation of "word of God," see *ibid.*, note #2, p. 86.

8. Wright, *The Theology of Prayer*, p. 130.

9. Shaw, *Saint Joan* (New York: Brentano's, 1924), p. 16.

10. Shaw, *Saint Joan* (New York: Brentano's, 1924), p. 86.

11. Many helpful books are now available to help develop this form of contemplative prayer. Among them are Morton T. Kelsey, *The Other Side of Silence: A Guide to Christian Meditation* (Paramus: Paulist-Newman Press, 1976); also Thomas Green, *Opening to God* (Notre Dame: Ave Maria Press, 1977). Also, on using religious symbols in discernment, see William C. Spohn, "The Reasoning Heart," *Theological Studies* 44 (March 1983): 40–45.

12. For a classical breakdown of these interior movements, see Hugo Rahner, "The Discernment of Spirits," *Ignatius the Theologian*, trans. by Michael Barry (London: Geoffrey Chapman, 1968), see especially pp. 152, 168, 169.

13. Fowler, *Becoming Adult, Becoming Christian: Adult Development and Christian Faith* (San Francisco: Harper and Row, 1984), pp. 103–105.

14. Larkin, *Silent Presence*, pp. 7–8.

# INDEX

Absolutes, 283; and formal norms, 286–289; and material norms, 292–294.

Affections, 14, 15, 187–188.

Aquinas, St. Thomas, 25, 43, 109; and natural law, 223–228; 236, 256; and epikeia, 257–258; and morality of act, 265–267, 270; and norms, 292; teleology in, 302; and prudence, 316.

Authority in the Church, response due, 155–161; presumption in favor, 157–159; as normative teaching, 159–161.

Autonomous ethics, 1, 47–48.

Basic freedom, 77; see also freedom of self-determination; core freedom.

Call-response, 6–7, 172.

Care, 14, 15.

*Challenge of Peace, The*, 19, 38, 206, 238, 274, 294.

Character, 7, 30, 71–72, 171, 186–188; faith and, 53; conscience and, 138–146; shaped by the Church, 200–202.

Character ethics, see ethics of being.

Christian ethics, see moral theology.

Church, 199–217; and character, 200–202; as bearer of moral tradition, 202–206; in the faithful, 202–203; in theologians, 203–205; in pastoral ministers, 203–205; in the hierarchy, 205–206; as community of deliberation, 206–215; aspects of exercising teaching authority, 215–217.

Circumstances, 267, 271–272, 275, 292, 302.

Civil disobedience, 259–261; criteria for, 259–261.

Classicist worldview, see worldview.

Conscience, 123–161; mature, 123–124; and superego, 123–130; in theological tradition, 130–135; as synderesis, 131–132; as moral science, 131–132; as judgment, 132–133; formation of, 136–150; and sources of moral wisdom, 137–138; and character, 138–146; and community, 142–145; and imagination, 141–146; and choice, 147–150; and Church authority, 152–161.

Consequences, 149, 243–244, 276, 277, 302, 303–304.

Consolation, 325.

Conversion, 100, 174, 176, 196, 286.

Core freedom, 77; see also freedom of self-determination; basic freedom.

Council of Trent, 25–26.

Covenant, 78, 91–99; and worth, 92–94; and solidarity, 94–97; and fidelity, 97–99; as revealed reality, 172–173.

Critical realism, 17–20.

Curran, Charles E., 47, 53, 211, 213, 234, 254, 258, 304, 308.

Decision making, methods of, 20–22, 300–306.
*Declaration on Abortion*, 2, 64, 254, 255.
*Declaration on Euthanasia*, 35.
*Dei Verbum*, 29, 34, 165.
Deontological method, 21, 301–302.
Desolation, 325.
*Dignitatis Humanae*, 130, 208, 252, 253, 254.
Discernment of spirits, 44, 53, 278, 314–328; meaning of, 314–317; importance of, 317; theological foundations of, 317–321; faith and, 317–318; God and, 318–319; Jesus and, 320; human person and, 320–321; process of, 321–326; prayer and, 321–323; gathering information and, 323–324; confirmation and 324–326; limits of, 326–328.
Discipleship, 189–197.
Dispositions, 187–188.
Dissent, 19, 207–215; reality of, 207–208; criteria for, 209–212; classes of, 211–212; guidelines for, 212–215.
Distinctiveness of Christian morality, 47–48, 54.
Double effect, principle of, 270–272.

*Economic Justice for All*, 19, 38, 64, 65, 170, 171, 206, 255.
Epikeia, 257–259.
Ethics of being, 7–8, 30; see also character ethics.
Ethics of doing, 8, 30.
Evans, Donald D., 49, 295.
Experience, 8, 10, 17, 18, 19, 38, 73, 228, 243; see also inductive method.

Faith and morality, 1, 46–56; linking of, 48–51; and character, 53; and actions, 53–54; critical-dialogical relationship, 54–56.
Foundational moral experience, 13–14.
Freedom, 75–83; of self-determination, 75–81; determinants of, 75–77; of choice, 81–83.
Fuchs, Josef, 47, 221, 257, 266, 268, 269, 292, 294, 295, 303.
Fundamental moral theology, 8, 9.
Fundamental option, 78–81, 110–111; theory of, 78–81.
Fundamental stance, 18, 79–80.

*Gaudium et Spes*, 28, 34, 37, 64, 67, 118, 130, 155, 171, 245.
God, 43–46, 51–52, 56, 77; as Trinity, 65–66; and discernment, 318–319.
Good, nature of, 43–44.
Great commandment, 179–181.
Gustafson, James M., 9, 44, 50, 51, 53, 54, 71, 138, 142, 169, 170, 185, 187, 304, 305, 310.

Häring, Bernard, 3, 29, 72, 78, 79, 80, 81, 90, 110, 113, 116, 166, 251, 308.
Heart, 13, 14, 15, 16, 78, 79, 86; as context for sin, 99–100.
Hierarchy, 205–206; see also magisterium.
Historical consciousness, 30, 31, 32, 33–36, 37; and natural law, 228, 235, 244.
Hope, 177.
Hospitality, 179–181.
Human action, morality of, 265–279.
*Human Life in Our Day*, 208.

Human nature, 63, 73.

Human person, 63–74; as image of God, 64–66; integrally and adequately considered, 66–72, 245; as relational being, 67–68; as embodied subject, 68–70; as historical subject, 70; as fundamentally equal but uniquely original, 71–72; as multi-leveled being, 77–78; and discernment, 320–321.

*Humanae Vitae*, 2, 152, 154, 159, 169, 209, 212, 232, 290, 308.

Idolatry, 93, 108, 262.

Image of God, 64–66.

Imagination, 49, 50, 71–72, 142, 171, 172, 182, 189, 200–202; conscience and, 145–146; and praying with Scripture, 181–182; and norms, 295–297; and pastoral moral guidance, 311; and discernment, 320–321, 324–325.

Inductive method, 37–39, 73.

*Instruction on Bioethics*, 2, 35, 36, 233, 254.

Intention, 187, 265, 266–267, 271–272, 275, 302.

Intrinsic evil, 227, 268–270, 276–277, 302, 308.

Janssens, Louis, 64, 66, 67, 73, 228, 265, 266, 269, 276, 287, 288, 289, 292.

Jesus, 185–197; as norm of moral life, 185–186; and moral character, 186–188; and action, 188–189; imitation of, 191; discipleship of, 191–197; and discernment, 320.

Keane, Philip S., 71, 279, 296, 297.

Knowledge, 83–87; conceptual, 83–84, 86; evaluative, 85–87.

Law, and sin, 91, 95–97; positive law, 250–263; nature of, 251–255; purpose of, 251–253; relation to value, 252–254; and morality, 253–255; and obedience, 255–263; binding power of, 255–263; and epikeia, 257–259; and civil disobedience, 259–261.

Legalism, 250, 252, 263.

Liturgy and ethics, 200–202.

Logic of self-involvement, 49–51.

Love, 14, 78, 80, 179–181, 285–286; see Great commandment.

*Lumen Gentium*, 155, 177, 209.

Magisterium, 153–155, 205–206; see also Authority in the Church

*Man for All Seasons, A*, 14–15, 133–134, 138–139.

Manuals, moral, 1, 7; purpose of, 26; limitations of, 26–28, 37, 45–46, 79, 208, 235, 293.

McCormick, Richard A., 47, 209, 212, 269, 273, 275, 276, 291, 292, 294, 295, 303.

Means, 265–267, 270–271, 274–275.

Method, of decision making, 20–22, 300–306; of theological reflection, 37–39.

Methodological presumption, meaning of, 157; applied to Church teaching, 157–159.

Moral analysis, four points of, 9–10, 305–306.

Moral philosophy, 6.

Moral theology, range of interest, 6–8, 29–30; divisions of, 8–9; structure of, 9–11; definition of, 6; characteristics of manualist era, 26–28; renewal of, 28–39.

Morality, 7–8, 13, 14, 44–45, 75.

Morals, 9–11.
Mortal sin, 108, 109–114; requirements for, 109–110; and fundamental option, 110–112.
Murray, John Courtney, 208, 252, 253.

Natural law, in tradition, 220–228; in antiquity, 221–223; in the Bible, 221; Greek influence, 221–222; Roman influence, 222–223; in Aquinas, 223–228; in magisterial documents, 231–233, 236–238; in contemporary theology, 235–236, 238–246; meaning of "natural," 220–221, 238–240; meaning of "law," 221, 240–241; definition of, 241; function of, 241–242; value of, 241–242; contemporary profile of, 242–246.
Niebuhr, H. Richard, 20, 90, 304.
Noninfallible teaching, 209–210.
Norms, 283–297; meaning and function of, 283–285; in relation to value, 284; and message of Jesus, 285–286; types of, 286–295; and imagination, 295–297; formal, 286–289; material, 289–295.

Obedience, nature of, 255–263; as virtue, 261–263.
Objectivity, 19, 23 n. 10.
O'Connell, Timothy E., 131, 242, 287, 289.
*Octogesima Adveniens*, 34, 237.
Ontic evil, see premoral evil.
*Optatum Totius*, 29, 165.
Order of nature, 223, 224, 225, 226, 231, 232, 233, 239, 268.
Order of reason, 223, 226, 231, 232–235, 236, 237, 239.
Original sin, 106–107.

Parables, 175–177.
*Pastoral Care of Homosexual Persons*, 2, 35, 167, 232.
Pastoral moral guidance, 160; and moral theology, 306–308; model of, 308–313; posture, 309–310; procedure, 310–312; judgment in, 312–313.
Penitential books, 25.
*Persona Humana*, 35, 110, 152, 169, 232, 286, 287.
Personalistic morality, 63–64, 66, 73–74; criterion of, 73.
Perspective, 187; see also vision, moral.
Philosophical ethics, see moral philosophy.
Physicalism, 226–227, 231, 232, 233, 234, 235; see also order of nature.
Pluralism, 215–216.
Power, and sin, 100–103; and discipleship, 192–196.
Practical absolute, 294–295.
Prayer, 15, 50, 182, 262, 321–323.
Premoral/ontic evil, 268, 269–270, 271, 272, 273, 276, 278, 290, 291, 292.
Presumption of truth, see methodological presumption.
Proof-text method, 166.
Proportionalism, 267, 272–279; definition of, 273; criteria of, 273–274; modes of knowing, 275–276; assessment of, 276–279; and material norms, 291–292.
Prudence, and discernment of spirits, 316.

Radical sayings, 177–179.
Rationalist, understanding of law,

256; understanding of epikeia,
257–258.
Reception, 217.
Recta ratio, 224, 235, 241.
Reflection, 16–20.
Reign of God, 174–177.
Relativism, social, 16; personal, 16–
17; emotivism, 17; and propor-
tionalism, 277–278.
Responsibility method, 21, 304–
305; and sin, 90; and conscience,
140.

Scandal, 213.
Scripture, 165–182; pre-critical use,
166; exegetical task, 167–168; hermeneutical task, 168–169; methodological task, 169–171; as revealed
morality, 169, 177–181; as revealed reality, 169, 172–177.
Sensitivity, 13–16.
Sermon on the Mount, 177; see also
radical sayings.
*Sharing the Light of Faith*, 101, 117,
156, 157.
Sin, 66, 89–121, 250–251; sense of,
89–103; biblical context for, 90–
100; as arrogance of power, 100–
103; original, 106–107; actual,
107–116; formal and material,
112; catalogues of, 113; mortal,
109–114; venial, 114–116; social,
116–121.
Social sin, 116–121; evolution of the

concept of, 117–119; notion of,
119–121.
*Sollicitudo Rei Sociales*, 95, 96, 119.
Special moral theology, 8–9.
Spiritual liberty, 323.
Subjectivism, and proportionalism,
277–278.
Superego, 123–130.
Synthetic terms, in moral norms,
288–289.

Teleological method, 21, 302–304.
Ten Commandments, 172–173.
Theological ethics, see moral theol-
ogy.
Three-font principle, 265–267.
*To Live in Christ Jesus*, 99, 101, 115.

Ulpian, 223, 224, 225, 226.

Virtue, 7, 30; see also character.
Vision, moral, 141–146, 200; see
also imagination and perspective.
Voluntarist, understanding of law,
256; understanding of epikeia,
257.

Walter, James J., 48, 55, 272, 276.
Will of God, and discernment of
spirits, 318–319.
Worldview, classicist, 30–33, 35–
36, 37, 234; modern, 31–36, 37;
see also historical consciousness.